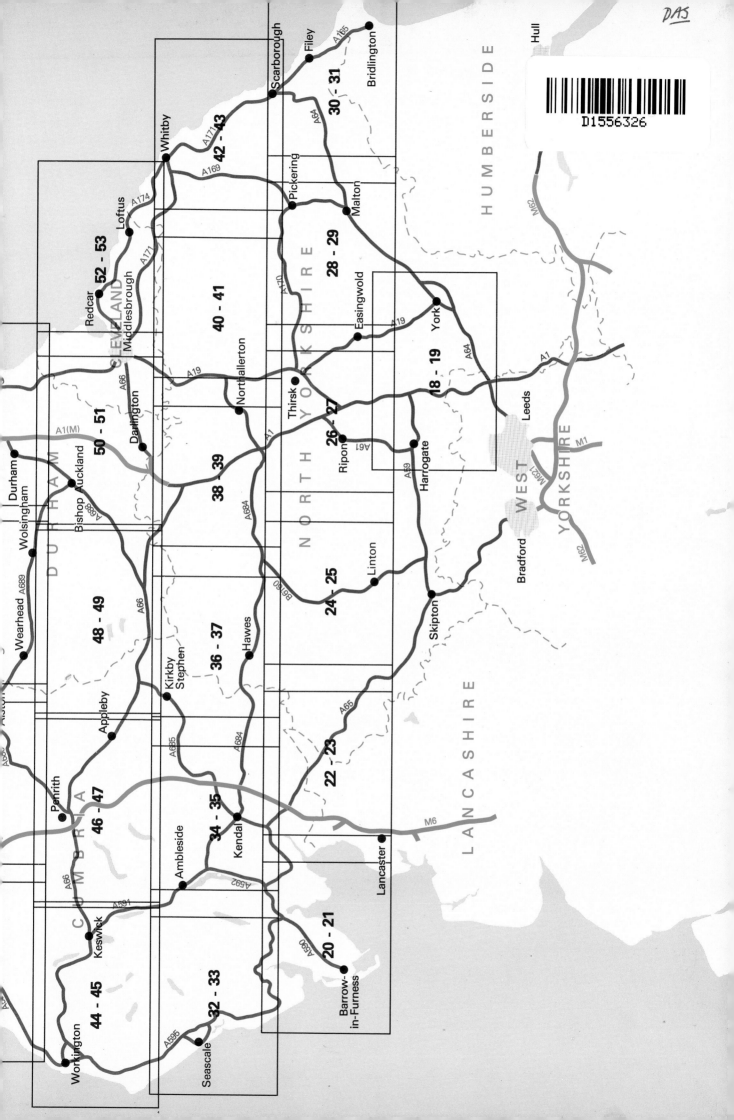

DAS

D1556326

Hamlyn
LEISURE ATLAS
North Country

Hamlyn
London·New York·Sydney·Toronto

The publishers would like to thank the following official tourist
boards for their help in the compilation of this book:

Northumbrian Tourist Board
Cumbria Tourist Board
Yorkshire and Humberside Tourist Board
North West Tourist Board

Compiled and edited by Colin Wilson

Gazetteer compilation: Julian Brown, Glyn Thomas.

The publishers are grateful to the following individuals and
organisations for the illustrations in this book: B. Boyd; British
Tourist Authority; Bruce Coleman Ltd.; Colour Library
International; Eric Crichton; Cumbria Tourist Board; W.F.
Davidson; Arnold Kidson; Bob Matthews; Colin Molyneux;
Spectrum Colour Library; York City Department of Tourism.

Previous page: Grasmere Water (map 33c).

Opposite: Durham Cathedral (60i).

First published 1982

Published by
The Hamlyn Publishing Group Limited
London • New York • Sydney • Toronto
Astronaut House, Feltham, Middlesex

Printed in Scotland by
John Bartholomew & Son Limited
Duncan Street, Edinburgh EH9 1TA

ISBN 0 600 34997 7

The representation in this atlas of any road or track, or the marking
of any object, is not an indication of the existence of a public right of
way. The contents of this atlas are believed correct at the time of
publication; while every effort has been made to ensure that the
information is accurate, no liability can be accepted by the publishers
for the consequences of any error. The latest position can be
checked with the appropriate Tourist Board.

Contents

4 How to use the Atlas

An Introduction to the North Country

5 Travel and Accommodation
6 Discovering the
North Country
9 History and Legend
12 Wildlife
14 National Parks
14 Long Distance Footpaths
16 Calendar of Events

Leisure Maps of the North Country

17 Key to symbols used
on the maps
18 1:100,000-scale
Leisure Maps (see endpapers
for page numbers)

Gazetteer of Activities

80 Countryside
(and picnic sites)
84 Gardens and Arboreta
86 Historical Sites
90 Museums and Art Galleries
93 Castles
94 Historic Buildings
97 Religious Places
102 Bird Watching
104 Industry Past and Present
107 Tourist Railways
108 Wildlife in Captivity
108 Cruising by Boat
109 Sailing and Boating
110 Water Sports
111 Fishing
116 Climbing and Skiing
118 Riding and Pony Trekking
119 Aviation and Motor Sport
120 Golf Courses
121 Activities of
Special Interest
122 Tourist Information Offices
123 Index to 1:100,000 maps

How to use The Leisure Atlas

The Hamlyn Leisure Atlas has been designed to be both comprehensive and flexible - there are a great many ways of using it. First and foremost, it offers a superb atlas of England's North Country, on an ideal scale of about 1·6 miles to the inch. The maps are detailed enough to show almost every tarmac road, however narrow, and a great many lesser tracks as well. With this atlas, there is no excuse for sitting in a main road traffic jam when attractive country lanes offer a more enjoyable and much less frustrating alternative.

Bartholomew's unique colour-coded height presentation provides a graphic picture of the geography of the region, while the maps show both natural and man-made features in remarkable detail. Careful interpretation of the maps themselves will do much to enhance any visit to the North Country.

Superimposed on these outstanding maps, however, are over 2000 symbols covering a range of 27 leisure activities and facilities, details of which can be found in the gazetteer section after the maps. The information represented by these symbols can also be used in many ways.

There are two basic ways of undertaking any holiday trip: you can plan every detail in advance, or you can simply turn up and find out what is available on arrival. This atlas works equally well in both cases.

For those who prefer to plan their holidays in advance, a brief perusal of the maps will quickly reveal those areas most richly endowed with one's favourite activities. Or one can browse through the gazetteer pages dealing with a particular pastime and thereby identify the map pages on which that pastime is best catered for.

The Atlas works just as well, of course, for the many people who prefer to take pot luck: after helping one reach the chosen destination, the appropriate map will reveal the full range of leisure activities available in that area.

Using the maps

Each map page is divided into six squares, marked with red grid lines. Each of these squares is identified throughout this Atlas by its page number and a letter between a and i: the key to these letters appears at the top of each page.

To find out about any chosen symbol, therefore, one must first work out the map reference of that symbol. The reference of Jervaulx Abbey in the example shown here is 25c; details about it can be found in the section on Religious Places on pages 97 to 101 of the gazetteer.

In addition to its map reference, each symbol is usually identified in the gazetteer by a name in bold type corresponding to the name found at or near the symbol on the map. This is particularly helpful when several identical symbols appear in one map square.

Wherever possible, each symbol appear exactly on its actual location. In some cases, such as in towns, this has proved impossible and the address or some other description of the actual location has therefore been included in the gazetteer.

There are also some locations with so many activities that it proved impossible to fit all the symbols onto the site. In such cases, the symbols have been grouped together in a box.

Where maps overlap, the extent of the duplication can be seen on the small diagrams at the top of each page. Where maps do overlap, some symbols will obviously appear on more than one map: when this occurs, the later entry is cross-referenced to the earlier one.

Finally, don't forget that events which occur only occasionally are not marked on the map, but appear (with their map references) in the Calendar of Events on page 16.

Using the Gazetteer

Each entry usually includes details of its opening hours and of other facilities available at the same site: these are shown by symbols after each entry, indicating that further information can be obtained in the relevant section of the gazetteer.

Opening times apply throughout the specified season unless otherwise stated. *Daily* means 7 days a week; *weekdays* means Monday to Friday. Most places are closed at Christmas and New Year - if you plan to visit then, telephone first.

Telephone numbers have been supplied wherever possible, together with the appropriate STD codes: where the exchange name differs from the location given for the activity, the name of the exchange is also given, so that local calls can be made.

Free means exactly that, but has only been specified where we have definite information to that effect. Many non-commercial sites - earthworks, walks, etc. - will also be free even when this is not specified, but you should be prepared to pay for anything not listed as *Free*.

☕ Indicates that refreshments are available on the site, although not necessarily throughout the stated opening period.

& Indicates that the attraction listed is suitable for disabled people. Other activities on the same site may not be suitable, however, and any cross references should be checked.

⊼ indicates a picnic site, for which no other details are given.

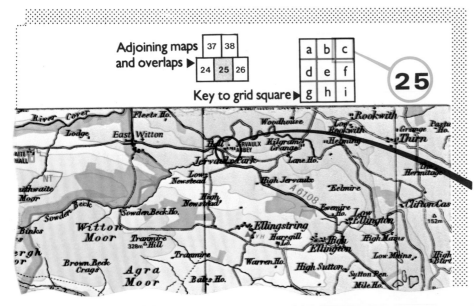

Religious

24i Linton: St Michael. Pleasant setting for church with Norman font and arcade, 14th century nave and 15th century chapels. Interesting Romanesque crucifix.

25c Jervaulx Abbey. Unspoilt ruins of 12th century Cistercian abbey. Charming setting. *Daily dawn to dusk.* ☕

25c Masham: St Mary. Mainly 14th century, this church has an interesting tower: lower half is 11th century, surmounted by a 15th century octagonal stage, topped by a spire. Saxon cross.

How to get there

With the M1/A1 road system serving the eastern side and the M6/A6 the western, all parts of northern England are easily and conveniently reached by car. The principal trans-Pennine roads in this area are A65, A66 and A69 and there are good main roads to virtually all parts of the coast.

Off-the-beaten-track roads are generally quiet with the exception of those in very popular touring areas like the Lake District, which get very busy at peak periods. In the more remote mountain and moorland areas garages may be few and far between so always ensure you have an adequate supply of petrol before setting out. Many of the hill roads are unfenced and it is important to keep a sharp lookout for sheep. Remember that they tend to move in the direction they are pointing rather than step neatly backwards like kerb-drilled humans.

There are excellent rail services to the north and with High-Speed Trains running from London to York, Darlington, Durham, Newcastle and Berwick, travelling time has been very much reduced. Cars can be taken by train on the Motorail service from London to Carlisle or Newcastle, from Newton Abbot in Devon to Newcastle or York, and from Inverness to York. Alternatively there are excellent car-hire facilities. Details of train services can be obtained from British Rail Travel Centres or any railway station.

National Express coaches run a wide range of services to the north. Details from any agent displaying the National Express sign or from National Travel offices.

There are air services from other parts of the UK to Blackpool, Teesside, Newcastle, Leeds (south of Harrogate on A658), and Carlisle. Details from travel agents or airways offices.

Useful Telephone Numbers

Weather Forecasts

Recorded forecasts giving the general outlook for North East England can be obtained by telephoning:

Newcastle ....(0632) 8091
Middlesbrough ....(0642) 8091

Motoring Information

Recorded details of road works, road conditions, etc., within a 50-mile radius of Newcastle can be obtained by telephoning:

Newcastle ....(0632) 8021
Middlesbrough ....(0642) 8021
   For the area within 50 miles of Leeds (which includes most of North Yorkshire), telephone:
Leeds ....(0532) 8021

Stockley Bridge (map 33a).

Tourist Information and Accommodation

There are over 70 Tourist Information Offices in the north run by local authorities and other bodies in accordance with standards laid down by the regional and national tourist boards. The staff at these centres can give advice on a wide range of subjects from accommodation and travel to local events and attractions. All these centres are listed on page 122.

Information on Northumbria (Northumberland, Durham, Tyne & Wear and Cleveland) can be obtained from the Northumbria Tourist Board, 9 Osborne Terrace, Jesmond, Newcastle upon Tyne NE2 1NT (tel. 0632 817744); on Cumbria from the Cumbria Tourist Board, Ellerthwaite, Windermere, Cumbria LA23 2AQ (tel.096 62 4444/7); on North Lancashire from the North West Tourist Board, The Last Drop Village, Bromley Cross, Bolton, Lancashire BL7 9PZ (tel. 0204 591511); and on Yorkshire & Humberside from the Yorkshire & Humberside Tourist Board, 312 Tadcaster Road, York, North Yorkshire YO2 2HF (tel. 0904 707961). All these organisations produce a wide range of publications giving details of holidays and tourist events and attractions.

All Tourist Information Offices have information on local accommodation and many provide a booking service for personal callers. Centres offering the Book-A-Bed-Ahead service can make a provisional reservation for accommodation at any other town that has a centre also operating the scheme, for the same or subsequent nights. Small fees may be charged for these services.

Discovering the North Country

The far northern counties of England are, on the whole, one of the least discovered parts of Britain. The Lake District, brought into romantic prominence in the first instance by the Lake School of poets (Wordsworth, Coleridge, Shelley and others) and the Yorkshire Dales are the exceptions to this and are generally well-known. Far too few people, however, are aware of the wild, green beauty of the North Pennines or the Cheviot Hills, where there are more sheep than people; the wooded valleys that cut deep into the heathery hills of the North York Moors; the fine cliffs of chalk and sandstone on the east coast; or the mahogany coloured rock at St. Bees Head in Cumbria. In thinking of the north, mountain and moorland may often spring most readily to mind, but there are also superb sea and skyscapes of cloud, water and distant hills across Morecambe Bay and the Solway Firth where skeins of wild geese fly in from the Arctic every autumn.

As well as a wide range of superb scenery that can rival any part of Britain, northern England has several cultural identities where traditions formed centuries ago are retained in an unselfconscious and uncommercial way and plenty of towns and cities that are both architecturally impressive and full of urban vitality. Indeed, the visitor can have the best of all worlds with scenic beauty and remoteness by day and a lively and interesting night-life in any one of a number of cities.

Heading north on the M6 from southern England the first dramatic change in the scenery occurs north of Lancaster when the whaleback moors of the Forest of Bowland suddenly loom to the east. Not a forest in the tree-covered sense, Bowland was originally a royal game reserve subject to Norman forest law. Further east, Ribblesdale divides Bowland from the Yorkshire

Dales and mile after mile of grassy limestone hills extend from here across half of North Yorkshire. This is the type of countryside that has been made famous through the veterinary stories of James Herriot. Narrow lanes wander up and down, often with dramatic steepness, between neatly repaired stone walls. Every so often there is a tiny village of dove-grey limestone or darker millstone grit carefully set off with patches of mown grass and hanging baskets of glowing red geraniums. Most of them have a small restaurant where the hungry traveller can sample ham and eggs or delicious home-made scones. This is a countryside on a very ample scale that cries out for one to leave the car and walk.

The dales themselves, long green valleys pushing deep into the hills, each have a special character of their own: Wensleydale is broad and well-populated with lush pastures and numerous villages; Langstrothdale has a totally different atmosphere, in this case an almost timeless isolation from the rest of the world.

Between the Dales and the North York Moors is a wide band of richly fertile farmland with red-brick market towns like Thirsk and Northallerton as centres. The Romans understood the strategic importance of this corridor of lowland between north and south and sited one of their major towns at Aldborough where the Brigantes, Britain's largest Celtic tribe, had their capital. Later the Ure was bridged by the Normans at Boroughbridge and the volume of trade enabled the town to boast twenty-two inns. At Ripon, one of Britain's smallest cities grew from Anglo-Saxon foundations and the Cistercian monks who built the magnificent Fountains Abbey understood well the advantages of combining arable ground for crops on the lowland and pasture for sheep in the dales.

The hill lover will find plenty more of interest in the eastern part of Yorkshire where the chalk Wolds, a northern kind of downland, and the North York Moors are divided by the now-drained marshland called The Carrs in the Vale of Pickering. The Wolds are mostly wind-smoothed pasture or ploughland that make a splendid playground for hares. The hills curve gently eastwards studded with villages whose names betray a strong Viking influence - Thwing, Langtoft, Helperthorpe - to the gull-thronged cliffs at Flamborough Head, the great breakwater sheltering Bridlington Bay. Up the

Grasmere (map 33c) seen from Helm Crag.

Sharp Edge, Saddleback (map 45f).

coast towards Scarborough the cliffs change from chalk to a golden rock which is the northern end of the great belt of Oolitic limestone that runs diagonally through England from Lyme Regis in Dorset. The Cotswolds are justly famous for their pretty villages of honey coloured stone, but many do not realise that Yorkshire can offer similar villages along the southern margin of the North York Moors. Scarborough, with its two bays, is an excellent centre for exploring the whole of this area and can offer much of interest in its own right.

The North York Moors have a unique dark and heathery quality. They are in effect a high table of hard stone into which many small rivers and streams have cut their way to make surprisingly sheltered and hidden valleys. At Rievaulx Abbey is perhaps the epitome of this, the noble ruins sheltering in a deep wooded ravine below the moorlands. Again, this is magnificent walking country where those with the greatest stamina have traditionally set out to see if they could reach the coast. And where the moors do reach the sea there is a wonderful stretch of coastal scenery with picturesque towns and fishing villages like Whitby, Staithes and Robin Hood's Bay nestling beneath the shelter of the hills. These hills are rich in minerals: the shopper will notice much jet on offer at Whitby - the stone is found in the neighbouring cliffs - and a reddish tint in some of the rock betrays the iron content that has provided the raw material for the steel towns along Teesside.

On the Durham side of the Tees are the coalfields that supplied fuel for the blast furnaces and much of the eastern part of this area is given over to industrial development. A strong reminder of pre-industrial days is found, however, in the city of Durham itself magnificently sited on a bend in the river Wear and with steep, cobbled streets running up to the castle and cathedral.

Further inland the industrial area is left rapidly behind as the wide Pennine Hills with lonely farmsteads and rolling open roads stretch towards the west. The two Durham valleys of Weardale and

Teesdale both have much to commend them and the latter is famous for its unique wildflowers. A very wide range of species has survived here, partly owing to agricultural techniques over the centuries and partly because of a special fast-draining soil called sugar limestone. It is in this area that the Whin Sill first makes its appearance. This hard ridge of congealed volcanic basalt has created the fine waterfalls of High Force and Caldron Snout as well as the foundation for the most dramatic stretch of Hadrian's Wall (at Housesteads) and the coastal scenery at Dunstanburgh where the castle stands on a 100ft basalt cliff.

England's central spine from Upper Teesdale to Hadrian's Wall is known as the North Pennines. It is a dramatic area with the highest public road in the country near Nenthead and vast acres of fell and fresh air where the wind orchestrates the calls of curlew and grouse with the distant bleating of sheep into wholly satisfying harmonies. Long ago lead and related minerals were mined in the area and the occasional sight of a now disused working, such as the restored waterwheel at Killhope, is a wistful reminder. Centre for much of the mining activity was Alston; small and remote but full of character, it is England's highest market town.

The South Tyne Valley from Hexham to Haltwhistle is the lowest route through this upper end of the Pennines, and as such was of great strategic importance to any military commander wanting to move troops with ease to counter any attack from the north. The Romans fully appreciated this and built one of their most famous monuments outside Italy - Hadrian's Wall - immediately above the South Tyne Valley. The way this extraordinary linear fortress snakes fluidly over the hills tends to belie the effort that must have gone into its making and it does help one appreciate how highly the Romans must have valued England to put such sterling endeavours into its defence. Looking from the wall today across the wilderness of bog and fell towards Wark Forest and the Scottish border one tries to imagine the feelings of a Roman legion brought from some remote part of the Empire. In those days the country was still quite heavily wooded, but the wind would still have rustled the brown summer grass and brought stinging flurries of sleet and snow in winter.

Beyond the new lake of Kielder Water surrounded by its man-made pine forest, now the largest in Europe, the Pennines merge almost imperceptably into the Cheviots. The hills here with names like Bloodybush Edge and Black Hag easily evoke the centuries of marauding and cattle rustling (or reiving as it was known locally) that went on among border families. The novels of Sir Walter Scott and the dozens of castles and fortified farmsteads with their pele towers bear witness to the past lawlessness and skullduggery of this area. Nowadays the local breed of white-faced Cheviot sheep and the hardy hill cattle can graze in peace.

The Roman wall and the hills have tended to draw attention away from the Northumbrian coast, an area full of historic interest. Highlight of the area is Holy Island (or Lindisfarne) where English Christianity was re-established by St. Aidan in the 7th century. Also important on a spiritual level are the Farne Islands, where St. Cuthbert went to study and meditate. The mighty castles of Bamburgh, Warkworth and Dunstanburgh and the walled town of Berwick-upon-Tweed all testify to the need to defend this part of England from attacks by the Scots and from across the North Sea.

St Aidan's statue, Holy Island (map 79e).

As well as Christian relics and fortifications there are several charming fishing villages: Craster is famed for its oak-smoked kippers, one of England's finer gastronomic achievements.

The very northernmost part of England is the fertile flood plain of the river Tweed lying between the Cheviots and the Lammermuir Hills of Scotland. The lovely and often peaceful river Tweed and its tributary the Till, two of Britain's finest salmon rivers, are like much of the rest of the county, well furnished with the castles and fortifications that are a reminder of more turbulent days. At Flodden a simple stone cross marks the bloody battle ground where in 1513 James IV of Scotland and many thousands of men were slaughtered, while Berwick-upon-Tweed was captured or sacked 13 times before it became English for the last time in 1482.

Cumbria is different in both culture and landscape from the rest of northern England. Geographically it consists broadly of a number of valleys, along with the lakes for which the region is famous, which radiate like the spokes of a wheel from a central dome of hard, glacier-scoured rock that makes up the Cumbrian Mountains. For the last two hundred years or so poets and painters have found great romantic inspiration in the mountains, lakes and valleys of the Lake District and have almost totally reversed our general attitude towards them. Today the blend of crag, woodland, sky and reflecting water garnished by the odd drift of wild daffodils is considered by most to be something approaching Elysium: before the artistic fraternity altered our perceptions such things were considered savage and gloomy, a grim reminder that untamed nature was utterly undesirable. It was this view that kept Cumbria relatively isolated from the rest of the country and allowed it to develop a distinctive culture of its own. Originally a Celtic kingdom -as hill names like Helvellyn and Blencathra testify - things like the little, brown Herdwick sheep, the traditional style of wrestling, the fox hunts conducted on foot, the distinctive soft dialect and a style of cookery still very much adhered to today, highlight a Cumbrian spirit that is alive and well.

Most people paying a visit to the area for the first time make quite understandably for the Lakes, each of which has a decided persona of its own. Windermere, as the largest, has a somewhat brash, 'I am the greatest' quality about it and the resort-like developments along it enable people to enjoy boating, swimming and a range of other waterborne activities. Ullswater has a wild and peaceful quality, Derwent Water is a tree-fringed watercolour, Coniston reminds one of Ruskin and water speed-record attempts, while Wast Water has a cold and beautiful mystery. Above them all tower the mountains - perhaps not high by Alpine or Himalayan standards, but nevertheless combining all the elements of cliff, scree and rocky outcrop, plus appropriate flora and fauna that make them real mountains rather than overgrown hills.

Here there is something for everyone; for those who like to admire the view from the safety of their car, for the lower slopes walker out for a turn after dinner, for the serious hill-walker and for the rock-climber intent on surmounting the insurmountable.

Such a concentration of riches in a relatively small area has tended to draw attention away from the parts of Cumbria on the periphery of the Lake District. This is a pity as much of this periphery is full of interest and would have been well-known in its own right had it been situated in a less varied area. To the south the coast juts out like a bunch of fat fingers into Morecambe Bay where the sea runs in long silver trails across vast areas of sand and mud. Views from here back towards the mountains are magnificent, especially when the setting sun sends red and orange reflections across the constantly shifting waters. The mountains and jagged coastline of Morecambe Bay have helped to isolate the west Cumbrian coast with its tiny resorts and the towns of Workington and Whitehaven. The latter was developed as a seaport from the late 17th century and has some fine Georgian architecture in a distinctive greyish-mauve local stone.

The coast curves gradually into the Solway Firth, designated an Area of Outstanding Natural Beauty largely because of the views across the estuary towards the hills of Dumfries. The wide plain to the east and the attractive Vale of Eden is guarded by the city of Carlisle with its red sandstone castle and cathedral.

History and Legend

The north of England has been inhabited since the earliest times and some of the limestone caves in the Yorkshire Dales or traces of small communities on the Wolds show that Stone Age hunters knew what would then have been endless forests and marshland teeming with game. The dry chalk country of the eastern Wolds was the easiest part of the north to clear and it was here that the first pastoral settlements developed in the early Bronze Age. The culture of this distant time is mysterious and too little remains for us to be able adequately to interpret it today. Some of the mass burials seem to indicate ritual human sacrifice, but no one is sure of the magical significance of the strange idols cut from chalk found in the grave of a five year old child at Folkton in the northern Wolds. Not far from here is the colossal monolith at Rudston, Britain's tallest; as with the Devil's Arrows, the impressive standing stones near Aldborough, their purpose can only be guessed at, although it was clearly religious.

Other centres of this early culture were in the most northerly part of England to the east of the Cheviots, where there are a number of the strange 'cup and ring' carvings (again with some seemingly magical significance) on large rocks and boulders; and on the fringes of the Lake District, as the stone-circles at Swinside and Castlerigg testify. The greatest centre of Bronze Age activity was, however, on the North York Moors where there are over 10 000 remains of one sort or another. As well as suiting these early people climatically and in other ways, this region probably had strategic importance in the trade of the times which was surprisingly extensive.

From here routes would have crossed England so that goods, in particular gold, could have been brought from Ireland, while the North Sea gave access to the whole of Europe and probably beyond. There is evidence to suggest, for example, that these early people were influenced by ideas from ancient Egypt.

The history of the Celts in the north can be divided into two major periods: before and after the Roman occupation. Today, perhaps, much of northern England seems primarily to have been moulded by Saxon or Scandinavian influences, but the Celtic underpinning is still very evident in the northern tradition. The fierce independence of Yorkshiremen or Northumbrians perhaps owes some of its origin to memories of the Brigantes, Britain's largest Celtic tribe in Roman times, who had their centre at Aldborough. They were a continuous thorn in the Roman flesh, being both cunning and warlike. One of the most evocative relics of their culture is the mighty fortified settlement on the gritstone plateau on the summit of Ingleborough. At 2373ft, this must be the highest place where people in England have lived and was probably the last stronghold of these fiercely independent northern Celts against the Romans.

After the Romans had left England, Celtic influence remained strong for many centuries, only gradually being overrun by pressures from the invading Angles, Saxons and Vikings. Indeed, the gentle lilt of the Cumbrian accent and many of the unique customs and traditions still current today derive from Celtic roots. These border peoples were culturally akin to the Welsh rather than to the Gaelic Scots or Irish, and there was considerable movement between north-west England and north Wales.

With the massive and impressive evidence of Hadrian's Wall running from Newcastle upon Tyne to the Solway Firth, it is clear that the Romans were very active in northern England. Unlike the south, the region was never comfortably colonized and all the existing remains testify to war, rebellion and struggle against a harsh environment and uncooperative people. The large number of northern place names ending in 'caster' or 'chester' (deriving from the Latin *castrum* meaning fort) indicate the high level of internecine strife during the Roman period. Despite this the Roman achievement was impressive: their roads struck northwards through the Vale of York (we now call this the A1), across the moors, as at Wheeldale on the North York Moors, and over mountains. Two of the most hair-raising roads in modern England, the Wrynose and Hardknott passes, are simply the route pioneered by the legionaries to their fort at Ravenglass on the Cumbrian coast.

The highlight of this mighty network of roads and forts is

Castlerigg stone circle (map 45f).

undoubtedly Hadrian's Wall and its associated bases. People often imagine it as a sort of solid barrier preventing marauders or invaders from Scotland from advancing. In fact it had several functions, its principal aim being to filter and control traffic.

After the Romans left England there was much warring in the north between Angles, Saxons and the older Celtic peoples, but in 643 King Oswald of Northumbria won a decisive battle over Cadwallon near Chollerford in Northumberland. Oswald was a Christian and his victory enabled monks from the Celtic monastery on Iona (off the west coast of Scotland) to establish a sister foundation on Lindisfarne. From this beginning an influential centre of Christianity grew in the north-east. St. Cuthbert lived as a hermit on the Farne Islands; the Venerable Bede, a monk from the twin foundations of Jarrow and Monkwearmouth, was famed as a scholar and wrote the first English history; and Alcuin of York, another monk, played a major role in the return to the Continent of the learning and culture that had been preserved in British monasteries.

Although originally the Celtic Church, influences from the south soon made themselves felt and, following the Synod of Whitby in 664, the Celtic Church returned to the ecclesiastical rule of Rome. The famous and beautifully illuminated Lindisfarne gospel, written after the monastery had returned to the Roman rite, shows a marvellous fusion of the imaginative Celtic style with the more realistic attitude stemming from Rome.

This flowering of Christianity and culture in the north was given a terrible setback when, one June morning in 793, Viking longboats appeared from the North Sea and the undefended monastery and church on Lindisfarne were plundered and burnt. The era of the Norsemen had begun and was to continue until after the Norman Conquest. During those turbulent centuries the north was attacked from the sea on innumerable occasions. Anglo-Saxons and Vikings battled with one another or made alliances to establish control over different parts of the country. Much of the north was eventually settled by people from Norway or Denmark (as the

place names testify), but their control was always precarious and life must often have been harsh and insecure. One of the last Viking invaders was Asbjörn, brother of Swein Estridsson of Denmark. Joining forces with Anglo-Saxons still smarting from the Norman Conquest, Asbjörn succeeded in capturing York in 1069. William the Conqueror thereupon laid waste large areas of the north by fire and general destruction in order to discourage the inhabitants from making other alliances designed to overthrow his regime. This brutal scorched-earth policy no doubt left a deep scar on the northern subconscious and much of the traditional independent-mindedness and impatience with outsiders shown by northerners, particularly in Yorkshire and Northumberland, could well have its roots in this terrible happening.

Although the Normans brought organisation and stability to most of England, the north remained turbulent for many centuries. Its people simply did not accept Norman rule and the forests and mountains made excellent hiding places for all kinds of outlaws and bandits (or resistance fighters, according to one's point-of-view). Stories such as those of Robin Hood, widespread throughout the north, are in many senses personifications of this hostility between the indigenous population and its Norman overlords.

Cumbria and Northumbria, because of their proximity to the Scottish border, had additional problems; the extraordinary number of castles and fortified houses demonstrate that everyone had to be prepared against sudden attack from the north. Such raids were often made by borderers who were simply out for plunder. Given luck and a following wind it would not have been too difficult to make a quick foray after cattle, sheep, women or anything else that came to hand and then return over the border to Scotland. Swift retribution and rough justice was usually the only means of retaliation and this gave rise to the long-standing family feuds so romantically captured in the Border novels and poems of Sir Walter Scott.

On a more organised level, too, the English and the Scots were often at loggerheads. Famous battles include that at Otterburn in 1388, celebrated in the Ballad of Chevy Chase, when the Scots under Douglas defeated the Percys; at Neville's Cross just outside

Hadrian's Wall near Housesteads (map 64e).

Durham in 1346 when the English army led (in true Christian spirit no doubt) by the Archbishop of York overwhelmed the Scottish invaders and captured their King David Bruce; and the Battle of the Standard fought near Northallerton in 1138, when David of Scotland was defeated by the northern barons. The most tragic battle of all was at Flodden, near the Scottish border, in 1513. Here the Scots under James IV fought stubbornly all day only to be defeated with the loss of their king, many of the nobility and between 5000 and 12 000 men, whereas the English are estimated to have had only 1000 dead.

The Wars of the Roses between the rival houses of York and Lancaster, each of which was vying for the English throne, also took their toll on the north. Essentially the struggle was waged between powerful members of the aristocracy who gathered large private armies around them and the 'wars' were by no means confined to Yorkshire and Lancashire. Towton, near York, was the scene in 1461 of the bloodiest battle ever fought on English soil, when 35 000 died in one day, the conflict securing the crown for Edward IV. Three years later, the Yorkists defeated the Lancastrians at the battle of Hexham in 1464.

The last battles to be fought on English soil were during the Civil War and Commonwealth period of the 17th century. Needless to say, the north saw its share of action and one of Cromwell's decisive victories was at Marston Moor (1644) near York when, assisted by the Scots, he defeated Prince Rupert.

One very noticeable thing about these northern battles is that almost all of them took place on the eastern side of the Pennines, largely because the route to the south was through the Vale of York, following the course the A1 takes today. Cumberland being relatively poor and mountainous was left much more to its own devices which helped in preserving its distinctive identity. The county was affected in the 18th century, however, by one of history's more remarkable characters, John Paul Jones. Born in southern Scotland he became captain of a Whitehaven slave ship and eventually settled in Virginia. During the War of Independence he undertook a number of adventures around the British coast and, in 1778 led an attack on the fort in his old home of Whitehaven. By 1779 he was commanding a French ship and fought and won a remarkable sea battle with a British ship off Flamborough Head. In 1788 he became an admiral for the Russians, but he died and was buried in Paris, although his body is now interred at the United States Naval Academy at Annapolis.

Once peace had been established in the north its economy was able to grow at a faster rate and its mineral wealth gave rise to enormous development during the Industrial Revolution. The iron and steel industry flourished along the mouth of the Tees through the combination of ore from the Cleveland Hills and coal from County Durham. Newcastle upon Tyne had the resources to develop many industries, in particular shipbuilding. Such activity naturally produced brilliant engineers, among the most famous being George Stephenson and his son Robert. George, after an inauspicious start in a poor home - he could not write his name until he was nineteen - made the world's first effective locomotive and, with his son, was instrumental in opening the famous Stockton to Darlington railway in 1825.

North Lancashire and Cumbria did not have mineral wealth to the same extent as the east. Iron was mined for many years at Millom on the Cumbrian coast, but its remoteness prevented it from developing into a major industrial centre. Shipbuilding grew at Barrow-in-Furness and, further north, Whitehaven became an important port and industrial town in the 17th century.

With its often violent history and admixture of many cultures, the north is rich in legend and superstition. In earlier times witches were plentiful and one of the most famous was Ursula Southeil, more commonly known as Mother Shipton, who was born in a cave at Knaresborough in 1488. She was a formidable woman whose main accomplishments were fortune telling and prophesy. Her supposed spell-casting capabilities were so feared in the neighbourhood that she succeeded in scaring the courts into leaving her alone. Ghosts are abundant in the region and there is scarcely a castle, battlefield or stately home that does not have one or more. Reports range from Roman legionaries observed around Hadrian's

Bamburgh Castle (map 79i).

Wall to the phantom army seen on several occasions in the 18th century on the summit of Souter Fell, Cumbria. The north east has a number of blood-chilling legends about creatures known as 'worms' which were elongated and slippery dragons, often of considerable size. The Lambton Worm used to coil itself three times round a small hill now known as Worm Hill until it came to a nasty end in the Middle Ages at the hands of the son of Lord Lambton, who covered his armour with sharp blades and fought it in the middle of a river so that it was cut to pieces and washed away. Unfortunately the local witch who had devised this ingenious means of combat put a curse on the family as her conditions had not been fully met (the son refused to kill his father) and from that day many of the Lambtons have met violent deaths.

York Minster and city walls (map 19f).

Wildlife

With its long and contrasting coastlines and extensive upland areas, the north offers a range of flora and fauna that is difficult to match elsewhere in England. The variety of wildlife is explained to some extent by the remoteness of much of the country; vast tracts of moorland, large areas of forest and unspoilt coasts have provided a sanctuary for the wildlife to live and breed in comparative safety, away from man's influence.

This is exemplified by the huge inter-tidal sands of Morecambe Bay. The bay, with its associated estuaries and marshes, is one of the most important areas in Britain for the observation of wildfowl and waders. It has been estimated that in the winter months between October and March it is possible to see concentrations of over 20 000 Dunlin and Knot on the mudflats, as well as large numbers of Oystercatcher, Shelduck and Wigeon. At the north-western corner of the bay is Walney Island which houses the most southerly breeding colony of Eider Duck in Britain. The Nature Reserve there also holds the largest assemblies of Lesser Black-backed Gulls and Herring Gulls in Europe. Further north the largest Black-headed Gull colony in England is on a Nature Reserve on the sand-spit at Ravenglass, known as the Drigg Dunes.

In the north-west the best place for watching cliff-nesting birds such as Guillemot, Puffin and Razorbill is St. Bees Head. Tiny Fleswick Bay between the twin headlands of St. Bees is a good spot to go in search of moonstones which can be found amongst the pebbles on the beach. The Solway Firth, besides attracting numerous waders and wildfowl, is renowned for its geese; in winter up to 4000 Pink-footed Geese may be present on the saltings and mudflats.

The north-east coast is noted for its seals, which may be seen from time to time in most places but particularly favour areas like the Farne Islands, where the Grey Seal breeds. The Farnes provide a home for many seabirds, with four breeding species of tern; there is also a chance of seeing rarities during the spring and autumn migration periods. The Eider Duck has bred here for centuries and with their alternative name of St. Cuthbert's Duck it is fitting that they should still breed at the place where the saint - a great lover of wildlife - had his hermitage.

To the south the Yorkshire and Humberside coasts, with their sandstone and chalk cliffs, have some fine seabird colonies, particularly those at Flamborough Head and along the Bempton Cliffs immediately to the north where it is estimated there are some 40 000 pairs of Kittiwake, as well as the only mainland breeding colony of Gannets in this country.

Inland the prime attractions for the naturalist are the upland areas of moor and mountain, such as the North York Moors, or the vast man-made forests, like the Kielder Forest in Northumberland. Large wilderness areas provide the best habitats for some of our more elusive mammals and, as well as the more familiar animals such as the Badger, there are other species with a particular preference for the northern wilds. Pine Martens still occur rarely in Cumbria and there are Blue Hares on some of the higher Pennine slopes. The Red Squirrel still occupies the pine forests and broadleaf woodlands in Cumbria and Northumberland whilst both our native deer - the Red and the Roe - are on the increase. On the fells Foxes are common where, instead of using the tunnelled earths of the lowlands, they live deep among the rocks on boulder-strewn hillsides. Among the more remarkable animals in the north are the white cattle of Chillingham Park, Northumberland. It is thought that the stock are descended from the Aurochs, or European Wild Ox, a species that has been extinct for several hundred years.

The birdwatcher will find many specialities both on the

This idealised lakeside shows some of the many species of birds which can be seen in such locations. **A:** Heron, which uses long legs and neck to catch fish in the shallows. **B:** Wigeon, whose strong jaws enable it to tear off leaves. **C:** Shoveler uses its large bill to sift food from the water surface. **D:** Moorhen feeds on land and water. **E:** Mallard is also versatile, being able to dive, feed from the water surface or graze on land. **F:** Tufted Duck dives to catch small invertebrates under water. **G:** Mute Swan feeds from the surface, but uses its long neck to reach far beneath the water. **H:** Coot dives for food.

mountains and moors and in the woods and forests. Grouse are found wherever there is any extensive heather cover, the lonely call of the Curlew can be heard in the more remote areas and Golden Plover can often be found on the higher moors. One of the more arresting sights is the Dipper; it seems as though every suitable stream has its own family bobbing about on the rocks and disappearing into the clear water to feed on aquatic larvae. Of the unusual birds it is possible to see species like the Ring Ouzel, Merlin, Peregrine Falcon and Raven in many of the region's less disturbed places.

The number of species of butterfly diminishes in northern latitudes, but the north has a few that are not found in the south. The Small Mountain Ringlet favours boggy places at high altitudes in the Lake District, the Large Heath prefers low-level bogs where its foodplant - the Beaked Rush - occurs, while the Scotch Argus has made incursions over the border at several places.

Plant life is also very varied. On some of the higher altitudes some alpine plants can be found as well as Dwarf species of Birch and Willow. The open fells have a thin acid soil which supports Bent-grasses and Fescues. The thin wiry grass *Nardus* is also common as it is scarcely touched by sheep: in it can be seen the pretty but tiny flowers of Tormentil and Heath Bedstraw and locally the bright yellow flowers of the Globe flower can also be found. The wetter parts of the fells are occupied by various mosses, particularly Sphagnum and Hair-mosses, and by two interesting small plants: the Sundew and Butterwort. Both plants obtain nutrients in which the soil is deficient by catching and absorbing insects.

The woodland, however, offers a habitat where more widespread plants grow. In the Lake District and Farndale in the North York Moors the glory of the woods is the Wild Daffodil. They survive in masses despite past depredations by the public. Every spring these areas also produce their fair shares of Primroses,

Cowslips, Violets and Bluebells. In the large man-made forests of Northumberland only the woodland rides produce any diversity of plant habitat. Here grow such attractive plants as the Devil's Bit Scabious, St. John's Wort and Cinquefoil. The keen botanist will also be able to seek out the rich variety of mosses, liverworts and lichens.

Country lanes are often sources of plants that give much pleasure: the Giant Bellflower with its luminous pale blue spikes; Bistort, or Sweet Dock as its sometimes known locally, with its bright pink spikes shaped like small red-hot pokers; and the lacy white flowers and ferny, aromatic leaves of Sweet Cicely. Of the more rare plants peculiar to the north are the Shrubby Cinquefoil, with its soft yellow flowers, which has its British stronghold in the Upper Tees Valley; Northumberland has several plants including Dwarf Cornel which are found mainly in the Cheviots.

The most remarkable wildlife area in the north is undoubtedly Upper Teesdale. Several different factors, especially a type of crumbly rock called sugar limestone, have combined to make this an area of high conservation value. The flora includes such delightful plants as the mauve-pink Birds-eye Primrose and the electric blue Spring Gentian. The remoteness of the habitat of these plants has helped them to survive and it is essential that visitors leave the wildflowers and their surroundings for others to enjoy.

To get the fullest enjoyment from the wildlife it is sensible to contact a local naturalists' trust or Nature Reserve Information Office. Wardens are normally pleased to advise anyone who shows some interest on where to look and how not to disturb the site. If every visitor shows reasonable respect for the countryside and tries to understand it, the work of the conservationists will be helped considerably and places will retain their interest for generations to come. Details of naturalists' trusts and much else relating to wildlife can be found at any Tourist Information Office (see p 122).

This idealised view of the shoreline shows some of the many species of birds which can typically be seen in such locations throughout the region. **A:** Curlew, with long bill for probing mud. **B:** Oystercatcher, with heavy bill for prising shells off rocks and crushing them. **C:** Bar-tailed Godwit, which probes mud for shellfish or worms. **D:** Redshank, with all-purpose bill able to probe for buried prey or snatch moving prey. **E:** Ringed Plover, with short bill for snatching small animals off the mud. **F:** Turnstone, which uses its short bill to do just that.

Long Distance Footpaths

The Pennine Way The first Long Distance Footpath to be so designated in Britain, it is also the second longest, stretching 250 miles from Edale in the Peak District to Kirk Yetholm north of the Scottish border. This atlas includes the section between Airton (24h) in North Yorkshire and the Scottish border (75a), winding through the Yorkshire Dales National Park and the Northumberland National Park on old packhorse tracks and drove roads, shepherds' tracks and Roman roads. It crosses such natural barriers as the Rivers Ure, Tees and Tyne and the Cheviot Hills as well as man-made structures like Hadrian's Wall. In fact, besides the great stretches of shaggy moorland, long ridges dipping sharply into valleys and the vast solitudes with no sound bar the tinkling of a brook or the rushing of wind through heather, there is much of historical and archaeological interest to be seen, including great earthworks, Norman churches and fine period houses, many of which are described in the gazetteer (sections ⋔, ⊞ and ✝). The Pennine Way is essentially a strenuous high-level path through predominantly wild country suitable only for walkers with some experience. Some of the route follows well trodden tracks marked with signposts, but in many places it crosses expanses of open moorland, devoid of prominent landmarks and consisting largely of peat, heather, bog and tussocks of rough grass. It is therefore vital to take heed of the safety advice given on this page.

An invaluable guide for anyone making a serious trek along all or part of the walk is 'The Pennine Way' (published by Her Majesty's Stationery Office) which provides detailed maps and general information on the walk. For the casual visitor or holidaymaker, however, the maps in this atlas are more than adequate; the path is clearly marked with a red dashed line.

The Cleveland Way This 93-mile path, the second to be officially opened, was completed in 1969 and is contained almost wholly within the North York Moors National Park. It stretches from Helmsley (28a) along the Hambleton and Cleveland Hills to the coast at Saltburn-by-the-Sea (52f) and then follows the coastline via Scarborough (43h), ending near Filey (30c). Although not one of the longest paths, it offers a great variety of scenery, ranging from the magnificent open moorland of the Cleveland Hills to the outstanding seascapes offered by some of the highest cliffs of the east coast. It also takes the walker past countless sites of archaeological and historical interest, such as Helmsley Castle (27c), Mount Grace Priory (40d) and the White Horse at Kilburn (27b), all described in the gazetteer section.

The route is readily accessible, even by car, and many sections are suitable for walking short distances. The entire length is marked with wooden signposts. Clothing should be suitable for both tough hill walking and muddy, overgrown and slippery ways, especially on the cliff section. An invaluable guide for the serious trekker is 'The Cleveland Way' (HMSO) which gives detailed maps and useful information; for the casual visitor or holidaymaker, however, our maps are more than adequate - the path is clearly marked on them with a red dashed line.

National Parks

The national parks of Britain are large areas, usually wild and sparsely populated, where special care is taken to conserve the natural landscape. However, very little of the land is nationally owned and even the open moorland usually belongs to someone, so that rights of access may be limited. National parks are jointly run by local planning committees and the Countryside Commission. They receive government aid for a range of activities: control of design and development of buildings; conservation measures such as the removal of eyesores, tree planting and laying out footpaths; and the provision of facilities like car parks, camp sites, information centres and country parks. The boundaries of all national parks are clearly marked on our maps with heavy green lines.

The waymark sign is used in plaque and stencil form by the Countryside Commission on long-distance footpaths

The National Parks and Long Distance Footpaths of the North Country, as described in the text on this page. The Parks are: **A** Lake District, **B** Yorkshire Dales, **C** North York Moors, **D** Northumberland, **E** Border Forest. The numbers indicate the relevant map pages.

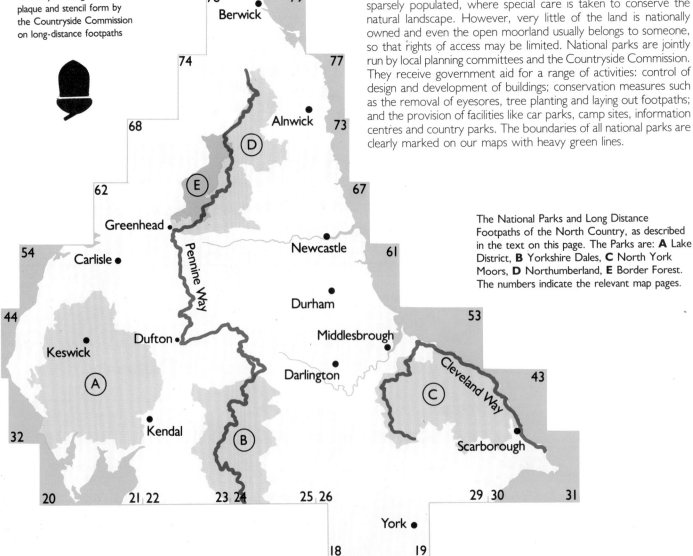

Stoney Cove and Thornthwaite Crag (map 34b).

The Lake District Some of the wildest, highest and most attractive mountains in Britain, as well as nearly all the largest lakes, are found within the 866-square miles of this spectacular national park. Lying wholly within the county of Cumbria, the park has three principal mountain ranges: the Skiddaw Slates, The Borrowdale Volcanics (including the famous 3200 ft Scafell Pike) and the Bannisdale Slates. The area is totally unspoilt and forms the most marvellous walking and climbing country with many paths and established routes to the summits or through the cols (see gazetteer sections ♣ and ▲).

The 463 mountain tarns combine with the 17 'waters' or 'meres' in the valleys to make an area which also abounds with boating and sailing activities (gazetteer entries under ⚲). Among the most notable lakes are the small and lovely Rydal Water, the 10½-mile-long Windermere and the serene Derwent Water with its many islands.

The Lake District is also famous for its association with such literary giants as Wordsworth, Coleridge, Beatrix Potter, Arthur Ransome, Ruskin and Hugh Walpole. Its historical and archaeological attractions include stone circles and barrows, early fortified village sites and Roman camps, dozens of which feature in the gazetteer (section ₥).

Yorkshire Dales A 680-mile-square park of mountains and moorland crossed by broad pastoral valleys. Its most remarkable features are the gritstone summits and the limestone escarpments that separate the deep green valleys. The scenery is magnificent: heather-clad moorlands, winding rivers, innumerable streams and waterfalls (known locally as 'forces'), pretty villages with many buildings of the traditional greystone, and green dales criss-crossed by drystone walls. Evidence of man's settlement from early times is seen in Bronze Age henges and tumuli, in Roman routes across the fells and in ruins like Rievaulx Abbey (27c), Middelham Castle (38h), details of which can be found in this gazetteer (sections ₥, ▥ and ✝).

Besides the Roman roads, there are many ancient tracks over the dales, making it a relative paradise for the serious walker and the casual rambler alike.

North York Moors This splendid park, with its boundary traced by the Cleveland Way, extends over 533 square miles from a rugged cliff-bound coastline, with some of the highest cliffs on the east coast, to the magnificent Vale of York. The central and northern moors are broad expanses of heather, over 1200 ft above sea level, which become purple and gold in late summer. Ideal for the walker, cyclist or motorist, the moors rise on their north-western border to the steep-sided Cleveland and Hambleton Hills, whose slopes carry extensive forests of larch and pine.

On the coast are precipitous fishing communities at Runswick, Staithes and Robin Hood's Bay whilst inland there are many well-proportioned villages of warm coloured stone. There are also many sites of historical and archaeological significance, including impressive ruined monasteries at Rievaulx, Byland, and Mount Grace, a Plantagenet castle at Helmsley, plus prehistoric burial places and a well-preserved Roman road near Goathland (see gazetteer sections ₥, ▥ and ✝ for details).

Northumberland Much of this remote and isolated park is high hill-country, embracing the Cheviot and Simonside Hills. A frontier region, the park has the added advantage of sharing its boundary with the Border Forest Park. Instead of offering the visitor a mere 398 square miles of worthwhile countryside, the combination gives 574 square miles of open leisure space, stretching from the Cheviots on the Scottish Border south to Hadrian's Wall. In between are open heather moors and wooded or grassy valleys of swift-flowing rivers like the Rede, Coquet and Tyne, all with much to interest both the casual visitor and the more serious walker. Although there are few through roads, most of the valleys are accessible by car for at least part of their length, after which there are excellent rights of way and footpaths, including the Pennine Way (see next page). There are excellent facilities for those interested in rock climbing (▲), fishing (⚲) or any field sport, while among the many interesting antiquities of the area are the large Roman fort at Housesteads (₥ 64e), the Temple of Mithras at Carrawburgh (₥ 65h), an array of mediaeval castles and towers set up in the troubled times of the Border Ballads, and - of course - Hadrian's Wall itself.

Border Forest Park (not a national park but large enough to be described in this section). This vast area of man-made forests extends over 300 square miles along the Cheviots and neighbouring hills in Northumberland, Cumbria and Scotland. There are in fact nine separate forests, the largest of which is Kielder - the biggest man-made forest in Europe. In Kielder is a new reservoir which is the largest man-made lake in Britain (equivalent in size to Ullswater in the Lake District). The whole area is run by the Forestry Commission who, to assist their work, have built over 500 miles of rough forest roads, many of which have since been turned into pleasant walks or drives for the public. In fact the park caters extensively for the walker, camper and casual day visitor: besides waymarked forest walks, exhibition centres, adventure playgrounds and camping sites, the Forestry Commission have provided facilties for trout fishing, deer stalking and game shooting. For the keen rambler and hill walker the forest roads lead to tracks linking the dales and the high hill ranges near the Scottish border. From the highest peak, the 1975 ft high Peel Fell (which stands right on the border) are excellent views of northern England and southern Scotland from the North Sea to the Solway Firth. For those interested in history the area abounds with hill forts, Roman camps, fortified farmsteads and castles, most of them reminders of troubled earlier times.

Calendar of Events

Events are listed by map reference, making it easy to discover what other attractions are available in any area at the same time. Remember that dates and times may vary from year to year and that you should always obtain more information before travelling, by telephoning either the number supplied or the nearest Tourist Information Office (see page 122).

January
42e Goathland: Plough Stots. A sword dance which celebrates an old ploughman's festival. *The Monday after Twelfth Night (6 January).*

May
42c Whitby: Planting of the Penny Hedge, Harbourside, Church Street. An old custom which originated in the Middle Ages when a hunting party of local lords mortally wounded the hermit of Eskdale. On his deathbed he spared their lives on condition that they carry out a penance; it was that they build 'with a penny knife' a hedge on the Whitby sands which would withstand three tides. *Eve of Ascension Day.*

79a Berwick-upon-Tweed: Riding the Bounds. A party of horsemen follow a ten mile route round the town's boundaries, a tradition which has continued since the reign of Henry VIII. *1st.*

June
18b Knaresborough: Bed Race, Conyngham Hall Grounds. *2nd Saturday 1300.*

47f Appleby: Horse Fair. Largest gypsy gathering of its kind. It has survived under the protection of a charter given by James II in 1685. Tel. (0930) 51177. *2nd Tuesday and Wednesday.*

48g Warcop: Rushbearing. Boys carrying rush crosses, and girls wearing crowns of flowers, proceed in procession through the village to the church where a short service is given. For details tel. Brough (093 04) 379. *29th, except when this falls on a Sunday when it is held on the previous Saturday.*

67g Newcastle: The Hoppings, Town Moor, Great North Road. A major gathering of many individual fairs from all over the country. *Mid-June to mid-July.*

July
18d Harrogate: Great Yorkshire Show, The Showground, Hookstone Oval. *2nd Tuesday to Thursday 0800-1900.*

33c Ambleside: Rushbearing. Procession through the town, led by a band, to St Mary's church for a short service, during which the Rushbearing Hymn is sung. After the service anyone who was carrying a rush cross is given a piece of gingerbread. For details tel. (096 63) 3205. *1st Saturday.*

48g Musgrave: Rushbearing (tel. 093 04 260). Procession to church where a short service is given and the rush crosses are presented to the clergy. Afterwards there is tea in the Village Hall and childrens' sports. *1st Saturday.*

55c Carlisle: Cumberland Show, Bitts Park. Tel. (0228) 710687. Major agricultural show. *3rd Thursday.*

60c Chester-le-Street: Durham County Agricultural Show, Lambton Park. *3rd Saturday.*

60i Durham: Miners' Gala. Colliery bands, etc. march through the city to The Sands for a mixture of festive and political events, usually including a speech by the leader of the Labour Party. *3rd Saturday.*

66b Whalton: Baal Fire Ceremony. This celebration, associated with fire-worship, has its origins in pagan times. Here a huge 'Baal Fire' is lit on the village green at sundown. *4th.*

67g Newcastle: The Hoppings. *See June.*

August
33c Ambleside: Sports. Popular day which includes track events, fell races, Cumberland and Westmorland wrestling and amateur cycling. Tel. Millom (0657) 2642. *Thursday before the 1st Monday.*

33c Grasmere: Rushbearing. Decorative procession around the village, of clergy and children carrying 'bearings', crosses made of rushes and flowers, to the church. After a short service, Grasmere gingerbread is given to all the children. For details tel. (096 65) 245. *Saturday nearest the 5th (St. Oswalds Day).*

33c Grasmere: Sports. Major Lakeland sporting fixture including fell races, Cumberland and Westmorland wrestling, hound trailing, pole leaping, high leaping and flat racing. For details tel. Ambleside (096 63) 2216. *3rd Thursday after 1st Monday.*

44c Cockermouth: Show. Agricultural show with livestock, produce and crafts; hound trails and Cumberland and Westmorland wrestling. For details tel. Maryport (090 081) 2925. *Saturday before 1st Monday.*

46b Skelton: Agricultural Show. Features a fancy dress competition, choosing the Country Princess, show jumping, pony sports, horse drawn vehicles and trade stands. For details tel. Penrith (0768) 62953. *3rd Saturday.*

46f Lowther Castle: Country Fair and Horse Driving Trials. Major four-in-hand driving event (Duke of Edinburgh usually competes), plus gymkhana, clay pigeon shoot, fishing demonstrations, etc. Details from estate office, tel. Hackthorpe (093 12) 392. *First or second weekend.*

46h Patterdale: Sheep Dog Trials, King George's Playing Fields. Tel. Glenridding (085 32) 266. Demonstrations and competitions as well as a terrier show, puppy trials, and a show of the Ullswater Foxhounds. *Bank Holiday Saturday.*

55c Carlisle: Great Fair. An old established fair of the which the centrepiece is an open air market with stall holders in period costume. Daily events detailed in information available from 𝒾 — tel. (0228) 25517. *Last week.*

69g Falstone: Border Shepherds' Show. *4th Saturday 0900.*

September
21f Urswick: Rushbearing. Procession from the old Grammar School in Little Urswick to Great Urswick. For details tel. Ulverston (0229) 56254. *Sunday nearest 29th (St Michael's Day).*

32a Egremont: Crab Fair. Tel. (0946) 820376. The fair, which dates back to 1267, begins with the distribution of apples to the public - crab apples were originally used, hence the name - in the main street. Features include greasy-pole climbing, 'World Gurning Championships' (the pulling of grotesque faces through a horse collar) and the 'Pipe Smoking' contest; also track and field events, shows and hound trails. *3rd Saturday 1230.*

33d Boot: Eskdale Show. Tel. Seascale (094 02) 333 ex. 240. In a magnificent setting amongst the mountains of the Hardknott Pass, this agricultural show is famous for its sheep sale. Other attractions include traditional singing and horn blowing. *Last Saturday.*

33f Hawkshead: Agricultural show famous for its exhibition of Herdwick sheep. Also features competitions, hound trailing and horse jumping. For details tel. (096 66) 292. *1st Tuesday.*

34i Kendal: Westmorland County Show. Tel. (0539) 23479. Recognised as one of the best one-day shows in the country, it features agricultural exhibitions, show jumping, wrestling, carriage driving and a Young Farmers 'welly race'. *2nd Thursday.*

43h Scarborough: Fair, William Street. Fair made famous by the old folk song. *Entire month.*

48h Brough: Hill Fair. A gypsy gathering about a mile outside Brough on the Appleby road which was once an important horse and cattle sale. For details tel. (093 04) 260. *30th.*

October
33a Wasdale Head: Wasdale Show. Tel. Ravenglass (065 77) 278. One of the premier sheep shows in Cumbria. Other activities include a tug-o'-war, pillow fights and fell races. *2nd Saturday.*

55d Wigton: Horse Sales. One of the largest one-day sales in the country, involving around 700 horses. For details tel. (096 54) 2202. *Last Wednesday.*

71a Alwinton: Border Shepherds' Show. Tel. Netherton (0669) 30246. One of the more famous shows in Northumbria, it features exhibitions of lambs and sheep, wrestling and hound trails. *10th.*

December
58b Allendale Town: Baal Fire Ceremony. Related to a similar ceremony in Whalton (see July), this ceremony happens round a huge bonfire. Costumed locals with blackened faces (known as Guisers) dance and parade carrying barrels of burning tar which are thrown onto the fire at midnight. *New Year's Eve.*

North Country - Key to map pages

Motorways	M5	National Parks		Battlefields	⚔
M'ways under const. & proposed		Forest Parks		Lighthouses	⍾
Motorway Junction Numbers	23 24 Restricted Access	Woods & Forests		Lightships	⚓
Motorway Service Areas	EXETER	Car Ferries	🚗	Summits	△ 672m
Dual Carriageways		Passenger Ferries		Spot Heights	. 223m
Dual C'ways under construction		Railways	STA L.C. (Level Crossing) Tunnel	Waterfalls	〜
Main Roads		Mineral Railways		Marshes	⚘
Secondary Roads		Disused Railways		Caves	⌒
Other Good Roads		Canals		Churches	+
Minor Roads & Tracks		Long Distance Footpaths		Coast Guard Stations	CG
Route Classification Numbers	A69 B631	Footpaths & Bridle Paths		Lifeboat Stations	LB
National Boundaries		Youth Hostels	▲ YH	Sandy Beaches	〜
County Boundaries		Airfields	✈	Rocky Foreshore	〜
Military Danger Zones	/////////	Windmills	⚑	Low Water Line	〜
National Trust Property	NT ●	Antiquities	∴	Cliffs	〜

HEIGHT OF LAND IN METRES AND FEET

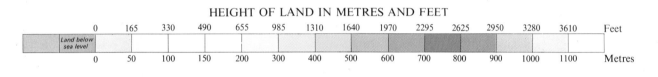

	0	165	330	490	655	985	1310	1640	1970	2295	2625	2950	3280	3610	Feet
Land below sea level															
	0	50	100	150	200	300	400	500	600	700	800	900	1000	1100	Metres

Activities covered in the gazetteer (with page numbers)

Where appropriate, these may be overprinted on the relevant black symbol above

- Countryside 80
- Picnic Sites 80
- Gardens and Arboreta 84
- Historical Sites 86
- Museums and Art Galleries 90
- Castles 93
- Historic Buildings 94
- Religious Places 97
- Bird Watching 102
- Industry Past and Present 104
- Tourist Railways 107
- Wildlife in Captivity 108
- Cruising by Boat 108
- Sailing and Boating 109

- Launching Slipways 109
- Water Sports 110
- Swimming Pools 110
- Fishing 111
- Skiing 116
- Climbing 116
- Riding and Pony Trekking 118
- Aviation 119
- Motor Sport 119
- Golf Courses 120
- Activities of Special Interest 121
- Towns Having Extensive Tourist Facilities
- Tourist Information Offices 122

18

a	b	c
d	e	f
g	h	i

26	27
18	19

0   1   2   3   4   5 Miles

0   1   2   3   4   5   6   7   8 Kilometres

High Gill Moor   Raventofts Hall   Markington   Monkton Mains   Newfields   Minskip   Heaton Ho.

Gill Moor   Hob Green   Hincks Hall   Park Ho.   Crow Ho.   Ornhams Hall   Grafton Lo.

Bowes Green   Shutt Ho.   "Barsneb"   High Cayton   Burton Leonard   Hall   Spellow Grange   Grafton

Bishop Thornton   South Stainley   HALL   Cayton Hall   Copgrove   Staveley   Marton   Marton Cot.

Black Ho.   Hardgate   Stainley Ho.   Grange   Spellow Hill   Brooms Ho.   Nineveh   Grassgills

Thornton B.   Shaw Mills   Scarah Moor   Cayton Grange   Hill Top   Walkingham Hill   Occaney   Loftus Hill   Forms Ho.   Lylands

Winsley   Hill Top   Newton Hall   Warren Ho.   Low Arkendale   Arkendale   Wall Close Ho.   Whixley Gr.

Bedlam   Broxholme Park   Nidd   Brearton   Farnham   Ferrensby   The Hoplars   Clareton

Burnt Yates   Moor   Brearton Grange   Hall   Gibbet Ho.   The Hollies   Claro Ho.   Coneythorpe   Allerton Park

Birstwith   Ripley   Malt Kiln Hill   Old Hall   Scotton   Linger Field   Hopewell Ho.   Gate Hill   Allerton Mauleverer

West Ho.   Clint Grange   Crag Hill   Killinghall   Niddmoor Ho.   Preston Ho.   90m Hosp.   Scriven   Flaxby

Clint   Track of Old Railway   Myer's Green   Spruisty   R. Nidd   Knaresborough   Hopperton

Hampsthwaite   Swincliffe   Sch.   Spruisty Hall Fm.   Knox Oak   Hall   Conyngham Hall   Goldsborough   A 59   Gelsthorp

West Syke Green   Levens Hall   Bilton   Park   Forest Lane Head   Well   Gallow Hill   Hall   Cattal Gran

Graytton Plain   Rowden   Oaker Bank   New Park   Abbey Mill Fm.   Oatlands   Northlands

HARROGATE   High Harrogate   Starbeck   Thistle Hill   Low Grange   Ribston Lo.   Highfield

White Ho.   Barracks   Sch.   Woodlands   Hospital   Scaliber   Plompton Hall   Park Ho.   Park

Holen Ho.   Oakdale   Birk Crag   The Stray   Oak View   Plompton Rocks   Loxley Grange   Little Ribston   Walshford

Harlow Hill   Pot Br.   Oatlands   Crimple Cot.   Crimple   Beck   Plompton Square   Walshford   Hunsin

Moor Park   Beckwithshaw   Pannal Ash   Govt. Offices   Ruddling Park   Braham Hall   Works   Cowthorp

Ten Acre Resr.   Beckwith Ho.   Lund   Rossett Green   College   All Saints' Court   Follifoot   Lo.   Crosper Ho.   Manor   North Deighton

Shaw Green   Pannal   Hill Top Hall   Day Cross   The Ridge   Aketon   Deighton Grange

Stainburn   Lanshaw Ho.   Tatefield Ho.   Brackenthwaite   Spofforth Moor   Ingmanthorpe

Cripple Head   MOOR   Spacey Houses   Swarth Hill   Oakwood Fm.   Haggs Fm.   Spofforth   Kirk Deighton

Briscoe Rigg   Spring Ho.   Nor Beck   Horn Bank   Sunrise   High Snape   Spofforth Park   Hall   Stockeld Grange

America   High Moor   Leyfield Ho.   Low Snape   Low Hall   Kirkby Overblow   Warren Ho.   Stockeld Park   Boggart Ho.

Braythorn   N. Rigton   Adlethorpe   Sicklinghall   Skerry Grange   Wetherby   Race Co.

Stainburn   Almscliff Crag   Spout Ho.   Dunkeswick Lo.   Lund Head   Stockeld Lo.   Parkhill

Banks   Huby   Swindon Hall   Barrowby   Linton Spring   Linton Hills   Flintmill Grange

Bogridge   Newby   Weeton Sta.   Healthwaite   Moor End   Swindon Grange   Morcar Hill   Kearby Town End   Wood Hall   Linton   Wetherby Grange

Riffa Ho.   Westfield   Weeton   Dunkeswick   Netherby   Clap Gate   Ho.   Whitwell Ho.

River Wharfe   Castley   Rougemont   Chapel Hill   Carlstonhill Fm.   Moor End   Collingham   Boston Spa

Arthington   Nunnery   Rawden Hill   Stank   Harewood   Stockton   Middlefield Far Field   Keswick Field   Grove   West Woods   Clifford

Creskeld Hall   Grange   Hewland Ho.   Weardley   Fish Pond   East Keswick   Rigton Hill   Compton

Staircase Ho.   Bank Foot   Bank End   Hollin Hall   Keswick Beck   East Rigton

Bramhope   Bank Side   Harewood Park   Lofthouse   Rigton Grange   Castle Hill

Breary Grange   Lineham   Bank Top   Stub Ho.   Bardsey   Hope Hall   Bramham

Eccup   Wike field Ho.   Biggin   Rigton Carr   Wothersome   Bramham Park

Camp Ho.   Black Hill   Owlet Hall   Wike   Low Green   Terry Lug   Well Hill

Eccup Resr.   Millfield Ho.   Manor Ho.   Black Moor   Scarcroft   Norwood Ho.   Kellfield Grange

ROMAN ROAD   Coolridge Hall   Alwoodley Old Hall   Brandon Ho.   Scarcroft Hill

Crag Ho.   Alwoodley   Alwoodley Gates   Brandon Ho.   East Rigton   Thorner   Bramham Park

Adel   Black Moor   Slaid Hill   Shadwell   Wigtofts   Kiddal Lane End

Cookridge Tower   Camp Town   Dunstarn   Grange Blackwood   Birkby Hill   Sand Hills   Kiddal Hall

HORSFORTH   Moor Allerton   Park Villas   Red Hall   Cobble Hall   Whin Moor   Saw Wood Ho.   Potterton Hall   Becca Hall

Megawood Park   Carr Manor   Roundhay Park   Bramley Grange   Arthursdale   Stockeld   Scholes   St. Johns

27	28
18	**19**

a	b	c
d	e	f
g	h	i

19

YORK

20

a	b	c
d	e	f
g	h	i

32	33
20	21

33	34
20	21	22

a	b	c
d	e	f
g	h	i

21

35	36
22	**23**	24

a	b	c
d	e	f
g	h	i

23

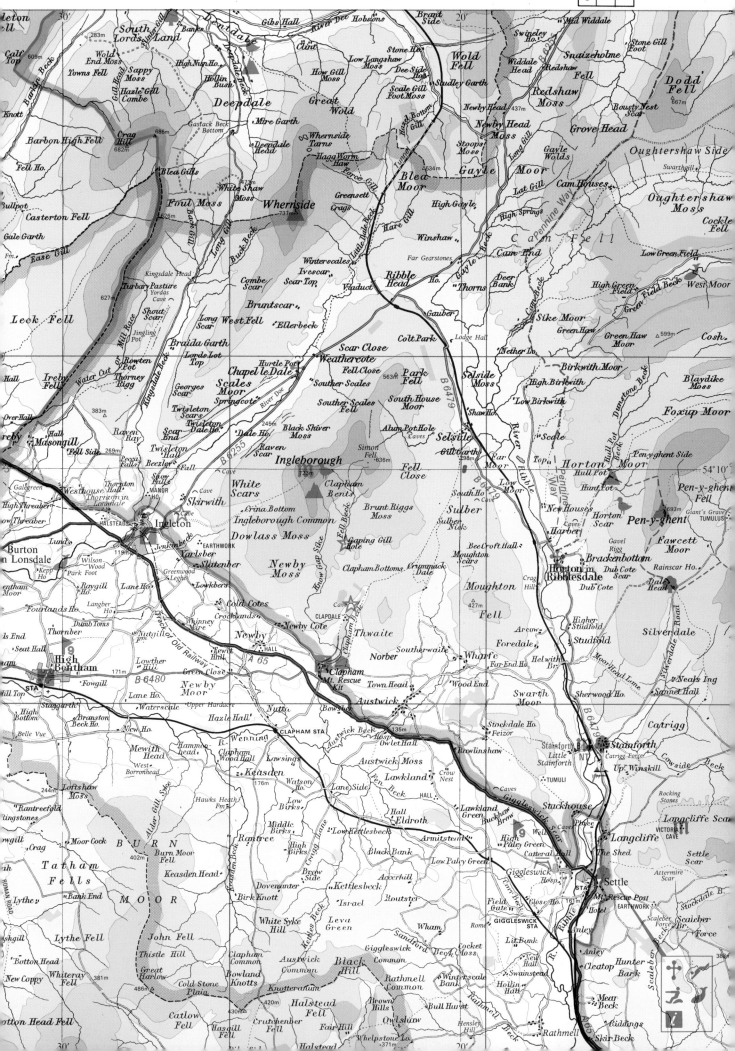

24

a	b	c
d	e	f
g	h	i

36	37
23	**24**	25

0 1 2 3 4 5 Miles
0 1 2 3 4 5 6 7 8 Kilometres

2°W

Pennine Way
Stone Gill Foot
Bousty Nest Scar
Grove Head
Dodd Fell
667m
Duerley Beck
Green Side
589m
Bardale Beck
Marsett
614m
Bella or Knight Close
Ch.
Raydale
Stalling Busk
Stake Fell
Side Head
Heck Brow
Haw Head
Littleburn
Forelands
Newbiggin
Blind Syke
New Gill Ho.
Cross Ho.
Bishopdale Beck
B 6160

Raydale Grange
Raydale Ho.
The Rookery
Ribba Hall
Myres Garth
Hargill Ho.
Haw Ho.
Doves

Fleet Moss
Tarn
Jeffery Pot
Billinside Moor
Cragdale Water
Thoralby Common
537m
Stake Fell
NT
Long Ridge
Riggs
Dewersit Moss
Bishopdale Edge
Walden Moor
Bridge End

Oughtershaw Side
Swarthgill
424m
Nethergill
Oughtershaw Tarn
Oughtershaw Beck
Cragdale Moor
West Side
Stake Moss
Kidstones
Kidstones Fell
Bishopdale Head
Dale Head
West Pasture Scar
Naughtberry Hill
Kentuckey Ho.
Walden Moor
Brad Mo

Cam Houses
Oughtershaw Moss
Cocklee Fell
Beckermonds Scar
High Bank
Oughtershaw
Hall
Cush Rigg
Yockenthwaite Moor
Chapel Moor
Cray Moss
Tarn
Bishopdale Gavel
Brown Haw

Low Green Field
Beckermonds
LANGSTROTHDALE
CHASE
Deepdale
R. Wharfe
Yockenthwaite
Cray
Buckden Pike
702m
Groove End
West Gill
Coverhead Fm

High Green Field
West Moor
Maze
Eller Carr Moss
Little Fell
Raisgill
Hubberholme Ch.
Cow Close
Out Moor
North Moor

Green Field Beck
Green Haw Moor
599m
Cosh
Cosh Beck
Eller Carr
605m
Horse Head Moor
Kirk Gill
285m
Wharfedale
Starbotton Fell
East Stone Gill
Great Hunters Stone

Dalnstone Beck
Blaydike Moss
Foxup
East Side
Kirk Gill Moor
Buckden
Shooting Ho.
504m
Tor Mere Top

Hull Pot
Foxup Beck
Halton Gill
Moss Top
Birks Fell
Birks Tarn
Cam Head
Earthwork

Horton Moor
Hull Pot
Hunt Pot
Foxup Moor
Hesleden High Bergh
R. Skirfare
Potts Moor
Out Moor
Firth Fell
Starbotton
Cam Gill Beck
River Wharfe

Up. Hesleden
Hesleden
Hesleden Beck
Middle Moor
Capple Stones
607m
Haw Fell
Moor End Fell
Moor End
West Scale Park
East Scale Park

Pen-y-ghent Fell
Pen-y-ghent Gill
Litton
Hall
Litton dale
Ackerley Moor
Old Cote Moor Top
704m
Great Whernside

Pen-y-ghent
693m
Giants Grave
TUMULUS
Dawson Close
East Garth
Cow Close
Old Cote Moor
B 6160

Horton Scar
Gavel Rigg
Fawcett Moor
Blishmire Ho.
624m
Cow Close Fell
Scoska Moor
Hay Tongue
Hay Dike

Dub Cote Scar
Newlaid Ho.
Dale Head
Pennine Way
Rainscar Ho.
Darnbrook Fell
668m
Fountains Fell Tarn
West Moor
Brootes Barn
Arncliffe
208m
Kettlewell
Crooka Well

YORKSHIRE
Silver dale
Fountains
Darnbrook Ho.
Field Ho. Barn
Blue Scar
Skirfare R.
Hawkswick Moor
Hawkswick
Conistone

Moor Head Lane
Silverdale
Out Fell
Fell
Thoragill Beck Ho.
Cowside Beck
Arncliffe Cote
Low Cote Moor
High Wind Bank
Mile Ho.

Neals Ing
Sannat Hall
Tennant Gill
593m
Knowe Fell
Flask
Parsons Pulpit
538m
High Cote Moor
Cote Gill Knotts
DOUKY BOTTOM CAVE
North Cote
Throstles Nest

Catrigg
Rough Close
Westside Houses
Stanggill Barn
Flock Rake
Hawkswick Clowder
Kilnsey Crag
Kilnsey
Gill Ho

Stainforth
Catrigg Force
Water Ho.
DALES
Nature Trail
NT
Middle House Fm.
High Mark
Kilnsey Moor
Conistone

Up. Winskill
Cowside Beck
Capon Hall
446m
Tarn Moss
Malham Tarn Field Centre
Malham Tarn
High Mark Brow
Chapel Ho.
Bare Ho.
396m

Cowside
Black Hill
Higher Trenhouse
Streets
Low Tran Ho.
Great Close
High Stony Bank
Mastiles Gate
Malham Moor
Waterfall
Bastow Wood
Yarnbury

Rocking Stones
Cave
Langcliffe Scar
VICTORIA CAVE
NT
Back Scar
Prior Rakes
Gordale Beck
396m
Mastiles
STONE CIRCLE
Grass Wood
SETTLEMENT

Langcliffe
The Shed
Grizedales
NATIONAL
Malham Lings
Lee Gate Ho.
Bordley Hall
Height Laithe
Netherside
297m
Spring Ho
High Garn Ho.
Grassington

Settle
Rescue Post
EARTHWORK
Settle Scar
Great Scar
553m
Ewe Moor
Malham Cove
Gordale Scar
New Houses
Firth Hill
Gryedale Ho.
Skythorns
Threshfield
Falls
Low Br.
Lythe Ho.

Attermire Scar
Stockdale
Kirby Fell
Rye Loaf Hill
Malham
Gordale Br.
The Weets
Know Bank
Threshfield Moor
Lainger Ho.
Linton

Scaleber Force
Scaleber Br.
Scaleber Force
High Side
Acraplatts
Kirkby Top
219m
Out Gang
Calton Moor
Hetton Common
Boss Moor
Langerton Ho.
Escoe Ho.
R.

Hunter Bark
Mear Beck
Scosthrop Moor
Ingle Beck
Kirkby Malham
Kirkby Beck
Hanlith Hall
Bark Lathe
Winterburn Moor
Captain Moor
Way Gill
Winterburn Resr.
Linton Moor
Threapland

Biddings Lane
Kir Beck
Crake Moor
Otterburn
Scosthrop
Calton
Winterburn Wood
Winterburn Beck
PARK
The Fleets
B 6265
Green
Cracoe
Burnsa Thorp

Skellands
Dykelands
Hellifield
In Fell
201m
506m
Cracoe Fell
2°W

CRAVEN

26

a	b	c
d	e	f
g	h	i

	38	39
25	26	27

0 1 2 3 4 5 Miles
0 1 2 3 4 5 6 7 8 Kilometres

Ripon

Masham

West Tanfield

Kirklington

Boroughbridge

Fountains Abbey

Studley Royal

Kirkby Malzeard

Sawley

Bishop Thornton

Markington

Ripley

Burton Leonard

South Stainley

North Stainley

Wath

Melmerby

Baldersby

Skipton upon Swale

Pickhill

Roxby

Sinderby

Burneston

Theakston

Snape

Well

Carthorpe

Galphay

Laverton

Grantley

Winksley

Sharow

Copt Hewick

Bridge Hewick

Littlethorpe

Bishop Monkton

Staveley

Farnham

Nidd

Scotton

Brearton

Thornton Watlass

Firby

Clifton Castle

High Ellington

Low Ellington

Thirn

Rookwith

39 40
26 27 28
18 19

a b c
d e f
g h i

27

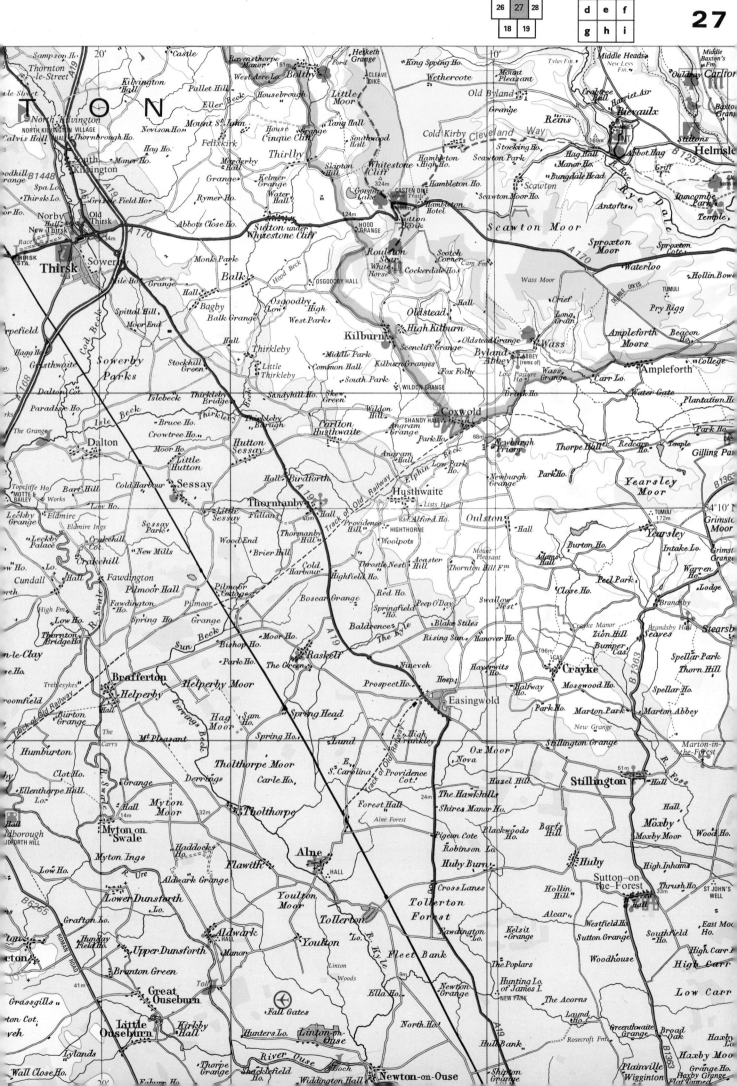

a	b	c
d	e	f
g	h	i

	40	41	
27	**28**	29
	19		

0   1   2   3   4   5 Miles

0   1   2   3   4   5   6   7   8 Kilometres

R Y E   D A

New Leys Fm.
Middle Heads
Ouldray Fm.
Carlton
Middle Barton's Fm.
Kirkbymoorside
MOAT
Spaunton Moor
Loand Ho.
50'
Pockley
Lund Head
Lund Co.
Ford
Starfits
Kirby Mills
Broats
Keldholme
Bogg Hall
TUMULI
Sinnington
Friarshill
Wr
abtree
Harriet Air
Rievaulx
ABBEY
Baxtons Grange
Cartoft
Manor Ho.
Keld Knowle
Abbot Hag
Griff
B 1257
Helmsley
CAS (rems of)
Duncombe Park
Temple
Hollin Bower
Beadlam
Nawton
A 170
Hall
Welburn
Lit. Edstone
Wythes
South Ings
Great Edstone
Sinnington Lo.
Sinnington Common
Cliff Ho.
Saltons
Breaks
Grange
Wombleton
40m
Harome Heads
Shaw Moor
Bowforth
Welburn Grange
Hill End
Marton
71m
Riseborough Hagg
Gallow Heads
Sykes
72m
proxton Moor
Sproxton Cote
A 170
Waterloo
Sproxton
Hall
Low Woods
106m
Rye Ho.
Harome
Aby Green
MOAT
Crook Ho.
Low Ground
Wombleton Grange
Sunley Hill
Sunley Co.
Riccal Moor
Southfield
Welburn Grange
White Thorn Ho.
Rook
Low Riseborough
Lance Butts
Low Riseborough
83m
Sparrow Hall
Highfield
Salton Lo.
Bridge Ho.
Normanby
Normanby Lo.
Manor
Throstle Nest
Golden Square
W. Newton Grange
Bank Top
NEWTON HALL
Nunnington
R. Riccal
Trowbridge
North Holme Ho.
Grange
Riccal Ho.
Low Woods
Muscoates
Grange
26m
Salton
Salton Grange
Hob Ground Ho.
Stainers
G! Carr
Ampleforth Moors
Beacon Ho.
Pry Rigg
DOUBLE DIKES
TUMULI
Double Dikes
Ampleforth
Oswaldkirk
College
Hall
Laysthorpe Lo.
Stonegrave
Nunnington
Highfield Ho.
River Rye
West Ness
East Ness
Waterholmes
Brawby Grange
Brawby
White Ho.
41m
Great Barugh
Little Barugh
42m
2m
Misp
Alma Fm.
rr Lo.
Water Gate
Plantation Ho.
B 1363
Caulkley's Bank
Caulkleys Grange
26m
Low Moors
Tuff
Redcarr Ho.
Temple
Park Ho.
Gilling East
Gilling Park
CAS
Low Warren Ho.
Hovingham Spa.
Cawton
Hol Beck
32m
Marrs Beck
Tuft Ho.
South Holme
Wath Beck
Slingsby Carr
Butterwick
Grange
Lit. Habton
Villa
Gosling
Sho
21m
Great Habton
Yearsley Moor
Syke Gate
"Stocking"
Hall
Hovingham
Temple
TUMULI
Haverfield Ho.
Barton Moor
Sleights
Manor Fm.
Ryton Grange
10'N
TUMULI
172m
Grimston Moor
Thorn Tree Ho.
Wool Knoll
TUMULUS
Temple
Fryton
Wath
CAS (rems of)
Slingsby
Wandale
Manor Ho.
Garr
Hazel H.
O
River
Yearsley
Intake Lo.
Grimston Grange
Coulton
Swathgill
Hovingham Lo.
EARTHWORK
TUMULUS
Barton-le-Street
B 1257
67m
Appleton-le-Street
Amotherby
Brot
! Park
Warren Ho.
Lodge
MAZE
Moor Ho.
Airyholme
TUMULUS
TUMULI
EARTHWORK
Swinton
Zion Hill
mper Cas.
Brandsby
Brandsby Hall
Seaves
Stearsby
Howardian Hills
MAZE
Cliff Field Ho.
107m
Dalby Bush
Wigganthorpe
Cotril
Howthorpe
Park Ho.
105m
Swinton Grange
Mo
Spellar Park
Thorn Hill
Skewsby
Dalby
Flat Top Ho.
Coneysthorpe
Eastthorpe Hall
Bog Hall
Hildenley
Trigger Cas.
Musley Bank
arton Park
Spellar Ho.
Foulrice
Deeply Ho.
Witherholm Hall
Whenby
Thorn Cot.
Ganthorpe
Great Lake
Obelisk
Castle Howard
Mausoleum
Gaterley
Roughborough Fm.
Bar Ho.
Marton Abbey
Clifton Ho.
Primrose Hill
Mowthorpe
Mowthorpe Dale
93m
Pyramid
Nod' Hill
Golden Hill
Porto
Stillington
31m
R. Foss
Marton-in-the-Forest
Hall
Cheese Vat Hall
Dudley Hill Ho.
Bulmer Beck
East Moor Banks
Welburn
Hutton Hill
High Hutton
A 64
79m
Low Hutton
Farlington
Cornbrough Hall
Stittenham
Bulmer
Mill Ho.
Monument
53m
Mt. Pleasant
Whitwell on the Hill
Elmire Fm.
Hall
Firby
Mr
Hall
Moxby
Up! Thowthorpe
Cornbrough Villa
Mt. Pleasant
Wheatclose Ho.
West Mill Ho.
Grange
Kirkham
PRIORY (rems of)
Westow
B 1363
Moxby Moor
Wood Ho.
Lt. Thowthorpe
Cornbrough Fm.
Westfield Ho.
71m
Sheriff Hutton
CAS
Sheepclose Ho.
Sheriff Hutton Park
Gower Ho.
Grange
Park Ho.
Whitwell
Cliff Ho.
Ch.
Brown Moor
St. John's Well
Moor Ho.
Bracken Ho.
West Lilling
Thornton le Clay
Lo.
Foston
Foston Rectory
Barton Hill
Pasture Ho.
Crambe
30m
Grange
utton-on-the-Forest
High Inhams
Thrush Ho.
53m
Low Roans
Lilling Hall
Thornton Cot.
Clay Hall
Penh
Hall
East Moor
High Roans Ho.
Lilling Green
E. Lilling Ho.
Grange
Red Ho.
Barton le Willows
Crambe Grange
R. Derwent
Gally Gap
75m
Busk Hi
Westfield Ho.
Sutton Grange
High Carr
Forest Carlton
Gennell Ho.
Leckby Ho.
Grange
Manor Ho.
Willow Bridge
Nearfield Ho.
Howsham
Howsham Br.
Oxfield Ho.
Middlefield Ho.
Woodhouse
Low Carr
Canal Head
Walbutts
DANGER ZONE
LC
B. Foss
Flaxton
Harton
Field Ho.
Lodges
Paradise
Grange
reenthwaite Ho.
Rosecroft Fm.
Broad Oak
Strensall
LC
B. Foss
White Averham
Bossall
Barnby Ho.
Leppington
Beck H.
Plainville
Wigginton
Haxby Moor
16m
Grange Ho.
Flat Topped
Haxby
Strensall Common
Claxton Hall
Claxton
Mt. Pleasant
Grange
Leppington Beck
Scrayingham
50'

41	42
28	29	30

a	b	c
d	e	f
g	h	i

29

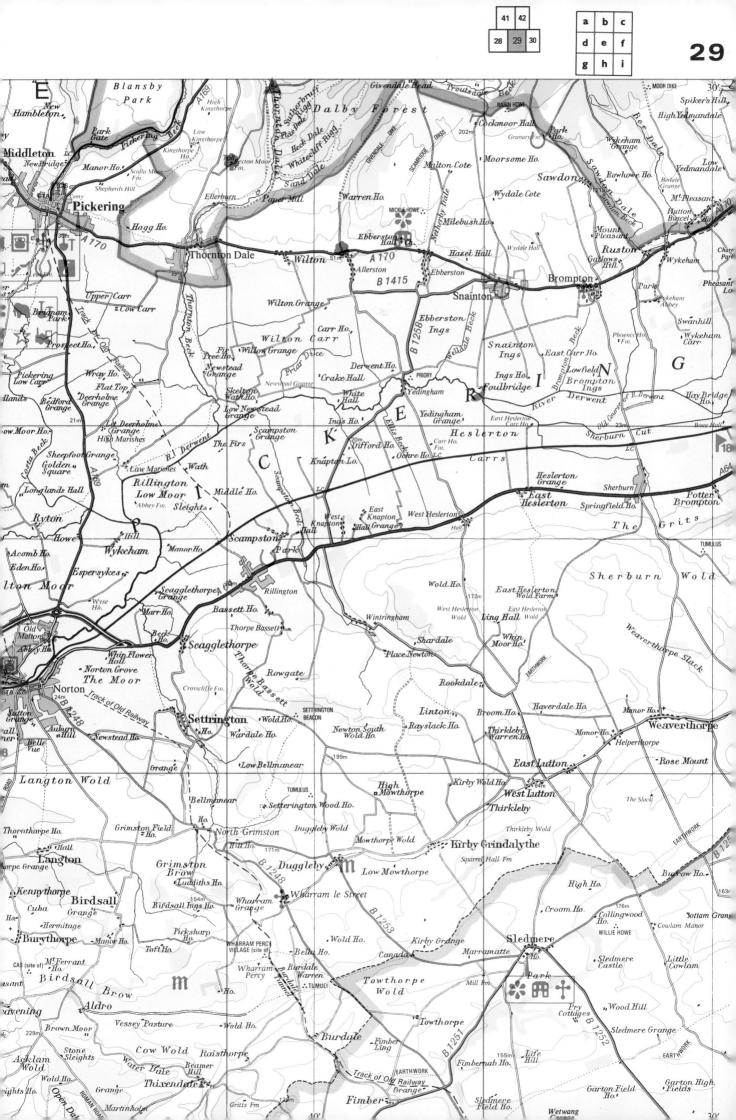

43
30 31

a b c
d e f
g h i

31

10'   0°

N   O   R   T   H

S   E   A

54°10'N

g & Queen Rock
Dulcey Dock
Speeton Cliffs
on   *Crab Rocks*
Speeton Moor   *Buckton Cliffs*
B 1229
Buckton Hall   *Bempton Cliffs*
Bempton
Grange   107m   *Cat Nab*
High Huntow   *Wandale*   *Gull Nook*
Fm   **Buckton**
L.C.   *"Metlands"*   *North Cliff*   *Thornwick Nab*
STA   **Bempton**   *LB*   *Breil Nook*
B 1229   B 1255   *CG*
Newsham Field   L.C.   *North Moor*   *Cradle H.d*
Norlands   *Lynhams*   **18**
North   *Field H.*   L.C.   STA   *TOWER*   *Selwicks Bay*
Mount   *Marton*   B 1255   *94m*
ntow   B 1255   B 1259   **FLAMBOROUGH HEAD**
ntow   *Ocean View*   *High Stacks*
Marton Lo.   *Nature*   *Dyke* **Flamborough**
The Grange   *Hall*   *Trail* *Cottages*
B 165   *Sewerby Fields*   *Danes Dyke*
Sewerby Cot.   **Sewerby Hall**   *South Landing*
B 1255   B 1255A   **Sewerby**
CG   *Sewerby*
Old Town   *Rocks*
North
14m   *Sands*
STA
BRIDLINGTON
165
LB
Hilderthorpe

B R I D L I N G T O N   B A Y

South
Sands

Wilsthorpe

VILLAGE
(site of)
orpe   *Fraisthorpe*
Sands

10'   0°

45	46
32	33	34
20	21

a	b	c
d	e	f
g	h	i

33

34

a	b	c
d	e	f
g	h	i

	46	
33	34	35
	21	22

Miles 0 1 2 3 4 5
Kilometres 0 1 2 3 4 5 6 7 8

Grasmere Rydal Ambleside Troutbeck Kentmere Mosedale

Hawkshead Windermere Bowness-on-Windermere Staveley Crook

SOUTH LAKELAND

Newby Bridge Backbarrow Levens

Cartmel Fell Whitbarrow Underbarrow Sizergh Castle

38

a	b	c
d	e	f
g	h	i

	49	50	
37	**38**	39
	25	26	

0 1 2 3 4 5 Miles
0 1 2 3 4 5 6 7 8 Kilometres

Thwaite · Scargill · Gutters · Barningham Park · Newsham Lo. · Nor Beck · Early Lo. · Newsham Ho. · Newsham · Sorrowful Hill · Carkin Fields · Park Ho.
Bragg Ho. · Barningham · Browson · West Layton · East Layton · Forcetts Barns · Langdale · Micklow
Barnathwaite · West Hope · Haythwaite · Park Ho. · Dalton Fields · Dunsa Bank · Green Bank · Fox Well · Carkin Grange · High Langdale · Low Hang Bank
East Hope Forest · Barningham Moor · Carter Ho. · Silverhill · Lands · Dalton Grange · Dalton · Dalton Beck · Carkin Moor · Low Grange · Brecon Ho. · Melsonby · Middle Caves
How Tallon · Newsham Moor · Windsor Lo. · △390m · Dousgill · Ravensworth · High Grange · Gatherley Moor · Kneeton Hall
Arndale Hill · Arndale Beck · Long Green Gate · Low Ho. · Crumma Ho. · Throstle Gill · Gayles · Hall · CAS · Kirby Hill · Blackhill · 189m · Hartforth Grange · High Merrybent
Kexwith Moor · Holgate Moor · Hornbriggs · Gayles Moor · DANGER ZONE · Pace's Ho. · Grove Gill Ho. · Whashton Green · Whashton · Hartforth · Rock Castle · Kirklands · Violet Grange
Moresdale Gill · Kexwith · 398m · High Waitgate · Grass Moor · Sturdy Ho. · Whashton Springs · Whashton Hag · Crabtree Ho. · Gilling West · Sedbury Park · Middleton Grange · Scotch Co
Moresdale Ridge · West Ho. · Cordilleras · High Feldom · Buddle Ho. · High Moor · Aske Moor · Gillingwood Hall · Gilling Grange · Sedbury
Hurst Moor · Hallgute · Helwith · Marske Moor · East Feldom · Jockey Cap Plant · Coalsgarth · Low Little Houses · Aske Hall · Temple · Mouldron · Oliver · Skeeby Mill · Morris
Fell End Moor · Shaw Moor · Shaw Beck · Shaw · Telfit · DANGER ZONE · Richmond Cut Moor · Aske Beck · 18 · Osythe · Skeeby · Scurray
Washfold · Hurst · Orgate · Park Top · High Gingerfield · Belleisle · Bend Hagg · High Wath Cote
Jingle Pot · Skelton Moor · Green Ho. · Rubbing Ho. · Jingle Pot · Applegarth · Swale · Richmond · Union Ho.
Owlands · Moor Ho. · Skelton · Clints · Thorpe under Stone · Vicars Green · A6108 · NT · Sandford · CAS · Easby
Marrick Moor · Wood Ho. · Copperthwaite · Hall · Huttons Moor · Downholme Park · Hudswell · St Martins · Wood Ho. · River Swale
Reeth · High Fremington · Hagg Cot. · Hollins · Deer Park · Sour Nook · DANGER ZONE · Sand Beck · Brokes · Holly Ho. · A6136 · Colburn · Thornbrough CATARACTONIUM
Grinton · 176m · Nun Cote Nook · High Oxque · Low · Ellerton Ho. · Hudswell Grange · Waithwith Bank · Hilltop Ho. · Catterick Camp · Hipswell · Harley Hill
Dike Ho. · Marrick · PRIORY · Marrick Park · Downholme Moor · Downholme · Scotton Hall · Breckenbrough
Cogden Hall · Ellerton Abbey · Stolerston Wood · 311m · Halfpenny Ho. · 305m · Hipswell Moor · Barden Fell · DANGER ZONE · Ulwith · Silver Hill · Manor Ho. · Tunstall
Cogden Moor · Stainton · Wath Gill · Coldstorms · Barden · Newfound England · Hauxwell Moor · Scotton · Scotton Beck · The Mound · High Field
Grinton Moor · Ellerton Moor · DANGER ZONE · WALBURN HALL · Crowhill · Boston · Halfpenny Moor · Barden Moor · Gandale · Belmount · Winterfield

R I C H M O N D S H I R E

Preston Moor · Peat Fell · Stainton Moor · Cross Gill Top · △411m · Spring Gill Beck · Barden Dykes · Glass Ho. · Cote Ho. · Hornby
Redmire Moor · DANGER ZONE · Black Beck · 259m · Skelton Cote · Barden · East Hauxwell · Wyrill Grange
Broomber Beck · Bellerby Moor · A6108 · Old Hall · Garriston Beck · Manor Ho. · Shindry · Arrathorne
Broomber Rigg · Bellerby · Leyburn Moor · Manor Ho. · Garriston · Hunton · Old Park Ho.
Castle Bolton · Scarth Nick · Preston under Scar · Washfold Ho. · Bellerby Beck · The Grotto · Brompton · E. Brompton
Castle Bank · Elm Ho. · Brookside · Intake Ho. · High Side · Crag · Wild Hill · Hesselton
Redmire · Hill Top · Rock Castle · Moor Ho. · Park Ho. · Burton Hall · Unthank · Akebar Fm · A684 · Patrick Brom
Low Bolton · Wood End · Westfield Ho. · Leyburn · 174m · Park Grange · Studdah · Constable Burton · Chapel Lane Ho. · Newton Beck · Butterwell
Redmire Force · Bolton Hall · Cliff Lo. · A684 · Stoop Ho. · Goods Line · Scrog Ho. · Finghall · Newton-le-
Swinithwaite · Wensley · River Ure · Harmby · How Hills · Spennithorne · Hutton Hill · Ruswick · Aysgarth School
Wanlas Park · West Witton · Gale Bank · A6108 · Eastfield Ho. · Low Hutton · Thornton Lo. · Lindale Lo.
Temple · Oaktree Ho. · Park Gate · The Park · Old Hall · Hallwith Ho. · Hutton Hang · Thornton Grange · Croft Ho.
Chantry · Spigot Lo. · Middleham · Hollins Ho. · Thornton Rust · High Marrifirth
Westwitton Moor · Middleham High Moor · Low Moor · Middleham · 236m · Hall · MOTTE & BAILEY · Danby Hall · Dantzic Ho. · Sand Hill · Highpond Ho.
Penhill Beacon · 546m · Ash Gill · Cotescue · Coverham Abbey · River Cover · Lodge · East Witton · Thornton Steward · Woodhouse · Rookwith
Hazely Peat Moor · Agglethorpe · Gilder's Beck Ho. · Braithwaite Hall · Fleets Ho. · Jervaulx Abbey · Jervaulx Park · Kilgram Grange · Helming
Burton Moor · Melmerby Moor · Melmerby · Caldbergh · East Scrafton · Braithwaite Moor · Low Newstead · High Jervaux · A6108 · Ewemire Low
Harland Hill · Carlton Moor · Carlton · Howden Lo. · Lanehb · Sowden Beck · Sowden Beck Ho. · Jervaulx · Eelmire · The Hermitage · Clifton Lo.

50 51
38 39 40
26 27

a b c
d e f
g h i

39

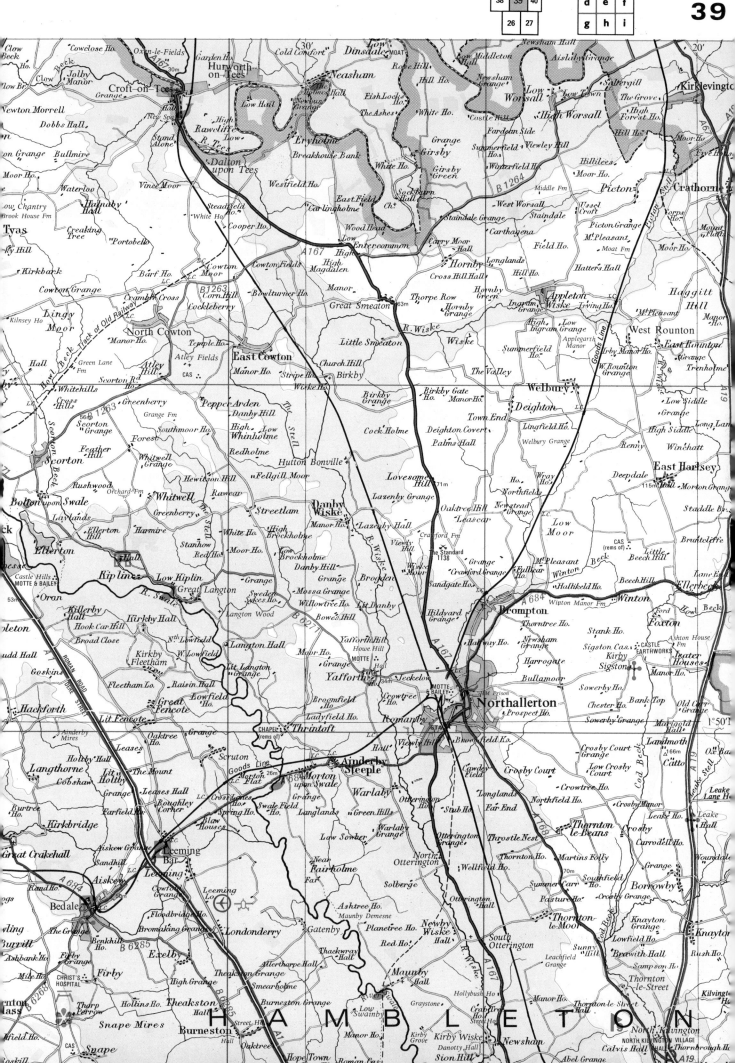

a	b	c
d	e	f
g	h	i

	51	52	
39	40	41	
	27	28	

0 1 2 3 4 5 Miles

0 1 2 3 4 5 6 7 8 Kilometres

Newsham Hall · Aislaby Grange · Low Worsall · Saltergill · Low T'n · The Grove · High Forest Ho. · Hall · Red Hall · White Hall · Hilton · Low Ho. · Howe Hill · Stanley Grange · Great Ayton · Cleveland Lo. · Rye Hill · Great Ayton Sta. · Little Ayton

High Worsall · Hill Ho. · Moor Ho. · Kirklevington · Middleton on Leven · Carr Ho. · Grange · Tanton · Manor Ho. · Grange · Woodhouse · Ayton Firs

Viewley Hill · Hillilees · Moor Ho. · Picton · Five Houses · Spyknave Hill · Windy Hill · Seamer · Seamer Hill · Tanton Dykes · Quakers Grove · Harland Hall · Easby

Middle Fm. · Staindale · Ussel Croft · Picton Grange · Mt Pleasant · Moor Ho. · Crathorne · Hunter Banks · Low Foxton · High Foxton · Goslingfire · Seamer Moor · Stokesley · Apple Grove · Tame Br. · Broughton · Prospect Hill · Mill Vale · Field Ho. · Pilly Hall · Drummer Hall · White Ho.

Field Ho. · Hatter's Hall · Haggitt Hill · R. Leven · Manor Grange · Hutton Rudby · Rudby · Sexhow · Thoraldby · Busby Ho. · Brawith · Broughton Br. Beck · Creyke Nest

Hill Ho. · Appleton Wiske · Irving Ho. · Mt Pleasant · Doddle Hill · Belle Vue · Broad Carr · Brook Ho. · Toft Hill · Over Green · Enterpen · Linden Grove · Lincoln · Carlton Grove · Great Busby · Dromonby Ho. · Kirby · Great Broughton · Ingleby Greenhow · Meynell Hall

West Rounton · East Rounton · Grange · Potto Grange · Raven Hill · Goulton · Faceby Grange · Carlton in Cleveland · Busby Hall · Bagdale Hill · Kirby Grange · Spring Ho.

Welbury · Deighton · East Rounton · Irby Manor Ho. · Trenholme · Wellington · Potto Carr · Potto Hall · Thorn Hill · Faceby · Underhill Ho. · Busby Moor · Cleveland Way · Hasty Bank · Garfit · The Holm

Lingfield Ho. · Welbury Grange · High Siddle · Long Lands · Summerfield Ho. · Springfield Ho. · Ingleby Arncliffe · Shepherd Hill · W. Lees · Whorlton · Swainby · Huthwaite Green · Live Moor · Broomflat · Staindale · Hall Garth · Cold Moor · Urra · Northwood

Low Siddle Grange · High Siddle · Winchatt · Renny · East Harlsey · Ingleby Cross · Arncliffe Hall · Hollin Hill · Sunny Side · Scugdale · Scugdale Hall · West Cote · Cote · Bank Ho. · Bilsdale Hall · Seave Green

Wray Ho. · Northfields · Deepdale · Hawknest · Morton Grange · Scarth Wood Moor · Near Moor · Harfa Beck · Harfa Bank · Crosslets · Holiday Ho. · High Ho. · Raisdale Beck · Ewe Hill · Cock Flat · Chop Gate

Low Moor · Staddle Br. · Cleveland Tontine · Mount Grace Priory · Black Shaw · Whorlton Moor · Shooting Box · Green Howe · Cairn Circle · Bride Stone · Ellermire

McPleasant · Fullscar · Braincliffe · Lady's Chapel · Osmotherley · Shooting Box · CLEVELAND · Orterley · Nab End Moor · Cam Ho.

Thorntree Ho. · Stank Ho. · Foxton · Lane End · Osmotherley Moor · Chequers · Snilesworth Moor · Prod Hills · High Farm · Arnsgill Ridge · Crooklet · Bilsdale West Moor · High Ewecote · Bracken

Newsham Grange · Sigston Cas. · Castle Earthworks · Ashton House · Slater Houses · Thimbleby Lo. · Oak Dale Res. · Moor Ho. · Douglas Ridge · Snilesworth Lo. · Low Arns Gill · Cow Ridge · Parci Gill · Fangdale Beck

Harrogate · Bullamoor · Kirby Sigston · Sigston Grange · Thimbleby · Thimbleby Moor · Dale Head · Low Cote · Wheat Beck · Scotland · High Thwaites · Wether Ho. · Malkin Bower

Chester Ho. · Sowerby Ho. · Old Carr Grange · Thimbleby Grange · Over Silton Moor · Nun Ho. · Black Hambleton · Lower Bocker · Hagg Ho. · Lane Ho. · Hazel Head · Hazelshaw Ho. · Helm Ho.

54° 20' N · Marigold Hall · Over Silton · Hunters Hill · Cow Wath · Hawnby Moor · Laverock Hall · Hagg End · New Ho.

Crosby Court Grange · Landmoth · Longlands · Greystone Ho. · Nether Silton · Arden Great Moor · Brewster Hill · Bumper Cas. · Ewe Cote

Low Crosby Court · Catto · Ox Bank · Hall · Manor Ho. · Brenk Hall · Nab Ho. · Kepwick Moor · Thorodale · Sportsman's Hall · St Agnes · Hill End Ho. · High Banniscue · Laskill

Crosby Court · Crowtree Ho. · The Grange · Leake Lane Ho. · Kepwick · Stay Ho. · Harker Gates · Arden Hall · New Hall · Low Banniscue · Feather Holme

Northfield Ho. · Crosby Manor · Leake Ho. · Leake Hall · Mill Ho. · Hall Park · Gormire Hill Ho. · Long Acres · Wass Ho.

Thornton le Beans · Crosby · Carrdell Ho. · Grange · Youndales · Obelisk · Cowesby Hall · New Hall · Hawnby · Risebrow · Broadway Foot · Rievaulx Moor

Martins Folly · Southfield · Low Ho. · Cowesby Moor · Dale Town Common · High Paradise · Dale Town · Sunnybank Fm.

Summer Carr · Pasture Ho. · Borrowby · Ruddings · Fox Hall · Boltby Moor · Lunshaw Ho. · Low Paradise · Murton Grange · Oscar Ho.

Thornton le Moor · Knayton Grange · Lowfield Ho. · Water Hall · New Building · Kirby Knowle Moor · Cleveland Way · Dale Town · Tylas Fm. · New Leys Fm.

Sunny Hill · Leachfield Grange · Brawith Hall · Sampson Ho. · Knayton · Rush Ho. · Upsall Castle · Kirby Knowle · Ravensthorpe Manor · Hesketh Grange · King Spring Ho. · Mount Pleasant · Barnclose Ho.

North Kilvington Village · Kilvington Hall · West Acre Lo. · Boltby · Cleave Dike · Ford · Wethercote

Manor Ho. · Thornton-le-Street Hall · Spital Beck · North Kilvington · Pallet Hill · Eller Beck · Little Moor · House · Cinque Cliff · Tang Hall · Southwood Grange · Old Byland · Reins

Abel Grange · Calvis Hall · B1448 · Thornbrough Ho. · Hag Ho. · Mount St John · Felixkirk · Thirlby · Marderby Hall · Hambleton · Cold Kirby · Scawton Park · Hag Hall

42

a	b	c
d	e	f
g	h	i

	53	
41	**42**	43
	29	30

0   1   2   3   4   5 Miles
0 1 2 3 4 5 6 7 8 Kilometres

NORTH YORK MOORS

NATIONAL PARK

Whitby

Saltwick Bay
Black Nab
Saltwick Nab
The Scar
West Cliff
Whitby Sands
Dunsley
Newholm
Ruswarp
Aislaby
Sleights
Briggswath
Ugglebarnby
Iburndale
Sneaton
High Hawsker
Low Hawsker
Normanby

Lealholm Moor
Danby Beacon Hill
Brown Rigg Howe
Black Dike Moor
Ugthorpe Moor
Ugthorpe
Lealholm
Lealholmside
Glaisdale
Egton
Egton Bridge
Grosmont
Egton Low Moor
Egton High Moor
Egton Grange
Hutton Mulgrave
Hutton Mulgrave Wood

Falling Foss
Low Moor
Ramsdale
Fylingdale Moor
Kirk Moor
Brock Hall
New May Beck

Pike Hill Moss
Three Howes
Julian Park
Goathland
Mallyan Spout
Beck Hole
Darnholm
Abbots Ho.
Partridge Hill
Widow Howe Moor
Goathland Moor
Sneaton High Moor
Blea Hill Howe
York Cross
Lilla Howe
Lilla Cross
Burn Howe Rigg
Jugger Howe
Fylingdales
River Derwent
Stony Rigg

Lyke Wake Walk
Wheeldale Moor
Wheeldale Howe
Nelly Ayre Force
Two Howes
Hunt Ho.
Hamer Moor
Low Hamer
Black Rigg
Rutmoor Beck
Gale Hill Rigg
Blawath Beck
Simon Howe Rigg
Craig Stone Rigg
Fen Moor
Newton Dale Sta.
Eller Beck Br.
Lilla Rigg
Tom Cross Rigg
High Woof Howe
Low Woof Howe
Louven Howe
Allerston High Moor
Langdale Forest
High Langdale End

Leaf Howe Hill
Leaf Howe
Brown Howe
Wardle Rigg
Lockton High Moor
Saltergate Moor
Carter's Ho. (Ruin)
Malo Cross
Mauley Cross
Scarfhill Howe
Stape
Gallows Dike
Saltergate
High Horcum
Blakey Topping

Cropton Forest
Keldy Castle
Rawcliff
Thornsby
Ellerton Lo.
Sutherland Lo.
Blackpark Lo.
Fall Rigg
Low Askew
Cropton
Cawthorn
Roman Camps
Whitethorn
Nova Ho.

Stony Moor
Newton-on-Rawcliffe
Cook's Grange
Keld Slack
Lockton
Levisham
Levisham Sta.
Skelton Tower
Levisham Moor
Low Horcum
Newgate Foot
Lockton Low Moor
Warren Ho.
East Toft Howe
Mount Pleasant
Low Staindale
Low Pasture Ho.
High Staindale
Dargate Dikes
Bickley
Deep Dale
Langdale End
Bickley Forest Toll
Troutsdale Moor

Pickering
Blansby Park
New Hambleton
Wrelton
Aislaby
Middleton
New Bridge
Manor Ho.
Kingthorpe
Saxton Moor
High Kingthorpe
Sand Dale
Dalby Forest
High Dalby Ho.
Seive Dale
Sneer Dale
Low Dalby
High Scamridge
Givendale Head
Hern Head
Troutsdale
Rock Ho.
Cockmoor Hall
Malton Cote
Moorsome Ho.
Sawdon

A169
A171
A174
A170
B1416
B1410
River Esk
Pickering Beck

a	b	c
d	e	f
g	h	i

42 **43**

30 31

43

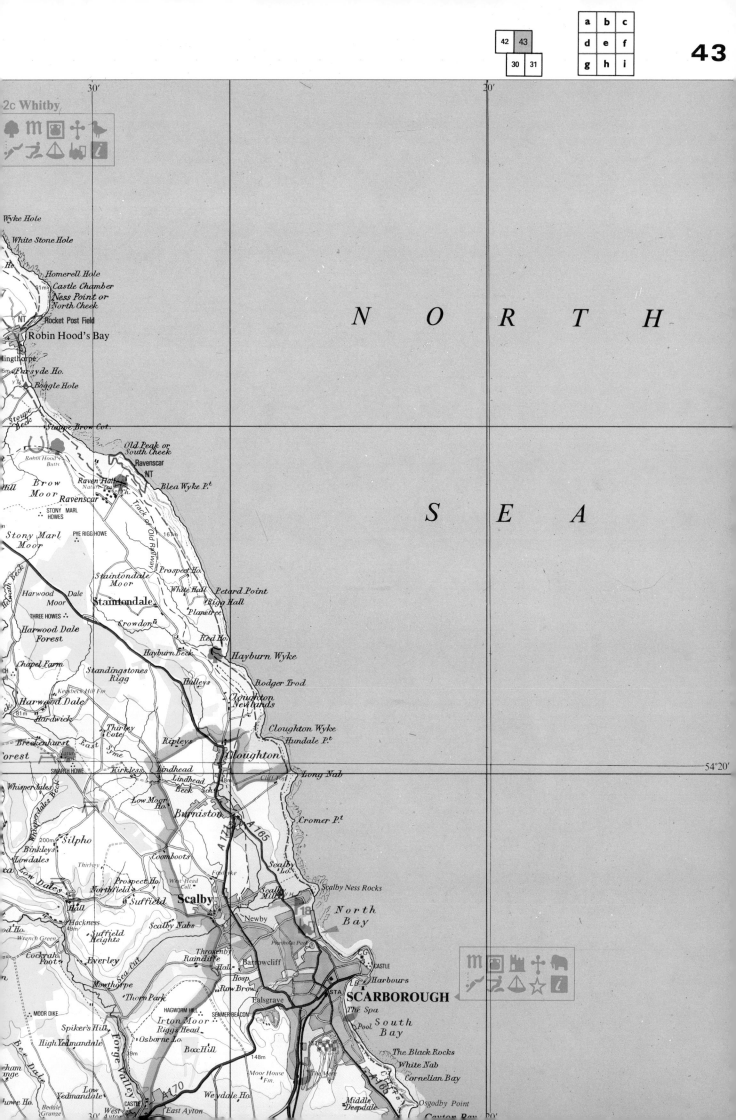

2c Whitby

Wyke Hole

White Stone Hole

Ho.

Homerell Hole

Castle Chamber

Ness Point or
North Cheek

NT   Rocket Post Field

Robin Hood's Bay

ingthorpe

Farsyde Ho.

Boggle Hole

Stoupe Brow Cot.

Robin Hood's
Butts

Old Peak or
South Cheek

Ravenscar

Brow   Raven Hall   NT
Moor
Ravenscar   Blea Wyke P.t

STONY MARL
HOWES

Stony Marl
Moor   PYE RIGG HOWE

Track of Old Railway

Prospect Ho.

Staintondale
Moor

Harwood   White Hall   Petard Point
Moor
Staintondale   Rigg Hall
THREE HOWES   Planetree

Harwood Dale   Crowdon
Forest

Chapel Farm   Red Ho.

Standingstones   Hayburn Beck   Hayburn Wyke
Rigg
Kegbeck Hill Fm   Hilleys

Harwood Dale   Rodger Trod

Hardwick   Cloughton
Newlands

Thirley   Cloughton Wyke
Cote
Breckenhurst   East   Ripley's   Syme   Hundale P.t
orest
SWARTH HOWE   Kirkless   Lindhead   Cloughton

Whisperdales   Lindhead   Long Nab
Beck   Sch.
Low Moor   CLIFF TOP
Ho.
Silpho   Burniston   A 171   A 165   Cromer P.t
Binkleys
Lowdales   Thirlsey   Coomboots   Scalby
Lo.
Prospect Ho.   West Head   Scalby Ness Rocks
Coll.
Northfield   Scalby   Scalby Mills
Hall   Suffield   Ho.
Hackness   Scalby Nabs   Newby   North
Suffield   Bay
Wrench Green   Heights
Cockrah   Everley   Throxenby   Barrowcliff   CASTLE
Foot   Raincliffe
Mowthorpe   Hall   Hosp.   Harbours
Thorn Park   Row Brow   STA   SCARBOROUGH
MOOR DIKE   Falsgrave   The Spa
Spiker's Hill   HAGWORM HILL   SEAMER BEACON   South
High Yedmandale   Irton Moor   Pool   Bay
Riggs Head
Osborne Lo.   Box Hill   The Black Rocks
Forge Valley   White Nab
Low   West   Moor House   Cornelian Bay
Yedmandale   Fm.
Bedale   East Ayton   Weydale Ho.   Middle
Grange   Deepdale   Osgodby Point
Cayton Bay

N O R T H

S E A

54°20'

44

a	b	c
d	e	f
g	h	i

54
44 45
32

0 1 2 3 4 5 Miles
0 1 2 3 4 5 6 7 8 Kilometres

3°30'W
ALAVNA ROMAN FORT
NETHERHALL
0m A 596
Birkby
Greengill
Row Hall
New Grange
Millstor
Tallen
Hill

Maryport
STA
Kirkborough
Netherton
Hall
Dearham
Hayborough
Townhead
Low House
Tallentire
West Ho.

Hosp
Ellenborough
Ewanrigg Hall
Craikhow Hall
Woodside
92m
A 594
A L

Risehow
Ewanrigg
Lineloot
ROMAN ROAD
Shepherd Hill
Broughton Moor
Broughton I.
Dovenby
Hosp
Bridekirk

New Ho.
Flimby
St Helens
8m
High Seaton
Line
Stockmoor
Little Broughton
Craggs
GreatBroughton
A 66
36m
East Ho.
Papcastle
Hame's Hall
OAS

Seaton
Camerton
Hall
Ribton Ho.
Ribton Hall
A 66
Brigham
EARTHWORK
Ellerbeck
Wellington
YH

Salmon Hall
Clifton
Hall
Tarn Bank
Greysouthen
The Dubbs
Waterloo
R. Coc

Dock
R. Derwent LB CG
Stainburn
A 66
Lit.Clifton
Bridgefoot
Eaglesfield
Moorland Close
Gree

WORKINGTON
STA
Schoose
West Leys
Losting Beck
Calva Hall
Mayfield
Gatefield
Eaglesfield Crag
Greentrees
Hi
High Dyke
'Bir

Westfield
14m
Hosp
Hunday
Winscales
Stargill
Gatebarrow
124m
Southfield
Gale Ho.
Deanscales
Eastho.
Woodside
Bir

B 52 96
Salterbeck
Midtown
A 596
127m
HALL
Branthwaite
Leegate
Dean
Pardshaw Hall
Mosser
Mosser Ma

High Harrington
103m
Wythemoor Ho.
Pardshaw
Beech Hill
Fellb

Harrington
STA
Grayson Green
Works
Branthwaite Rigg
Ullock
A 5086
Sosgill
Mossergate
Fellb

Westgill End
Lodge Cas
Distington Hall
Kelmore Hill
Colingate
Gilgarran
Mockerkin
231m
Mockerkin How
Fangs
Iredale Place
Lowesw
Waterend

Park Ho.
Distington
Sike Whins
HAYES CAS (rems of)
Stubsgill
Fm
Dean Moor
Deancross
Havercroft
144m
Ringcroft
Holedale
Holme
Wood

Cunning Pt
Lowca
Common End
Boon Wood
Pica
Wilson Park
Wright Green
Wooden
Benthow
Burnbank Fell
Watergate

Providence Bay
Moresby
West Croft
Green Spot
247m
Mosses
Lamplugh
Carling Kno
Lowes

Parton Bay
STA
Parton
51m
Rose Hill
The High
Startoes
Tatehill
Dub Hall
Brownrigg
Asby
Hall
Felldyke
Sharp Knott
Congra Moss 572m
Blake Fell

Tanyard Bay
Briscoe Bank
Redness Pt
Rowton Syke
Beck
Dub
Arlecdon Hill
Arlecdon
Lund
Smithwaite
446m
Murton Fell
Gavel Fell
Whi

WHITEHAVEN
STA
Harras Park
A 595
Round Close
Low Harras
Priest Gill
Kekle Beck
Bogholes Fm
Kelton Head
296m
Kirkland
255m
Sadler's Knott
Kelton Fell

Hosp
CORKICKLE ST
75m
Yew Bank
Weddicar Hall
Hall
Bleak Ho.
A 5086
Rowrah
Old Quarry
Hawes
Stockhow Hall
Ghyll Fm
Croasdale
Floutern Tarn
NT

Kells
Hensingham
B 5294
Threapthwaite
Frizington
Rheda
Frizington Parks Rly
Quarry
Eskett
R. Ehen
Croasdale Beck
Crofoot
How Hall Fm
NT
Mireside Fm
616m
NT

Saltom Bay
Hosp
Birks
Track of
Old
Ennerdale Bridge
Mireside
Bowness
Ennerdale
Water

Sandwith
Mire Ho.
Ingwell
55m
B 529
Cleator Moor
Swinside
Fellend
NT
Angler's Crag
Craghill
Enne

North Head
Summer Hill
High Ho.
Byerstead
Bell Ho.
Moor Row
Wath Brow
Mills
Graystone
Flat Fell
Meadley Resr
Grike
Crag Fell
The Side

t. Bees Head
30'N
141m
Linethwaite
B 5345
Springfield Bigriggs
Loc
Cleator
345m
Long Barrow
Blakeley Raise 390m
R. Calder
Black Pots
NT

South Head
Rottington
High Walton
Woodend Sike Ho.
Nook
A 595
Cobra Castle
Wilton
High Ho.
541m
Lank Rigg
Long Grain
633m

4h Egremont
35m
Loughrigg
S Bees
Gillfoot
Moss Dalts
Uldale Fm
85m
Latterbarrow Beck
Kinniside Common
NT

Egremont
Marlborough Hall
3°30'W
Grange

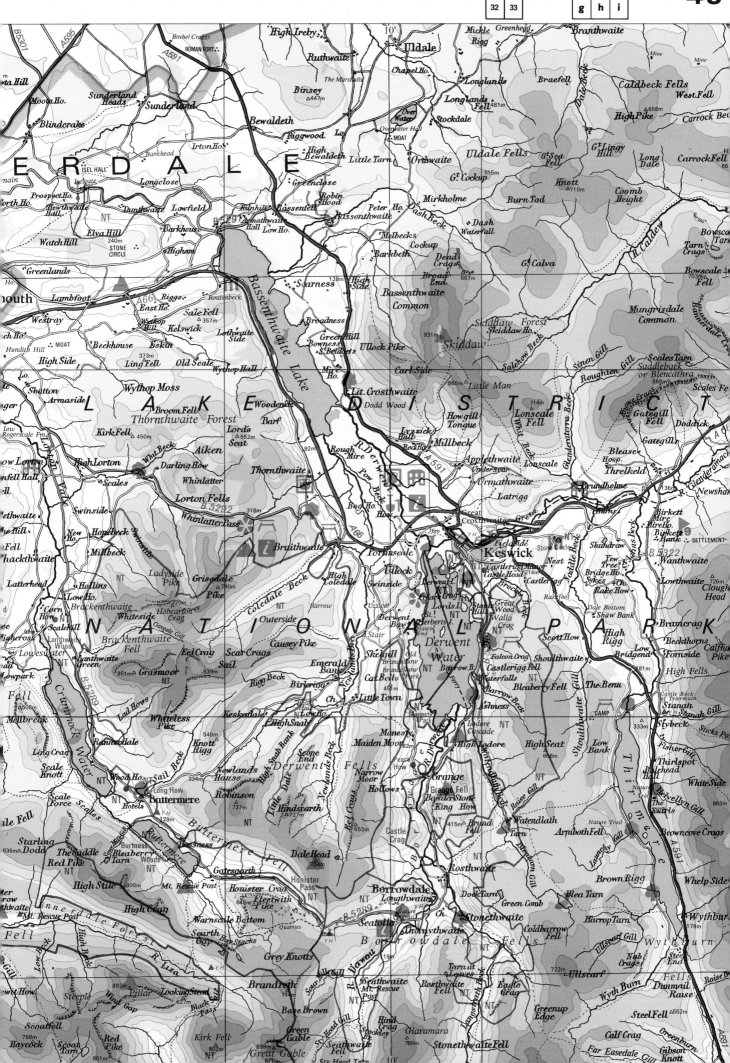

54 55
44 45 46
32 33

a b c
d e f
g h i

45

56	57
46	47	48
35	36

a	b	c
d	e	f
g	h	i

47

Gt. Salkeld 40'
Robberby
Coulston
Cuns Fell
Gale Hall
Green Fell △740m
Brown Hill
Lambgreen Hills
617m
Crossgill Head
Nunwick Hall
Lit. Salkeld
Gawtrechouse
Dale Beck
Skirwith Fell
Cross Hall Mine
Cottages or Gregs Hut
Rake End
Hunsonby
Sootyhill
Shire
Muska Hill
Fellside
Thack Moor
Fallow Hill
Winskill
Crewgarth
Bradley
Row
High Cap
893m
△ Cross Fell
River Tees
Tees Head
Swath Beck
Hard Hill △678m
Bank
Briggle
Gillbank
Townhead
Ardale Beck
Kirk Dale
Grey Scar
Milburn
Langwathby 144m
Briggle Beck
Skelling
Burrellhill
Bank Hall
Wildboar Scar
Middle Tongue
Forest
86m
Luhay
Skirwith Hall
Skirwith Beck
Kirkland
Grimply Hill
Great Dun Fell
Edenhall
Abbey
Ranbeck
Crowdundle Beck
Iron Howe
Mine
Green Castle
 hilt
Dolphenby
Staingills
Willickeld Sike
Hanging Walls of Mark Anthony
Blencarn
Knock Fell
ydepark
Whins Pond
Udford
Underwood Loscars EARTHWORK
High Slack
Burney Hill 427m
Knock Ore Gill
772m
dthorn
Udford Ho.
High Scald Fell
R. Eamont
Ch.
Hornby Hall
Winderwath
Culgaith
Millburn
HOWGILL CAS
Pennine Way
BROCAVVM ROMAN FORT
A 66
ROMAN ROAD
Woodside
LC
Newbiggin
Gullom Holme
Milburn Grange 398m
Knock Pike
Swindale Beck
Gt. Rundale Tarn
Whinfell
Whinfell Ho.
Ash Hill
Houtsay
Low Abbey
189m
Knock
Brownber Hill
699m
Seamor Tarn
Haversheaf Hall
Temple Sowerby
Hale Grange
Far Close
481m
Dufton Pike
Bluethwaite Hill
Lit. Rundale Tarn
689m
Highground
Whinfell Forest
Whinfell Park
Julian Bower
Marton Moor
Ch.
Peeping Hill
Backstone Edge
Melkinthorpe
Town Head
Track of Old Railway
119m
Kirkby Thore
Mine
Sleastonhow
Dufton
YH
Town Head
Greenhow
Harthwaite Cot.
Keisley
High Cup G
Abbott Lo.
Cliburn
R. Leith
Brigham Bank
R. Eden
Long Marton
Dudmire
Brampton
Burthwaite
Harbour Flatt
Woodside
Wood Ho.
Crossing Hall
Eden Grove
Redlands Bank
Powis Ho.
Inn
Croft Ends
594m
Murton Pik
Brackenthwaite
Street Ho.
Hesley
Eddy Ho.
Bolton
Roman Road
Scrog Bank
Flakebridge
Murton
Bradley
Gt. Strickland
Greengill Sike
Woodhead
.131m
Crackenthorpe
Hanging Shaw
Low Barn
Shepherd's Cot.
Hilton
Field Head
Morland
Keld
Bolton Lo.
BEWLEY CAS (rems of)
Colby Laithes
Appleby
Gale
Kirkber
Langton
Hall
Sheriffs Park
Sandriggs
Newby
Highfield
King's Meaburn
Sockenber
Penny Hill
Colby
CASTLE
Brackenber Moor
Brackenb
Bankwood
Hall
Thrimby
Lit. Strickland
Ford
Burwain
203m
Jerusalem
B 6542
Lowfield
Coupland
Sandford Thorn
Out Scar
Towcett
Turnbank
Crabstack
Wickerfield
Hoff Beck
Southfield
Scarside
Longlands 294m
Barnskew
Lankaber
Hoff Row
Burrells
Great Ormside
New Hall
A 66
dale
Threaplands
Reagill
Grayber
Barwise Hall
Hoff
R. Eden
Rosgill Hall
Wintertarn
Ploverigg
Trainlands
Dryvers
Lookingflatt
Low Rutter
Gill Ho.
Lit. Ormside
Sandford
R. Lowther
Rayside
REAGILL GRANGE
Maulds Meaburn
Drybeck
Newlands
Hadderdale
Ford
Rowbridge Ho.
Heights Castle
Helmbeck
Birks
Shap
308m
Wickerslack
SETTLEMENT
Glass Ho.
B 6260
Dry Beck
Helm
Blacksyke
Shap Abbey
Low Harberwain
Hulls
Highfield
Scaleback
174m
Breaks Hall
Birks Head
Keld
Keld Chapel NT
Hardendale
Crosby Ravensworth
Haber
Woodfoot
Gaythorne Hall
Hall
Crow Hill
Bleatarn
Thrnshp
M6
39
Oddendale
SETTLEMENT
SETTLEMENTS
G. Asby
High Grisenill
Sawbridge Hall
Hull Bank
Forest
Kemp Howe
STONE CIRCLES
Crosby Lo.
Whitewall
SETTLEMENT
Asby Mask
Dona Close
Grassgill La
264m
Long Mire
Gills
Blasterfield
Asby Winderwath Common
Fell Head
Whygill Head
Water Houses
Grange
Wet Sleddle Resr
Shap Thorn
Coalpit Hill
Roman Road
Asby Grange
Muddy Gill
Stockbar
Low Fell
Shap Summit
B 6261
401m
Crosby Ravensworth Fell
Orton Scar
344m
Great Asby Scar
High Pike
Burtree
Grange Scar
Little
Crosby Garrett
M6
30'
54°30'

58	59
48	**49**	50
37	38

a	b	c
d	e	f
g	h	i

49

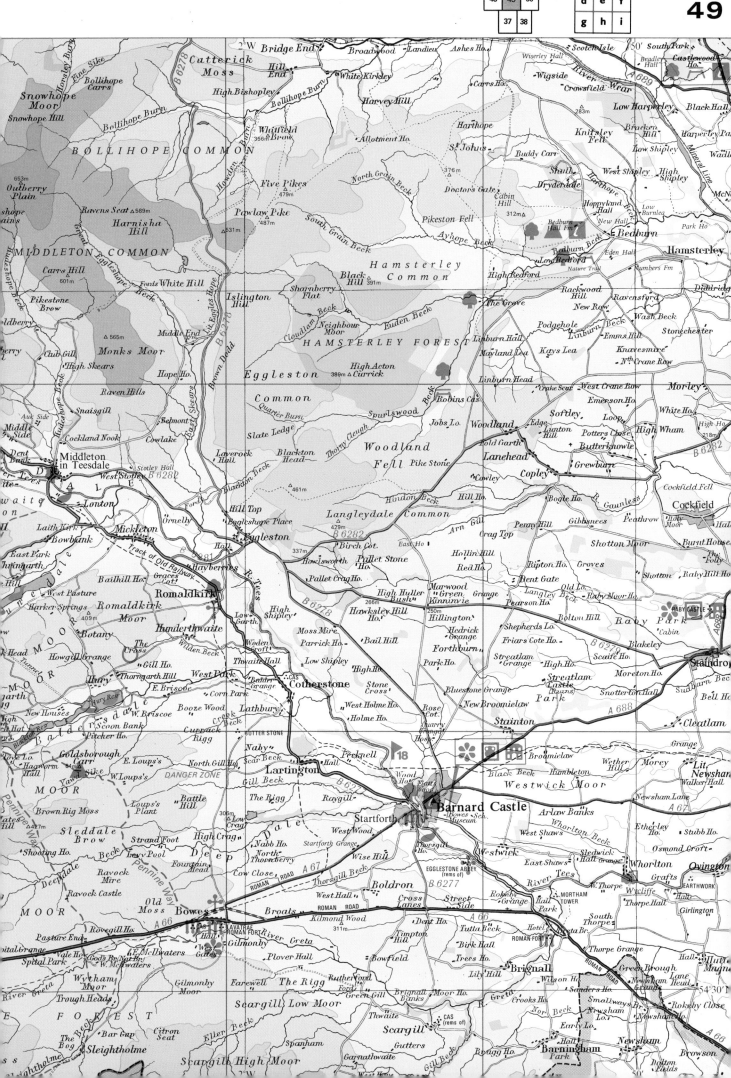

60 61
50 51 52
39 40

a b c
d e f
g h i

51

Church Kelloe
Town Kelloe
Hall
Garmondsway
Trimdon Grange
Langdale
Trimdon
Colliery
Trimdon
Rodridge
Hutton Ho.
Hutton Henry
141m
Hilam
Nesbitt Hall
Middlethorpe
Crimdon Ho.
North Sands

182m
The Grange
Park Ho.
Hurworth Bryan
White Hurworth
Catlaw Hall
South Wingate
Sheraton
East Grange
Nelson
North Hart
Springwell
Parton Rock

Garmondsway
50m
Moor
Mahon Ho.
Trimdon
Trimdon Ho.
Hope Ho.
West Car Side
Dropswell
Hurworth Burn Resr
156m
Sheraton Grange
Whelly Hill Ho.
Naisberry
Throston Grange
High Throston
HARTLEPOOL
Middleton

116m
Farnless
Fishburn
Mine
Galley Law
Murton Blue Ho.
119m
Middleton Ho.
Hall
Elwick
Dove Cote
Dalton Piercy
Hartlepool Bay

Bishop Middleham
Holdforth
Bridge Ho.
River Skerne
Murton Hall Fm
Pawton Hill
Stotfold Moor
Long Scar

Hardwick
Green Knowles
Hardwick Hall
Spruceley Hosp.
Hosp.
Ryal
Weterton Cot.
117m
Butterwick
Embleton
Old Hall
Crookfoot Resr
High Stotfold
Amerston Hall
Middle Stotfold
Brierton
Owton Grange
Blue Ho.
Seat Care

Temple
A 689
Donnewell
111m
Redcar Ho.
High Swainston
Middle Swainston
76m
Gunnersvale
Low Stotfold
31m
Works

Sedgefield
Beacon Hill
Oldacres Hall
Close Ho.
Red Gap
44m
Claxton Grange
Tofts
Hunter
B1276

Sands Hall
Glower o'er Him
Race Co
Mordon Moor
Diamond Hall
Cowley Ho.
Salter Ho.
Newton Hanzard
Woodside
Anniggate Ho.
North Burn
Newton Bewley
Field Ho.
Greatham
Graythorp
Greenabella Fm
GREATHAM STA

Harpington Hill
Southfield Ho.
Layton Ho.
96m
Brierly Wood
Wynyard Park
Hall
A 689
Wolviston
Marsh Ho.

Hepper Ho.
West Layton
81m
South Layton
Shotton Beck
Grindon
Thorpe Leazes
Fulthorpe
Wilmire Ho.
Bottle Hill
High Grange
Cowpen Bewley
A1185
Cowpen Marsh
Seal Sand

Elstob
Elstob Hall
Elstob Hill
Goods Line
Whitton Three Gates
Thorpe Thewles
Blakeston Hall
Low Middle Field
View Hill
9m
Salt Holme

Lea Close
Stillington
Whitton
West Ho.
Greystone
Carlton Grange
Howden Hall
Brieringham Beck
Billingham
Haverton Hill
Salt Holme
Refinery
Port Clarence

Great Stainton
Bishopton
Downland Fm
Carlton
Roseworth
Newton
4m

Little Stainton
Redmarshall
Hill Ho.
Castle Hill
MOTTE & BAILEY
Hardwick Field
Mount Pleasant
Cargo Fleet
North Ormesby
A175

Stony Flat
Coalgarth Ho.
Grassy Nook
Jack Eye Ho.
STOCKTON-ON-TEES
MIDDLESBROUGH

Gilly Flat
Sauf Hall
Fairfield
Whinny Hill
River Tees
13m
Normanby

East Newbiggin
West
Elton Moor
23m
Hartburn
Linthorpe
Berwick Hills

63m
Hill Ho.
Long Newton Grange
Sandy Leos
Hartburn Grange
Hartburn
A 66
Thornaby-on-Tees
Acklam
Easterside
Ormesby

Salter Carr
Bewley Hall
Newton Grange
Viewley Hill
35m
Elton
Red Ho.
Hospital

Hang Thorn
Spring Ho.
Long Newton
Coatham Stob
Cowley Moor Ho.
Bowesfield
Preston on Tees
Preston Hall
Stainsby Grange
Thorn Hill
Coulby Manor
Tollesby
Nunthorpe

Bumper Hall
Hard Stones
Spring Ho.
Street Ho.
White Ho.
Witham Hall
East Gate
Eaglescliffe
Barwick
White Ho.
Low Fm
A174
Stainton Vale
Industrial Estate
Stainton
Hemlington
Hendington
Coulby

West Moor
Call Hill
Urlay Nook
ALLENS WEST STA
Nature Trail
Thornton
Stainton Grange
Hosp.
Newham

DINSDALE STA
Oak Tree
Middleton St George
Middleton One Row
Foster Ho.
High Goosepool
Low Goosepool
TEESSIDE AIRPORT
Aislaby Grange
Aislaby
Egglescliffe
Yarm
Old Hall
Betty's Close
Ingleby
Sober Hall
White Ho.
Thornton Grange
Low Thornton Moor
Newham Hall

MOTTE
Over Dinsdale Grange
Featherstone Ho.
West Moor
Tees
B1265
Field Ho.
Rose Hill
Kirklevington
High Leven
Leven Br
7m
Hilton House Fm
Greenfield
Newby

Low Dinsdale
MOAT
Middleton
Newsham Hall
Aislabygrange
Clock Ho.
Friarage
Hilton
Middleton upon Leven
Howe Hill
Tanton

a b c
d e f
g h i

52 **53**

41 42

53

1° W

50'

N O R T H

S E A

40'

Brough Ho.
166m
High Cliff
Hummley Hall
Shepherds Ho.
Hall
burn
A 174
ge
A 173
Brotton
Carlin How
Cleveland
Way
Skinningrove
Works
Upton
208m
Boulby
Bias
Sear
Cowbar Nab
North
Skelton
Loftus
Loftus Grange
Deepdale
A 174
Staithes
Cliff Fm.
Brackenberry
Wyke
Kilton
Cock
Shote
Ings Ho.
Mine
Dalehouse
Piers
Kilton Thorpe
South Loftus
Easington
Seaton Hall
Port Mulgrave
Stank Ho.
Liverton Lo.
Rose Croft
Borrowby
Grange
Plumtree
Ho.
Hinderwell
Lit.
Moorsholm
Lane Ho.
Oaks Fm.
Stanghow
Park Ho.
Warren
Ho.
Liverton
Roxby
Dale
Grasshill
Ho.
Runswick
Runswick
Bay
Kettle Ness
Handale
Borrowby
Low
Borrowby
LB
Hob
91m
Holes
Kettleness
abtree
Hagg
North
Lane Ho.
B 1366
Grinkle
Park
Park Ho.
America Ho.
Newton
Mulgrave
Low Ho.
Old Railway
Goldsborough
Loop Wyke
e Ho.
Moorsholm
High Waupley
Green Howe
Birchall Ho.
Ellerby
Northfields
Brockrigg
Overdale
Overdale Wyke
South
Lane Fm.
Lane
Head
Stang Howe
Roxby Low Moor
Ellerby
Bank Top
Track
Westfields
Deepgrove
Deepgrove Wyk
Sandsend Nes
Moorside Ho.
Scaling
Newton Mulgrave
Moor
B 1266
Upton Hall
198m
Lythe
Sandsend Wyk
Ivens Ho.
Waupley
Moor
Scaling Dam
Land o'nod
Farm
Mickleby
West
Barnby
East
Barnby
Mulgrave Cas.
54° 30' N
Freebrough
Hill
Gerrick
Liverton
Moor
Scaling Res.
Roxby High Moor
Mickleby Beck
High Leas
CASTLE
Mulgrave
Woods
Robinson
Sandsend
East
Row
Moorsholm
Moor
Gerrick Moor
236m
Easington High Moor
High Tranmire
Fm.
Newton Mulgrave
Broom
Ho.
Hermitage
Rock Head
Raithwaite
Hall
JOB CROSS
Robin
Hood's
Butts
Ugthorpe
Moor
Ugthorpe
Lo.
Ugthorpe
East Row Beck
Holy Well Ho.
Birk Head
Heulah
Greystone
WHITE CROSS
Siss Cross
TUMULI
Black
Dike Moor
224m
A 171
Hutton
Dunsley
Newholm
dale
DANBY LOW MOOR

54

a	b	c
d	e	f
g	h	i

| 54 | 55 |
| 44 | 45 |

0 1 2 3 4 5 Miles

0 1 2 3 4 5 6 7 8 Kilometres

Middle Bank

Cardurnock Flatts

Campfield

Rogersceugh

Bowness Common

NT

Cardurnock

Anthorn

F I R T H

S O L W A Y

Low Water Mark

30'

20'

Moricambe

Grune Pt.

Newtonholme

Newton Marsh

Newton Arlosh

Shaw

Angert

Skinburness

East Cote

Skinburness Marsh

Calvo Marsh

Wath

Seaville Cote

Hartlow

Whinclose

Border

River

Whitehill

B 5307

Silloth

Holiday Camp

5m

Calvo

Salt Cotes

Sleightholme

Causewayhead

Greenrow

B 5302

Blackdyke

Seaville

Red Flatt

Selby Ho.

Browrigg

Moss Side

Wedho

18

Blitterlees

B 5301

B 5300

Balladoyle

7m

Dryholme

Kingside Hill

Raby

High. Ho.

Hall

Wolsty

Hayrigg

Abbey Cowper

Abbeytown

Abbey Ho.

Kelsick

MOAT

Swinsty

9m

Dundra

New Ho.

Foulgyke

Highlaws

Longburn

Bankhead Moor

4°50' N

Beckfoot

Pelutho

Aldoth

Hall

11m

Wheyrigg

B 5302

Mawbray Hayrigg

West Ho.

Grayson Ho.

Smarthill

Souherfield

Blencogo

Newtown

Lowsay

Roundall

Weary Hall

Crooklands

42m

Hall

Cowgate

Tarns

Cobble Hall

Mereside

Crummock Beck

Greenrigg Villa

Holme St. Cuthbert

35m

Common Moss

Croft Ho.

Bromfield Hall

Thornby End

Mawbray

Goodyhills

Overby

Holme Dub

Clappers

Low Scales

Seymour Ho.

Hailforth

Jericho

Aikshaw

Mealrigg

Greenah

Langrigg

Gill Ho.

High Scales

Leegate Ho.

Dubmill Pt.

Salta

Edderside

New Cowper

Whinbank

B 5301

Housenrigg

Goosegreen

Low Row

Aiki

Salta Moss

Black Dub

Howrigg

Stubbs gill

Heathfield

Crookdale

High Aketon

North Lo.

Brownrigg Hall

Westnewton

Yearngill

Fletchertown

Allonby

Newtonfield

Warwick Hall

Brayton Park

74m

B 5299

Washhill

Priestcroft

Leesrigg

Allhallows

Bowscale

Crookhurst

Crookhurst Beck

Aiglegill

Whitelees

Aspatria

Harriston

Baggrow

Blennerhasset

White Hall Cas

Allonby Bay

Staith

Mealo Ho.

Mealo Hill

CAS

STA

R. Ellen

Fitz

Kirkland Guards

Torpenhow Par

A 596

A 595

Hayton

Hall Bank

Gill Gooden

Lowfield

Overgates

Bluedial

Prospect

Ellen Villa Hall

Arkleby

Threapland

Bothel

Old Quarry

Whitr

Allerby

Oughterside

Moorgill

Parsonby

Plumbland

Wharrels Hill

Stangerhill

Crosscanonby

Low Leathes

Gilcrux

B 5301

ENCLOSURE 285m

Cemetery

Crosby Villa

Springwell Ho.

Ewelose

Bothel Craggs

Birkby Lo.

Crosby

Wardhall Common

ROMAN FORT

ALAVNA ROMAN FORT

0m

Birkby

Greengill

251m

Maryport

NETHERHALL

Kirkborough

Hall

New Grange

Millstonemoor Tallentire Hill

Moota Hill

Sunderland Heads

Sunderland

A 591

Netherton

Dearham

Hayborough

Low House

Moota Ho.

STA

Ellenborough

Townhead

Tallentire

West Ho.

Blindcrake

Ewanrigg Hall

Craikhow Hall

A 595

Risehow

Woodside

91m

Irton Ho.

A 594

30'

A L L E R D A L E

55

62
54 55 56
45 46

a b c
d e f
g h i

Glasson
Glasson Moss
Lowflow
Whitriggmoor Ho.
Whitriggs Ho.
Drumburgh
Walker Ha
Easton
Bousteard Hill
Longburgh
Shield
HADRIAN'S WALL (course of)
Dykesfield
NT
Burgh Marsh
R. Eden
King Edward's Monument
NT
Priesthill
Bankend
High Grindledike
Priesthill
Harker
Knells
Harker Grange
Houghton Hall
Houghton
A74
A7
Brunstock
Drumburgh
Moss
Whitriggmoor Ho.
Fingland
Greenspot
Whitrigglees
Kirkbride
Fingland Rigg
Haverlands Ho.
Studholme
Longrigg
Laythes
Eastholme
Ploughlands
Laverickstone
Little Bampton
Westfield Ho.
New Bampton
Wampool
Mossend
Low Eskrigg
Biglands
Aikton
Fisher Gill
Gamelsby
EARTHWORKS CASTLE
Eskrigg Ho.
Tarnrigg Moor
Tarnside
Middlemoor Ho.
Moorhouse
Oulton Ho.
Oulton
Dockraybank
Dockrayrigg Ho.
Woodside
Lowfield Ho.
Aikhead
Hover Br.
Longhead
Wigton
Kirkland
Greenwood Ho.
Low Houses
Bushgillhead
Highmoor
Forest Hall
Sandybrow
HighLongthwaite
Old Carlisle
ROMAN FORT
Cunningarth
Warblebank
Crags
Red Dial
Wray
Rase Lo.
Stoneraise Place
Tracentree
Greenhill
Intack Fm.
Wiza
Beck
Westward
Park
Bolton
New Houses
Islekirk Hall
Westward
Bolton
New Houses
Thackthwaite Hall
Boltonwood Lane
High Hall
Reathwaite
Broadmoor
Seberham Cas. Fm.
Boghall
Clea Hall
Hazelsprings
Brocklebank
Hallbank
Lanehead
Wellrash
Catlandshill
Bolton Park
Angerton Bank
Pow Heads
Faulds Brow
Roundhill
Waverhead
Hazelgill
Ellenbank
Sandale
Newlands
Rash
Daleside
Snowhill
Thistlebottom
Ireby
Aughertree
ENCLOSURES
Townhead
Green How
Mickle Rigg
Greenhead
Branthwaite
Ruthwaite
Uldale
Chapel Ho.
Longlands Fell
Longlands
Braefell
Caldbeck Fells
West Fell
The Marshalls
Stockdale
Over Water
Overwater Hall
MOAT
Uldale Fells
Gt. Sca Fell
Gt. Lingy Hill
Long
Carrock Fell
High Pike
Carrock Beck
Stone
FORT
Linewath
Hutton Roof

CARLISLE
Moorpark
Thurstonfield
Moorhouse
B 5307
Kirkbampton
Oughterby
Thurstonfield Lough
Box
Roblow
Wiggonby
Blackbrow
Rickerby Ho.
Woodhouses
Orton Rigg
Dow Hall
Wiggonrigg
Lonning
Hardcake Hall
Pow
Drumleaning
Greyrigg Hall
Thornby
High Whinnow
Parton
Mickletbwaite
Crofton
Thursby
Eveninghall
W. Curthwaite
Westend
W. Woodside
Gaterigg
Ghyll Head Fm.
Howrigg
Lowling
Kirkstead
Rosleyrigg
Lower Green Quarries
Rosley
Chalk Beck
Welton
Broadmoor
Caldewbeck
Bellbridge
Warnell Hall
Sebergham
Warnell Fell
Low Browrigg
Paddigill
Ratten Row
Whelpo
B 5299
Caldbeck
Townhead
Hesket
Newmarket
Parkend
Nether Row
Hudscales
Woodhall
FellSide
Fauld
Faulds
Parkend Beck
Dale Beck
Mine
Mine
Calebrack
Haltcliff View
High Row
Townend
Thornthwaite Hall

CARLISLE
Brisco
Currock
Upperby
Blackwell
Netherton
Brisco
Durdar
Lough
Burthwaite Hill
Blackhall Wood
Durdar Ho.
Blackhall
Burthwaite
Blackhall Park
Bankdale Fm.
East View
Monkcastle
Raughton
Longrigg Cot.
Foulbridge
Highbridge
Thethwaite
Ivegill
Low Braithwaite
Middlesceugh Hall
Scales Hall
Sowerby Row
Richmond Plains
Howgill
Nook
Southerby
Roe Ho.
Hewerhill
Skelton Wood End
Hollyhill
Askrigg
Woodclose
High Dean Chapter
Pringle Ho.
Sowerby Row
Lamonby
Newsham
Lamonby Fm.
Wharton
Field Ho.
High Row
Inglewood Edge

KESWICK
NATIONAL PARK
DISTRICT

	63	64	
56	57	58	
	47	48	

a	b	c
d	e	f
g	h	i

57

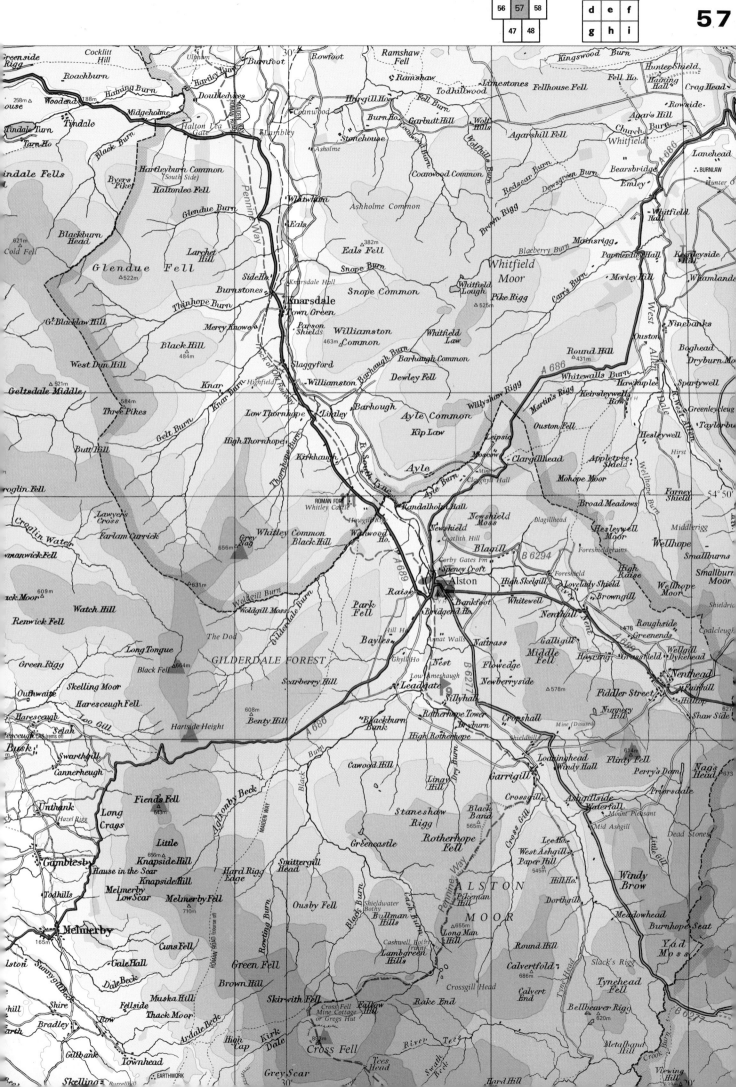

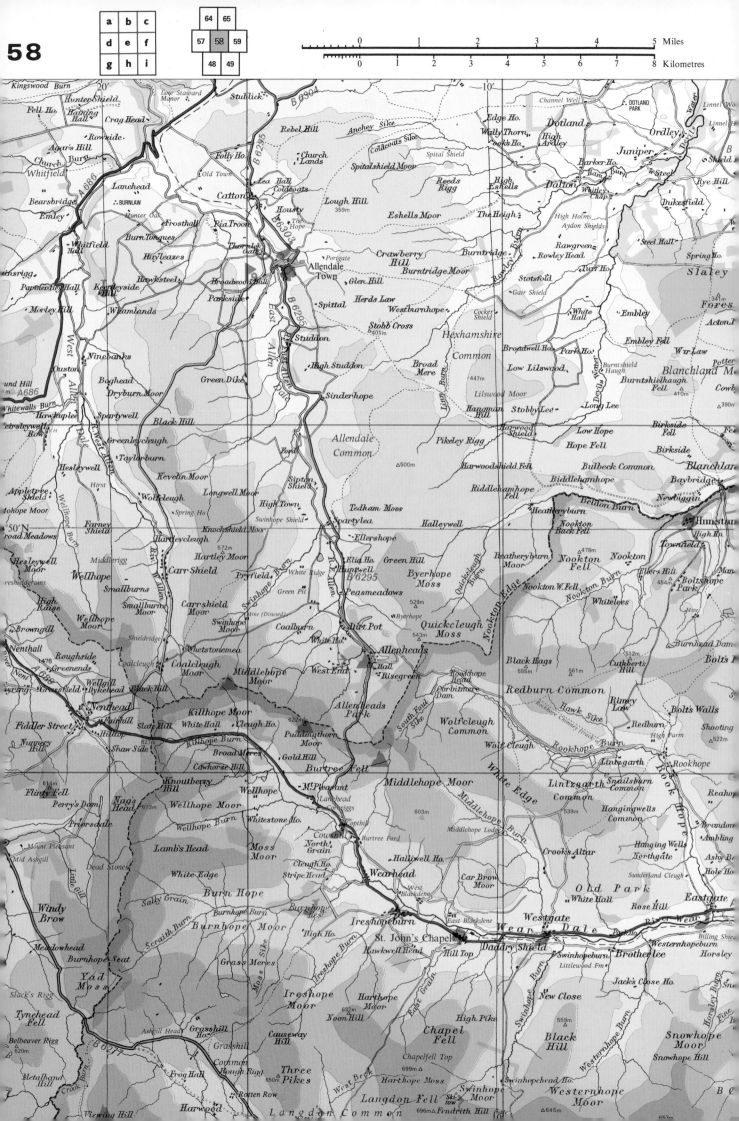

66 67
59 60 61
50 51

a b c
d e f
g h i

61

DURHAM
Scale
0 ½ Mile

Hosp.
County Hall
River Wear
To A1(M) A69
WESTERN HILL
NEWCASTLE ROAD
A691
LOW DRYBURN RD
FLEGHOUSE LANE
WESTERN HILL
FRAMWELLGATE PETH
GPO
P St P
CLAYPATH
Hosp.
CROSSGATE PETH
MARCERY LANE
PIMLICO ROAD
GROVE
CROSSGATE
NEVILLE'S CROSS BANK
DARLINGTON RD
A167
A690
NEVILLE'S CROSS
POTTERS BANK
QUARRYHEADS LANE
Castle
University
Cathedral
LEAZES RD A690
NEW ELVET
HALLGARTH ST
CHURCH ST
STOCKTON RD
A1050
Police Station
SHINCLIFFE PETH

Downhill Ho.
93m
Mundles
A1018
Cemetery
Fulwell STA
Seaburn
Whitburn Bay
Roker
Monkwearmouth CG
HYLTON CAS
Castletown
Southwick
R. Wear
231
Power Sta
SUNDERLAND
Hylton
South Hylton
L.C.
Hosp.
STA
LB
Dock
Hendon
Grindon
B1300
A89
Thornley Close
B1405
Middle Herrington
Mine
Ryhope Colliery
Salterfen Rocks
E Herrington
New Silksworth
Kenstall
Silksworth
delphia
B1286
Tunstall
Lo.
Ryhope
Stony Gate
Low Haining
Thristley Ho.
Burdon Hall
Hosp.
A1018
Burn Hall
Seaham Grange
B1281
wbottle
Haining
Warden Law
197m
Old Burdon
A19
Field Ho.
Murton
L.C.
45m
Hosp.
Mine
FeatherBed Rocks
HOUGHTON LE-SPRING
B1404
Sharpley Hall
B1404
STA
L.C.
SEAHAM
White Ho.
Warden Law
Bank Top
B1404
LB
New Town
Dean Ho.
High Sharpley
Stotfold
B1285
Nose's Point
Haining Grove
Hetton Downs
163m
Mine
Slingley Hill
Haverley Ho.
Dalton-le-Dale
G. Eppleton
Dalton Moor
Hetton-le-Hole
Murton
Cold Hesledon
Hesledon East Ho.
ton
Eppleton Hall
L.C.
B1283
Ghyll
Tower
Chourdon Pt
Lyons
Hawthorn Hive
Low Moorsley
Easington Lane
B1281
Hesledon Moor Ho.
Mineral Line
Hawthorn Burn
Hawthorn
Shippersea Bay
Hetton le Hill
B1280
South Hetton
135m
Eagle Hall
Beacon Ho.
Shot Rock
Elemore Vale
Coldwell Burn
Coop Ho.
Loom
Elemore Hall
Low Haswell
Duncombe Moor
Hallfield
A182
B1432
Holm Hill
Low Grounds
Easington Colliery
Fox Holes
Elemore Grange
High Haswell
171m
Holy Cross
B1283
Littletown
Haswell
Pespool Hall
Easington
Little Thorpe
Horden Pt
149m
High Ling Ho.
Strawberry Hall
urn Hill
152m
Haswell Plough
B1283
West Horden
Mine
Horden
Ludworth
Haswell Moor
Low Hills
Shadforth
Ludworth Tower
Hare Hill
Dene Mouth
Shotton Colliery
Fatclose Ho.
A1086
Dene Holme
Thornley
Swan Cas.
PETERLEE
Shotton Hall
Dene Ho.
Blackhall Colliery
High Croft Ho.
B1279
Oakerside
Castle Eden Burn
Hardwick Hall
Black Halls Rocks
Wheatley Hill
White Ho.
New Winning
Castle
B1281
Dene Leazes
B6291
A181
18
Castle Eden
High Hesleden
Thornley Hall
B1278
Wellfield Ho.
Hesleden
Twedale
Black Halls
Wingate
Old Wingate
Eden Vale
Benridge
Monk Hesleden
Hall
Filpoke
Carrington Hill
Mine
Thornbush
Stationtown
Hutton Ho.
Hulam
Nesbitt Hall
Middlethorpe
39m
Crimdon Ho.
Town Kelloe
Trimdon Grange
Hutton Henry
141m
Nelson
North Hart
Springwell
18
Trimdon Colliery
Langdale
Rodridge
Thorpe Bulmer
HARTLEPOOL
182m
The Grange
Hurworth Bryan
South Wingate
Sheraton
East Grange
Hart
Middle Warren
North Sands
Parton Rocks
Carmondsway
Park Ho.
White Hurworth
Catlaw Hall
Black Hurworth
Sheraton Grange
Whelly Hill Ho.
A179
A1049
Soft Lees Haven
Trimdon
Trimdon Ho.
A179
Dropswell
Hurworth Burn Resr
B1280
156m
Throston Grange
CG

60i DURHAM

54° 50′

68 69
62 63 64
56 57

a b c
d e f
g h i

63

BORDER FOREST PARK

Glendhu Hill 513m
Kershopehead
English Kershope
Glen Dhu
Davy's Round
Black Hill
Reamy Rigg
Skelton Pike 342m
The Beck
Shuels
Stelshaw
HOPE
Blacklyne Ho.
Blacklyne Common
Bewcastle Fells
Kettle Hall (ruin)
Black Knors
Baileyhead
Coldside
Broadside
Woodside
White Lyne
The Flatt
Holmhead
Stubb
Mid Todholes
Crook
Murrayholme
Bankhead
Dirtup
Oakshaw Ford
Brownhill
Ann's Hill
Roadhead
Parknook
Parkhead
Crossgreens
Peel O'Hill
Bewcastle
Greenholme
Scotstown
Bogside
Lyneholme
Low Floweryhirst
Show Burn
Wintershields
Allergarth
Askerton Park
Low Park
N Greenhill
Bellbank
Cracrop
High Green Hill
Rinkton Hills
Greensburn
Torties
Craigburn
Howdale
Kirkcambeck
Askerton Cas.
Lees Hill
Knorren Lodge
West Hall
Moorguards
Hillhouse
White Hill
Burtholme
Boothby
Gt Easby
Cotehill Fm.
Naworth Castle
Brampton
Warren Ho.
Milton Hall
BRAMPTON JUNC STA
Kirkhouse
Hallbankgate

Long Rigg
Lishaw Burn
Yate Burn
Christianbury Craig
Sighty Crag 518m
Whitelyne Common
Smuggy's Pike
Sloty Crag
Long Crag
Greyfell Common
456m
Crew Crag
Crew Ruin
Gaylock Hill
White Preston 422m
Black Preston
Cock Play
Highgrains Waste
Hazelgill Crag
Hazel Gill
Leafy Rigg
High Grains
Barron's Pike 355m 343m
Yellow Fawns
Low Grains
Borderrigg
BEW CAS
Shopford
Woodhead
Bushley Bank
High Ho.
Side Fell
Gillalees
Lynes
Cocklet Rigg
The Beacon
Spadeadam Fm.
Dumblar Rigg
King Water
Highstead Ash
Snowden Close
Palmer Hill
Waterhead Common
Clark's Hill
Park Nook
Triermain
Craigsike Ford
Miller Hill
Birdoswald
Camboglanna Roman Fort
Wall Bowers
Appletree
Upper Denton
Laneton
Chapelburn
Lanehead
Closegill
Naworth Castle Park
Tortie
Highfield
Denton Hall
Denton Ho.
Cleugh Head
Whamoss Rigg
Denton Fell 256m
Back Dike
Carnetley
Brackenside
Milton
Low Lonning Fm.
Silver Top
Greentarn Rigg
Greenside Rigg
Cocklitt Hill
Moss Hill
258m Woodend 188m
Tarnhouse Rigg
Bowbank
Roachburn
Haining Burn
Midgeholme

High Long Ho.
Rough Pike
Lewis Burn
Greens' Gears
Broomy Hill
Broomylinn
Gill Pike
Stot Crags
Gray Mare's Crags
Horse Head
The Knares 461m
Stripe Sike
Tarn Beck
Cammock Rigg
Foulbog Sike
Urthing Head
Paddaburn Moor
Paddaburn
Johnny's Crags
Chainsike
R. Irthing
Potsloan
Hen Hill
Blackshaws Hill
Butter Burn
The Gair
Hen Hill
Berry Hill 299m
DANGER ZONE
FOREST
SPADEADAM
Caud Beck
Watch Rigg
Deer Hill
Tip Hill
Green Side
White Rigg
Green Rigg 265m
Middle Shield Park
Round Rigg
Forster's Hill
Candel Linn
R. Irthing
Thirlwall Common (North Side)
Moss Peteral
Wandrew Convalescent Home
Gilsland Spa
Greengate Well
Irthing Ho.
Baron Ho.
Breckney Bed
The Hill
Orchard Ho.
Gilsland
B 6318
MILECASTLE
CAMP
L.C.
Thirlwall Castle
Carvoran Roman Fort
CAMP
Greenhead
New Angerton
Showfield
Blenkinsopp Castle
Weydoncleugh Side
Hot Moss
Blenkinsopp Common
Wain Rigg
Featherstone Common
Hartleyburn Common (North Side) EARTHWORK
Hartley Burn
ROMAN ROAD
Kellah
Doubledykes

THE RIGG
Jocks Pike 349m
Reeker Pike
Humble
Humble Hill 490m
Black Knowe
Bolts Law 395
Hopehouse
Chirdon Burn
Clintburn 318m
Little Dodd Hill
Whitehill Moor
Whitehill
Shankle End
Spy Rigg 313m
Butterburn Flow
Gowany Knowe
Butterburn
Lampert
Black Fell
Gaylock Hill
Newhouse
Hummell Knowe
Rutheryhaugh
Wileysike Ho.
White Rigg
Hugh's Hill
Black Rigg 242m
Tipalt Burn
Farglow
High Tipalt
Hangingshields Rigg
Chesters Pike
Cockmount MILECASTLE
Walltown
AESICA Roman Fort
VALLUM
Sunny Rigg
Edge Hill
Haltwhistle
Bellister Castle
Wydon NT
Wydon Eals
Bridge End
Park
Kellah Featherstone Castle
Burnfoot
Ramshaw Fell
Ramshaw
Qwanbury
A69

B6318
A69

75
70 71
65

a b c
d e f
g h i

71

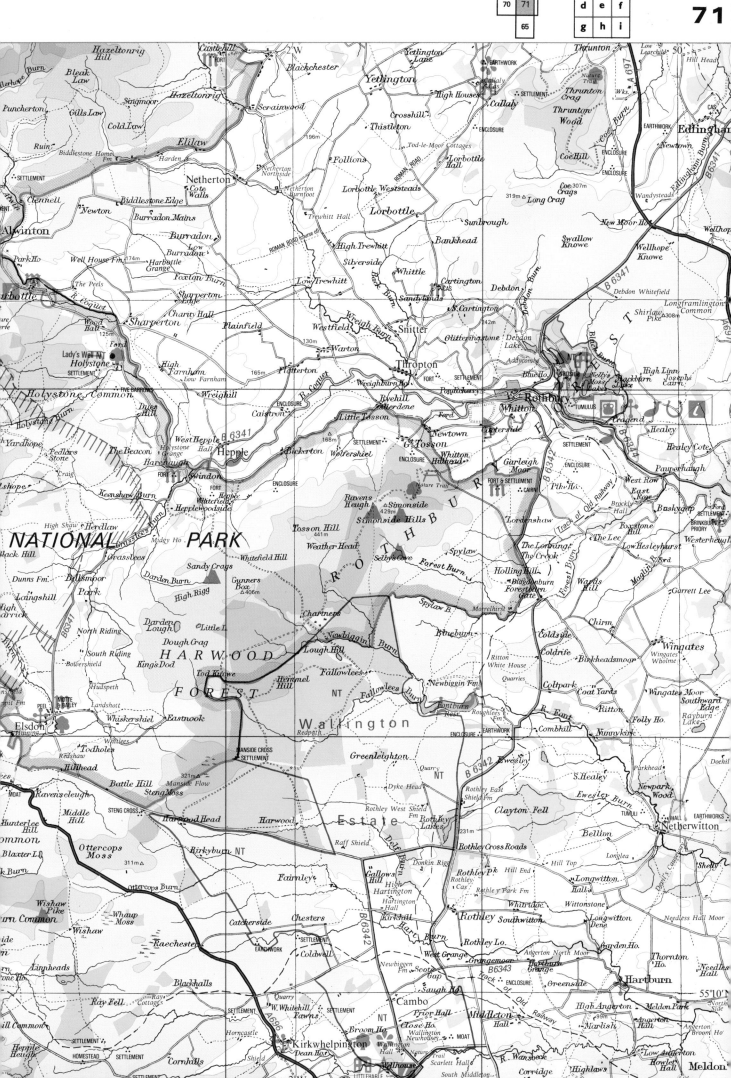

a	b	c
d	e	f
g	h	i

	76	
72	73	
65	66	

0   1   2   3   4   5 Miles
0 1 2 3 4 5 6 7 8 Kilometres

Castlehill FORT
Blackchester
Yetlington Lane
Thrunton
Low Learchild
Hill Head
Overthwarts
Corby's Crags
Alnwick or Aydon
St Mar

Singmoor
Cold Law
Hazeltonrig
Scrainwood
Yetlington
High Houses
Callaly Cas
SETTLEMENT
Callaly
EARTHWORK
Thrunton Crag
Thrunton Wood
Nature Trail
A 697
Wks.
CAS.
Edlingham
Black L.
Freem

Eliław
Harden
Netherton Northside
Netherton Burnfoot
Crosshill
Thistleton
Tod-le-Moor Cottages
Lorbottle Hall
ENCLOSURE
196m
Coe Hill
ENCLOSURE
Newtown
EARTHWORK
Wandysteads
ENCLOSURE
CAS
Black Burn

Netherton
Cote Walls
Follions
Lorbottle Weststeads
Lorbottle
Long Crag
319m
Coe 307m Crags
New Moor Ho.
Glantlees Hill 260m
Wellhope
Snook Bank
Glantl

Biddlestone Edge
Burradon Mains
Trewhitt Hall
ROMAN ROAD
Sunbrough
Bankhead
ROMAN ROAD course of
B 6341
Swallow Knowe
Wellhope Knowe
Wellhope Knowe
Debdon Whitefield
Canada

Burradon
Low Burradon
High Trewhitt
Silverside
Whittle
Cartington CAS
Debdon
Debdon Burn
Longframlington Common
EARTHWORK
Overgrass

174m
Harbottle Grange
Foxton Burn
Low Trewhitt
Sandylands
S. Cartington
242m
Shirlaw Pike 308m
Newmoor Hall
A 697
Embleton Stead
Swanlan

Sharperton Lane
Charity Hall
Plainfield
Westfield
Wreigh Burn
Snitter
130m
Glitteringstone
Debdon Lake
Addycombe
Black Burn
WEST
A 697
Smalldene

Sharperton
Ford
High Farnham
Low Farnham
165m
Flotterton
Warton
Thropton
FORT
Glitteringstone
Pondicherry
Rothbury
Blue Ho.
Nelly's Moss Lakes
High Linn
Joseph's Cairn
Besom Barn
North End
Embleton Hall
172m
Longframling

Five Barrows
Dues Hill
Wreighill
Caistron
ENCLOSURE
Little Tosson
Ryehill
Allerdene
Ford
Whitton
Carterside
Rothbury
TUMULUS
Cragend
i
Devil's Cau

West Hepple
Holystone Grange
Hepple Hall
B 6341
Hepple
Bickerton
Wolfershiel
G. Tosson
ENCLOSURE
Newtown
Whitton Hillhead
Garleigh Moor
FORT & SETTLEMENT
SETTLEMENT
ENCLOSURE
Healey
Healey Cote
Framlington Villa
Cockshot
Low Tou

The Beacon
Harehaugh
FORT
Swindon
Hepple Whitefield
Hepplewoodside
Keenshaw Burn
Crosslees Burn
ENCLOSURE
Ravens Heugh
Nature Trail
Simonside 429m
Simonside Hills
CAIRN
Pike Ho.
Lordenshaw
West Row
East Row
Pauperhaugh
Brockly Hall
Foxstone Hill
Ford
SETTLEMENT
Todstead
Low Healey
High Healey

Midgy Ho.
Tosson Hill 441m
Weather Head
Selby's Cove
Forest Burn
ROTHBURY
Spylaw
The Lorbing
The Crook
The Lee
Low Hesleyhurst
Westerheugh
R. Ford
Maglin Burn
Tod Burn

Darden Burn
High Rigg
Sandy Crags
Whitefield Hill
Gunners Box 406m
Spylaw B.
Morrelhirst
Blueburn
Holling Hill
Blagdonburn
Forestburn Gate
Wards Hill
Garrett Lee
North Birks
Lindenlane
Hillhead
Todburn

Darden Lough
Dough Crag
Little L.
Chartners
Newbiggin Burn
Lough Hill
King's Dod
Tod Knowe
Hemmel Hill
Fallowlees
Newbiggin Fm
Ritton White House
Quarries
Coldside
Coldrife
Birkheadsmoor
Chirm
Wingates
Wingates Wholme
Viewlaw
TOWER

HARWOOD
FOREST
Eastnook
Whiskershiel
Redpath
Wallington
Fallowlees Burn
NT
Fontburn Rest
Roughlees Fm
Combhill
Coltpark
Coat Yards
R. Font
Folly Ho.
Ritton
Nunnykirk
Wingates Moor
Southward Edge
Rayburn Lake
West Moor
Todburn Moor
Muckley
Faxti

Battle Hill
321m
Manside Flow
Steng Moss
Steng Cross
MANSIDE CROSS
SETTLEMENT
Greenleighton
QUARRY
NT
Dyke Head
Ewesly
B 6342
EARTHWORK
ENCLOSURE
S. Healey
Parkhead
Newpark Wood
Doehill
High Trewitley
Beacon Hill
CROSS
Stanton Ho.
190m
Whinney Hill
Haredene

Harwood Head
Harwood
ESTATE
Rothley West Shield Fm
Rothley East Shield Fm
Rothley Lakes
231m
Clayton Fell
Ewesley Burn
TUMULI
Netherwitton
Gallowshaw
Selby Hill
Stanton
Bellim
Berry
Hall

311m
Kirkyburn NT
Fairnley
Raff Shield
Delf Burn
Donkin Rigg
Rothley Cross Roads
Rothley Pk
Rothley Cas
Hill End
Hill Top
Longwitton Hall
Longlea
Shelly
Ford
Stantonven
Wood Ho.
Maid Hall

Ottercops Burn
Whaup Moss
Raechester
Catcherside
SETTLEMENT
EARTHWORK
Chesters
Coldwell
Gallows Hill
High Hartington
Hartington Hall
Kirkhill
Rothley Hare Burn
Rothley Southwitton
Whitridge
Longwitton
Longwitton Dene
Wittonstone
Needless Hall Moor
Longshaws
Buckshaw Hall
Nunriding Hall

Blackhalls
Ray Cottages
A 696
Coldwell
B 6342
West Grange
Scots Gap
Grangemoor
B 6343
Fenham Grange
Greenside
Argerton North Moor
Garden Ho.
Thornton Ho.
Hartburn
Quarry Ho.
Newton Underwood
Throphill
B 6343
R. Wansb

SETTLEMENT
Cornhalls
W. Whitehill
Fawns
SETTLEMENT
QUARRY
Cambo
NT
Prior Hall
Middleton Hall
Track of Old Railway
ENCLOSURE
SETTLEMENT
Needless Hall
Meldon Park
North Side
Newton Red Ho.
Meldonpark Fm.
Molesdo

Horncastle
Kirkwhelpington
Dean Ho.
Shield
Broom Ho.
Close Ho.
Wallington Newhouses
MOAT
Wallington Hall
Nature Trail
Scarlett Hall
South Middleton
LITTLEHARLE TOWER
Corridge
99m
Angerton Hall
Low Angerton
Howley Hall
Meldon
W. Col

Wallhouse
R. Wansbeck
Highlaws
50'

77
72 73
66 67

a b c
d e f
g h i

73

40'
30'

Cawledge Middle Park
Bilton
Alnmouth
ALNMOUTH
BAY

Longdyke
Bilton Banks
Waterside Ho.
Denwmoor
Townfoot
High Buston
Wooden
NT
Buston Barnes Fm.

Shilbottle
Wood Ho.
Hillhead
Northfield

Low Whittle Mine
99m
Southmoor
Eastfield Hall
Shortridge Hall
Low Buston

Southside
Sturton Grange
LC
Birling

Newton Low Hall
Brotherwick
Warkworth
9

Newton-on-the-Moor
Bank Ho.
Howlet Hall
Hermitage Cas.
20m

Villa Fm.
East Ho.
Warkworth
Old Barns
Jaudin

Hazon High Houses
Walksmill
New Barns
Gloster Hill

Chesterhill
Hazon Lee
Guyzance
Morwick Hall
New Hall
Warkworth Harbour
CG
LB
North Steel
Coquet Island

Common Swarland Estate
Lawrance Lee
Mere Burn
Brainshaugh
Hall
Whirleyshaws
R. Coquet
Link Ho.
Amble
South Steel

Acton Dene
PRIORY
Hope Ho.
Moor Ho.
Hauxley
12m
Hauxley Haven

East Ho.
Acton Ho.
56m
Cavil Head
Chester Ho.
North Togston
Low Hauxley
Radcliffe
Bondicarr

Acton Hall
Old Felton
Acklington Park Fm.
Acklington
Low Park
Togston
Broomhill
Low Hall
DANGER
Bondi Carrs

Swarland
8th Acton
ACKLINGTON STA
(Heliport)
Hadston Carrs

Swarlanddean
Mouldshaugh
High Park
B 6345
38m
Hadston Fm.
South Broomhill
ZONE

Felton
Cheeveley
HM Prison
Hadston Link Ho.
Chevington Drift

Cowslip Hill
Thirston Ho.
Woodside
Red Row
Chevington
E. Chevington

Felton Park
West Thirston
East Thirston
Maidens Hall
Whitefield Ho.

Hemelspeth
Thirston New Houses
The Brocks
Shaw
Bullock's Hall
DRURIDGE

Wintrick
ESHOTT CAS (site of)
W. Chevington
N. Steads
High Chibburn
BAY

Blackbrook Fm.
Longdike Burn
Hall
Eshott Heugh
Eshott
Low Chibburn
NT
Druridge Bay

BOCKENFIELD
Eshott Birnie
Chevington Moor
Druridge

Burgham Fm.
104m
Helm
LC
Widdrington

Longdyke
West Forest
E. Forest
W. Stobswood
Mine
S. Steads
Hemscott Hill

Causey Park
Earsdon Hill
Peth Hills
Stobswood
Houndalee
The Scars

Causey Park Bridge
E. Stobswood
B 1337
Blakemoor Fm.
Brig Hd.

Fieldhead New Houses
Earsdon
WIDDRINGTON STA
Cresswell
TOWER
Seal Skears

Tindale Hill
Earsdon Moor
Northwood Fm.
Fernybeds Fm.
Highthorn
Snab Point

Tritlington Broom Fm.
Ulgham Park
Hagg Fm.
Cresswell Ft.
Headagee

Fenrother
Tritlington
R. Lyne
Ulgham Grange
N. Linton Fm.
Ellington
Mine

Fenrother Lane
Ulgham
S. Linton
Linton Burn
R. Lyne

Shield Green
The Cockles
Ulgham Fence Fm.
Crowden Hill Fm.
Linton Colliery
West Moor
Lynemouth

Herons Close
Cockle Park
TOWER
Ulgham Broom Fm.
East Moor
Aluminium Works

Low Espley
Espley Hall
Blubbery
Broomhill Fm.
Old Moor Stead
Potland Fm.
Power Sta.
Lyne Sands

High Highlaws
Hebron
Hebron Hill
Longhirst Lane Fm.
Old Moor
Lynefield Ho.
Blue Holes
10m
Beacon Pt.
18

Low Heighley
Longhirst
Middle Moor
LC
Third Ho.
A 189

Warreners Ho.
West Shield
Hosp.
Longhirst Grange
Butterwell Fm.
Longhirst Brocks
Potland Burn
ASHINGTON
Woodhorn
Woodhorn Demesne
Outer Carrs

Pegswood Moor
Fawdon Ho.
Newbiggin-by-the-Sea

West Benridge
m
Fulbeck
Pegswood
STA
Bothal Park
A 197
Causey Garth
Hirst
Spital Carrs

Hosp.
Bothal
Bothalhaugh
Whitefield
Ashington Fm.
North Seaton

Dean Ho.
Spittal Hill
Grange Ho.
Morpeth
Park Ho.
Shadfen Park Ho.
R. Wansbeck
Sheepwash
Industrial Estate
North Seaton Colliery

NEWMINSTER
CAS
STA
Shadfen
Guide Post
Stakeford
A 196
W. Sleekburn

Mitford Steads
High Church
High Ho.
CAS
Hepscott Red Ho.
North Choppington
Healeywood
Bomarsund
Scotland Gate
B 1334

Tranwell
High Common
Stobhill
Hepscott
Catchburn
Coalburn
Choppington
Cambois

55°10'

76

a	b	c
d	e	f
g	h	i

78	79
76	77
72	

0   1   2   3   4   5 Miles
0   1   2   3   4   5   6   7   8 Kilometres

Milfield
Fenton Town
Fenton Demesne
Nesbit
Hetton Hall
THE RINGSES
EARTHWORK
North Hazelrigg
Sionside
Belford Moor
South Hazelrigg
North Lyham
Lyham Moor
Newlands
Newlands West Lodge
Old Lyham
Warenton
Sandy Ho.
Galewood
Thirlings
Newtown
Doddington
Horton Moor
ENCLOSURE
SETTLEMENT 199m
Dod Law
EARTHWORK
West Horton
East Horton
Spylaw
South Lyham
ENCLOSURE
Marleyknowe
Ewart Park
River Till
Doddington Br.
Weetwood Hall
Heatheryhall
West Lyham
Alloy or Lyham Burn
SETTLEMENT
Linkeylaw
Lanton
Coupland
rknewton
B6351
Glen
Heavering
Akeld Steads
Track of Old Railway
Turvelaws
B6348
West Weetwood
SETTLEMENT
Fowberry Tower
Herlaw
Greendykes
Chatton Moor
Brownridge
R. Glen
Yeavering Bell
Akeld
Humbleton Buildings
Hamildon Hill 1402
Humbleton
Humbleton Hill
Wooler
Weetwood Moor
Chatton
58m
Wandon
Shielhope
Amersidelaw
celhouse
Gleadscleugh
MOTTE
Waud Ho
Coldmartin
Fowberrymoor
Broomhouse
Sandyford Moor
CAIRN
Chatton
Tom Tallon's Crag
Gains Law
Wooler W.
Tower Martin
Blakelaw
Willie Law
ommonburn Ho.
Common Burn
SETTLEMENT
Wishing Well
Ford
Earle
Haugh Head
ENCLOSURE
Chillingham
Great Moor
Broadstruther
Earlehillhead
Lilburn Hill
Newtown
Lilburn Grange
Chillingham Park
Wildlife Park
CAS
Chillingham Park
Ross Castle
FORT
NT
Botany
ulburn air
Havelly B.
Snear Hill
Middleton Hall
Ford
Lilburn Tower
Lilburn B.
Hepburn
eston Hill 825m
Cold Law 452m
Brands Hill
North Middleton
East Lilburn
Hepburn Bell
Hepburn Wood
Quarryhouse
Langlee
Middleton Old Town
164m
South Middleton
Lilburn Glebe
Bewick Folly
Blawearie
Bewick Moor
SETTLEMENT
Cateran Hill 267m
Broadhope Hill
Rackside
Ilderton
Roseden Edge
Bewick Br.
99m
Old Bewick
30'N
Langlee Crags
Middleton Crags
FORT
Roseden
FORTS
Scald Hill
Langleeford
Lang Crags
Dod Hill
EARTHWORK
Roddam B.
Roddam Hall
Wooperton
Track of Old Railway
New Bewick
Harehope Hill
Harehope Hall
Langleeford Hope
Harthope Burn
Threestoneburn Ho.
Threestone Burn
Heddon Hill
277m
Ford
Roddam
Hedgeley Moor 1464
PERCY'S CROSS
B6346
Tarr
Eglin
Harthope Linn aterfall)
Hedgehope Hill
Kelpie Strand
Harelaw B.
The Dod
Calder
Roddam Rigg
River Breamish
Beanley Moor
650m
mb Fell
Standrop Rigg
Dunmoor Hill
Reaveley Greens
Brandon White House
Low Hedgeley
Beanley
EARTHWORK
Kimm
Standrop B.
Het B.
Dunmoor B.
Reaveley Hill
Reaveleyhill
Heddon
Brandon
Hedgeley Hall
ielcleugh Edge
Collaw B.
Linhope
Linhope Burn
SETTLEMENT
CAIRNS
Reaveley
Ford
TOWER
Powburn
Titlington Pike
SETTLEMENT
Titlington Mou
High Cantle
High Bleakhope
Breamish
Linhope Spout (Waterfall)
Linhope
SETTLEMENTS
Hartside Hill
East Hill
Branton Buildings
Greenfields
Shawdonwood Ho.
Titlington
Hall
Low Bleakhope
Greensidehill
Hartside
SETTLEMENTS
Ewe Hill
SETTLEMENT
Fowberry
ROMAN ROAD
Branton Middlesteads
Glanton
Shawdon Hall
Woodh
Shill Moor
Alnhammoor
SETTLEMENTS
FORT
SETTLEMENT
Glanton Pyke
EARTHWORK
West Bolton
Bolton
Cushat Law
Scaud Knowe
Chesters
Cobden
Cochrane Pike
EARTHWORK
EARTHWORK
SETTLEMENT
Mile End
Shawdon Hill
R. Aln
Low Barton
Low Broomepark
Low Broom
Shank B.
Fore B.
Leafield Edge
Ewe Hill
The Mill
Howbalk Mountain
Rothill
Sting Head
Shank Ho.
High Knowes
Great Ryle
Eslington Hall
Whittingham
Battle Bri
Hogdon Law
Spartley B.
Prendwick
Eslington Lowhill
Eslington Highhill
Thrunton
Low Learchild
Hill Hea
Dryhope Hill
Milkhope
Northfieldhead Hill
Unthank
Little Ryle
Yetlington Lane
EARTHWORK
Nature Trail
Hazeltonrig Hill
Castlehill
FORT
Alnham
Alnham Ho.
Blackchester
Yetlington
CAS
SETTLEMENT
Thrunton Crag
Thrunton Wood
Puncherton
Gills Law
Singmoor
Hazeltonrig
Scrainwood
High Houses
Callaly
Coe Hill
Bleak Law
Cold Law
Elilaw
Crosshill
Thistleton
ENCLOSURE
EARTHWORK
Newtown
Edl
Allerhope Burn
Ruin
Biddlestone Home Fm
Harden
196m
Tod-le-Moor Cottages
Follions
Lorbottle Hall
Coe Burn
ENCLOSURE
SETTLEMENT
Clennell
Newton
Biddlestone Edge
Netherton
Cote Walls
Netherton Northside
Netherton Burnfoot
Lorbottle Weststeads
Lorbottle
Coe 307m
Long Crag
319m
Wandysteads
Burradon Mains
2°W
Trewhitt Hall
B624

	79	
76	77	
	73	

a	b	c
d	e	f
g	h	i

77

78 79
76 77

a b c
d e f
g h i

79

Farne Islands
East of Bamburgh (79i)

55° 40' N

Knivestone
Longstone
N. Wamses
S. Wamses
Big Harcar
Oxscar or
S. Goldstone
Glororum Shad
Brownsman
Elbow
Gun Rock
Staple I.
Megstone
Islestone Shad
Skeney Gar
Callers
Crumstone
Staple
Sound
Fang
Knocks Reef
Knockbn Ends
FARNE ISLANDS
The Kettle
Lit. Scarcar
NT
Nature Trail
The Bush
Farne I.

's Bay
ye
otherston's Hole
Sharper's Head
Berwick
upon-Tweed
CG
Pier   Meadow Haven
Sandstell Point
Spittal

Redstan Cove
Borewell
L.C.
Old Colliery Row
Hill
Cheswick Black Rocks
Nabhill
Cheswick Sands
Cheswick
Cheswick Ho.
Ladythorne
18
Cheswick Buildings
Windmill Hill
Goswick
ncroft
Broom House
Sand Ridge
Snipe Pt.
Coves Haven
Keel Hd.
erryburn
dgemill
Haggerston Cas.
Brockmill
Snook Pt.
The Snook
Emanuel Head
ringtons hill
The Barns
The Links
HOLY ISLAND
Berrington
New Haggerston
Causeway
(Lindisfarne)
The Lamb
3m
L.C.
Beal
Beal Sands
Holy Island Sands
Holy Island
Lindisfarne Cas.
55° 40'
Lickar
Low Lynn
Mount Hooley
PRIORY
NT
The Harbour
Kentstone
Fenhamhill
Burrows Hole
Hunting Hall
Kyloe Cot.
Fenham
Guile Pt.
wick Northfield
82m
B 6353
Lowick Low Steads
West Kyloe
Fenham Flats
Old Law
Lowick
Fenwick
East Kyloe
Fenwick Stead
Wide Open
Skate
Lowick High Stead
SETTLEMENT
Kyloe Hills
Bogle Houses
Fenham le-Moor
Road
Moorhouse
Shepherdskirk Hill
EARTHWORK
Buckton
Ross Links
Low Water Mark
Brownridge
Shiellow Crags
EARTHWORK
Ross Back Sands
Barmoor Red Ho.
Sneafield
Elwick Burn
Elwick
Ross
Biteabout
Laverock Law
EARTHWORK
Coal Burn
205m
Greensheen Hill
Kettleburn
Detchant
Low Middleton
Ross Back Sands
Megstone
h Moor
Holburn
ST CUTHBERTS CAVE
Middleton
Easington Grange
Budle Bay
Budle Pt.
18
Inner Sound
rangham
Hetton Steads
Holburn Grange
Cockenheugh
211m
Swinhoe Fm.
Craggyhill
Easington Demesne
Easington Chesterhill
Heather Cottages
Hall
Easington
Waren Mill
Budle
CAS.
North Hazelrigg
Hetton Hall
Plantation Fm.
Westhall
Hall
B 1342
Bamburghfriars
Bamburgh
THE RINGSES
EARTHWORK
Redsteads
Hetton Law
Belford
Sionside
Outchester
Spindlestone
B 1347
Glororum
Burton
Greenhill
Fowberry
Saddlershall
CG
ington
199m
Horton Moor
ENCLOSURE
South Hazelrig
North Lyham
Belford Moor
Lyham Moor
Belford Mains
Newlands
New Mousen
Newlands West Lodge
Newlands Burn
Bradford
Springhill
50'

Countryside

Nature trails, scenic walks, country parks, field and nature study centres and areas of outstanding natural beauty, including woods, waterfalls, moors, coastline and interesting natural features. For more arduous hill walking, orienteering, etc. see page 116.

Country Code

Throughout the North Country, especially in the national parks, efforts are being made to maintain a balance between the interests of those who work and those who play in the countryside. Visitors must remember that much of the land, the mountains and the hills also provide farmers' livelihoods. So whenever and wherever you are out walking, please follow these simple rules:

* Guard against risk of fire
* Close all gates behind you, especially those at cattle grids, etc.
* Keep dogs under control
* Keep to the paths across farmland - you have no right of way over surrounding land
* Avoid damaging fences, hedges and walls
* Leave no litter - take it away with you
* Safeguard water supplies
* Protect wildlife, plants and trees - do not pick flowers, leave them for others to enjoy
* Drive carefully on country roads
* Respect the life of the countryside - and you will be welcomed

20a Whicham. Footpath north to the summit of Black Combe. Spectacular views.

20c Foxfield. Walk of 4¾ miles south along the Duddon Sands, a vast area of mudflats where many birds can be seen. 🐦

20h Walney Island. Nature reserve with large numbers of birds and interesting shore vegetation. *By permission only.* 🐦

21a High Hay Bridge: Nature Reserve. Tel. Greenodd (022 986) 412 or 283. Two trails around deer enclosures, woodland, marsh and tarns. No dogs. *By appointment only.* 🐖🐦

21b Fell Foot. An 18-acre country park with fine trees, open parkland, superb views and many facilities for the visitor. 🐦⛺🛶

21b Grange-over-Sands. Nature trail of 2 miles through deciduous woodland and open limestone fell to the summit of Hampsfell.

21c Arnside. Nature walk of 2 miles with wide views of the Kent estuary, Morecambe Bay, the Lakeland mountains and the Pennines.

21d Bardsea. Country park with fine views across Morecambe Bay, attractive walks in woodland and excellent bird watching. 🐦♨🐦

21e Holker Hall. Tel. Flookburgh (044 853) 328. Herds of fallow, sika and red deer can be seen in the park. *Easter to early October 1100-1800.* 🐦✻🖼🖻⚘☆

21f Arnside Knott. Small but beautiful tract of coastline owned by the National Trust. See 21c.

21f Castlebarrow. Nature trail of 1½ miles through Eaves Wood with interesting flora on limestone pavement. Guide from National Trust, Silverdale.

21i Lancaster: Hornsea Pottery. Tel. (0524) 68444. 42 acres of landscaped parkland with leisure park containing rare farm animal breeds. 🐦⛺♨🐘

22a Arnside. See 21c.

22a Dallam Tower. Deer park which can only be viewed from the road or footpaths of the area.

22b Field End. Nature trail north along a short length of the Lancaster/Kendal Canal showing nature's adaptation of a man-made waterway.

22d Arnside Knott. See 21f.

22d Castlebarrow. See 21f.

22g Lancaster. See 21i.

23a Dent. Footpath south to White Shaw Moss (23b) with panoramic views over the Yorkshire Dales.

23e Clapham: Yorkshire Dales National Park Information Centre. Tel. (046 85) 419. Permanent exhibition about the national park. Many walks start from here, including the Reginald Farrar Trail and an 8 mile trek north to Ingleborough Summit. 🛈

23f Dale Head. Footpath to the summit of Pen-y-ghent, incorporating part of the Pennine Way.

23i Stainforth Bridge. Footpath following the banks of the River Ribble south to Langcliffe.

23i Settle. Walk east along Attermire Scar to Victoria Cave, where many notable archaeological treasures were found in the early 19th century.

24d Dale Head. See 23f.

24e Buckden. Footpath up to the 2302ft Buckden Pike and along Starbotton Fell. Beware -the walk is arduous and may take all day. ♨

24g Stainforth Bridge. See 23i.

24g Settle. See 23i.

24h Malham Tarn Field Centre. Tel. Airton (072 93) 331. Holiday courses arranged in natural history subjects, including ecology, birds, photography, geography, meteorology. Minimum age 16 years for unaccompanied children. *February to November.* 🐦🛶

24h Prior Rakes. Walk east to Kilnsey (24i) on Mastiles Lane, an old drover road once used by monks from Fountains Abbey (see ✝ 26h).

Picnic Sites

These are usually situated in areas of natural beauty, often with a nature trail or walk nearby. They generally consist of wooden tables, log seats, litter bins (please use) and, if near a road, parking spaces. Do not expect any conveniences or other facilities. Although mainly run by the Forestry Commission, others are maintained by local councils, National Parks, the National Trust and by private concerns.

Although the blue symbol above is used to indicate a picnic site on the maps, many locations are marked 'on the ground' with signs bearing the symbol shown here.

24h Gordale Scar. Footpath leads to impressive waterfall which cascades over a limestone cliff. Most spectacular after heavy rain.

24h Malham: Yorkshire Dales National Park Centre. Airton (072 93) 363. Exhibitions and displays about the park. Many walks from here to Malham Cove and Malham Tarn. *April to end September, mid-morning to mid-afternoon.* ♿ 🛈

24i Grassington: National Park Centre, Hebden Road. Tel. (0756) 752748. Display features conservation and park management. *April to end September, mid-morning to mid-afternoon.* ♿

25c High Knowle. Short walk through Druid's Wood with fine views over the Pennines. ♨

25e Lofthouse. Footpath north through the spectacular wooded gorge of How Stean.

25h Pateley Bridge. Footpath to Yorke's Folly and Heyshaw Moor via Grassington.

25i Brimham Rocks Country Park. 362 acres of open moorland which includes an area of grotesquely shaped rock formations. Information centre in old shooting lodge. 🐦

26e Studley Park: Studley Royal Country Park. 650 acres of landscaped parkland and magnificent woodland with herds of deer. *Daily, dawn to dusk.* ✻ ✝

26g Brimham Rocks. See 25i.

27b Boltby. Footpath south over moorland and through woods to Southwood Hall.

27b Sutton Bank: Garbutt Wood. Nature trail of 2½ miles leads north through old birch woods and along a jurassic rock escarpment.

White Horse Walk follows the Cleveland Way south above the Kilburn White Horse, carved on limestone hillside, with wide views over Vale of York. ⅲ

27b White Horse. Walk north from Sutton Bank. See previous entry.

27c Rievaulx: Rievaulx Terrace. Delightful grass covered terrace, backed by woodlands, with classical 18th century temples and splendid vistas over the Abbey, Ryedale and Hambleton Hills. *April to end October, daily 1030-1800.* 🖻 ✝

27c Helmsley: Freedom of Ryedale Holidays, 23a Market Place. Tel. (0439) 70775. Multi-activity holidays include hill and fell walking. 🐦 ∪

Start of the Cleveland Way Long Distance Footpath (see page 14).

27c Castle. Footpath from Helmsley, through woods onto the Whinny Bank and the Cleveland Way. Magnificent views of Ryedale. ⅲ

27c Wass. Footpath leads north to Oldstead (27b) and an observatory from which there are fine views of the Vale of York. Passes Byland Abbey. ✝

28a Rievaulx. See 27c.

28a Helmsley. See 27c.

28a Castle. See 27c.

28a Riccal Dale. A beautiful tree-clad valley with footpaths up both sides. Especially worth visiting in autumn. ⅲ

28b Ford. 6½ mile walk up the valleys of Kirkdale and Sleightholme Dale, both heavily wooded and containing many interesting flowers. ✝

29b Allerston. Long distance walk (about 7 hours) through Langdale and Dalby Forests to Reasty (43d). Views of Derwent Valley and Vale of Pickering.

29b Pexton Moor Farm: Dalby Forest Drive. Forest road, upgraded for public use as a toll road, which winds through some of the most varied forest scenery in the North York Moors.

    Bridestones Moor. Nature reserve with curiously eroded rock formations and interesting flora and fauna. Access from the toll road.

30c Filey Brigg. Country park comprising an extensive grass-covered cliff top with magnificent views towards Flamborough Head. 🏕 🦅

31d B1255: Dane's Dyke. Country park with nature trail leading to popular beauty spot. The dyke is a huge Bronze Age ditch and embankment.

32a St Bees. Cliff walk on 300ft sandstone headland with fine views over Solway Firth. Also good for bird watching (see 🦅44g).

32c Wasdale Head. 3½ mile nature trail north along the lake shore and riverside, through plantations by a tarn and areas of bog.

32c Strands. 4½ mile walk north into Nether Wasdale where there are pleasant views from the common.

32e Ravenglass. 4 mile walk through woodland, containing hardwoods and evergreens, to Muncaster Castle (32f).

32f Eskdale Green. Attractive walk of ¾ mile along paths winding through young larches and old beech woods, known as Giggle Alley.

32f Muncaster Castle. Nature trail through rhododendron walks with fine views of the Esk Valley; also passes a heronry. *Easter to early October, Saturday to Thursday 1200-1700.* ☕ ❀ 🏕 ♿ 🐘 📷

33b Stickle Gill. Footpath to Stickle Tarn via the beautiful Dungeon Ghyll waterfalls.

33c Rydal Water: White Moss Common. Woodland walk used by Wordsworth. Splendid views of Rydal and Grasmere; notable for bluebells in May. 🏕

33c Ambleside. 2½ mile walk west over Loughrigg Fell with superb views of Rydal and Windermere. Footpath also leads east to Stockghyll Force (34a), a fine waterfall, particularly after heavy rain.

33d Dalegarth Station. Nature trail south through glaciated valley, mixed woodland and a gorge to several waterfalls.

33d High Ground. 3 mile walk up to and around the isolated Devoke Water; best seen on a fine day.

33d Birks. 6 mile walk south through the Duddon Valley. Starts in woodland, emerges on fell-land, descends to the river and finishes among farm fields. 🏕

33f A593. Short walk west to Stand End and Low Oxen Fell, mostly on hard-surfaced tracks.

33f Tarn Hows. Nature trail through mixed woodlands with good botanical interest and outstanding scenery. *(By permission only).*

33f High Wray. Attractive lakeside walk via Belle Grange (34d) and Windermere to Wray Castle.

33f Hawkeshead. A 1 mile footpath to Hawkeshead Hill; gives splendid views of nearby mountain ranges.

33f Brantwood. Nature trail from Ruskin's home through oakwoods, pastures by a deep gorge, waterfalls and open fells with superb view of Coniston Water and the mountains beyond. ☕ 🏕 ❀ 📷

33f Nature Trail: Bogle Crag. Three way-marked walks through typical Lakeland forest. 🏕

33f Grizedale: Visitor Wildlife Centre. Tel. Satterthwaite (022 984) 273. Wildlife displays, information room, forest theatre. *Easter to October 1000-1700; November to Easter 1100-1600.* ☕ 📷 ℹ

    Millwood Forest Trail alongside a stream through old oak, Douglas fir and Norway spruce.

    Spruce Knott Observation Tower for wildfowl on nearby water, and forest fauna in this conservation area.

33g Foxfield. See 20c.

33i High Hay Bridge See 21a.

34a Rydal Water. See 33c.

34a Ambleside. See 33c.

34d A593. See 33f.

34d Tarn Hows. See 33f.

34d High Wray. See 33f.

34d Hawkeshead. See 33f.

34d Nature Trail. See 33f.

34d Grizedale. See 33f.

34d Ferry House: Claife Nature Trail. Lakeside and woodland walk. Leaflet from National Trust.

34e Brockhole: Lake District National Park Centre. Tel. Windermere (096 62) 2231. Audio-visual displays, films and information room. *Mid-March to mid-November, daily from 1000.* ☕ ♿ ❀ 📷 ℹ

    Nature Trail shows lakeshore and woodland habitat, including globe flowers and red squirrels, and marvellous panoramic views. *Same times as above.*

34e Windermere. Zig-zag walk up to Orrest Head, north of the town, providing superb panoramas.

34e Belle Isle. Nature trail around the island amongst a variety of trees; fine views of Windermere. *Mid May to mid-September; Monday, Tuesday, Thursday and Sunday 1030-1700.* ☕ ❀ 🏕

34g High Hay Bridge. See 21a.

34g Fell Foot. See 21b.

34h Town Head. Footpath north to Gummer's How, an excellent viewpoint. 🏕

34h Sow How. Attractive walk east through woodland plantations past two delightful tarns to St Anthony's Chapel in Cartmel Fell.

34i Kendal. Nature trail west through Serpentine Woods with fine views of Kendal. Interesting flora.

34i Field End. See 22b.

35h Sedbergh: Yorkshire Dales National Park Information Centre. Tel. (0587) 20125. Displays, books, maps etc. *Easter to October, daily 1100-1700.* ℹ

35i Dent. See 23a.

36g Dent. See 23a.

36i Hardraw Force. Footpath behind this 100ft-high waterfall.

37h Bear Park: National Park Centre. Tel. Aysgarth (096 93) 424. Interpretation centre with displays, books, etc. Mini nature trail to Aysgarth Falls starts here. *April to end September.* ℹ

40e Osmotherly: Lyke Wake Walk. Start of this famous long distance path which passes through 40c, 41d, 41e, 41f, 42d, 42e and 42f. The path, named after a Cleveland dirge, crosses heather, bracken and bog nearly all the way on a 40-mile route to Ravenscar (43d). To qualify for membership of the Lyke Wake club, who meet at Queen Catherine's Hotel, Osmotherly, the journey has to be covered in 24 hours.

40f Lane House. 6 mile walk north along the Cow Ridge to High Farm and back down Arnsgill Ridge. Beautiful, open, heather-covered moorland.

40h Boltby. See 27b.

40i Laskill. 4½ mile walk west to and around Easterside Hill, a 'hump' of open moorland.

40i New Hall. Path leads west through woods into the beautiful bracken-covered valley of Thorodale. Splendid views of Vale of Mowbray and Pennines.

40i Rievaulx. See 27c.

41a Gribdale Terrace: Captain Cook's Boyhood Walk. Runs south to Cook's Monument, then north over Great Ayton Moor to Roseberry Topping. 🏕

41a Ford. 4¾ mile walk through little-known Baysdale to beautifully situated Baysdale Abbey, the remains of a 12th century Cistercian nunnery.

41b Danby Lodge National Park Centre. Tel. Castleton (028 76) 654. Former shooting lodge adapted as a visitor centre for the North York Moors. The 13-acre grounds include gardens, woodland and a riverside meadow. Also slide shows, exhibitions etc. *Easter to October daily 1000-1800; November to March weekends 1000-1700.* ☕ 📷 ℹ

41b Ainthorpe. 7 mile walk south east to Little Fryup Dale over Danby Rigg, an area littered with Bronze Age cairns. Good views into Eskdale.

41c Lealholm Side. Pleasant 6¼ mile walk north west through Park Head and onto Danby Beacon, one of the best all round viewpoints on the Moors.

41c Ash House. Short walk around the top end of Farndale, an area famous for daffodils.

41d Cowl House. Moorland walk of 3 miles north to Stump Cross and Bransdale along good tracks to a position which gives superb views of the high moors.

41e Trough House. Footpath north east to the head of Great Fryup Dale. Marvellous scenery with crags, shapely hills, streams and waterfalls.

41e Rosedale Abbey. Short walk in the secluded, peaceful Northdale and Rosedale.

 This symbol is often used 'on the ground' to mark the route of nature trails

Nature Reserves
Nature reserves, and the nature trails which run through them, exist for several reasons: the area may be of scientific or educational interest; or a particular kind of habitat or species of wildlife needs to be preserved. The reserves are controlled by such organisations as the RSPB, the Nature Conservancy Council or a County Naturalists Trust, but these bodies often do not own the land, so that access is frequently limited. It is, therefore, vital when visiting a nature reserve to keep to the marked path or trail and to observe the Country Code (see page 80). For details of any particular reserve contact the organisation concerned or the nearest ℹ (see page 122).

41f Nature Trail: Newtondale. Interpretative forest trail leads east showing varied tree species and different stages of the forest's development.

41g Helmsley. See 27c.

41h Farndale. Nature reserve where wild daffodils can be seen each spring in an abundance once common in Britain.

41h Lowna. Several footpaths north into Birch Hag Woods and Farndale. Leaflet from local National Park Information Centres.

41h Ford. See 28b.

41i Sutherland Lodge Activities Centre. Tel. Cropton (075 15) 228. Multi-activity holidays include field courses, ecology, etc. 🐾▲〇

42a Lealholm Side. See 41c.

42c Whitby: Northern Field and Activity Centres, Larpool Hall. Tel. (0947) 4073. Holiday courses in ecology, geography, geology, fossils, botany. 🐾

42c Falling Foss. Two attractive walks in pleasant valley of mixed woodland. Short walk goes through mainly broadleaved woodland to The Hermitage and a waterfall viewpoint; long walk continues over open farmland and moors past wildlife ponds. ⌐

42d Nature Trail. See 41f.

42e Moors: Newtondale Station. Three walks of various lengths start from this new station on the North York Moors Railway. All give fine views. ⌐🚂

42e High Horcum. Walk south to Hole of Horcum and over Levisham Moor to Dundale Pond. Plenty of prehistoric earthworks and tumuli to see.

42f Nature Trail: May Beck Farm. Trail through traditional moorland sheep farm. No dogs. Guide from National Park Centres.

42g Sutherland Lodge. See 41i.

42h Newgate Foot. 4 mile walk north over Hazelhead Moor to Blakey Topping, a 300ft 'sugar loaf' with extensive views.

42h Lewisham Station: Cropton Forest Drive. 5½ mile drive on forest roads through attractive mixed coniferous woodland with fine views of Newtondale.

42h Seive Dale. Three walks in Dalby Forest, all starting from car park on Forest Drive. ⌐

42h Snever Dale. Forest trail winds through varied forest to a commanding viewpoint. ⌐

42i Howden Hill. 5 mile walk north up Langdale Rigg and into Langdale Forest, a Forestry Commission plantation. Fine views before entering the forest.

42i Nature Trail. Three waymarked walks in Wykeham Forest. All go through the forest nursery and give superb views over Troutdale. ⌐

43d Robin Hood's Butts. Walk north along the cliff, waymarked as part of the Cleveland Way. Beautiful coastal scenery.

43d Ravenscar. 3 mile geological trail shows the varied geology of the area; fossils may be found. Leaflet from National Park Centres.

Cliff Walk. Footpath leads along the cliff to Stoupe Beck Wood and back over Brow Moor. Fine coastal scenery over Robin Hood's Bay.

43d Nature Trail. Long distance walk (about 7 hours) through Langdale and Dalby Forests to Allerston (29b). Magnificent views.

Slipho Forest. Two walks along a plateau past Bronze Age burial mound and nature reserve. ⌐

43d Hayburn Wyke. 65 - acre property includes an important nature reserve, woodland paths, a stream and access to the shore.

44f Loweswater. Walk of 4 miles around lake and through Holme Wood. The view epitomises all that is best about Lake District landscape.

44g St Bees. See 32a.

44i Bowness: Smithy Beck Trail. Leads along the edge of Ennerdale Water and climbs into the forest, past the site of a mediaeval settlement.

Nine Becks Walk along cleared trails and forest roads through larch and spruce woods; magnificent views over Ennerdale from Great Gable tower.

45d Whit Beck. Steep footpath west into the woods around Spout Force. Spectacular scenery.

45e Mire House: Dodd Wood Trail. 1½ miles through spruce and larch woods, giving superb views across Bassenthwaite Lake to Whinlatter, Keswick and Derwent Water. Some paths are steep.

45e Whinlatter Pass Visitor Centre. Tel. Braithwaite (059 682) 469. Displays and audio-visual presentation on local forestry. *Easter to October, daily 1000-1700.* 🐦⌐▲ℹ

Comb Trail. Rugged and often steep walk through spruce, Douglas fir, western hemlock and larch. Fine views of Bassenthwaite Lake.

45e Braithwaite: Noble Knott Walks. Series of waymarked trails of varying length and steepness wind through old oakwoods, firs, larch and spruce. ⌐

45e Derwent Island: Friar's Crag. Lakeside and woodland nature walk, including Ruskin's memorial and Friar's Crag viewpoint.

45e Ashness. 3 mile walk leads south through woods to the Lodore Cascades (waterfall). One of the 'classic' views of Derwent Water.

45f Walla Crag. Footpaths lead east through woods overlooking Derwent Water; splendid views.

45f Camp. Footpath west through woods to an ancient hill fort high above Thirlmere.

45g Buttermere. 3½ mile walk north over Rannerdale, a rarely visited yet delightful and typical Lakeland dale. Excellent views. Also a 4½ mile walk around Buttermere offering fine scenery.

45h Seatoller: Johnny's Wood. Nature walk through woodland and open fell; interesting woodland flora. Superb view from 1050ft High Doat.

45h Stonethwaite. A level and pleasant walk south along the banks of the River Derwent.

45i Nature Trail: Swirls Forest Trail. Shows examples of forestry practice along a ¾ mile waymarked walk.

45i Launchy Ghyll. Forest trail of 1 mile on a steep hillside illustrates landscape development and modern forestry and woodland management.

45i Brown Rigg. Pleasant but steep footpath leads up through woods to Harrop Tarn. Views of Thirlmere.

46e Lyulphs. Footpaths lead up to Aira Force (waterfall) and then west into Gowbarrow Park, old park land with good views of Ullswater.

46e Howtown. Footpath covering 6½ miles along the eastern shore of Ullswater to

Patterdale; the walk typifies the beauty of the Lake District. 🛥

46f Dalemain Country Park. Tel. Pooley Bridge (085 36) 450. Deer park with fallow deer; woodland. *Easter to end September, Saturday to Thursday 1400-1715.* 🐦⌐❋▣🏠

46h Wintercrag. Footpath up Martindale onto Hallin Fell, one of the National Park's best viewpoints.

46h Hartsop. Two footpaths leading to good Lakeland walks: one west to Brother's Water, and one east to Hawes Water. Both offer good views.

47f Appleby Castle. Nature trail through grounds amongst a collection of waterfowl and rare farm animals. *Easter, then May to end September; daily 1030-1700.* 🐦🏠🐘🐾

Woodland Nature Trail with good variety of trees, including riverside species. Leaflet from ℹ *May to September.*

48b Cauldron Snout. Footpath to highest waterfall in England, which cascades 200ft into a gorge.

48c High Force Hotel. Footpath through pine and beech woodlands to High Force (see entry below) and Ettersdale.

48c High Force. Spectacular moorland waterfall drops 70 ft over steep cliffs. Path leads to open moorland above the fall.

49b The Grove: Redford Walk. Waymarked walk (purple arrows) on rough tracks up the Euden Valley. Fine views from the top of the Bedburn Valley. ⌐

49c Castlewood House: Collier Wood. Nature trail through attractive wood with permanent display boards on route. ⌐

49c Toll: Hamsterley Forest Drive. Attractive 4½ mile drive through mixed woodland, following the course of Bedburn Beck. Also, at Information Centre, displays on the forestry and wildlife of the area. ▲ℹ

49c Bedburn Beck. Crossfield Walk. 2½ mile waymarked walk (white arrows) along forest road and rough tracks through woodland. ⌐

Postman's Route. Waymarked walk (blue arrows) showing many features of Hamsterley Forest. ⌐

49d Middleton in Teesdale. Walk along the banks of the River Tees to Newbiggin and then back along the Pennine Way. Some of the finest riverside scenery in England.

49d Romaldkirk. Footpath south into the beautiful valleys of Teesdale and Baldersdale.

49e Spurlswood Beck Walk. Forest road and paths (waymarked with green arrows) through mixed woodland of oak, beech, larch and Douglas fir. ⌐

High Acton Walk. 8 mile forest walk, (waymarked with orange arrows) through the Euden and Spurlswood Beck valleys to the more remote part of Hamsterley Forest. ⌐

49h Barnard Castle. Footpath north through the ancient parkland of Marwood Chase, now known as Flatts Wood; fine views of the River Tees.

50a Castlewood House. See 49c.

50b Bishop Auckland. Pleasant 4 mile walk along the banks of the River Wear to Escomb.

50b Auckland Park. Nature trail through this large public park with its unusual 18th century deerhouse. Interesting flora and fauna described in leaflet available from gateway. 🐦🏠🐾

50e Heighington. Short, picturesque walk west through open farming country to Houghton-le-Side.

50h The Holmes. Nature trail along the River

Tees from Broken Scar to Blackwell. Leaflet describing the walk from Town Hall, Darlington.

50i Darlington: South Park. Circular ½ mile nature trail has much of interest, including several types of tree and many species of waterfowl.

51a Hardwick Hall Country Park. Tel. Sedgefield (0740) 20745. Nature trail on wooden walkway explores the once magnificent 18th century pleasure gardens; wealth of wildlife in lake and woods. 🐷 🛖 ❄

52f Saltburn-by-the-Sea: Valley Gardens. Waymarked circular nature trail through wooded and formal gardens.

52h Gribdale Terrace. See 41a.

55c Belah: Kingmoor Nature Trail. 1½ mile walk through nature reserve with a variety of habitats ranging from oak woodland to heath.

55c Carlisle: Eden Riverside Trail, west from Eden Bridge. Leaflet describing the various habitats from 🛈 at Old Town Hall.

56a Belah. See 55c.

56a Carlisle. See 55c.

56c Talkin Tarn Country Park. Tel. Brampton (069 77) 3129. Woodlands and open pastureland around a popular and attractive lake, with the accent on leisure activities connected with the lake. 🐷 🛖⛵

58b Allendale Town. Trail of 4½ miles north to the Hope and Cose Hole. Riverside scenery and high views over the valley.

58f Hunstanworth. Footpath west into the valley of Nookton Burn, with views of wild, rolling moorlands.

58h St John's Chapel. Pleasant walk west to West Blackdene along the bank of the River Wear. Good views of Upper Weardale.

59a Pow Hill Country Park. Small area of moorland with great views of Derwent Reservoir. 🛖

59c Hooker Gate. Three walks in Chopwell Woods which extend into the Derwent Walk Country Park (see later entry). 🛖

59c Rowland's Gill: The Derwent Valley and Gibside Trail. Walk through Gibside Estate (60a) with excellent views of the Derwent Valley.

59c Bentfieldside: Derwent Walk Country Park. Woods and parkland along the route of a disused railway line which runs north to Swalwell (66i). A nature trail extends the length of the park, in which can be seen many trees, shrubs and wildflowers.

59g Stanhope. Waymarked walk of 2 miles to Linkirk Cave in a delightful wooded ravine. Fine views.

59h Wolsingham. Many footpaths lead north through woods and farmland to the picturesque Tunstall Reservoir; good views. 🛖

59i Castlewood House. See 49c.

60a Rowland's Gill. See 59c.

60b Beamish Hall. Woodland around the Hall has been acquired to create a country park. 📷 🛗 🦉

60c Penshaw. Waymarked country trail of 3½ miles passes the Penshaw Monument and runs along the banks of the River Wear. 🏰

60e Waldridge Fell Country Park. Open moorland designated a Site of Special Scientific Interest.

60i Sunderland Bridge. Pleasant and easy walk through the Croxdale Estate high above the wooded slopes of the River Wear. Excellent views.

61h Peterlee: Castle Eden Dene. Waymarked

walk into this 500 acre nature reserve in the largest coastal ravine in County Durham. Most of the area is woodland with a wide range of wildlife.

61h A1086. Two waymarked walks into Castle Eden Dene (see Peterlee, above).

61h New Winning. Waymarked walk of 1¼ miles into Castle Eden Dene (see Peterlee, above).

61h Castle Eden. Four waymarked walks into Castle Eden Dene (see Peterlee, above).

63g Talkin Tarn. See 56c.

63i Bridge End. Footpath west to Kellah among the woods and fields of the South Tyne Valley.

64e Stonehaugh: Warksburn Forest Walks. Three waymarked walks along attractive burn through surrounding woodland. Boards describe trees and wildlife. 🛖

64g Earthwork. Footpath leads south west over Plenmeller Common, an area of open moor and rough grass pasture.

64i Ridley: Allen Banks Nature Reserve. 194 acres of hill and river scenery. Many miles of paths lead through the deciduous woodland by the river. 🛖

64i Nilston Rigg. Footpath north west to Lough Green (Plankey Mill) and then south on the eastern banks of the River Allen. Some of the finest views in the county.

65c Wallington Hall. Three nature trails through 100 acres of woodland, lakes and gardens in the Estate. 🐷 ❄ 🏛 ☆ 🛈

65h A695. Short walk through Swallowship Woods and along a river bank.

66a Bolam Lake. Country park of small lake surrounded by mature woodland in a landscape of scattered farms. Nature trail. 🛖 ⛵ 🦆
Bolam Lake Information Centre. Tel. Belsay (066 181) 81234. Displays of the geology and natural history of the area. *Daily 1100-1200, 1500-1600.*

66a Wallington Hall. See 65c.

66i Swalwell: Derwent Walk Country Park. Woods and parkland along route of disused railway line which runs south to Bentfieldside (59c). Nature trail extends the length of the park in which can be seen many trees, shrubs and wildflowers.

66i Rowland's Gill. See 59c.

67a Country Park: Plessey Woods. Sheltered woods in the valley of the River Blyth surrounded by open farmland. Nature trail shows the diversity of the wildlife and evidence of former mining activities.
Plessey Woods Information Centre. Tel. Bedlington (0670) 824793. Displays of the geology and natural history of the area. *Daily 1100-1200, 1500-1600.*

67a Sheepwash: Wansbeck Country Park. 143 acres of woodland and grass with the tidal section of the Wansbeck converted into a fine stretch of water for leisure activities. Boats for hire; nature trail. 🛖🦆

67e St Mary's Island. Nature trail featuring the island at low tide; interesting rock pools, many species of seabirds and varied flora and fauna. 🦆

67i Marsden. Coastal walk of 6½ miles to Marsden Rock and Whitburn and then inland into the Cleveland Hills; waymarked.

68f Kielder Castle Visitor Centre. Tel. Bellingham (0660) 50209. Displays of natural history and forestry work in the area. *April to end September; weekdays 0900-1600; weekends 1100-1700.* 🐷 ♿ 🛖🦆 🛈
Kielder to Blakehopeburnhaugh (69e) Forest Drive. Twelve miles of forest road through wild and remote border forest and moorland.

Suitable for normal cars if driven with care. 🛖
Duchess Drive Walk. Circular waymarked trail up Kielder Burn and round Castle Hill.

69e Blakehopeburnhaugh. Forest drive to Kielder Castle (68f) through remote and wild border forest and moorland. Suitable for normal cars if driven with care. 🛖🦆
Redesdale Forest. Short riverside nature trail from picnic place. 🛖

69h Sidwood. Short waymarked walk in mixed woodland alongside Tarset Burn. 🛖

70e Blakehopeburnhaugh. See 69e.

70h Sidwood. See 69h.

71a Holystone Forest. Two distinct walks start from the picnic site: Lady's Well Walk through young spruce, along line of Roman road, and over open farmland to the well; and Farm Walk through mixed woodland including tall oak coppice, past a hill farm and down attractive burnside. An extension of the farm walk runs to Dove Crag, a viewpoint and fine waterfall. 🛖

71c Nature Trail: Thrunton Wood. Crag Tip Walk is an easy uphill stroll to a panoramic viewpoint; Castle Hill Walk extends Crag Tip Walk onto moorland and Macartney's Cave. 🛖

71c Cragside. Tel. Rothbury (0669) 20333. Country park of 900 acres, famous for its magnificent trees and rhododendrons; also has lakes, waterfalls and streams. Four waymarked walks lead from the three main car parks. *April to October daily; November to March weekends only.* 🏛 🛗 🛈

71d Elsdon. Short, pleasant walk to Hudspeth in the north east and then south to Eastnook. Suitable for summer afternoons.

71e Nature Trail: Simonside Forest. Three waymarked walks through the forest offering superb views of the Simonside Hills and Coquetdale. 🛖

71h Wallington Hall. See 65c.

72a Holystone Forest. See 71a.

72b Nature Trail. See 71c.

72b Cragside. See 71c.

72e Nature Trail. See 71e.

72h Wallington Hall. See 65c.

73e Blakemoor Farm Countryside Trail. Incorporating a farm trail, the circular walk includes a tour of livestock, farm buildings, hedgerows and farm patterns. 🦆

73h Sheepwash. See 67a.

76c Hepburn. Three waymarked walks: Woodland Walk through larch wood; Hepburn Crag Walk to open moorland and a small Iron Age camp; Ros Castle Walk to a fine viewpoint of the Cheviots and Northumbrian coast. 🛖

76i Nature Trail. See 71c.

77f Craster. Walk of 5 miles along one of the finest stretches of Northumberland coastline to Dunstan Steads. Landscape dominated by Dunstanburgh Castle (see 🏰).

79a Berwick-upon-Tweed. Signposted walk along the south bank of the River Tweed, one of the finest salmon rivers in Britain.

79c Staple Island. Nature Trail. Leaflets available from 🛈 at Seahouses or from National Trust. 🦆

79c Farne Island: Inner Farne. Nature reserve and nature trail. Large colony of Atlantic Grey Seals. Contact National Trust or 🛈 at Seahouses for trail leaflet and details of boat services. *Accessible by permission only.* 🦆

79i Bamburgh. Walk of 5½ miles north along the coast to Warren Mill in Budle Bay and then back through Spindlestone. Good coastal scenery.

Gardens and Arboreta

Cultivated, wild and herbal gardens, including privately owned ones which open at specific times of the year; formal arboreta; floral displays. For country parks see the section on the Countryside (pages 80-83).

18a Ripley Castle. Tel. Harrogate (0423) 770152. Extensive grounds laid out by Capability Brown, with flowering shrubs, a garden temple and many fine trees. Walled flower garden; Palm House. *Good Friday to end September daily 1100-1800.* 🍵🏛

18d Harlow Car Gardens. Tel. Harrogate (0423) 65418. 60 acres of ornamental and woodland gardens, including a rose garden, herbaceous borders, rock gardens, peat beds and glasshouses. Model fruit and vegetable plots. *Daily, 0900-dusk.*

18d Harrogate: Valley Gardens. Sheltered gardens with fine flowerbed displays, well-kept lawns, rock gardens, lily ponds and magnificent trees.

18e Rudding Park. Gardens closed in 1982.

18h Harewood House. Tel. Harewood (0532) 886225 or 886331. Park landscaped by Capability Brown; extensive lawns; large herbaceous border; shrubberies and fine rose displays. *April to end October: daily from 1000.* 🍵👟🏛🐾🎪

18h Roundhay Park. Landscaped grounds with two fine lakes as well as pleasure, canal and rose gardens. *Daily, dawn to dusk. Free.* 🏊18

18i Bramham Park. Tel. Boston Spa (0937) 844265. Extensive grounds landscaped in French style, with magnificent hedges, tree lined walks, ornamental cascades and ponds. *Easter to end September: Tuesday to Thursday, Sunday and bank holiday Mondays; 1315-1730.* 🍵🏛

19c Sutton-on-the-Forest: Sutton Park. Tel. Easingwold (0347) 810249. Medium-sized garden with terraces, woodland walks, border and rose gardens, lily pond and ice house. *Easter, then May to end September: Sunday, Tuesday to Thursday and bank holidays: 1400-1800.* 🍵🏛

19f Heslington: University of York Gardens. New garden of trees and river-like lake joined to an 18th century topiary garden by canal pool. *Daily, dawn to dusk. Free.*

19f York: Yorkshire Museum Gardens. Interesting specimen trees including a large monkey puzzle tree. *Daily 1000-dusk.* 🏛

21d Conishead Priory. Tel. Ulverston (0229) 54019 or 54029. Large grounds with beach, tunnel to artificial lake, shrubberies, rose and rock gardens and extensive woods. *Wednesday, Thursday and weekends 1400-1700. Free.* 🍵🏛

21e Holker Hall. Tel. Flookburgh (044 853) 328. 22-acre garden with exotic flowering trees, exceptional magnolias, rose garden, cherry and woodland walks. Lakeland Rose Show in mid-July. *Easter to end September: Sunday to Friday, 1100-1715.* 🍵👟🌲🏛⚘☆

22a Levens Hall. Tel. Sedgwick (0448) 60321. Famous 17th century topiary garden. Also formal flower beds, herbaceous borders and beech circle. Plant centre. No dogs. *Daily (except winter weekends) 1000-1700.* 🍵🏛🚂

22d Leighton Hall. Tel. Carnforth (0524) 734474. Extensive grounds with lawns, long herbaceous border and shrubbery walk. Fine views. No dogs. *May to September: Tuesday to Thursday and Sundays, 1400-1630.* 🍵🚃🏛🐾☆

23e Ingleborough Hall (now a school). The gardens contain an exotic collection of bushes, trees and plants, many of them from the East.

25g Percival (Parcevall) Hall. Tel. Burnsall (075 672) 214. Beautiful gardens in hillside setting. *Easter to end September: daily 1000-1800.* 🍵

26a Thorp Perrow. Tel. (0677) 22710. Sixty-acre grounds include a lake, wild garden and an arboretum with over 2000 species of trees and shrubs. *Easter to November: daily 0900-dusk.* 🚃

26e Norton Conyers. Tel. Melmerby (076 584) 252. 18th century walled garden. Plant shop. *Weekdays 0900-1700, Sundays 1400-1730.* 🍵🏛

26e Studley Park: Studley Royal. Ornamental gardens laid out in the 18th century with ponds, statues and monuments leading up to Fountains Abbey (see ✝ 26h.). *Daily from 0930 (winter Sundays from 1400).*

26h Ripley Castle. See 18a.

26i Newby Hall. Tel. Boroughbridge (090 12) 2583. Garden sloping down to river, with long herbaceous borders. Several seasonal gardens; rock gardens; many unusual trees and shrubs; beautiful statuary. *April to end September: Tuesday to Sunday 1100-1730.* 🍵🚃 🏛

27c Duncombe Park. Large garden with 18th century terraces and woodland rides; formal and secret gardens. *May to August: Wednesdays 1000-1600.*

27f Newburgh Priory. Tel. Coxwold (034 76) 435. Wild water garden, walled garden and collection of rock plants. *Mid May to late August: Wednesdays 1400-1800.* 🍵✝

27i Sutton-on-the-Forest. See 19c.

28a Duncombe Park. See 27c.

28f Castle Howard. Tel. Coneysthorpe (065 384) 333. One of the most important and earliest landscape gardens in the country, with lakes, bridges and temples. Also a more formal garden and two rose gardens added later. *Easter to October: daily 1100-1700.* 🍵👟🏛🎪

28g Sutton-on-the-Forest. See 19c.

29a Zoo: Flamingoland. Tel. Kirby Misperton (065 386) 287. Grottoes and ornamental walks; ponds with water lilies; rose gardens; many fine trees. *Early March to end October: daily 1000-1600.* 🍵👟🚂🐾🐟☆

Sutton Park (19c)

29b Ebberston Hall. Tel. Scarborough (0723) 88516. Half the original features remain of fine early 18th century water gardens. *Mid-April to mid-September: daily 0930-1730.* ⌂

29i Sledmere House. Tel. Driffield (0377) 86208. 1000 acre park laid out by Capability Brown. Italian garden, rose beds and good statuary. *Easter, then Sundays only until early May. May to late September: Tuesday to Thursday, weekends and bank holidays, 1330-1700.* ☕⌂✝

30i Burton Agnes Hall. Tel. Burton Agnes (026 289) 324. Formal gardens with sweeping lawns, clipped evergreens and lily ponds; woodland garden. *April to end October: Weekdays: 1345-1700; Sundays 1345-1800.* ☕⌂✝

31g Sewerby Hall. Tel. Bridlington (0262) 73769. Large grounds with formal walks, terraces and statuary. Many mature trees; notable 'Old English' walled garden. *Daily 0900-dusk.* ☕▣🐘

32f Muncaster Castle. Tel. Ravenglass (065 77) 614. Magnificent gardens containing one of the finest collections of rhododendrons in Europe. *Saturday to Thursday 1200-1700.* ☕♿♣🐘⌂

33c Rydal Mount. Tel. Ambleside (096 63) 3002. Wordsworth's garden, said to be one of the finest small gardens in England. *March to October: daily 1000-1730. November to mid-January: Thursday to Tuesday 1000-1230, 1400-1600.* ☕⌂

33c Clappersgate: White Craggs Garden. Now Closed.

33c Ambleside: Stagshaw. Tel. (096 63) 2109. Garden is planted mainly with trees, shrubs and bulbs; good rhododendrons. *Daily in daylight hours.*

33f Brantwood. Tel. Coniston (096 64) 396. Garden created by the writer Ruskin. Many exotic trees; woodland paths with fine Lakeland views. *Easter to end October Sundays to Fridays 1100-1730.* ☕♣🪑▣

33i Graythwaite Hall. Tel. Newby Bridge (0448) 31333. A 7-acre garden, largely with flowering shrubs, particularly rhododendrons and azaleas. *April to June: daily 1000-1800.*

33i Rusland Hall. Tel. Satterthwaite (022 984) 276. Many fine specimen trees in landscaped grounds. Large numbers of daffodils and bluebells in spring. *April to end September: daily 1100-1730.* ♿▣⌂

34a Rydal. See 33c.

34a Clappersgate. See 33c.

34a Ambleside. See 33c.

34d Ferry House: Ash Landing. Garden contains the largest collection of hardy heaths and heathers in the world. Also fine trees, shrubs and herbaceous plants. *Weekdays 1400-1700, Saturdays and bank holidays 1000-1700.*

34e Hole Hird: Lakeland Horticultural Society Garden. Contains fine collection of rhododendrons, azaleas, conifers and ornamental and flowering shrubs. *Daily at reasonable times. Free.*

34e Brockhole. Tel. Windermere (096 62) 2231. Gardens and grounds stretch down to lake shore. Formal gardens; terraced rose gardens; shrubs. *End March to November: daily from 1000.* ☕♿♣🪑▣

34e Belle Isle House. Tel. Windermere (096 62) 3353. Small formal garden and rhododendron walk. *Mid-may to mid-September: Monday, Tuesday, Thursday and Sunday, 1030-1700.* ☕♣⌂

34g Graythwaite Hall. See 33i.

34g Rusland Hall. See 33i.

34i Sizergh Castle. Tel. Sedgwick (0448) 60285. Garden, laid out in 18th century, contains rock

Castle Howard (28f)

and rose gardens and many daffodils. *April to end September: Wednesday, Thursday and Sunday. October: Wednesday and Thursday; 1400-1745.* 🏰⌂

34i Levens Hall. See 22a.

38f Richmond: St Nicholas. Tel. (0748) 2328. Medium-sized garden of horticultural interest; shrubs, rock garden, topiary work. *April to October: daily 1000-1900.*

38h Constable Burton Hall. Tel. Bedale (0677) 50428. Large, mainly informal garden with woodland walk. Rock garden, herbaceous borders, fine daffodils in spring. *April to mid August: daily 0900-1830.* ⌂

39g Thorp Perrow. See 26a.

45e Friar's Crag: Lingholm. Tel. Keswick (0596) 72003. Formal and woodland gardens, garden shrubs, rose garden; exceptional views. *April to end October: Monday to Saturday 1000-1700.* ♿

46f Dalemain. Tel. Pooley Bridge (085 36) 450. Parts of the historic Elizabethan gardens and summer house still remain; wild garden with superb trees. *April to end September: Saturday to Thursday 1400-1715.* ☕♣▣⌂

47b Acorn Bank. Tel. Ambleside (096 63) 3003. Walled garden; good collection of herbs. No dogs. *April to end October: Tuesday to Sunday 1000-1730.*

49f Raby Castle. Tel. Staindrop (0833) 60202. Fine mid-18th century gardens with terraces and yews. Deer park. *April to June, Wednesday and Sunday; July to end September, Sunday to Friday; also Easter and bank holiday weekends; 1300-1730.* ☕▣⌂

49h Bowes Museum. Tel. Teesdale (0833) 37139. Set in 20 acres of parkland, the museum is surrounded by rockeries and formal flowerbeds. *Daily from 1000.* ☕▣⌂

50d Raby Castle. See 49f.

51a Hardwick Hall. Tel. Sedgefield (0740) 20745. Part of the country park is being developed as an arboretum; exotic trees join fine specimens of beech, yew, chestnut, etc. *Daily. Free.* ☕♿♣🪑

56b Corby Castle. Tel. Wetheral (0228) 60246. Early 18th century grounds with fine woodland walks beside the River Eden. *End March to end October, 1400-1900.* 🏰

60c Washington: Old Hall. Tel. (0632) 466879. Rose garden; lower garden with shrubs and many herbaceous perennials. *March to October:*

Wednesday to Monday 1300-dusk: November to February: weekends 1400-1600. ⌂

60i Durham: University of Durham Botanic Garden, Palace Green. 10 year old garden built for research and teaching; European, North American and Sino-Himalayan collections. *Daily 0900-1600. Free.*

60i Elvet Hill: St Aidan's College Grounds. Tel. (0385) 65011. Well-landscaped grounds which are best in July. Also laburnum walk and reflecting pool well stocked with aquatic plants. *Daily 0900-dusk. Free.*

64h Vindolanda: Museum Garden. Tel. Bardon Mill (049 84) 277. Many fine trees and flowering shrubs surround the museum. *Daily 1000-1800.* ☕♿🏰▣

65c Wallington Hall. Tel. Scots' Gap (067 074) 283. Fine gardens with unusual walled garden and conservatory filled with fuscias. *Daily.* ☕♣⌂☆ℹ

66a Wallington Hall. See 65c.

66g Jesmond Dene. Gardens planted with many exotic trees and shrubs; rhododendron display in spring very fine. *Daily dawn to dusk. Free.* ☕

71c Callay Castle. Tel. Whittingham (066 574) 663. Garden consists of lawns, herbaceous borders, shrubs, woodlands and lakes. No dogs. *May to September: weekends and Bank Holidays, 1415-1730.* ☕⌂

71h Wallington Hall. See 65c.

72b Callay Castle. See 71c.

72h Wallington Hall. See 65c.

76i Glanton: World Bird Research Station. Tel. Powburn (066 578) 257. Arboretum contains every species of tree native to Northumberland. Children can feed tame research birds while walking round. *Late May to mid-September: daily 1400-1700.* 🐦

76i Callay Castle. See 71c.

77e Howick Hall. Tel. Longhoughton (066 577) 285. Formal terraces in grounds of 18th century mansion. Informal woodland garden with many shrubs. *April to end September: daily 1400-1900.*

79e Lindisfarne Castle. Tel. Holy Island (0289) 89244 during opening hours only. Small walled garden designed by Gertrude Jekyll. *April to end September: Saturday to Thursday 1100-1230, 1400-1700, when tides permit.* 🏰⌂✝🪜ℹ

Historical Sites

18b Knaresborough: Castle. Tel. Harrogate (0423) 68954 ext. 251. Mainly 14th century castle captured and demolished by the Parliamentarians during the Civil War. Scattered ruins include the keep, dungeon and a secret passage. *Easter, then Spring Bank Holiday to late September; daily 1000-1700.* 🖼

Chapel of Our Lady of the Crag. Unique mediaeval shrine cut into cliffs above the River Nidd, with grotesque faces carved in the cave walls.

Mother Shipton's Cave. Alleged birthplace in 1488 of the famous witch and prophetess, once better known than Nostradamus.

18h Harewood Castle. Unsafe Norman ruins with 14th century additions. *View from the outside only.* 🍺🚠❀🎡🎯🎿

19f York: Legionary Fortress Wall, Yorkshire Museum Gardens. York was the military capital of Roman Britain but little remains today; here can be seen a small but well-preserved section of the fortress wall. *Daily from 0800. Free.* 🖼

Multangular Tower, Yorkshire Museum Gardens. A 4th century polygonal tower 35ft high; the top of its walls have clearly been repaired by mediaeval stone-masons. *Daily from 0800. Free.* 🖼

Roman Sewers, under Swinegate and Church Street. Part of the ancient Roman system, consisting of a main channel less than 5ft high and about 150ft long with six side channels. *Visits by small parties only; write to Yorkshire Museum.*

City Walls. Virtually all of the city's mediaeval walls are still intact. **Baile Hill to Lendal Bridge:** this passes over Micklegate Bar, the most important city gate, on which the impaled heads of traitors were displayed. **Bootham Bar to Foss Bank:** Bootham Bar still retains its portcullis; the next gate, Monk Bar in Monkgate, is the best preserved. It is vaulted with three floors and also has a portcullis in working order. **Red Tower to Fishergate Postern Tower:** Red Tower dates from 1490 and is the only major part of the wall in brick. The next gate - Walmgate Bar in Walmgate - still has its barbican, wooden doors and portcullis. Fishergate Bar in Paragon Street is a small gate between Walmgate Bar and the Postern Tower in Fishergate, where the wall ends. The latter was built in 1505 and once stood on the River Foss. *The walls are open 0930-dusk. Free.*

19g Towton: Battlefield. Scene of the bloodiest battle ever fought on English soil. Here on 29 March 1461 the armies of York and Lancaster clashed, cramming more than 100,000 men into a battlefront less than 1000yds long. As the Yorkists advanced, the Lancastrians were trapped with their backs to the River Cock. It became a massacre with no quarter given; over 25 000 Lancastrians were killed for the loss of 'only' 8000 Yorkists.

20b Millom. Group of 5 prehistoric stone circles, notably an oval with a central stone and an avenue of stones to one side.

20f Dalton-in-Furness Castle. A 14th century pele tower built by the monks of Furness Abbey (see ✝). Now contains a collection of armour and old documents. *Any reasonable time: key from 18 Market Place.*

20f Little Urswick. Iron age stone wall 10ft thick that once enclosed several huts. Nearby are the scant remains of a later rectangular settlement, probably Roman.

Glossary of terms

Stone Age (or Palaeolithic): characterised by the first use of tools, including stone axes, etc. Normally taken to date from about 650,000 to 8000 BC.

Neolithic: late Stone Age, characterised by the use of polished tools usually flint, the first domestic animals and the beginning of agriculture. From about 8000 to 4000 BC.

Bronze Age: the first use of metal for tools and weapons (also to time of ancient Troy) from about 4000 to 800 BC.

Iron Age: officially the age in which we still live, it began about 800 BC.

Prehistoric: a general term covering all the above Ages; often used on these pages to describe sites whose precise origins are hard to date.

Mediaeval (or Middle Ages): an ill-defined historical period, usually taken to run from about 1000 AD (the fall of Rome, the Norman Conquest of England) to about 1500 (the start of the Tudor era in Britain).

Barrow. Mound of earth, stones, etc., covering a burial chamber, usually containing several graves.

Henge. Monument comprising a circular embankment of one or more ditches, often with a stone circle within. Usually dates from the Neolithic or Bronze Age.

Hypocaust. Roman system of under-floor heating.

Motte and Bailey. Standard Norman system of castle building, with a high mound (the motte) surrounded by a ditch or moat, and a separate protected enclosure (the bailey), often containing a stone keep.

20i Piel Castle. Built in 1327 by the monks of Furness Abbey (see ✝). In June 1487 Lambert Simnel, Pretender to Henry VII's throne, landed from Ireland and held court here. The motte-and-bailey castle was partly restored in the 19th century. Access by boat from Roa Island. *Summer only. Free.*

21a Ulverston: Hoad Hill Monument. Huge stone replica of Eddystone Lighthouse commemorating Sir John Barrow, founder of the Royal Geographical Society, who was born in the town in 1764.

21d Birkrigg Common. Five prehistoric barrows.

21d Stone Circles. Two concentric circles, the outer with 14 stones, the inner with 10. 🍀🐓

21f Arnside Tower. Ruins of a mediaeval defence tower constructed by the powerful Stanley family, who once owned the Isle of Man and later became the Earls of Derby.

22c Middleton: Roman Milestone, south of the church. One of the few still outdoors, it bears the inscription *MP LIII* - 53 miles from Carlisle.

22d Arnside Tower. See 21f.

22d Warton Crag Hill Fort. Roughly triangular prehistoric stronghold defended by three earth ramparts.

22f Gressingham Castle. Scant remains of a Norman motte-and-bailey.

22h Crossgill. Stump of a Saxon cross with weathered carvings around its base.

23e Ingleborough: Hillfort. Standing at 2373ft, it is the highest in England and was a major stronghold of the Brigantes tribe until captured by the Romans in the 2nd century AD. Parts of the wall are still 12ft thick. 🐦▲

23i Stainforth. Fine packhorse bridge built in 1670. 🍀

23i Victoria Cave. Neolithic hunters lived here over 5000 years ago, and in 450 AD British refugees hid from Anglo-Saxon invaders. 500yds north, in Jubilee Cave, pottery has been found from the Neolithic, Bronze, Iron and Roman eras.

24b Deepdale: 20 limestone boulders forming the base of an unfinished prehistoric cairn.

24g Victoria Cave. See 23i.

24g Stainforth. See 23i.

24i Thorpe. Cave on the west slope of Elbolton Hill inhabited by nomadic neolithic hunters about 2300 BC.

25h Pateley Bridge: Bridge. Mediaeval foundations underly the much later bridge.

26b Camp House: Henges. 3 Bronze Age stone circles, each over 800ft in diameter with an inner embankment and inner and outer ditches. The most northerly is the best preserved, the middle one is the easiest to reach.

26e Ripon: Market Cross, Market Square. This 90ft obelisk dates from 1780; each night at 2100 a hunting horn is sounded at its base.

26i Boroughbridge (A1): Devil's Arrows. Three gigantic standing stones of about 2000 BC. It is said that the Devil shot them at a local church but missed.

27b White Horse. Carved in 1857, it stands 684 hands (228ft from hoof to shoulder).

27c Helmsley Castle. Ruins of a 12th century fortress. There are substantial remains of the huge keep and tower, which are surrounded by a moat and extensive earthworks. *Daily from 0930 (winter Sundays from 1400).* ♣

27g Aldborough: Isvrivm. Scant remains of an early Roman town, including traces of the boundary wall and three mosaic pavements, one in perfect condition. *Daily from 0930.* 🖼

28a Helmsley Castle. See 27c.

28a Grange. Remains of a Roman villa including a geometric mosaic.

28h Sheriff Hutton Castle. Tel. (034 77) 341. Ruinous 12th century castle with a 100ft tower and a dungeon. *Daily from 0930.* ♿

29a Pickering Castle. An important 12th century motte-and-bailey; substantial parts of the outer walls and keep survive and the chapel has been restored. Henry I, John and Edward II all stayed and Richard II was imprisoned here. The castle has seen much action: it was besieged in the Magna Carta War (1215-16) and badly damaged in the Civil War. *Daily from 0930 (winter Sundays from 1400).*

29g Wharram Percy. A line of six prehistoric barrows running from north-east to south-west.

29h Duggleby: A neolithic round barrow 20ft high and over 100ft in diameter.

30e Willy Howe: Bronze Age round barrow.

30f Argam Dikes: northern end of a 5-mile dyke, probably an Iron Age defensive earthwork.

30h Dane's Graves. Iron Age cemetery with

over 200 round barrows. Like Danes Dyke (31g) it existed much earlier than the Danes after whom it is named.

30i Rudston Churchyard. This Bronze Age monolith, at over 25ft, is the tallest standing stone in Britain. It was brought here from at least 10 miles away.

31e Flamborough Head: Monument. Commemorates the battle off the Head in 1779 between British and American ships (under John Paul Jones). It gives the directions and distances of local towns and foreign countries.

31g Danes Dyke. A substantial bank and ditches running to Cat Nab (31d), cutting off 5 square miles of headland. Celts created it about 100 BC as a defensive fortification, but like Dane's Graves (30h) it somehow was named after the Danes who invaded the country nearly 1000 years later.

32a Egremont Castle. Mound and some stonework remains of a 12th century castle.

32e Walls. Remains of the Roman fort of Glannaventa the best preserved of which are the 12ft high bath house walls.

32f Birkby Fell. The foundations of several stone huts and, to the east, more than 300 heaps of stones cleared from mediaeval fields.

33a Cairns and Stone Circles. A group of circles; the largest has 42 stones (only 8 are still standing), with 5 cairns inside it.

33b Three Shire Stone. This marked the border of Cumberland, Lancashire and Westmorland before the county boundary changes of 1974.

33d Hardknott Castle: Mediobogdum Roman Fort. This high fort is one of the most outstanding in Britain. Still visible are traces of the granary, headquarters, commander's house and walls and - outside the fort - the bath house and parade ground. *Any reasonable time. Free.*

33g Swinside: a fine 3500-year-old circle marked out by 55 stones. *Private land; view from nearby footpath.*

34b Thornthwaite Crag. A 14ft high stone cairn shaped like a column. Although obviously important, its builders are unknown. It lies at the southern end of High Street (See 46f).

34e Reservoir: Prehistoric Settlement. Scant remains of circular huts surrounded by a drystone wall on a prehistoric bank.

34i Kendal Castle. Scant remains of a 12th century motte-and-bailey; birthplace in 1512 of Katherine Parr, Henry VIII's sixth wife.

35b Bland House: Stone Circle. Remains of a prehistoric stone circle 138ft in diameter.

35h Middleton. See 22c.

36b Pendragon Castle. Remains of a single great tower, allegedly the home of Uther Pendragon, father of King Arthur. In fact it was constructed much later, during the 12th century. *By permission of the landowner. Free.*

36c Nine Standards Rigg. Several stone cairns up to 12ft high and of unknown origin.

37f Maiden Castle. A prehistoric circular embankment connected by a short avenue to a large round barrow 100yds to the east.

37g Bainbridge: Virosidum Roman Fort. Scant remains of this fortress, which was in use for more than three centuries. *By appointment.*

37h Ivy Scar. Fallen stones surrounding a prehistoric oval embankment.

37h Aysgarth Bridge. Single-arched stone bridge over the River Ure. Built in 1539, it gives a good view of the well-known Aysgarth waterfalls.

37h Castle Dykes. Oval neolithic embankment, probably a henge monument, with an internal ditch and an entrance to the east. The other gaps in the embankment are probably modern.

38b Throstle Gill. Ruined Brigantian hillfort with a stone rampart, ditches and bank.

38h Middleham: Motte-and-Bailey. All that remains of this castle, built soon after the Norman Conquest, is the 40ft high mound and some of the defensive earthworks. About 1190 it was abandoned for the stone castle nearby (see 🏰 for details).

Bridge. Built in 1831 this oddity has a narrow central span supported by 2 buttressed crenellated towers connected by arches that give only 13ft of headroom. Arrow-slits add a final touch of Gothic eccentricity.

40b Whorlton Castle. 13th-century gatehouse is all that survives of this building.

40h Cowesby Moor. Prehistoric shallow barrow over 100ft long. At least 5 people were buried here.

41a Captain Cook's Monument. Here once stood the cottage where Cook lived as a boy. In 1934 it was shipped to Australia and replaced by this replica of the obelisk that marks his first landfall there.

41b Tumulus. Neolithic hillfort with a stone wall, banks and ditches guarding 300 small cairns.

41e Loose Howe. 60ft wide barrow of about 1700 BC. Originally it contained a coffin and a dug-out canoe made from tree-trunks, but why they were there is a mystery as this upland site is several miles from any navigable water.

41g Helmsley Castle. See 27c.

42b Mulgrave Castle. Ruins of a 13th century castle consisting of a great tower enclosed by an outer wall.

42c Whitby: Cook Memorial, Khyber Pass. Bronze statue of Captain Cook; on one side of its pedestal is a representation of *Resolution*, in which he sailed from Whitby.

Caedmon Memorial Cross, Church Street. a 20ft tall cross dedicated to the earliest English Christian poet, who died in AD680. Several carved religious panels adorn its stone base.

42e Wheeldale Beck: Roman Road. The best preserved section of Roman road in Britain. It was part of a road from Malton (29d) to Whitby (42c) and was possibly constructed for military use in about AD 80 but was abandoned within 50 years. The road is 16ft wide and in places the original kerb stones remain. Although the top surface of gravel or small stones disappeared long ago, the large foundation stones remain.

42g Pickering Castle. See 29a.

42i Grain Beck. Over 100 small neolithic mounds.

43h Scarborough: site of Roman Signal Tower, east of the castle. It was built in 370 to warn of Saxon pirate raids. The outline of the station has been marked out in concrete and its defensive ditch excavated on the south. 🏰

44b Alavna Roman Fort. Built in AD 110 to prevent Hadrian's Wall being outflanked by sea, it was in use until the 4th century. Traces of its platform and ditches can be seen.

44h Egremont Castle. See 32a.

45b Bassenthwaite Lake: Castle How hillfort. This small stronghold was inhabited in Roman times. There are 4 banks and ditches to the west.

45e Derwent Isle: Follies. Built by a local eccentric in the 1770s, they include a Druids' circle, a fort and a church. Now owned by the National Trust. 🛥

45f Castlerigg Stone Circle (also known as Druids Circle or the Keswick Carles). Created in about 1500 BC, this magnificent circle is 100ft in diameter and consists of 38 stones; inside are another 10 stones forming an oblong. In his poem 'Hyperion' Keats called it "a dismal cirque of

Druids stones upon a forlorn moor". Spectacular views. *Any reasonable time. Free.*

46a Carrock Fell Fort Remains of the largest hillfort in Cumbria (280 × 130yds), thought to have been a stronghold of the Brigantes. Fallen masonry mark what were probably the gateways.

46c Penrith Castle. South wall plus remains of two towers. It was built in the 14th and 15th centuries and was added to by Richard III. *Any reasonable time. Free.*

46c Henge. Neolithic stone circle and its large rampart surround a 10ft tall standing stone.

46f Tirril: High Street Roman Road. Footpath from Brocavum Roman fort (47a) to Troutbeck (34b). This was once an important highway, hugging the ridgetops to avoid possible ambushes in the thickly wooded valleys and hillsides.

46f Lowther Castle. Only the facade survives of this 19th century castle. Out of bounds but visible from the Wildlife Park. 🐘 🏛 🐘

46f Tumuli. Group of small prehistoric stone circles, stone avenues, cairns and barrow tombs.

46h Thornthwaite Crag. See 34b.

47b Milburn. A village whose street plan survives intact from the 12th century. The houses, most of which are modern, surround a green; the narrow roads could be barred to defend the village or prevent cattle wandering.

47e Roman Milestone, in lay-by on the north side of A66. One of the very few still on its original site.

47h Settlement: Ewe Close. Substantial remains of an important Iron Age town; the Roman road from Lancaster (22g) to Carlisle (55c) made a detour to visit it.

47h Settlements: Ewe Lock. Traces of Iron Age huts and paddocks.

48g Brough Castle. Imposing ruins of a Norman castle. The keep is largely intact as are parts of the bailey walls and the south-east cylindrical tower. Standing on one of the main north/south routes near what was then the Anglo-Scottish border, its history was turbulent: it was captured several times and burned down twice. The castle was abandoned in 1666 after the second fire. *Daily from 0930 (Sundays from 1400).*

48i Beldoo Moss: Roman Signalling Station. Four stony banks mark the station's defences. This 4th century station, which was garrisoned by up to 50 men, would have used fire, smoke or semaphore to pass messages along a chain of similar stations between the Roman forts at Brough (48g) and Bowes (49g).

48i Rey Cross Roman Camp. The best preserved Roman marching camp in Britain: large sections of the camp's defensive rampart can be seen. Rey Cross probably accommodated the tents of the Ninth Legion during its successful campaigns against the Brigantes in AD 72-73.

49g Bowes Castle. The ruins of a single great tower built in the 12th century to guard against Scottish raiding parties. *Daily from 0930 (Sundays from 1400). Free.*

49g Lavatrae Roman Fort. Rampart mounds and traces of the bath-house are visible.

49h Barnard Castle. Ruinous 12th-to-14th century castle dominating the town from a clifftop high above the Tees. Its round tower and north wall are largely intact. The castle was partially demolished in 1630. *Daily from 0930 (winter Sundays from 1400).*

49i Roman Fort: Maglona. Only traces of the fort can be seen.

50b Vinovia Roman Fort, Binchester Hall Hotel car park. Well-preserved foundations of a 4th-century Roman bath-house. *By permission of the hotel:* Tel. Bishop Auckland (0388) 604646.

50g Forcett: Hillfort. The largest in Britain, covering 850 acres, although only the section east of the church can be visited. It was the base of Venutius, king of the Brigantes, during his revolt after Nero's suicide in AD 68; the Ninth Legion marched from York and captured it in AD 72.

50h Piercebridge: Roman Fort. Remains of the walls and flanking towers.

Roman bridge, between the Roman fort and the Tees. Parts of the stone foundations, piers and abutment remain.

52h Captain Cook's Monument. See 41a.

53i Mulgrave Castle. See 42b.

55c Carlisle: Cross, by the old town hall. Ancient cross topped by a fierce lion. Here in 1745 the Young Pretender proclaimed his father King, and declarations are still made beneath it.

55d Old Carlisle Roman Fort. Part of the ditches and rampart of Derventio, a cavalry camp.

56a Carlisle. See 55c.

56c Cumrew Fell: prehistoric cairn 70ft wide.

56e Armathwaite Castle. A 15th-century pele tower with four storeys.

56i Kirkoswald Castle. Ruinous tower and scattered masonry of an early 13th-century moated castle. *By permission of the landowner. Free.*

56i Long Meg and Her Daughters. Standing stones erected in about 1500 BC. Long Meg is a 12ft high column of red sandstone with various markings including a spiral and a cup-and-ring. To the west the daughters form a large circle of 59 stones; two of the biggest, to the east and west of the circle, mark the spring and autumn equinoxes. Only Stonehenge and Avebury are more important prehistoric circles.

57e Whitley Castle Roman Fort. Only the magnificent defensive ditches (especially to the south-west) are visible. This 2nd century fort guarded the road from Kirkby Thore (47e) to Hadrian's Wall and protected the local lead mines.

59c Vindorama Roman Fort. Scant remains of a Roman bath-house. *Any reasonable time.*

59f Lanchester: Roman Altar, All Saints Church porch. In the 3rd century, Roman soldiers from Swabia (Germany) dedicated this altar to their goddess Garmangabis. ✝

59g Stanhope: fossilised tree stump. At least 250 million years old, it stands at the gateway of the Church of Saint Thomas.

60c Penshaw Monument. A replica of the Temple of Thesis in Athens, visible for many miles from its high location. This colonnaded building was erected in 1844 in honour of the 1st Earl of Durham. *View of outside only.*

60d Lanchester. See 59f.

60i Durham: Framwelgate Bridge, North Road. Stone bridge over the River Wear built in 1128 and rebuilt in 1388-1405. *Pedestrians only: any time. Free.*

Elvet Bridge, off New Elvet. 12th century stone bridge widened in 1805. *Pedestrians only: any time. Free.*

Marquess of Londonderry, Market Place. Equestrian statue of the 3rd marquess (1778-1854) in plaster electroplated with copper. Local folklore has it that the sculptor committed suicide because he forgot to give the horse a tongue!

Neville's Cross, St John's Road, off Crossgate Peth. Ruined cross commemorating the famous defeat of a Scottish army under King David Bruce on 17 October 1346.

60i School of Agriculture: Maiden Castle hillfort. Neolithic hillfort overlooking the River Wear, protected on three sides by steep slopes and on the west by a 6ft high embankment.

61a Hylton Castle. Built in 1395-1410; only the shell of the gatehouse tower survives. *Daily from 0930 (Sunday from 1400).*

61a Thorney Close. Prehistoric round barrow.

61d Houghton-Le-Spring: Neolithic Barrow, Copt Hill. Eight cremations and burials were added to it in the Bronze Age.

62d Scots' Dike. Earthwork constructed after the Agreement of 1552 to mark the western edge of the Anglo-Scottish border. It consists of a bank between two ditches.

Hadrian's Wall

When the Romans invaded Britain in AD 43, their highly trained army, which had already conquered much of the known world, came up against ill equipped, poorly organised barbarians. Within 40 years, only Wales, south-west England and the highlands of Scotland remained unconquered. During their march north, various forts and defensive lines were established, one of them along a new military road, Stanegate (stane = stone; gate = way), which linked the major forts at Carlisle and Corbridge.

In AD 118, there was a full-scale uprising by the northern tribes. This was put down, but when the Emperor Hadrian visited Britain in AD 122 he ordered that a permanent barrier be built across the narrowest part of England, roughly along the line of the Stanegate.

Even by Roman standards, the wall was a massive undertaking, covering 73 English miles (80 Roman miles), from the lowest ford on the Solway Estuary at Bowness to the equivalent point on the River Tyne, at what later became Wallsend.

Although it made as much use as possible of natural features, running along the valleys of the Tyne and Irthing rivers and across the top of rocky crags, its construction involved the movement of over one million cubic yards of stone.

Wherever the terrain demanded it, a great V-shaped ditch was built north of the wall, to blunt any attack. The wall itself stood 16ft high and 10ft wide (some of the later parts were slightly narrower, while the section west of the Irthing was initially built of turf, and was rebuilt in stone about AD 180). Milecastles were built at every Roman mile (1620 yds), each housing about 50 men; between these, at every third of a mile, were look-out turrets. This meant that all parts of the wall were under constant observation by troops.

The area south of the wall was completely cleared and was declared a military zone. The southern boundary of this zone was marked by a massive ditch - the vallum - with earth

mounds on either side. This could be crossed only at guarded causeways opposite each fort and was intended simply to keep the conquered civilian population away from the wall itself. A new military supply road, with a hard, all weather surface about 15 yds wide, was then built between the wall and the vallum.

The main fighting garrisons were to have been housed in the old forts along Stanegate, but it was later decided that they should be kept nearer the wall. Several of the milecastles (eventually 17 of them) were therefore much enlarged, to 3½ acres for 500 infantry, or to 5½ acres for 1000 infantry or 500 cavalry. The total garrison on the wall therefore amounted to over 13,000 men. These troops, incidentally, were not the crack legionaries who had built the wall, but more lightly armed auxiliaries, drawn from the European nations conquered by Rome.

Although the wall represented a formidable obstacle to the local tribes, it was never intended as a fighting platform. Rather, it was a secure border - in peaceful times, each milecastle acted as a customs post - from whose gates troops could descend upon any troublemakers.

In this capacity, Hadrian's Wall was manned for over 250 years, although it fell into disrepair between AD 140 and AD 196, during which time the empire's northern boundary moved to the Antonine Wall, between the firths of Forth and Clyde in Scotland. A major revolt in AD 196 saw the Romans forced to retreat,

however, and Hadrian's Wall was thoroughly rebuilt; it was manned thereafter until its final abandonment in AD 383.

For the next 1500 years, the wall was left to the ravages of nature and of man: local farmers used its stones, as did the builders of the Military Road (now B6318), themselves trying to pacify the Scots after the 1745 rebellion of Bonnie Prince Charlie.

Despite this, substantial parts of the wall and of its associated civil and military buildings can still be seen. The route of the wall, the vallum and the older Stanegate are marked on the main maps, starting northwest of Glasson (55a) and running east via Carlisle (55c), Aesica (63i), Housesteads (64e) and Carrawbrough (65d) to Heddon-on-the-Wall (66h); east of that, the exact line is uncertain, although it ended on the River Tyne at Wallsend (67h).

Virtually nothing remains west of Birdoswald (63h) or east of Chesters (65d), but between these places a surprising amount has survived. Where significant remains do exist, they are marked on the maps with the m symbol and specific entries on these pages describe what can be seen.

Opening times vary, but are given in the gazetteer. For those dependent on public transport, the wall is not easy to visit (other than on foot - it makes a popular long distance walk). However, daily bus services to the wall, plus park and ride services between the main sites, are run from Hexham *(late July to early September only)*; contact Hexham ℤ for details.

◀ South

Wall

North ▶

Vallum and earth mounds

Military Way

North Ditch

Cross section of Hadrian's Wall and its associated earthworks

63d Bew Castle. Scant remains of the walls and tower. It was built by Beuth, a Scandinavian settler of the 9th century, and was destroyed by Cromwell in 1641. *By appointment.*

Bronze Age Hut, south of the Kirk Beck. Scant traces only.

63h Birdoswald: Camboglanna Roman Fort. Travelling from the west, this fort stands astride the first substantial section of Hadrian's Wall. Large parts of the fort itself remain, notably the south and east gates. *Any reasonable time.*

63h Gilsland: Milecastle 48. Best preserved of all the Hadrian's Wall milecastles; remains of two stone barrack blocks and a staircase to the rampart walk can be seen. *Daily from 0930 (Sundays from 1400).*

63i Thirlwall Castle. Ruins of a rectangular fortified manor house built in 1360 with stone taken from nearby sections of Hadrian's Wall. Despite this, from here east to Aesica is the best preserved section of the Wall.

63i Aesica Roman Fort. The best preserved section of Hadrian's Wall is that running from here west to Thirlwall Castle.

Milecastle 42, ½ mile east, straddles an excellent stretch of wall. Built by the 2nd Legion, its massive south gate still stands over 6ft high. *Daily from 0930 (Sundays from 1400).*

64c Bellingham: Gingall, outside the town hall. This large musket, which was fired from a rest, was brought back following the Chinese Boxer Rising in 1900-1901.

64e Housesteads Fort, Hadrian's Wall. Known as Vercovicium, this infantry fort held a garrison of 1000 men. There are remains of all four gates, the west gate still being very tall. Inside the fort are substantial remains of the commandant's house, the barrack block and granaries. In addition, there are the foundations of the only known Roman hospital in Britain and the only Roman latrine in Britain (which even had flushing water!). Magnificent views along the Wall. Housesteads is the most popular fort on Hadrian's Wall and may be very crowded in summer unless visited early. *Daily from 0930 (Sundays from 1400).*

64f Goatstones. Prehistoric stone circle; the top of the eastern stone has 13 cup markings upon it.

64f Simonburn Castle. Ruins of a 13th century tower house.

64g Thirlwall Castle. See 63i.

64g Aesica Roman Fort. See 63i.

64h Vindolanda Roman Fort. Remains of a fort and border settlement on the Stanegate, the military road south of Hadrian's Wall. There are remains of the headquarters building and of a civilian settlement west of the fort; also full-scale reconstructions of the Turf Wall, a turret from the Stone Wall and a timber gate tower. *Daily from 1000.*

65b Carrawbrough: Roman Temple. Remains of a small temple dedicated to Mithras, the favourite god of Roman soldiers. Replicas of its three magnificent altars can be seen here; the originals are in the Museum of Antiquities at Newcastle (see 67g.). *Any reasonable time. Free.*

65d Cilurnum Roman Fort: Chesters. The best preserved Roman cavalry fort in Britain; it held a garrison of 500. Like all other such forts, three of its four gates were positioned north of Hadrian's Wall to let the cavalry make quick sorties against hostile natives. The remains include foundations of the headquarters building, commandant's residence and the bath house. *Daily from 0930 (Sundays from 1400).*

65g Queen's Cave. Reputed hiding place of Margaret, wife of Henry VI, and her son after the Lancastrian defeat in the Battle of Hexham (1464) during the Wars of the Roses.

65h Aydon Castle. Substantial sections of a 13th-century manor house survive in the present building. *Daily from 0930.*

65h Corstopitum Roman Fort. One of the original forts built to defend the Stanegate military road, it later became a flourishing town and served as a supply depot for the garrison on Hadrian's Wall. The remains include the best preserved Roman granaries to be seen in Britain. *Daily from 0930 (Sundays from 1400).*

65h Dilston Castle. Ruins of a large mansion whose last occupant was James Radcliffe, Earl of Derwentwater. It was demolished after his execution following the unsuccessful 1745 Jacobite Rebellion, in which he took part.

66c Mitford Castle. Possibly the only mediaeval 5-sided great tower in England. *Not open.*

66c Morpeth Castle. Traces of motte castle erected in the 1090s, plus remains of a 13th-century stone castle.

66g Nafferton Farm. Castle ruins stand next to a stone bridge built with blocks taken from it.

66h Prudhoe Castle. Tel. (0661) 32303. Remains of a huge 12th-to-14th century castle. Access to the pele yard only. *Daily from 0930 (Sundays from 1400).*

67i Roman Fort. Foundations of a 1st century fort converted during the 3rd century into a supply depot. *Monday to Saturday from 1000; also summer Sundays from 1400.*

68f Kielder Stone. Large block of sandstone marking the mediaeval England-Scotland border, used as a pillar box. Messages were left in a small hole to be collected by the enemy clans. The stone is marked D (for Douglas) and N (for Northumberland).

69b Roman Camps. Overlapping earthworks of 4 forts that were staging-posts for troops marching north along Dere Street.

69f Bellshiel Law. Prehistoric long barrow surrounded by a stone kerb.

69f Bremenium Roman Fort. Stone remains of what was once the most northerly occupied fort in the Roman Empire. It was finally abandoned in AD 343 after a local rebellion.

69i Bellingham. See 64c.

70b Roman Camps. See 69b.

70e Bellshiel Law. See 69f.

70e Bremenium Roman Fort. See 69f.

70h Bellingham. See 64c.

71a Castlehill Fort. Large Prehistoric hillfort surrounded by three ramparts and ditches. The entrance was on the east.

71a Harbottle Castle. Remains of a Plantagenet motte-and-bailey with a later rectangular tower. *Not open.*

71b Cartington Castle. Ruins of a tall rectangular tower erected in the 15th century.

71d Harehaugh Fort. Iron Age hillfort with ramparts and ditches to the east and west.

71d Elsdon Castle. A well-preserved 11th century motte-and-bailey, abandoned in 1156.

71f Fort and Settlement. Remains of an Iron Age hillfort; inside are the faint outlines of Roman stone huts. South-west of the fort are two rock outcrops carved with the cup-and-ring motifs common in the Bronze Age.

72a Castlehill Fort. See 71a.

72b Cartington Castle. See 71b.

72d Harehaugh Fort. See 71d.

72e Fort and Settlement. See 71f.

72f Tower. Substantial remains of 16th century pele tower.

73g Cockle Park Tower. Three-storey tower house of the 15th century. *Unsafe.*

73g Mitford Castle. See 66c.

73g Morpeth Castle. See 66c.

74i Roman Camps. See 69b.

75b Yeavering Bell: Prehistoric Hillfort. Single stone rampart; inside are the sites of more than 130 circular huts.

75c Dod Law: Settlement. Traces of 3 prehistoric settlements; in these camps can be found many rocks with carvings.

75c Wooler. Prehistoric oval fort bisected by triple ramparts.

75h Settlements. Widespread group of sites of about 40 Iron Age huts.

75h Castlehill Fort. See 71a.

76a Yeavering Bell. See 75b.

76b Dod Law. See 75c.

76b Wooler. See 75c.

76c Chillingham Castle. Impressive but ruinous castle with four huge 14th century corner towers and 17th century connecting wings.

76g Settlements. See 75h.

76g Castlehill Fort. See 71a.

77a Preston Tower. Tel. Chathill (066 589) 227. Rectangular 14th century pele tower bearing a clock installed in 1864.

77h Denwick: Percy Tenantry Column. A fluted doric pillar 83ft high surmounted by the lion of the Duke of Northumberland; it was erected in 1816 by the duke's tenants in gratitude for his reduction of their rents. Allegedly, however, the rents were cut only after being quadrupled and the duke had to pay much of the cost of the column himself.

78g Wark Castle. Ruins of a 14th century motte.

78h Etal Castle. Ruinous rectangular great tower dating from the 14th century.

78h Flodden. A granite cross commemorates "The Brave of Both Nations" who died here during the battle of Flodden Field on the evening of 9th September 1513. An invading Scottish army under James IV was heavily defeated by troops under the command of the Earl of Surrey (who was charged with defending England in the absence of Henry VIII). The English army were cleverly led, outflanked the Scots and attacked from the north, cutting off their retreat. Their archers and cannon proved superior and over 10 000 Scots were killed, including James himself and almost every important Scots leader.

78i Ford Castle. All that survives of the original building is the King James Tower, built in 1338; originally the castle had four towers.

78i Roughting Linn: Inscribed Slab. A rock slab (60ft × 40ft) with over 60 cup-and-ring markings from about 1500 BC. This is the best example in Britain; they are common at Bronze Age sites and were probably religious symbols.

79a Berwick: Castle. Ruins of a 12th century castle now largely built over by the railway station; its Great Hall is now the station waiting room!

Edwardian Walls, near Royal Border Bridge (see). Scant remains of the mediaeval city walls, built in 1295 in Edward I's reign.

Elizabethan Walls. One of the finest and most complete city walls in Europe. They were built in 1558-66 and were among the first designed to act as a defence against gunpowder warfare; consequently they are rather squat, very densely compacted and up to 10ft thick. There are three main bastions: Cumberland's Bastion, Brass Mount and Windmill. The wall ramparts, which are open to the public, form a circuit over 2 miles long. *Daily from 0930 (Sundays from 1400).*

79g Dod Law. See 75c.

Museums and Art Galleries

Collections of almost every size and kind are listed here, other than those of a purely industrial nature, which are described in the section on Industry Past & Present on pages 104-106. Many stately homes also contain fine collections of objets d'art which are described in the section on pages 94-96.

18b Knaresborough: Old Courthouse Museum, Castle Grounds, tel. Harrogate (0423) 504684. Local history and a mock-up of a courtroom. *Monday to Saturday from 1000, Sundays from 1400 (closed winter Mondays, Thursdays and Fridays).* m

18d Harrogate: Art Gallery, Victoria Avenue, tel. (0423) 502744. Collections of oils and water colours. *Mondays to Wednesday and Fridays 0930-1900; Thursdays 0930-1700; Saturdays0930-1600; Sundays 1400-1700. Free.*

Royal Pump Room Museum, opposite Valley Gardens, tel. 503340. The spa's original sulphur well; also exhibits of costume, pottery and local history. *Monday-Saturday 1000-1700; Sundays 1400-1700.*

19f York: Castle Museum, Tower Street, tel. (0904) 53611. Two 18th century prisons have been merged into this outstanding folk museum. Reconstructions include a water-driven cornmill, a Victorian street and period rooms (including a 1950's living room!); also costumes, agricultural equipment and militaria. *April to September: daily 1000-1800. October to March: daily 1000-1630.*

City Art Gallery, Exhibition Square, tel. 23839. European and British paintings since the 14th century; also local works of art and modern stoneware. *Monday to Saturday 1000-1700; Sundays 1430-1700.*

Heritage Centre, Castlegate, tel. 28632. Exhibits of the social and architectural history of York. See ☆ for details.

Impressions Gallery of Photography, 17 Colliergate, tel. 54724. Displays of photographic equipment and photographs. *Tuesday to Saturday 1000-1800. Free.*

Minster Library, York Minster. Temporary exhibitions of books and manuscripts. *Weekdays 0900-1700.* ✝

National Railway Museum, Leeman Road, tel. 21261. Enormous collections of locomotives, rolling stock and other railwayana. See ⬇T for details.

Racing Museum, Racecourse Grandstand, tel. 22260. Unique collection of horse racing memorabilia. *Open on racedays.*

Yorkshire Museum, Museum Gardens, tel. 29745. Collections of archaeology, geology, natural history and the decorative arts. *Monday to Saturday 1000-1700; Sundays 1300-1700..*

Hospitum, Museum Gardens. Once the 15th century gatehouse of St Mary's Abbey, this now contains Roman antiquities. *Easter to September: Monday to Saturday 1000-1700; Sundays 1300-1700.*

19g Tadcaster: Ark Museum, Kirkgate. Sponsored by John Smith's Brewery Ltd., it is the only British museum of brewery equipment. Also has a local history section. *Tuesday to Thursday 1400-1600. Free.*

20e Barrow-in-Furness: Furness Museum, Ramsden Square, tel. (0229) 20650. Archaeological and local history exhibits, including the Vickers-Armstrong collection of ship models. *Monday to Saturday from 1000 (closed bank holidays). Free.*

21a Ulverston: Laurel and Hardy Museum, 7 King Street, tel. (0229) 52292. The only museum devoted to the memory of Stan Laurel and Oliver Hardy. There are over 2000 photographs on display as well as personal possessions, film props and films. Every month the 'Sons of the Desert'

(their fan club) meet here, and this will be the venue of an international convention of fans in 1984. *Mondays, Tuesdays, Thursdays and Fridays 1000-1600.*

21b Cartmel: The 1658 Gallery, Grammar School Road, tel. (044 854) 392. This 17th century coach house contains a collection of carved wood sculptures by Michael Gibbon. *Monday to Wednesday and Saturdays 1000-1730; Sundays 1300-1800.*

21e Holker Hall: Lakeland Motor Museum. Tel. Flookburgh (044 853) 509. More than 60 historic cars, motorcycles and bicycles; there are also collections of automobilia and a full size replica of Sir Malcolm Campbell's *Bluebird* World Land Speed Record Car. *Easter to early October: daily 1100-1800.* 🍷 🌸 ❄ 🏠 ☆ ☆

21i Lancaster: City Museum, Market Square, tel. (0524) 64637. Collection of archaeological remains; also the museum of the King's Own Regiment. *Weekdays 1000-1700.* 🏛

Museum of Childhood, Judges Lodgings, tel. 2808. Displays on past Lancashire childhood, including life at home, at play and at school; also a fine collection of dolls. *Easter to end October: daily 1400-1700.* 🏛

25h Pateley Bridge: Nidderdale Museum, Council Offices, tel. (0423) 711225. Located in an old workhouse, the displays cover many aspects of local history. *Easter to Spring Bank Holiday: weekends 1400-1700. Spring Bank Holiday to September: daily 1400-1700. October to Easter: Sundays only 1400-1700.* ⬇T

26e Ripon: Wakeman's House, Market Place, tel. Harrogate (0423) 504684. A 16th century house containing period furniture and items of local history and archaeology. *May to September: Monday to Saturday 1000-1700; Sundays 1400-1700.* ℹ

27c Rievaulx Terrace and Temples. Two 18th century garden temples and some fine fresco paintings; also an exhibition on English landscape design. *April to October: daily 1030-1800.* ♣ ✝

27g Aldborough: Roman Museum. Archaeological remains, including pottery, glass and coins, from the Roman town of Isurium. *Monday to Saturday 0930-1600 (1830 in summer); Sundays 1400-1600 (1830 in summer).*

28f Castle Howard. Tel. Coneysthorpe (065 384) 333. The magnificent house contains an outstanding collection of paintings by artists such as Holbein (whose famous portrait of Henry VIII is on display), Rubens, Tintoretto, Van Dyck, Reynolds and Gainsborough. There are also classical and Ancient Egyptian sculptures, a fine collection of ceramics, and excellent Soho tapestries. The Costume Gallery in the Stable Court has the largest private collection of 18th-to-20th century costumes. *Good Friday to end October: daily 1130-1700.* ☕ ♿ ✿ 🏛 ✕

29a Pickering: Beck Isle Museum of Rural Life, tel. (0751) 73707. Excellent folk museum showing local activities of the last 200 years. Many reconstructions and displays include a wheelwright's shop, a blacksmith's forge and a display on surgery and quackery. *Easter to mid-October: daily 1030-1230, 1400-1700 (August 1030-1900).* 🍷 ⬇T

29d Malton: Museum, Market Place, tel. (0653) 5136. Extensive collection of local Roman finds as well as prehistoric and mediaeval material. *Easter to end September: Monday to Saturday 1000-1600;*

Sundays 1400-1600. Afternoons only in winter.

31g Sewerby Hall. Tel. Bridlington (0262) 73769. Local and natural history, archaeology and works of art; also an exhibition about Amy Johnson, the famous pilot. *Easter to September: Sunday to Friday 1000-1230, 1330-1800.* 🍷 ✿ 🐘

31g Bridlington: Harbour Museum. History of the harbour from the 17th century; also an aquarium. *April to September: daily 0900-2100.*

33c Dove Cottage: New Grasmere and Wordsworth Museum, tel. Grasmere (096 65) 464. Former coach house containing manuscripts and other possessions of the poet William Wordsworth: and also contemporary portraits from the National Portrait Gallery. *March to October: Monday to Saturday 0930-1630.* 🍷 🏛

33e Coniston: Ruskin Museum. Yewdale Road, tel. (096 64) 359. Exhibits on the life and work of John Ruskin, the famous Victorian writer and art critic; also local history. See also 33f Brantwood. *Easter to October daily from 1000.*

33f Brantwood. Tel. (096 64) 396. John Ruskin's home 1872-1900: there are many of his pictures, manuscripts, furniture and other memorabilia. See also 33e Coniston. *Easter to October: Sunday to Friday 1100-1730.* 🍷 ♣ ⌂ ✿

33f Grizedale Visitor and Wildlife Centre. Tel. Satterthwaite (022 984) 276. A deer museum with large photographic dioramas of animal life. *Daily from 1000.* 🍷 ♣ ℹ

33i Rusland Hall. Tel. Satterthwaite (022 984) 276. Georgian mansion with a mechanical music exhibition, including an automatic grand piano; also a display of vintage photographic equipment. *April to September: daily 1100-1730.* ♿ ✿ 🏛

34a Dove Cottage. See 33c.

34g Rusland Hall. See 33i.

34i Kendal: Museum of Archaeology and Natural History, Station Road, tel. (0539) 21374. Dioramas show the natural resources of the Lake District; also a mammal collection and archaeological and local exhibits. *Weekdays 1030-1230, 1400-1600; Saturdays 1400-1600. Free.*

Abbot Hall Art Gallery. Tel. 22464. Georgian house with 18th century paintings, furniture and objets d'art, and also changing exhibitions of modern paintings, sculpture and ceramics. *Weekdays 1030-1730; weekends 1400-1700.* 🍷 ♿ 🏛

Museum of Lakeland Life and Industry, Abbot Hall, tel. as above. Local trade and industry displays. See ⬇T for details.

Studio Pottery, Wildman Street. Permanent collection of lakeland stone pottery and paintings by local artists.

36i Hawes: Upper Dales Folk Museum, Station Road, tel. (096 97) 494. Folk museum with a wide range of exhibits on the life and crafts of the Dales; one display shows how Wensleydale cheese is made. *April to September: Monday to Saturday 1000-1300, 1400-1700; Sundays 1300-1700. October:Tuesdays and weekends only.*

National Park Centre, Station Yard, tel. 450. Display relating the Wensleydale railway line to the social history of the area. *Easter to early November: daily mid AM-late PM (according to demand). Free.* ♿ ⬇T ℹ

37f Reeth: Swaledale Folk Museum, Reeth Green, tel. (074 884) 373 (*evenings*). Illustrates many aspects of local life including children's games, Swaledale housewifery, and local buildings. See ↓T for details.

37h Aysgarth Falls: **Yorkshire Museum of Carriages and Horse-Drawn Vehicles.** Tel. Richmond (0748) 3275. Old stone mill with about 50 horse-drawn vehicles and much ancillary equipment. *Easter to September: daily 1100-1700.*

38d Reeth. See 37f.

38f Richmond: **Green Howards Museum,** Holy Trinity Church, tel. (0748) 2133. The oldest church in Richmond, now the regimental museum of the Green Howards, containing more than 10,000 items. There is a special section on the 18 Green Howards who have won the Victoria Cross. Religious services are still held in a chapel within the church and the curfew bell is rung daily. *April to October: Monday to Saturday 1000-1630; Sundays 1400-1630. November, February and March: Monday to Saturday 1000-1630.*

40c Great Ayton: **Captain Cook Schoolroom Museum.** Tel. (0642) 723017. Small exhibition of maps, books and pictures about the famous explorer. See also 51i Captain Cook Birthplace Museum. *April to October: weekdays 1030-1200, 1400-1630: weekends 1400-1630.*

41b Danby **Lodge National Park Centre,** Lodge Lane,tel. Castleton (028 76) 654. Indoor exhibits, films and talks about the North York Moors National Park. *April to October: daily 1000-1700. November, February and March: weekends only 1000-1700.* 🍽 ♣ 🇮

41h Hutton-le-Hole: **Ryedale Folk Museum.** Tel. Lastingham (075 15) 367. Excellent collection of 18th century buildings housing exhibits on the origins, superstitions, crafts and pastimes of the local people since prehistoric times. Also an open-air industrial section (see ↓T for details). *End March to end October: daily 1100-1800.*

42c Whitby **Museum,** Pannett Park, tel. (0947) 602908. Fine collection of fossils; also prehistoric and Roman archaeology, local history and a shipping gallery with relics of Captain Cook. *May to September: Monday to Saturday 0930-1730; Sundays 1400-1700. October to April; weekdays (not Wednesdays) 1030-1300; Wednesdays and Saturdays 1030-1600.*

Pannett Art Gallery, Pannett Park, tel. 2908. Water colours and oil paintings including works by Turner. *Open as museum (above).*

Royal National Lifeboat Institution Museum, Pier Road, tel. 602001. Has the last lifeboat to be pulled by oars; also many photographs, anchors and pieces of equipment. *Easter weekend 1000-1530. Whitsun to September: daily 1000-1600.*

43h Scarborough: **Woodend Museum,** The Crescent, tel. (0723) 67326. Former home of the Sitwell family, containing their paintings and first editions, plus collections of British and foreign natural history, Yorkshire geological samples and an aquarium. *Tuesday to Saturday 1000-1300, 1400-1700; also summer Sundays 1400-1700.*

Three Mariners Inn, 49 Quay Street, tel. 75201. Former inn dating from the 14th century, once a smugglers' den. Collection of local history exhibits and a special section on John Paul Jones (see page 11) *Whitsun to mid September: daily 1030-1800.*

Crescent Art Gallery, The Crescent, tel. 67326. Permanent collection, plus temporary exhibitions. *Open as Woodend Museum. Free.*

Rotunda Museum, Vernon Road tel. 67326. Archaeology from the North East, plus local history. *Open as Woodend Museum. Free.*

44a Workington: **Helena Thompson Museum,** Park End Road, tel. (0900) 62598. An 18th century house with collections of costumes, decorative art, social and local history. *Tuesday to Saturday 1000-1200, 1400-1600. Free.*

44b Maryport: **Maritime Museum,** Senhouse Street, tel. (090 081) 3738. Local history and a collection of maritime models. *Tuesday to Saturday 1000-1600. Free.*

44g Whitehaven: **Museum and Art Gallery,** Market Place, tel. (0946) 3111 ext. 289. Ground floor has collections of locally made pottery, local history and archaeology; also temporary exhibitions. *Monday to Saturday 1000-1700. Free.* ↓T

45e Thornthwaite: **Gallery.** Tel. Braithwaite (059 682) 248. A 17th century lakeland barn containing original paintings, sculpture, jewellery and craftwork, all by local artists. *March to October: Monday to Saturday 1000-1730.* 🍽 ᵫ

45f Keswick: **Fitz Park Museum and Art Gallery,** Station Road, tel. (0596) 72363. Collection of original manuscripts by Wordsworth, Southey and other writers with local connections; also a large scale model of the Lake District, plus sections on geology, birds, dolls, etc. *April to October: Monday to Saturday 1000-1200, 1400-1700.*

Pencil Museum, Southey Works. A museum devoted to the origin and development of the pencil. See ↓T for details.

46b Gill: **Beckstones Gallery.** Tel. Greystoke (085 33) 601. Converted stable displaying original paintings by local and national artists. *April to December: Tuesday to Sunday.*

46f Dalemain: **Westmorland and Cumberland Yeomanry Museum.** Regimental museum in the base of a pele tower. Also a **Countryside Museum,** with exhibits about the countryside and a collection of agricultural tools. *Easter to September: Saturday to Thursday 1400-1715.* 🍽 ᵫ ♣ 🚌 ✿🏚

49f Raby Castle. Tel. Staindrop (0833) 60202. Contains many fine paintings by such masters as Claude, Reynolds and Teniers; also ceramics, including Chinese porcelain and Meissen birds from the Japanese Palace at Dresden. In the coach house is a collection of antique horse-drawn vehicles, including the state coach of the Dukes of Cleveland. *April to end June, Wednesdays and Sundays; July to end September, Sunday to Friday; also bank holidays; 1400-1630.* 🍽 ✿ 🛒 🏚

49h The Bowes Museum, tel. Barnard Castle (0833) 37139. Ornate French Renaissance-style chateau built in the late 19th century by John Bowes to house his superb collection of art treasures. Complete period rooms from 1570-1870; galleries of outstanding European paintings, with one of most magnificent groups of Spanish art in Britain (including 'St Peter' by El Greco); also collections of tapestries, silver and porcelain. *Monday to Saturday 1000-1600 (later in summer); Sundays 1400-1600 (later in summer). Closed Christmas week.* 🍽 ᵫ ✿

50d Raby Castle. See 49f.

50e Shildon: **Timothy Hackworth Museum,** Soho Street. The home of an early railway pioneer now featuring local and railway history. See ↓T for details.

50i Darlington: **Museum,** Tubwell Row, tel. (0325) 63795. Collections of local, social and natural history; children especially like the collection of birds' eggs. *Monday to Saturday from 1000. Free.* ☆

Art Gallery, Crown Street, tel. (0325) 62034. Permanent and temporary exhibitions of pictures. *Monday to Saturday from 1000 (not bank holidays) Free.* ᵫ

Railway Museum, North Road Station. Large collection of rolling stock, engines and other railwayana. See ↓T for details.

51c Hartlepool: **Gray Art Gallery and Museum.** Clarence Road, tel. (0429) 66522. Paintings and local history and natural history exhibits; also a reconstructed blacksmith's shop. *Monday to Saturday 1000-1730; Sundays 1400-1700.*

Maritime Museum, The Docks. Ship models and displays relating to all aspects of the town's maritime history.

51e Billingham **Art Gallery,** Town Centre. Modern gallery with monthly exhibitions of works of art. *Monday to Saturday 1000-1730.*

51f Middlesbrough: **Art Gallery,** Linthorpe Road, tel. (0642) 247445. Exhibitions of modern British art. *Monday to Saturday 1000-1800. Free.*

Dorman Museum, Linthorpe Road, tel. (0642) 813781. As well as a permanent display of regional and Linthorpe pottery, there are collections of local and natural history including a children's gallery with a small aviary and aquariums. *Weekdays 1000-1800; Saturdays 1000-1700. Free.*

51h Preston Hall, Yarm Road, tel. Stockton (0642) 781184. The theme of the museum is Victorian social history, brought to life by a reconstructed street of the 1890s and several period rooms. Also collections of armour, pewter, toys, costumes and sewing machines. *Monday to Saturday 1000-1800; Sundays 1400-1800.* 🍽 ↓T

51i Marton: **Captain Cook Birthplace Museum,** Stewart Park, tel. Middlesbrough (0642) 311211. Modern building containing memorabilia of the explorer and exhibitions about his life and voyages. A room has been modelled to resemble one of his ships below decks. *Daily from 1000.* 🍽 ᵫ 🏠

52a Hartlepool. See 51c.

52d Middlesbrough. See 51f.

52f Redcar: **RNLI Zetland Lifeboat Museum,** King Street, tel. (064 93) 71921. On show is *Zetland,* the world's oldest surviving lifeboat; also exhibits about fishing and seaside entertainment. *Monday to Saturday 1100-1600. Free.*

52g Marton. See 51i.

52h Great Ayton. See 40c.

52i Guisborough: **Gallery.** Now closed.

54g Maryport. See 44b.

55c Carlisle: **The Guildhall.** Greenmarket, tel. (0228) 34781. Restored mediaeval half-timbered town house, once the meeting place of the city's eight guilds; now has exhibitions on their history and on the history of Carlisle. Displays include a mediaeval pillory and stocks, guild silver, civic regalia and an iron-bound chest dated 1400. *October to April: Monday to Saturday 1000-1600. May to September: Monday to Saturday 1000-1800. Bank holiday weekends 1430-1700.*

Museum and Art Gallery, Castle Street, tel. 34781. Excellent Jacobean house with a wide range of exhibits, including collections of archaeology (with Roman remains from Hadrian's Wall), local geology and British birds. Also pre-Raphaelite and other British paintings, a fine set of English porcelain and displays of costumes, musical instruments, toys and dolls. *Monday to Saturday and bank holidays, 0900-1700. (1900 in summer).*

Border Regiment and King's Own Royal Border Regiment Museum, The Castle, tel. 32774. The history of the regiment from 1702; four Victoria Crosses, battle trophies, uniforms and records. Two dioramas show famous battles in which the regiment fought. *Daily from 0930 (but winter Sundays from 1400).*

56a Carlisle. See 55c.

60b Beamish: **North of England Open Air Museum.** The theme of this superb museum is the social and industrial development of England. See ↓T for details.

60i Durham: **Gulbenkian Museum of Oriental Art,** Elvet Hill, tel. (0385) 66711. The only British museum entirely devoted to Oriental art. Collections of Chinese ivories, jade carvings, porcelain and textiles; also items from the Middle

92

and Far East, including 50ft-long carved teak panelling from a Burmese palace and a Tibetan magician's apron made from human bones. *Weekdays 0930-1300, 1415-1700. Also Easter to Christmas: Saturdays 0930-1200, 1415-1700; Sundays 1415-1700.*

Durham Light Infantry Museum and Arts Centre, Aykley Heads, tel. 42214. Modern building tracing the story of the regiment from 1758 to 1968. On display are medals, weapons, uniforms, photographs and equipment; particularly popular is a Bren carrier (onto which children can climb) and life-size dioramas of famous DLI feats of heroism. Changing exhibitions of arts and crafts, concerts, films and other activities. *Tuesday to Saturday 1000-1700; Sundays and bank holiday Mondays 1400-1700.*

Durham Cathedral Treasury Museum, tel. 44854. Relics of St Cuthbert, the 7th century bishop of Holy Island (79e); also plate silver, manuscripts, robes, etc. *Monday to Saturday from 1000; Sundays from 1430.*

Monks' Dormitory, now the cathedral library, has Anglo-Saxon carved stones and is also used for temporary exhibitions. *Monday to Saturday 1030-1600; Sundays 1400-1600.*

Fulling Mill, The Banks. Exhibition of archaeological remains excavated in the city. *Tuesdays, Thursdays and Fridays from 1000; Wednesdays from 1300. Free.*

61a Sunderland: Grindon Museum, Grindon Lane, tel. (0783) 6306. Reconstructed 19th century rooms: dentist's, doctor's surgery, pharmacy, cobbler's, living room, kitchen and two bedrooms. Connecting corridors are lined with contemporary advertisements. *Mondays, Wednesdays and Fridays 0900-1800; Tuesdays and Thursdays 0930-1700; Saturdays 0930-1600; June to September Sundays 1400-1700. Free.*

Museum and Art Gallery, Borough Road, tel. 41235. Collections of ship models, pottery and English silver; also sections on natural history, archaeology and British art. *Weekdays 0930-1800; Saturdays 0930-1600; Sundays 1400-1700; bank holidays 1000-1700. Free.*

61i Hartlepool. See 51c.

63g Banks: LYC Museum, tel. Brampton (069 77) 2328 LYC stands for Li Yuan-Chia, an artist himself, who founded the museum. There are collections of Roman and oriental antiquities, and contemporary works of art ranging from concrete pottery to kinetic sculptures. *Daily 0900-1900.*

63i Carvoran: Roman Army Museum. Tel. Gilsland (069 72) 485. Converted farm buildings house displays on Hadrian's Wall and the Roman soldiers' everyday life. Many reconstructions include a scale model of the nearby Magna fort and models of a mounted cavalry officer, and of soldiers on and off duty. Audio/visual programmes. *March to end October: daily 1000-1830 (1700 in October).*

64e Housesteads (Vercovicium) Fort: Roman Wall Museum. Tel. Bardon Mill (049 84) 363. Collection of finds excavated from the fort and Hadrian's Wall. *Daily from 0930 (winter Sundays from 1400).*

64g Carvoran. See 63i.

64h Vindolanda Roman Fort Museum, tel. Bardon Mill (049 84) 277. Superb museum with archaeological remains from the fort and Hadrian's Wall. Among many documents is a letter from a protective Roman mother to her son serving in the wilds of Britain: "I have sent you two pairs of sandals and two pairs of underpants. Greetings to Elpis, Tetricus and all your messmates..." There are also special displays on Roman transport and cookery and some full-scale reconstructions (see m for details). *Daily from 1000.*

65d Chesters (Cilurnum) Roman Fort Museum, tel. Humshaugh (043 481) 379. Roman antiquities from the fort and from Hadrian's Wall. *Daily from 0930 (winter Sunday from 1400).*

65h Hexham: Middlemarch Centre for Border History, Manor Office, tel. (0434) 604011. Exhibits on Border history. *July to September: weekdays 1000-1700; weekends 1400-1700.*

Moot Hall Exhibition Gallery, Market Place, tel. 604011. Temporary displays. *May to October.*

65h Corstopitum Roman Fort Museum. Tel. Corbridge (043 471) 2349. Collection of carved stones, altars, metalwork and other remains excavated from the fort. The most famous exhibit is 'The Corbridge Lion', a fine Romano-Celtic carving of a lion devouring a stag. *Daily from 0930 (winter Sundays from 1400).*

65i Newton: Hunday National Tractor and Farm Museum. A stone farmhouse is the nucleus of a large collection of tractors and farm equipment. See for details.

65i Branch End: Stocksfield Art Gallery, tel. Stocksfield (066 15) 3065. Paintings by local and national artists. *Mondays, Wednesdays and Fridays from 1000 (closed bank holidays).*

66f Ponteland: Callerton Gallery, County High School, Callerton Lane, tel. (0661) 24711. Occasional exhibitions of works of art. *Weekdays during termtime: 1000-1600.*

66g Branch End. See 65i.

67c Morpeth: Cameo Gallery, King Edward VI School, Cuttingwood Lane, tel. (0670) 55415. Temporary exhibitions. *Weekdays during school term from 0930.*

67f Tynemouth: Watch House. Contains the museum of the Tynemouth Volunteer Life Brigade with numerous relics of shipwrecks. *Monday to Thursday 1030-1530; Sundays 1030-1200.*

67g Newcastle upon Tyne: Laing Art Gallery, Higham Place, tel. (0632) 327734 or 326989. Collections of British silver, ceramics, glass, metalware and paintings, particularly water colours; also Japanese prints. *Monday to Saturday 1000-1800; Sundays 1430-1730.*

Side Gallery, 9 Side, tel. 322208. Photographic arts centre featuring work mainly from the North East; also temporary exhibitions and screenings of early, contemporary or local films. *Tuesday to Saturday 1100-1800; Sundays 1100-1600. Free.*

John George Joicey Museum, City Road, tel. 324562. Collections of local history, armour and period furniture in a 17th century almshouse. *Monday to Saturday 1000-1800.*

Hancock Museum, Barras Bridge, tel. 322359. Collections of natural history, including notable displays of British mammals; also 'A picture of Northumberland' and tropical and cold-water aquaria. *Monday to Saturday 1000-1700; summer Sundays 1400-1700.*

Blackfriars, Friars Street, tel. 615367. Almost intact Dominican friary containing a permanent exhibition about the development of the city, plus several craft shops. *April to September: Tuesday to Friday and bank holiday Mondays 1000-1800; weekends 1000-1630. October to March: Tuesday to Saturday 1000-1300, 1400-1630.*

Museum of Science and Engineering, West Blandford Street, tel. 326789. Scientific and engineering displays plus temporary exhibitions. *Monday to Saturday 1000-1800. Free.*

Keep Museum, St Nicholas Street. Part of the New Castle has collections of mediaeval material. *Tuesday to Saturday 1000-1600; Mondays 1400-1600 (later in summer).*

Northumberland Record Office, Melton Park, Gosforth, tel. 362680. Includes displays about local history. *Monday to Thursday 0900-1700; Fridays 0900-1630. Free.*

National Bagpipe Museum, The Black Gate, Castle Garth. See ☆ for details.

Newcastle University, tel. (0632) 328511. In the University Quadrangle are several museums open to the public. **Museum of Antiquities.** (tel. ext. 3844 or 3849) has archaeological exhibits including a fascinating reconstruction of the Temple of Mithras at Carrawburgh (see m 67g.) and a scale model of Hadrian's Wall. **Hatton Gallery:** (tel. ext. 2053) has paintings, drawings and sculptures from the 14th century onwards, including a large relief by Kurt Schwitters. **Greek Museum** (tel. ext. 3966) displays Ancient Greek and Etruscan art. *All three museums are open weekdays 1000-1630 (later in some cases).*

67g Gateshead: Shipley Art Gallery. Tel. (0632) 771495. Permanent displays and temporary exhibitions. *Monday to Saturday and bank holidays 1000-1800; Sundays 1400-1700.*

67h Jarrow: Bede Monastery Museum, Church Bank, tel. (0632) 892106. Displays on the life of the Venerable Bede, the famous 7th century historian, and on early Christianity in the North East. *Tuesday to Saturday 1100-1630 (1730 in summer); Sundays 1430-1730.*

67i South Shields: Museum and Art Gallery, Ocean Road, tel. (089 43) 568740. Collections of social and natural history, fine and applied art. *Monday to Saturday 1000-1800; Sundays 1400-1700.*

Arbeia Roman Fort, Baring Street, tel. 561369. Collection of memorial stones and other exhibits found on the site. *Easter to September: Monday to Saturday 1000-1800; Sundays 1400-1700. October to April: weekdays 1000-1600; Saturdays 1000-1200.*

71f Rothbury: Coquetdale Gallery, Church House, tel. (0669) 20327 or 20534. Temporary exhibitions of works of art.

72a Rothbury. See 71f.

73g Morpeth. See 67c.

73h Woodhorn: Church, tel. Ashington (0670) 814444. Occasional exhibitions. *Tuesday to Saturday 1000-1600; summer Sundays 1400-1700.*

75c Wooler: Cheviot Field Centre and Museum, Padgepool Place, tel. (066 82) 711. Displays of the archaeology, geography and history of the area.

76b Wooler. See 75c.

77g Alnwick Castle, tel. (0665) 602722 or 602207. Border stronghold containing the regimental museum of the Royal Northumberland Fusiliers. Also an archaeological museum with prehistoric and Roman antiquities, and a coach house containing the state coach and other carriages of the Dukes of Northumberland. *May to September: Sunday to Friday 1300-1630.*

79a Berwick-upon-Tweed: Museum, 32 Marygate, tel. (0289) 7320. Collections of applied art and local history. *Summer: weekdays 1400-1700; Saturday, 0900-1200. Free.*

King's Own Scottish Borderers Regimental Museum, The Barracks, tel. 7426. The oldest barracks in the country, with uniforms, arms, models and other militaria depicting the history of the regiment. *Weekdays 0930-1200, 1315-1630; Saturdays 0930-1200.*

79i Bamburgh: Grace Darling Museum. In 1838 Grace Darling and her father rowed a coble to the shipwrecked SS Forfarshire and saved the lives of nine people. This museum commemorates that famous exploit. *April to October: daily 1100-1800.*

Castles

18e Spofforth Castle. Substantial remains of a rectangular 13th-to-15th century fortress, reputedly the birthplace of Harry Hotspur. *Daily from 0930 (Sundays from 1400). Free.*

19f York: Cliffords. Tower. Compact but well fortified tower of 'quatrefoil' shape built in 1244 by Henry III. Already ruined when garrisoned by Royalists during the Civil War, in 1644 it was bombarded into submission by Roundhead troops. Restored by Charles II in 1660, it was again damaged in 1684, this time by its own garrison, who set fire to it in protest at their quarters! *Daily from 0930.*

21i Lancaster Castle. This 12th-to-15th century castle is one of the largest in England, with a magnificent twin turreted gatehouse and 80ft square great tower. Part of it is in regular use as a courthouse, which restricts access at times.

22g Lancaster. See 21i.

33f Wray Castle. Magnificent 'replica' castle built in the mid 19th century, now a Merchant Navy training school. *View from footpath.*

34d Wray Castle. See 33f.

34i Sizergh Castle. Tel. Sedgwick (0448) 60285. Impressive house incorporating a 14th century pele tower 60ft high, with 10ft thick walls, a dungeon and battlements, built to withstand raids by the Scots. The domestic wings were added later. *April to end September: Wednesdays, Sundays and bank holiday Mondays (also Thursdays in July and August) 1400-1745.* ❧ ⌂

37i Castle Bolton: Bolton Castle. Tel. Wensleydale (0969) 23408. Attractive rectangular fortress with large corner towers, built in 1379 and notable for its well defended entrance and the many portcullises which protect the inner reaches. Mary Queen of Scots was imprisoned here for 5 months in 1568/9; in 1644 the garrison held out for a year against Cromwell. Now houses a small folk museum including a 19th century Dales kitchen. *Tuesday to Sunday from 1000.* ☕

38f Richmond Castle. The well preserved ruins of this massive triangular castle dominate the town. One of the oldest in Britain, with parts dating from 1080, its main feature is the 100ft high 12th century keep. The castle never saw action, its decline being due entirely to neglect. *Daily from 0930.*

38h Middleham Castle. Substantial ruins of a conventional 12th/13th century square castle with high walls enclosing a central keep. It was a favourite residence of Richard III and survived until the Civil War, after which it was slighted. *Daily from 0930 (Sundays from 1400).* ⌂

43h Scarborough Castle. Standing high on a rocky headland, this 12th century castle was twice besieged by rebels in the 16th century, twice captured by Roundheads during the Civil War and was further damaged by heavy German shelling in 1914. Since then, the North Sea has claimed parts of the curtain walls, but Henry II's great keep remains, along with the impressive triangular barbican. *Daily from 0930.*

44c Cockermouth Castle. Well preserved 12th-to-14th century castle. It was attacked by Scots under Robert the Bruce, by Yorkists during the Wars of the Roses and by Royalists in the Civil War. Now the home of Lord Egremont. *Not open.*

46e Dacre Castle. Tel. Pooley Bridge (085 36)

375. Massive 14th century pele tower restored in 1675 and still lived in. *Summer only: by written appointment.*

47a Brougham Castle. Tel. Penrith (0768) 62488. Imposing 12th-to-14th century square castle with 4 storey great tower. *Daily from 0930 (Sundays from 1400).*

47f Appleby Castle. Tel. (0930) 51402. Moated castle with ruined outer walls and well preserved 80ft high square keep dating from 1170, with spiral staircase. Main buildings not open. *Easter weekend, then May to end September: daily 1030-1700.* ▼ ♣ ⌂

49f Raby Castle. Tel. Staindrop (0833) 60202. Majestic 14th century fortified manor house with 9 towers, outer curtain walls and separate gatehouse. *April to June Wednesdays and Sundays; July to end September Sunday to Friday; also bank holiday weekends; 1400-1700.* ▼ ❋ ▣ ⌂

50a Witton Castle. Mediaeval fortified manor with three towers, two gateways and keep. ⌂

55c Carlisle Castle. Tel. (0228) 31777. Well restored border stronghold, parts of which date from 1092. Robert the Bruce twice failed to take it, and its stormy history continued in the Civil War (when it was captured by both sides) and the 1745 Jacobite rising (during which it was again taken by each side). Intact but gloomy keep has carvings by condemned prisoners. *Daily from 0930 (Sundays from 1400).* ▣

56a Carlisle. See 55c.

60f Lumley Castle. Tel. Chester-le-Street (0385) 883267. Square fortified manor house dating from 1390, with corner towers and interesting gatehouse. Now a hotel offering Elizabethan evenings (see ☆ for details).

60h Brancepeth Castle. 19th century restoration of a 14th century castle. *Not open.*

60i Durham Castle. Tel. (0385) 65481. Norman Castle built for the Bishop of Durham in the days when he enjoyed secular as well as religious power, it commands the neck of the peninsula surrounded on three sides by the River Wear; now part of Durham University. *July to September: Monday to Saturday 1000-1200, 1400-1630; Sundays 1400 -1700. October to June: Mondays, Wednesdays and Saturdays 1400-1600.* ⌂ ✝

64i Langley Castle. Tel. Haydon Bridge (043 484) 481. Four storey H-shape tower with corner turrets, built in the 14th century and badly damaged by Henry IV in his 1404 campaign against the Percys. Now restored as a restaurant offering mediaeval banquets.

65d Chipchase Castle. Substantial 14th century tower 50ft high, with corner turrets and oak portcullis. The mansion house was added in Jacobean times. *Not open.*

65e Cocklaw Tower. 15th century pele tower with 3 floors and walls thick enough to house a spiral staircase.

65h Corbridge: Vicar's Pele. Simple 3 storey tower, with 1 room per floor, which was built in 1300 and later became the vicarage. Now a tourist information centre (see ⓘ).

66b Belsay Castle. Large 14th century rectangular tower, 70ft high and with 9ft thick walls. The adjoining mansion is a 17th century addition. *Not open.*

67f Tynemouth Castle. 14th-to-16th century curtain wall, barbican and impressive gatehouse and tower, built to defend the adjacent priory. *Daily from 0930 (winter Sundays from 1400).* ✝

67g Newcastle upon Tyne Keep. Great tower (with mural gallery on top floor), curtain wall and renovated great hall with well, all dating from the reign of Henry II. The castle saw much action in wars against Scotland and during the Civil War. *Mondays 1400-1600, Tuesday to Saturday 1000-1600 (later in summer).* ▣ •

73b Warkworth Castle. Tel. Alnwick (0665) 711423. Substantial 12th and 14th century stronghold with unique multangular great tower, gatehouse and great hall. Setting for Shakespeare's Richard II and now better preserved than the bard's description of it as "this worm eaten hold of ragged stone". In real life, its main enemies were the Scots, who failed to capture it in 1327, but succeeded in 1644. *Daily from 0930 (winter Sundays from 1400).* ✝

77e Dunstanburgh Castle. Dramatic ruins of an 11 acre castle founded in 1316 and sited on high cliffs facing the sea. It was captured twice during the Wars of the Roses and afterwards left to decay; chief remains are of the extensive curtain wall and gatehouse, with twin D-shape towers. *Daily from 0930 (winter Sundays from 1400).* ↳

77g Alnwick Castle. Tel. (0665) 602207. Restored Norman border fortress with a splendid array of high walls, towers, gatehouses and an impressive keep, almost rivalling Windsor as an example of mediaeval fortification. Its fine condition is the result of much 19th century work, the castle having seen extensive action, especially in the 12th century wars with Scotland. *May to late September: Sunday to Friday 1300-1630.* ▣ ⌂

78e Norham Castle. Tel. (0289) 82329. Ruins of a 12th century border fortress built to guard one of the River Tweed fords; a massive rectangular great tower remains, with traces of other buildings around it. Its location obviously made it a prime target for Scots marauders through the ages, most recently in 1513, when James IV of Scotland used artillery (including the famous Mons Meg) to capture it, only to perish at Flodden a few days later. *Daily from 0930 (Sundays from 1400).*

79e Lindisfarne Castle. Tel. Holy Island (0289) 89244. Tiny, 20-man fortress built on a rocky crag by the Tudors against attacks from the French or the Scots, neither of whom ever arrived. It never did see action and in 1903 was ingeniously converted to a private house (see ⌂). *April to end September: Saturday to Thursday 1100-1300, 1400-1700. October: weekends only 1400-1700.* ❋ ⌂ ✝ ⌊ᴛ ⓘ

79i Bamburgh Castle. Tel. (066 84) 208. Magnificently sited on a sheer-sided 150ft volcanic outcrop, this large mediaeval fortress was built during the 12th century on a site defended since Iron Age times. It was captured in succession by Normans, Scots, and by Henry II; in the Wars of the Roses it was held by Lancaster and twice besieged, in 1464 suffering the dubious distinction of being the first English castle to succumb to artillery when it fell to the Earl of Warwick. It was much restored in the 18th and 20th centuries, however, and is now virtually intact. Collections of armour, weapons, china and tapestry. *April to end October daily from 1300.* ☕

Historic Buildings

Including stately homes, historic houses and non-military buildings with interesting architectural features. Some castles which boast fine interiors have their rooms described here, although their military histories will be found in the section on Castles (page 93).

18a Ripley Castle. Tel. Harrogate (0423) 770152. Home of the Ingilby family since 1350, although the present buildings date from the 18th century. Collections of Civil War armour and weapons; also fine furniture, pictures and a priest's hiding hole. The only military part is the 15th century turreted gatehouse. *Easter to September: weekends plus some weekdays in summer, 1400-1800.* 🍷 ❋

18e Stockeld Park. Tel. Wetherby (0937) 62376. Small 18th century Palladian mansion with oval hall and magnificent crinoline staircase. *March to October: by appointment only.* 🍷

18h Harewood House. Tel. (0532) 886225. Superb 18th and 19th century home of the Earl of Harewood. Robert Adam interior has fine ceilings and plasterwork plus magnificent Chippendale furniture. Collections of Sèvres and Chinese porcelain, English and Italian paintings. Historical exhibition in stable block; children's adventure playground. *April to end October, daily from 1100; limited winter opening.* 🍷 ⌂ ❋ m 🐘 ❋

18i Bramham Park. Tel. Boston Spa (0937) 844265. Queen Anne mansion with fine furniture, pictures and porcelain. *Easter to end September: Sundays, Tuesday to Thursday and bank holiday Mondays 1315-1700. Closed for horse trials early June.* 🍷 ❋

19b Beningbrough Hall. Tel. York (0904) 470715. Immaculate 18th century house in Baroque style with notable woodcarvings and, in the principal rooms, some 100 famous paintings on loan from the National Portrait Gallery. Victorian laundry, plus audio/visual displays of domestic life. *April to end October: Tuesday to Thursday, weekends and bank holiday Mondays, 1100-1800.* 🍷 ⌂

19c Sutton-on-the-Forest: Sutton Park. Tel. Easingwold (0347) 810249. Georgian house with Cortese plasterwork, furniture by Chippendale and others, and fine porcelain, clocks and paintings. Ice house in grounds; souvenir shop. *Easter weekend, then May to end September: Tuesday to Thursday, Sundays and all bank holidays 1400-1800.* 🍷 ❋

Levens Hall (22a)

19f York: Guildhall, Coney Street, tel. (0904) 59881. Restored 15th century building with timbered roof and underground passage to the river. *Weekdays from 0900; also May to October Saturdays from 1000, Sundays from 1400. Free.*

Treasurer's House, Chapter House Street (behind the Minster), tel. 24247. Fine 17th century town house with furniture, paintings and audio/visual display about personalities linked with the building. *April to end October: daily 1030-1730.*

Kings Manor, Exhibition Square, tel. 59861. Restored 15th-to-17th century house much used by royalty; now part of the University. *Daily 0900-1700. Free (report to porter).*

Merchant Adventurer's Hall, Fossgate, tel. 54818. Timber framed 15th century great hall with some later additions; fine paintings, trade guild banners, oak furniture, etc. *Monday to Saturday from 1000 (when not in use)*

Merchant Taylors Hall, Aldwark, tel. (agents) 55452. Restored mediaeval guild hall with fine oak timbered roof. *May to September weekdays 1000-1200, 1400-1600 (when not in use). Free.*

St Anthony's Hall, Peasholme Green, tel. 59861 ext 274. This 15th century building now houses many important church documents. *Weekdays 0930-1300, 1400-1700. Free.*

Black Swan Inn, Peasholme Green. Converted 15th century merchant's house; one room has mediaeval painted panels and fireplace.

Mansion House, Coney Street. Private home of the Lord Mayor, this 1725 Georgian building houses the city plate and regalia.

Old Starre Inn, Stonegate. Oldest pub in York, in use at least since 1644.

The Shambles, near the market. Famous cobbled street of well preserved mediaeval buildings.

Twelfth Century House, off Stonegate. Restored remains of a Norman residence.

Assembly Rooms, Blake Street, tel. 24604. Colonnaded Georgian ballroom by Burlington. *July and August weekdays 1000-1600. Free.*

St William's College, College Street, tel. 37134. Building with 1453 timbered frontage, once the home of chantry priests from the

Minster. Now houses a brass rubbing centre. *Daily from 1000 (Sundays from 1230).*

20f Dalton-in-Furness: Tytup Hall. Tel. (0229) 62929. Small 18th century house with notable painted panels. *By appointment only.*

Town Trail. Starts from the railway station and covers 1½ miles, including Georgian and Victorian town houses and Market Square, which has 17th century cottages. Leaflet from 🛈.

21d Swarthmoor Hall. Tel. Ulverston (0229) 53204. Restored Elizabethan house with oak floors and staircase, mullion windows and fine panelled rooms. Birthplace of George Fox, founder of the Quakers, and still owned by them. *Mid March to mid October: Monday to Wednesday and Saturdays 1000-1200, 1400-1700. Free.* Nearby, to the east, is Swarthmoor Meeting House, a preserved 17th century Quaker hall.

21d Conishead Priory. Tel. Ulverston (0229) 54019. Victorian Gothic-style house with plaster ceilings, marble fireplaces and much wood panelling. Now a Buddhist college. *April to October weekends 1400-1700.* 🍷 ❋

21e Holker Hall. Tel. Flookburgh (044 853) 328. Victorian wing of 16th century stately home with notable woodcarvings and fine furniture and paintings. *Easter to end September: Sunday to Friday (plus some summer Saturdays) 1100-1715.* 🍷 ♿ ♣ ❋ ▣ ⌂ ☆ ☆

21i Lancaster Old Town Hall. Georgian building now housing a museum. *Daily.* ▣

Judges Lodgings. Tel. (0524) 2808. A 17th century town house once used by visiting Assize Court judges. Now a museum. *Easter to September: Monday to Saturday and bank holidays 1400-1700.* ▣

22a Levens Hall. Tel. Sedgwick (0448) 60321. Norman pele tower much expanded into an Elizabethan manor house with fine plasterwork, panelling and furniture. No dogs. *Easter Sunday to end September: Sundays, Tuesday to Thursday and bank holiday Mondays 1400-1700.* 🍷 ❋ ↓T

22b Hall: Preston Patrick Hall. Tel. Crooklands (044 87) 200. Manor house built in the 14th

94

century with good tracery windows. Now part of a working farm. *By appointment only. Free.*

22d Leighton Hall. Tel. Carnforth (0524) 732729. Country house built in 1760 with later neo-Gothic facade. Fine interior has early Gillow furniture, good paintings, clocks etc. Guided tours by the family. No dogs. *May to September: Sundays, Wednesdays, Thursdays and bank holiday Mondays 1400-1630.* ♥ ⌂ ❀ ♞ ☆

25b Braithwaite Hall. Tel. Wensleydale (0969) 40287. Built in the 17th century; now a working farmhouse standing in 748 acres. *By appointment.*

26e Norton Conyers. Tel. Melmerby (076 584) 252. Jacobean family house said to be the "Thornfield Hall" of Charlotte Brontë's 'Jane Eyre'. Family pictures, furniture, small collections of toys, dresses and Brontë relics. *Early May to mid September: Sundays, July Saturdays and bank holiday Mondays 1400-1700. Also open Boxing Day.* ♥ ❀

26h Markenfield Hall. Tel. Ripon (0765) 2928. Finest surviving example in the north of a moated manor house; built in the 14th to 16th centuries. *May to September: Mondays 1000-1700.*

26h Ripley Castle. See 18a.

26i Newby Hall. Tel. Boroughbridge (090 12) 2583. Famous 17th century Robert Adam house, recently refurbished. Treasures include collection of classical sculpture, Gobelins tapestries, Chippendale furniture, porcelain, china, etc. Adventure garden for children. *Easter to end September: Wednesdays, Thursdays, weekends and bank holidays (also Tuesdays and Fridays from June to August); 1330-1730.* ♥ ⌂ ❀ ♞

27e Shandy Hall. Tel. Coxwold (034 76) 465. Unusual timber framed mediaeval house full of books, pictures and Laurence Sterne relics. *June to September: Wednesdays 1400-1800.*

27f Gilling Castle. Tel. Ampleforth (043 93) 238. Original Norman keep with 16th and 18th century additions, including Elizabethan panelled great chamber. Now a preparatory school. *Monday to Saturday 1000-1600. Free.*

28b Nunnington Hall. Tel. (043 95) 283. Large 16th century manor with magnificent hall and staircase; panelled bedrooms; tapestries. *April to end October: Tuesday to Thursday and weekends 1400-1800; bank holiday Mondays 1100-1800.* ♥ ☆

28d Gilling Castle. See 27f.

28f Castle Howard. Tel. Coneysthorpe (065 384) 333. Magnificent 18th century palace on a grand scale, with chapel, domed great hall and vast state rooms; collections of furniture, porcelain, tapestry, and paintings by Rubens, Reynolds, van Dyck, Gainsborough and others. 1000 acre grounds include an italianate temple and a Hawksmoor mausoleum. *Good Friday to end October: daily 1130-1700.* ♥ ❀ ▣ ⚒

28h Foston Rectory. Tel. Whitwell (065 381) 240. Pink brick building of 1814 by Sydney Smith. *June to September: Sunday PM only by written appointment.*

29b Ebberston Hall. Tel. Scarborough (0723) 85516. Early 18th century Palladian villa with family paintings and furniture. *Easter to mid September: daily 0930-1730.* ❀

29i Sledmere House. Tel. Driffield (0377) 86208. Georgian house built in 1751-87, with famous 100ft library, furniture by Chippendale and others, Turkish room; children's playground. *Easter weekend, then Sundays until early May, then Tuesday to Thursday, weekends and bank holiday Mondays until late September; 1330-1700.* ♥ ❀ ✝

30i Burton Agnes Hall. Tel. (026 289) 324. One of the least altered Elizabethan country houses in Britain; fine impressionist paintings, carved ceilings, tapestries and china. *April to end October: weekdays 1345-1700, Sundays 1345-1800.* ♥ ❀ ✝

Raby Castle (49f)

Norman Manor House. Nearby remains dating from 1170 include original piers, plus old donkey wheel. *Any reasonable time. Free.*

32f Muncaster Castle. Tel. Ravenglass (065 77) 614. Magnificent 13th-to-19th century home with fine furniture, 6000-book library and paintings by van Dyck, Reynolds, Gainsborough and others. One corner of the house is a 13th century pele tower. Teenage commando course. *Easter to early October: Sundays, then Tuesday to Thursday 1400-1630.* ♥ ♿ ♣ ❀ ♞

33c Dove Cottage. Tel. Grasmere (096 65) 418. Home of the poet Wordsworth from 1799 to 1808, preserved as it was then with his furniture and personal belongings. *March to October: Monday to Saturday from 0930 (1000 in March and October).* ▣

33c Rydal Mount. Tel. Ambleside (096 63) 3002. Wordsworth's home from 1813 until his death in 1850; contains many possessions and first editions of his work. Building is a 16th century farmhouse with 18th century additions. *March to October: daily 1000-1700. Also limited opening November to January.* ♥ ❀

33f Hawkshead: Grammar School. Attended by William Wordsworth and maintained as it was then, including a desk on which he carved his initials. *Any reasonable time: ask locally.*

Courthouse, ½ mile north on B5286. Tel. Ambleside (096 63) 3003. Only remnant of the 15th century manorial buildings of Furness Abbey. Now a museum (see ⚒ for details).

33f Near Sawrey: Hill Top. Tel. Hawkshead (096 66) 334. Small 17th century farmhouse where Beatrix Potter wrote many of her famous books; now contains her china, paintings, furniture and some of her original drawings. No indoor photography; no electric lighting; no dogs. Very busy at peak times. *April to end October: Monday to Thursday 1000-dusk, Sundays 1400-dusk.*

33i Rusland Hall. Tel. Satterthwaite (022 984) 276. Georgian mansion with period panelling, furniture, paintings, sculpture and clocks. *April to September: daily 1100-1730.* ♿ ❀ ▣

34a Rydal. See 33c.

34d Hawkshead. See 33f.

34d Near Sawrey. See 33f.

34e Hall: Townend. Tel. Ambleside (096 63) 2628. Lakeland farmhouse with original 17th

century furniture. No electricity; no dogs. *April to October: Tuesday to Friday, Sundays and bank holiday Mondays, 1400-dusk or 1800.*

34e Belle Isle. Tel. Windermere (096 62) 3353. Unique circular Georgian house built 1778, with Gillow furniture, family paintings and much else. Children's playground. Access by boat from far end of Bowness Promenade. *Mid May to mid September: Mondays, Tuesdays, Thursdays and Sundays 1030-1700.* ♥ ♣ ❀

34g Rusland Hall. See 33i.

34i Kendal: Abbot Hall. Tel. (0539) 22464. Fine 1759 house with restored ground floor rooms containing pictures, furniture and other objets d'art. Modern galleries upstairs (see ▣). *Weekdays 1030-1730; weekends 1400-1700.* ♥ ♿ ▣ ⚒

Castle Dairy. Wildman Street, tel. 21170. Oldest habitable stone house in the area, this well preserved Tudor building has oak beams and a hand carved four-poster bed. Now a restaurant. *Easter to September Wednesdays 1400-1600.*

34i Sizergh Castle. Tel. Sedgwick (0448) 60285. Large 15th-to-18th century home with Tudor great hall, fine ceilings, panelling, tapestry and furniture; collections of silver, china, Stuart and Jacobite relics. *April to end September: Wednesdays, Sundays and bank holiday Mondays (also Thursdays in July/August) 1400-1745.* ❀ ♞

34i Levens Hall. See 22a.

38c Moulton Hall. Tel. Barton (032 577) 227. Manor house rebuilt 1650 with fine carved wood staircase. *By appointment only. Free.*

38f Richmond: Georgian Theatre, Victoria Road, tel. (0748) 3021. Built in 1788 and still used, this is now the oldest theatre in Britain in its original form, with a unique intimate Georgian interior. New theatre museum contains the oldest complete set of scenery in Britain. *May to end September: daily 1430-1730.*

38h Constable Burton Hall. Tel. Bedale (0677) 50428. John Carr 18th century house with contemporary furniture and paintings. *Telephone for opening times.*

38h Braithwaite Hall. See 25b.

39d Kiplin Hall. Tel. Richmond (0748) 818290. Jacobean building of 1620 with furniture, tapestries and pictures. *Spring Bank Holiday to mid September: Sundays, Wednsdays and bank holidays 1400-1730.*

39g Bedale Hall. Tel. (0677) 23131. Georgian mansion with fine ballroom, plus room containing domestic and craft exhibits. *May to September:Tuesdays 1000-1600. Free.*

44c Cockermouth: Wordsworth House, Main Street, tel. (0900) 824805. Birthplace in 1770 of the famous poet. House dates from 1745 and has original staircase, nine rooms furnished in 18th century style, audio/visual show in old stables and Wordsworth relics. *April to end October: Friday to Wednesday 1100-1700.* 🍵

45d Low Lorton: Lorton Hall. Tel. (090 085) 252. Fine 17th century house with oak panels, Jacobean furniture, priest's holes, plus attached pele tower and chapel. *By appointment only.*

45f Keswick: Mirehouse. Tel. (0596) 72287. House noted for its literary connections, with manuscripts and pictures linked with Bacon, Carlyle, Tennyson and the Lake Poets. *April to October: Sundays and Wednesdays PM.* ♿

45f Brundholme: Old Windebrowe. Tel. Keswick (0596) 72112. Building with relics of the Lake Poets, plus kitchen restored to 1794. *Easter to end October: Wednesdays 1400-1630.*

46b Hutton-in-the-Forest. Tel. Skelton (085 34) 207. Mainly 17th century house with later additions, built around a 14th century pele tower. Contains furniture, paintings, china, armour and tapestries; formal gardens with lake and woodland. No dogs. *Late May to September Thursdays, Sundays in August and all bank holiday Mondays: 1400-1700.* 🍵 ⌂

46f Dalemain. Tel. Pooley Bridge (085 36) 450. Mediaeval pele tower much extended since, with Georgian facade, Tudor plasterwork, Queen Anne furniture, Chinese wallpaper, oak panelling, etc. *Easter Saturday to late September: Saturday to Thursday 1400-1715.* 🍵 ♿ ♣ ⌂ ❋ 🖼

47h Flass House. Tel. Ravensworth (093 15) 278. Fine Palladian manor of 1851. *Not open to the public.*

49f Raby Castle. Tel. Staindrop (0833) 60202. The only stately home in County Durham open to the public, this extensive mediaeval castle has an opulent 18th/19th century interior, including a massive great hall, period furniture and fine paintings. *April to June Wednesdays and Sundays; July to end September Sunday to Friday; also bank holiday weekends; 1400-1700.* 🍵 ❋ 🖼

49h The Bowes Museum. Tel. Barnard Castle (0833) 37139. Ornate French-style chateau built by John Bowes in 1869 to exhibit his many collections. See 🖼 for details.

50b Auckland Castle. Tel. Bishop Auckland (0388) 663063. Official home of the Bishop of Durham. Parts date back to the 12th century, but the building was Gothicised in the 18th century. Unusual deerhouse in grounds. *Guided tours by appointment. Free.* 🍵 ♣ 📍₁₈

50d Raby Castle. See 49f.

51i Ormesby Hall. 18th century mansion with fine plasterwork and opulent decoration. Small garden; courtyard used by mounted police. *April to end October: Wednesdays, Sundays and bank holiday Mondays 1400-1800.* ♿

52e Kirkleatham: Sir William Turner's Hospital, Tel. Redcar (0642) 471757. Finest almshouses in the north, founded by Charles II in 1676. Courtyard open any reasonable time. ✝

52g Ormesby Hall. See 51i.

55c Carlisle: Guildhall, Greenmarket, tel. (0228) 34781. Mediaeval timbered town house recently renovated and now containing a local museum (see 🖼 for details).

Parish Hall, near the cathedral. Stone 15th century tithe barn with massive roof beams.

Priors Tower, Cathedral Grounds. A 13th century pele tower with a first floor room decorated by 45 panels bearing local coats of arms. *Monday to Saturday 1400-1700 (also AM in summer).* ✝

55h Hesket Newmarket: Hesket Hall. Odd 12-sided building with circular roof. *Not open.*

56a Carlisle. See 55c.

56h Hutton-in-the-Foreset. See 46b.

60c Washington Old Hall, The Avenue (A182). Tel. (0632) 466879. Restored home of George Washington's ancestors, now containing period furniture, Delft ware and Washington relics. US Independence Day celebrated every 4th July. *March to end October: Thursday to Tuesday 1300 -sunset. November to end February: weekends only 1400-sunset.* ❋

60i Durham: Castle. Tel. (0385) 65481. Interior now has splendid apartments, including Senate Room with 16th century Flemish tapestry, magnificent 1322 Great Hall with banners and carvings, and the 4 storey 1663 Black Staircase. *July to September: Monday to Saturday 1000-1200, 1400-1630. October to June: Mondays, Wednesdays and Saturdays 1400-1600.* 🛅 ✝

Town Hall, Market Square. Traditional Victorian building containing city plate and regalia; also relics of Count Boruwalski, a violin playing Polish dwarf. *Monday to Saturday office hours.*

65c Wallington Hall. Tel. Scots Gap (067 074) 283. Built in 1688 but greatly altered in the 1740s. Elaborately decorated interior with exceptional rococo plasterwork, fine porcelain and furniture and pre-Raphaelite wall paintings. Rooms range from an early Georgian salon to late Victorian nursery and kitchen. Collection of coaches. *Mid April to end September: Wednesday to Monday 1300-1730. October: Wednesdays and Weekends 1400-1630.* 🍵 ♣ ❋ ☆ 🛈

66a Wallington Hall. See 65c.

66h Wylam: George Stephenson's Cottage. Tel. (066 14) 3457. Stone cottage built 1750; birthplace in 1781 of the famous railway pioneer. Access on foot only. *April to end October: Wednesdays and weekends 1400-1700.*

67e Seaton Delaval Hall. Tel. (0632) 481493. Magnificent Vanbrugh building in Baroque style, with Doric facade and two wings, built in the 18th century. Paintings, furniture, statuary and historical documents. *May to end September: Wednesdays, Sundays and bank holidays 1400-1800.* ☆

71c Callaly Castle. Tel. Whittingham (066 574) 663. A 17th century mansion incorporating a 13th century pele tower. Exceptional salon has notable Italian plasterwork; ballroom has tapestry panels from Versailles; there are collections of paintings, porcelain, furniture and silver. *May to September: weekends and bank holidays only 1415-1730.* 🍵 ❋

71c Cragside. Tel. Rothbury (0669) 20333. Magnificent Victorian mansion created for armaments king Lord Armstrong. It was the first house in the world to be lit by water-generated electricity. Eccentric interior includes comfortable rooms with pre-Raphaelite paintings and original furniture, and such gadgets as hydraulic lifts, Turkish baths and scientific apparatus. *April to end September: Tuesday to Sunday and bank holidays 1300-1730.* ♣ 📍 🛈

71h Wallington Hall. See 65c.

72b Callaly Castle. See 71c.

72b Cragside. See 71c.

72h Wallington Hall. See 65c.

76i Callaly Castle. See 71c.

77g Alnwick Castle. Tel. (0665) 602207. Rich Renaissance interior belies warlike exterior; staterooms house many treasures, including paintings by Titian, van Dyck, Canaletto and others, together with fine furniture, porcelain, armour, books and other heirlooms. This is the second largest castle in England. *Early May to late September: Sunday to Friday 1300-1630.* 🛅

79a Berwick: Town Hall. Tel. (0289) 6332 ext 50. Council chamber, guildhall and old jail in mainly 18th century building. *By appointment only: the Clerk of the Trustees.*

79e Lindisfarne Castle. Tel. Holy Island (0289) 89244. In 1903 the ruins of this tiny 16th century fortress were converted into a luxurious private home by Sir Edwin Lutyens, who installed a series of bedrooms and living rooms linked by rock passages. These have been well preserved, with Flemish and English oak furniture and an interesting collection of prints. *April to end September: Saturday to Thursday 1100-1700. October: weekends only 1400-1700.* ❋ 🛅 ✝ 📍 🛈

Cragside (71c)

Religious Places

Cathedrals, churches, chapels, abbeys and monasteries are open all year unless marked otherwise; if a church is locked enquire at the vicarage for the key. Also included here are holy wells, ecclesiastical ruins and other places of religious significance.

18b Knaresborough: St John the Baptist. Mainly Early English and Perpendicular parish church in prominent setting. Notable tower; 17th century woodwork and monuments; poor box dated 1600; Pre-Raphaelite glass work.

18c Goldsborough: St Mary. 12th to 15th century village church with fine monuments and heraldic glass dated 1696.

18d Stainburn: St Mary the Virgin. Primitive Norman church in isolated setting with arcaded Norman font, 17th century pews and pulpit.

18f Cowthorpe: St Michael. Remote 15th century church with fine font, unusual tower and wooden chest with gabled roof.

18g Bramhope: St Giles. 17th century chapel in grounds of Hall. Unusually complete Puritan furnishings; font dated 1673.

18g Adel: St John the Baptist. Small church, one of finest examples of Norman work in Yorkshire. Notable carvings on south portal; rich chancel arch with interesting capitals.

18h Bardsey: All Hallows. Interesting Saxon tower with traces of gabled porch; Norman arcade and doorway; 14th century chancel.

18i Collingham: St Oswald. Early church heavily restored by Victorians. Two interesting Saxon crosses: Apostles Cross of about 800 and another of the late 9th century.

18i Bramham: All Saints. Fine Norman tower with Perpendicular spire. Remarkable early 20th century panelling and screen in the chancel.

19a Aldwark: St Stephen. Unusual mid-19th century church by Lamb. Exterior walls are a combination of pebble-stones, herringbone brickwork and stone dressings; elaborate timber roof.

19a Little Ouseburn: Holy Trinity. 13th to 15th century church; tall Norman tower with Perpendicular pinnacles; late 18th century domed Tuscan rotunda mausoleum in the churchyard.

19a Nun Monkton: St Mary. Fine church in delightful setting. Nave is part of a 12th/13th century Benedictine nunnery. Interior is good with interesting lancet windows and arcades; some glass by William Morris.

19e Nether Poppleton: St Everilda. Pleasant rural church hidden behind farm at end of village. Galleried interior; mediaeval glass; 17th century monuments; painted rood screen.

19f York: Minster. The cathedral church of St Peter is a magnificent structure in Early English to Perpendicular styles. Built between 1220 and 1470, its architecture is fine: the richly decorated west front is without doubt the best in England after Beverley, with its marvellous twin pinnacled towers and central window, known as the Heart of Yorkshire. In contrast is the massive and simple central tower, the largest in England. Inside is the highest and broadest nave in the country which is similarly simple. However, the glory of York is in its glass: the development of English glass can be traced through three centuries. The earliest glass (13th century) is in the north transept in five tall lancet windows known as the Five Sisters; in the aisles and nave are 14th century windows. The finest glass is that of the east end, however: this glorious sea of coloured glass was completed in 1405 and is one of Europe's finest windows, with panels telling the story of the Bible from the Creation to the Apocalypse. Other notable features of the Minster: octagonal chapter house; fine 15th century choir screen; recently excavated undercroft housing a permanent exhibition of the Minster's history.

All Saints, North Street, Micklegate. Late Norman church noted for its slender 120ft spire and exceptional stained glass of the 14th and 15th centuries.

All Saints, Pavement, Coney Street. This church has a fine octagonal lantern tower and a 15th century lectern with a rare chained book.

St Cuthbert, Peasholme Green, Foss Islands Road. Ancient church, York's oldest, with good 15th century oak doors and an 18th century brick vestry with pantile roof.

St Denys, Walmgate. Noted for its richly carved Norman doorway and fine 12th century glass, some of the oldest in York.

St Helen, St Helen's Square, Petergate. Dating from the 14th century, it is the civic church of York. Good 15th century glass.

Holy Trinity, Goodramgate, Lord Mayor's Walk. 13th to 15th century church with saddleback tower and 18th century box pews.

Holy Trinity, Micklegate. Fragment of Norman Priory church, with transitional Norman pillars; ancient stocks in churchyard.

St Lawrence, Lawrence Street. Early English church with the 12th century doorway of a destroyed church in churchyard.

St Margaret, Walmgate. Church with late 17th century stone and brick tower and exceptionally fine Norman porch.

St Martin-cum-Gregory, Micklegate. Church dates from early 13th century and is both archaeologically and architecturally interesting. Now an Anglican Youth Centre.

St Martin-le-Grand, Coney Street. Mainly 15th century church gutted in 1942. It has been partly reconstructed; the rest of the area is now a garden of remembrance.

St Mary, Bishophill Junior, Micklegate. Ancient church with fine Saxon work, especially in the tower and windows.

St Mary, Castlegate. Large church restored by Butterfield in 1870; fine tower has an octagonal upper stage.

St Mary's Abbey, Museum Gardens. Mediaeval remains of important Benedictine monastery on the foundations of a Norman building.

St Michael-le-Belfrey, Petergate. Fine tudor church of about 1536 with fine altar rails and altarpiece of 1732. Guy Fawkes was christened here.

St Michael, Spurriergate, Coney Street. Ancient church with excellent 12th century arcades inside. Many other fine details.

St Olave, Marygate, Bootham. Church, dating from 11th century, but used as a gun emplacement during Civil War. Largely rebuilt in 18th century.

19f Fulford: St Oswald Old Church. Small mid-14th century church with tiny, ivy-covered brick tower. Now converted into a house. *By appointment only.*

19g Wighill: All Saints. Mediaeval church, with 12th century arcade, in pleasant setting. Superb Norman doorway; Jacobean furnishings.

19g Newton Kyme: St Andrew. Set beside a Regency Hall, the church has Transitional arcades and 15th century tower; old heraldic glass; curious carvings on porch; monuments.

19g Tadcaster: St Mary. Mostly Perpendicular church rebuilt in late 19th century out of reach of flood waters. Fine, buttressed tower; exceptional 20th century woodwork.

19h Bolton Percy: All Saints. Striking mid 15th century limestone church in a remote setting. Exceptionally fine interior: glass in east window is original; fine chancel, sedilia and piscina; 15th century roof and rood screen; 17th century pews.

19h Ryther: All Saints. Rural church with an early Norman chancel arch, 13th century nave and 14th century south aisle. Remarkable monuments; four mediaeval altar slabs.

20b Millom: Holy Trinity. Late Norman church with some later mediaeval work. Nave has fine black and white roof with Norman piers.

20f Great Urswick: St Mary and St Michael. Massive 13th century tower; box pews and gallery; fine wood carving; fragments of ancient crosses of Saxon and Viking origin.

20f Furness Abbey. Cistercian abbey with extensive remains of the church - the western tower, transepts and choir are nearly their original height. Parts of the chapter house, parlour and cloisters also remain. For leaflet about abbey trail contact ⓘ. *Daily from 0930 (Sundays from 1400).*

21b Cartmel: St Mary the Virgin. Massive 12th century church, once part of an Augustinian Priory. Central tower is unusual, with another tower set diagonally on top of it. Other features include: fine Perpendicular windows; magnificent Renaissance screens and stalls; 14th century canopied monument. The greatest mediaeval church in Cumbria.

Priory Gatehouse. Only other remains of the Augustinian Priory; now a shop. *March to Christmas, daily at reasonable hours. Free.*

21c Witherslack: St Paul. Mid 17th century church in romantic wooded setting. Fine classical interior with canopied pulpit.

21i Lancaster: St Mary. Large and impressive Perpendicular church with rich furnishings, especially the Decorated stalls and 17th century pulpit.

22a Beetham: St Michael and All Angels. Early mediaeval church with 12th century tower. Panels of good mediaeval glass, one incorporating a portrait of Henry IV.

22c Kirkby Lonsdale: St Mary the Virgin. Inspired by Durham Cathedral, this mainly Norman church has one of the finest churchyards in the country - praised by Ruskin and painted by Turner.

22f Tunstall: St John the Baptist. Mainly 15th century church in pastoral setting. Fine Perpendicular porch; 15th/16th century glass from the Netherlands; large buttresses.

22g Lancaster. See 21i.

23e Chapel-le-Dale: St Leonard. 17th century church in remote and magnificent setting under Ingleborough.

23e Clapham: St James. Pleasant early 19th century church with Perpendicular tower. Lofty nave arcades; Decorated windows.

23d Burton-in-Lonsdale: All Saints: Impressive late 19th century church with tall spire and stone-vaulted chancel.

23d Ingleton: St Mary. Late 19th century church with Perpendicular tower and fine arcaded Norman font with thirteen figures.

23f Horton-in-Ribblesdale: **St Oswald.** Sturdy church in rugged setting; Perpendicular tower; Norman font; fragments of mediaeval glass.

23i Giggleswick: **St Alkelda.** Perpendicular church with handsome 17th century pulpit, lectern and altar rails. Good lychgate.

24d Halton Gill: **St John the Baptist.** Tiny church of 1626 with adjoining school room.

24e Arncliffe: **St Oswald.** Magnificent dale setting. 15th century tower; Royal Arms of 1797; list of men of dale who fought at Flodden Field.

24h Kirkby Malham: **St Michael.** Regional Perpendicular-style church in beautiful setting. Low exterior belies spacious interior. Transitional font; 17th century balustraded pews; unusual niches in columns of arcades.

24i Linton: **St Michael.** Pleasant setting for church with Norman font and arcade, 14th century nave and 15th century chapels. Interesting Romanesque crucifix.

25c Jervaulx **Abbey.** Unspoilt ruins of 12th century Cistercian abbey. Charming setting. *Daily dawn to dusk.* ☕

25c Masham: **St Mary.** Mainly 14th century, this church has an interesting tower: lower half is 11th century, surmounted by a 15th century octagonal stage, topped by a spire. Saxon cross.

25g Burnsall: **St Wilfrid.** 15th century church with Saxon fragments and two hogback tombs. Norman font; 15th century alabaster panel; Jacobean pulpit; 17th century lychgate.

26a Masham. See 25c

26b West Tanfield: **St Nicholas.** Chiefly 15th century church with interesting 14th century altar tomb - complete with its wrought iron hearse - of the Marmion family.

26e Ripon **Cathedral.** Built in the 13th century, the cathedral stands on a site that has been used for religious buildings since the 7th century. The oldest part is the crypt which belonged to the church of St Wilfrid of about 670. The squat exterior belies its size; the central tower lost its spire in 1660 and the spires on the two west towers were dismantled for safety reasons. If the towers had been replaced, the proportions of the cathedral would be among the best in England. The west front, however, still retains much fine work, as does the 16th century Gothic nave. Other features: good 13th and 14th century glass; 12th century and octagonal late mediaeval fonts; Lady Chapel famous for its collection of early printed books and manuscripts; ornate Gothic sedilia; late 15th century choir stalls with exceptional misericords.

26e Studley Royal: **St Mary the Virgin.** Late 19th century church by William Burges with commanding spire and notable sculpture over the east window. ♣ ❋

26h Fountains **Abbey.** Magnificent ruins of a great Cistercian abbey dating from 1132, standing in beautiful Studley Park. Probably the best example of a monastic ruin in Western Europe; not to be missed. *Daily dawn-dusk.* ☕

26i Roecliffe: **St Mary.** Tiny mid-19th century church in Norman Revival style. Interior contains 17th century woodwork, a vestry door from York Minster and splendid altar rails and pulpit.

27a Thirsk: **St Mary the Virgin.** The main body of the church was built in 1420 and is a good example of fully developed Perpendicular. The interior is grand with a magnificent altar table.

27c Rievaulx **Abbey.** Magnificent Cistercian abbey, begun about 1132, in beautiful setting. Earliest large Cistercian nave in Britain. Also extensive and well-preserved ruins of monastic buildings. View from Rievaulx Terrace (see ♣). *Daily from 0930 (winter Sundays from 1400).* ♣ ▣

27c Byland **Abbey.** Ruins of one of Yorkshire's three great Cistercian monasteries. Buildings date from late 12th and early 13th centuries. Well preserved glazed tiles. *Daily from 0930 (Sundays from 1400).*

27e Coxwold: **St Michael.** Mainly Perpendicular church with octagonal tower. Interesting 17th/18th century furnishings including box pews, the pulpit, the west gallery and monuments in the chancel.

27e Raskelf: **St Mary.** Largely rebuilt in the 19th century, the church retains a 15th century timber tower and pyramid cap. Also: Norman font, 11th century arcade, 17th century baluster screen.

27e Thormanby: **St Mary.** In isolated setting, the church has squat brick tower and unusual porch. Externally very attractive.

27f Newburgh **Priory.** Tel. Coxwold (034 76) 435. Originally a 12th century Augustinian Priory with later additions. *July to end August, Wednesdays 1400-1800.* ☕ ❋

27f Brandsby: **All Saints.** Late 18th century church set in undulating and wooded country. The interior is a fine example of Classical architecture; notable 18th century baluster font.

27g Aldwark. See 19a.

27g Little Ouseburn. See 19a.

27h Alne: **St Mary.** The church has interesting mixture of styles: the tower with mediaeval ground stage and Renaissance upper stages in brick; Norman font and doorway; 15th century aisle and nave; Jacobean pulpit; and pleasant 18t century panelling.

27i Stillington: **St Nicholas.** Charming church in village setting. The cream-washed interior contains good box pews, arcades with octagonal piers, and red brick floors.

27i Marton-in-the-Forest: **St Mary.** Striking exterior with 12th and 15th century work, especially the gables. Interior features: 13th century font; fragments of 15th century glass; 17th century altar rails and benches.

28a Rievaulx Abbey. See 27c.

28a Sproxton: **St Chad.** Small 17th century church moved from West Newton in 1879. Pleasant windows, grey stone roof and good entrance gate.

28b Ford - Kirkdale: **St Gregory.** Small Saxon church in superb setting. Chiefly known for its remarkable pre-Conquest sundial, the finest of its kind in Britain, which is set above the southern doorway. ♣

28d Brandsby. See 27f.

28e Hovingham: **All Saints.** Victorian church with pre-Conquest tower and Saxon reredos in south chapel.

28g Stillington. See 27i.

28h Sheriff Hutton: **St Helen and the Holy Cross.** Pleasant exterior of sandstone and limestone. Interior full of good furnishings, plus the tomb of Richard III's son.

28h Foston: **All Saints.** Norman church with fine south doorway, chancel arch and piscina.

Glossary of Terms

Shown here is the ground plan of a typical mediaeval cathedral. Most of the cathedrals and churches described on these pages were started and/or completed during the mediaeval period, and their general layout will be similar.

Apse. Vaulted recess, usually at one end of the choir.
Arcade. Range of arches carried on piers or columns, either free-standing or attached to a wall.
Baluster. Small ornate pillar or column.
Barrel Vault. Semi-circular vault in the roof; also known as a tunnel vault.
Chancel. The area in which the altar stands.
Clerestory. Upper storey of the nave walls, pierced by windows.
Corbel. Block of stone projecting from a wall to support some horizontal feature.
Corbel Table. Series of corbels just below the roof eaves; often seen in Norman buildings.
Decorated. English Gothic architecture dating from (roughly) the first half of the 14th century.
Early English. English Gothic architecture dating from (roughly) the 13th century.
Fan Vault. Chamber whose supporting ribs spread out in the shape of an open fan.

Lancet Window. High narrow window with sharply pointed arch.
Lady Chapel. Usually named for its dedication to the Virgin Mary. See plan.
Lychgate. Wooden structure at the churchyard entrance providing cover for a coffin.
Misericord. Small hinged wooden seat, used in the choir stalls to give some support to a person standing up; often elaborately carved.
Perpendicular. English Gothic architecture dating from (roughly) 1350 to 1530.
Piscina. Basin for washing Communion vessels; usually set in a wall near the altar.
Reredos. Structure above and behind the altar.
Rood Loft. Loft or gallery built above a rood screen (see below).
Rood Screen. Separates the nave from the chancel or choir; incorporates a large rood (crucifix).
Sedilia. Seats for priests (usually 3) on the south side of the chancel.
Tester. Horizontal canopy over the pulpit.
Tympanum. A triangular space above the main door, usually highly decorated.
Undercroft. Vaulted room below a church or chapel.
Vault. Arched room or passageway, often underground.

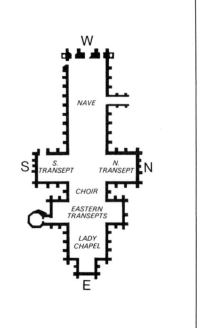

28i Kirkham Priory. Beautifully situated by the River Derwent, with a 13th century gatehouse ornamented with heraldic shields. *Daily from 0930 (Sundays from 1400).*

28i Bossall: St Botolph. 12th century cruciform church with a central tower and a fine 13th century doorway, sheltered by a 19th century porch. Also a superb 18th century font cover, Royal Arms of 1710 and a good 20th century reredos.

29a Pickering: St Peter and St Paul. 12th and 14th century church with much restoration. Inside details are good: 15th century wall paintings, 18th century brass chandeliers and pulpit, 20th century Jacobean style screen.

29c Brompton: All Saints. 14th to 15th century church with octagonal spire. Porch is a memorial to an early experimenter with flying machines. Wordsworth was married here in 1802.

29d Old Malton: St Mary. The church is a fragment of the Gilbertine Priory church. There is much interesting 11th and 12th century work, especially the west front.

St Mary's Priory. Last remaining Gilbertine monastery in regular use in England. Fine misericords. *Dawn to dusk. Free.*

29h Wharram-le-Street: St Mary. Interesting church with unrestored early Norman tower and a Saxon nave and west doorway.

29i Sledmere: St Mary. One of the best village churches in the county, with restored mediaeval tower. 🍺 ✳ 🏛

30a Ganton: St Nicholas. Mainly 13th century church in very pleasant setting. Tower has small octagonal spire; very fine mid-18th century monument in the south transept.

30c Filey: St Oswald. Mainly 12th and 13th century cruciform church in a wooded setting overlooking a ravine.

30i Boynton: St Andrew. Chiefly Classical church with a Perpendicular west tower. Of interest is the Strickland mortuary chapel which lies beyond the altar and a lectern by William Strickland, shaped like a turkey to commemorate the introduction of the bird to this country.

30i Burton Agnes: St Martin. 13th to 14th century church with a fine late 15th century tower. Many interesting monuments. 🍺 ✳ 🏛

30i Harpham: St John of Beverley. Norman church remodelled in the 14th century. Fine collection of mediaeval and 18th century monuments.

31e Flamborough: St Oswald. Mediaeval church much restored in 19th century. Rich interior noted for early 16th century rood screen and loft retaining traces of the original colour. Also Norman tub font and mediaeval crucifix in the south chapel.

31g Bridlington: St Mary. Church consists of nave and two west towers of a 12th century Augustinian Priory. Fine 13th and 14th century arcades and north porch. *May to September, Mondays to Saturdays from 1000; usual Sunday services. Free.*

31g Bessingby: St Magnus. Successful 19th century version of a late 14th century church. Fine Norman font and several good monuments. Beautiful setting on the Wolds.

32a St Bees: St Mary and St Bega. Partly Norman church with a central tower of 1200 and a clerestoried nave of 1250. Splendid Norman doorway with rich mouldings; two rose windows and many lancets.

32a Beckermet: St John the Baptist. Fine small Victorian church set high above the confluence of two streams. Pleasing and well designed interior. Unusual collection of ancient stones in porch and on window sills.

32b Calder Abbey. Ruins of the cloister, nave and some church aisles are all that remain of an abbey founded in 1135 for the order of Savigny. *Not open.*

32b Gosforth: St Mary. Church rebuilt, in Decorated style of late 19th century. Churchyard contains Gosforth Cross, an important 10th century monument. Many Saxon fragments.

32c Strands. Small, partly Georgian church in a beautiful setting. Oak panelling comes from York Minster; 14th century cherubs on the roof.

32e Hewrigg: Irton Cross. In the churchyard of Irton church stands 1000-year-old Anglian cross, with delicate decorations of interlacing and complicated knot work.

32e Waberthwaite: St John the Baptist. Remote and strange church with 15th century windows, a Norman font, a pulpit of 1630 and Saxon crosses. Excellent views from the churchyard.

33c Grasmere: St Oswald. Massive church dating from 11th, 13th and 17th centuries. Wordsworth and members of his family are buried here; monument to the poet by Woolner.

33g Ulpha: St John. Built of local stone, the church is in a beautiful setting by the River Duddon. Fragments of 18th century decoration and timber in the roof.

34a Grasmere. See 33c.

34g Cartmel Fell: St Anthony. Early 16th century church built on fell-side. Low mullioned windows and saddle-back tower; good Flemish and English mediaeval glass; pre-Reformation figure of Christ from vanished rood screen; two screened pews.

34h Witherslack. See 21c.

34h Tarnside: St Kentigern. Mid-16th century church built on ancient site. Unusual collection of Tudor consecration crosses; 15th century effigies; finely carved 14th century font; and many curiosities.

34i Kendal: Holy Trinity. Perpendicular church enlarged in mid-19th century, mostly in Early English style. Interesting 16th and 17th century monuments.

35c Crosby Garrett: St Andrew. Mainly Norman church on a steep hill with fine views.

36b Kirkby Stephen: St Stephen. Stately and impressive church founded in 8th century and rebuilt in the 13th and 15th. Embattled 16th century tower; fine monuments.

37e Healaugh: St John the Baptist. Norman church with fine door, corbel tables and unusual carving on the chancel arch.

37f Grinton: St Andrew. Chiefly 15th century church with austere exterior. The interior contains much of interest: early font with 15th century cover; early 18th century pulpit with tester; good monuments including a wooden mural tablet of 1698.

37f Marrick: St Andrew. Remains of Benedictine nunnery, part now a farmhouse. Chancel in ruins; nave pulled down and rebuilt in 1811.

38d Grinton. See 37f.

38d Marrick. See 37f.

38e Downholme: St Michael. Small 17th century church that suffered much in 19th century, but the porch, rood loft window and some other windows still remain. Also notable 18th century painted texts on the arcades inside as well as an interesting font.

38f Easby Abbey. Sited on the banks of River Swale, considerable ruins remain including 14th century gatehouse, chapter house and cloisters. *Daily from 0930 (Sundays from 1400).*

St Agatha. The church, close to the ruins, has a commanding view of Richmond and is long and low and of beautiful weathered stone. The interior has interesting Norman font, 19th century nave roof and pews, and some excellent wall paintings.

38f Hornby: St Mary. Attractive church with campanile-type tower. Inside there is a Norman arcade, elegant 19th century font, some mediaeval monuments and brasses, and some early 16th century painted panels.

38g Wensley: Holy Trinity. Church that is pleasant both inside and out. Internally there is much to see: 15th century screen with Jacobean extras; font and cover of 1662; 13th century sedilia; 15th century stall ends; and a Flemish brass of 1395.

38h Middleham: St Alkelda and St Mary. Largely 14th to 15th century collegiate church. By legend, St Alkelda was a Saxon princess martyred in about 800 and buried here.

38i Jervaulx Abbey. See 25c.

39a Croft-on-Tees: St Peter. Mostly 14th century church of colourful local stone with good buttresses and tracery. Piece of Romano-British sculpture in south wall; tomb and monuments to Milbanke family.

39f Kirby Sigston: St Lawrence. Well restored church of Transitional period. Notable 17th century pulpit and font; good 20th century screen and stalls.

39g Bedale: St Gregory. Large church with impressive semi-fortified west tower. Other interesting features include a barrel vaulted porch, 14th century tombs and a fine 20th century wrought iron gate to the crypt.

39i Leake: St Mary. Mediaeval church with Norman tower in pretty setting. Two 15th century stall-ends with fine carving.

40b Whorlton: Holy Cross. Isolated church with roofless 12th century nave. The 12th century tower and 13th century chancel are intact. Interesting canopied wall tombs.

40c Stokesley: St Peter and St Paul. Church with 15th century tower and mediaeval chancel; attractive setting.

40d Kirby Sigston. See 39f.

40d Mount Grace Priory. Best surviving example of a Carthusian foundation in Britain. Unusual layout of monastic quarters was governed by the need for each brother to remain isolated from his fellows, a peculiarity of the Carthusian order. *Daily from 0930 (Sundays from 1400).*

40e Arncliffe: All Saints. Small 18th century chapel rebuilt in 1821 in Classical style. Interior is white with red box pews; a Scandinavian ship hangs from the roof.

40i Rievaulx Abbey. See 27c.

41b Danby: St Hilda. Moorland church with detached Perpendicular tower. Most of the church was rebuilt in the 18th century and 'mediaevalised' by Temple Moore in 1903. Good 17th and 18th century monuments.

41g Leake. See 39i.

41h Lastingham: St Mary. Norman abbey church remodelled in 1228. Chiefly remarkable for Abbot Stephen's crypt of 1078-85; fragments of Saxon sculpture.

41h Ford. See 28b.

41i Appleton-le-Moors: Christ Church. Mid-19th century church in French Gothic of satisfying proportions. The interior shows good use of iron work and glass.

42c Whitby: St Mary. Massive church that stands on hill above town. The tower and south doorway are mid-12th century. Good interior remodelled in the 18th century; the chancel is unspoiled 12th century.

42c Whitby Abbey. Considerable remains of fine church dating from 13th century. Damaged by shellfire in the 1914-18 War. *Daily from 0930 (winter Sundays from 1400).*

43g Hall - Hackness: St Peter. Mainly 15th century church with tower and spire of about 1200. Notable tower arch; Saxon cross; early 16th century font cover; 15th century stalls; unusual candlesticks.

43h Scarborough: St Martin, Albion Road. Mid-19th century church in French style and of good proportions inside and out. Notable work by Pre-Raphaelites; superb organ case.

St Mary, Castle Road. Under the lee of the castle, the church suffered much during the Civil War. Most interesting remains are the 12th/13th century arcades, piers, wall shafts in the nave and the clerestory. Also notable is the 19th century glass. Anne Brontë is buried here.

44c Dearham: St Mungo. Norman church with 12th and 13th century additions. Collection of fragments of Anglo-Danish sculpture.

44c Brigham: St Bridget. Late Norman church rebuilt in early 15th century. Interesting saddle-backed roof added in 19th century.

44g Whitehaven: St James, Queen Street. Mid-18th century church with the finest Georgian interior in the county. Altarpiece by pupil of Correggio; 18th century pulpit.

44g St Bees. See 32a.

45a Iselgate: St Michael. Largely Norman church with embattled pele tower in river setting. Of interest are a 15th century window with three sundials to mark monastic hours; pre-Norman stones; Saxon cross.

46b Greystoke: St Andrew. Mostly late Perpendicular, the church has a Transitional chancel arch and was made collegiate in 1382. Twenty canon stalls with interesting misericords; 15th century glass.

46c Penrith: St Andrew. Stately early 18th century Classical church which retains Norman tower of red sandstone. Interesting Tuscan-columned doorway dates from 1720. Saxon crosses in churchyard.

46c Eamont Bridge: St Wilfred. Ancient chapel restored in 1658 and in 19th century. Inside there is cathedral opulence; it is full of carved oak: elaborate organ casing, tall pews, grand screen. The reredos is gilt oak and includes a magnificent 15th century altarpiece. Well worth a visit.

47a Edenhall: St Cuthbert. Small, mediaeval, red sandstone church with squat Perpendicular tower, surmounted by stunted spire. 14th century glass inside as well as 17th and 18th century memorials. Beautiful setting.

47a Ch.: St Ninian. Mid-17th century church built on site of Saxon and Norman churches. The interior is all original; the setting of the church by River Eamont is beautiful.

47e Bolton: All Saints. Small church with much Norman work, especially the fine relief over the north door. Unusual chancel screen of late 18th century with open tracery.

47f Appleby: St Lawrence. Large, mainly Early English and Perpendicular church with splendid gargoyles and battlements. Beautiful setting between Norman castle and the river. Contains the oldest working organ in England.

47g Shap Abbey. Tel. Shap (093 16) 670. Small abbey of the Premonstratensian order founded in 1201. The cloister buildings are laid out in detail but the abbot's house is still in use as a farm. *Daily from 0930 (Sundays from 1400). Free.* &

47g Keld Chapel. Small, pre-Reformation building in which occasional services are held. *For access see notice on chapel door.*

47h Crosby Ravensworth: St Lawrence. Originally a 12th century church in Early English style. Set in lovely valley.

47i Great Ormside: St James. Church with strong fortified tower, Norman nave arcade and chancel arch with scalloped capitals. Also: some fine Perpendicular roofs; complete 17th century furnishings.

48g Crosby Garrett. See 35c.

49d Romaldkirk: St Romald. Church with 13th century transept, 14th century chancel and transept, and 15th century tower. Interesting wall painting fragments and plaster roof.

49f Staindrop: St Mary. Small church of Anglo-Saxon origin in pretty setting. West tower, aisles and arcades are Norman; south aisle and porch were added in 14th century. Contains the only pre-Reformation screen in the county.

49g Bowes: St Giles. 14th to 15th century church with Norman doorways; 12th/13th century fonts; some Roman inscriptions on church wall.

49h Egglestone Abbey. Remains of abbey founded in 1189 for Premonstratensian canons. Picturesque setting on bank of River Tees. *Daily from 0930 (winter Sundays from 1400). Free.*

50b Escomb. Bare and simple church virtually unaltered since Saxon times, except for the insertion of windows. Curious sundial above porch; inscribed stone from Roman fort at Binchester in north wall.

50d Staindrop. See 49f.

50i Haughton le Skerne: St Andrew. Mediaeval church with some Norman work. Beautifully furnished in post-Reformation manner with Cosin woodwork. Some interesting carved stones.

50i Darlington: St Cuthbert. Beautiful Early English church between Market Place and River Skerne. Some mediaeval stalls with good misericords, plus a superb Cosin font cover.

50i Croft-on-Tees. See 39a.

51a Sedgefield: St Edmund. Mediaeval church with fine tower; interior contains good Cosin woodwork; epitaph on tablet in chancel is dated 1708, as are the organ case and font.

51e Billingham: St Cuthbert. Ancient church that combines Saxon work - tower and nave - with 20th century Perpendicular.

51h Stockton-on-Tees: St Thomas. Spacious Classical church built in early 18th century. Imposing pulpit; 18th century altar with reredos from wood of Captain Cook's *Resolution*.

51h Egglescliffe: St John the Baptist. Mainly Perpendicular church in fine setting above the Tees. Woodwork in style of Cosin. Chained books include *Eikon Basilike*.

52e Kirkleatham: St Cuthbert. Mid-18th century church with mediaeval core. Two rows of Tuscan columns carry the nave roof; wealth of original furniture and 14th century chest. Extraordinary Baroque octagonal mausoleum of the Turner family on north side of the chancel.

Sir William Turner's Hospital. Splendid chapel with fine fittings and glass. *Daily.* ⏍

52i Guisborough Priory. Ruins of a 12th century Augustinian priory, which include a gatehouse, dovecote and the east end of 14th century church. *Daily from 0930 (Sundays from 1400). Free.*

54f Abbeytown: St Mary. Base of church is 12th century nave of Holm Cultram Abbey. Rich Norman west portal; 16th century porch.

54g Crosscanonby: St John the Evangelist. Norman church built with Roman stones. Interesting pre-Norman hogback gravestone carved like house of the dead. Good pew carving.

54g Dearham. See 44c.

54i Plumbland: St Cuthbert. Norman church rebuilt in 1870 but retaining 12th century door and chancel arch, 13th century piscina and vestry door. Hogback stone in churchyard.

54i Torpenhow: St Michael. Much restored Norman church with superb views. Preserved Norman door, arches and chancel arch. Late 17th century decorated nave ceiling.

55c Carlisle Cathedral. Begun in 1123 as a Norman church, it is the second smallest cathedral in England. It boasts one of the finest stained glass windows - the east - in the country. Other features include carved choir stalls with good misericords, and a painted barrel-vault ceiling. ⏍

55h Caldbeck: St Kentigern. Large, mostly early 16th century church which was well restored. Gravestone of John Peel.

56a Carlisle. See 55c.

56b Warwick: St Leonard. Fine Norman village church with superb 12th century apse and tower arch.

56e Armathwaite: Chapel of Christ and St Mary. Originally a 12th century chapel which fell into ruin and was rebuilt in 1688. Built in plain stone, it has a chancel, nave and small western turret with one bell.

56i Kirkoswald: St Oswald. Church through which a spring flows, issuing into a drinking well outside the west wall. The late 19th century tower stands at top of hill 200 yds away from the church.

59d Blanchland Abbey. 13th century church incorporates remains of the old abbey church built in 12th century by Premonstratensians. The Lord Crewe Inn also has remnants of the old abbey, including abbot's lodging, the guest house and the abbey kitchen.

59f Lanchester: All Saints. Mainly Norman and Early English church. Interesting features include a Roman altar in the porch, superb Norman chancel arch, and 13th century glass. m

60a Gibside Chapel. The mausoleum of the Bowes family, built in Classical style in 1760; an outstanding example of Georgian church architecture. *April to September, Wednesday to Monday; March and October, Wednesdays and weekends; from 1400.*

60d Lanchester. See 59f.

60f Chester-le-Street: St Mary and St Cuthbert. Early mediaeval church with curious tower combining octagonal storey with a fine spire. Contains an Anchorite's cell and effigies of the Lumley family.

60f Finchale Priory. In picturesque position on banks of River Wear are the considerable remains of the 13th century church of a Benedictine priory. *Daily from 0930 (Sundays from 1400).*

60f Pittington: St Lawrence. Originally an Anglo-Saxon church, it has a fine 12th century arcade, composed of six round arches with bold zig-zag carving. Norman font.

60h Brancepeth: St Brandon. Gothic church of various dates is memorable for a complete set of 17th century woodwork, partly of 1638 and partly post Restoration, donated by Bishop Cosin, who was rector here.

60i Durham: Cathedral. One of the finest Romanesque buildings in existence, the cathedral stands on a loop of the River Wear. Started in 1093 and consecrated in 1133, the cathedral incorporated, for the first time, the three classic elements of Gothic architecture: rib vaulting, pointed arches and flying buttresses. This is best seen in the lofty nave, with its great round piers and high vault. Other notable features: a superb 12th century bronze sanctuary knocker; the Galilee Chapel containing the tomb of the great Saxon historian Bede; the reredos, known as the Neville Screen, dated 1380; the 13th century Chapel of Nine Altars; the tomb of St Cuthbert, with his coffin, maniple and cross; a collection of gravestones (from Saxon times onwards); superb manuscripts and early crosses. Treasury Museum has displays of cathedral silver plate and other valuables. Superb views from the belfry. Not to be missed. 🍵

St Mary-le-Bow, North Bailey. At the eastern end of the cathedral; church was rebuilt in 1685. Contains important Cosin woodwork, especially rood screen.

Durham Castle. Tiny Norman chapel whose crypt has six carved pillars which provide some of the most interesting Norman sculpture in existence. For details of the castle see 🏰 and 🏛

St Giles, Gilesgate. 12th-to-13th century church in commanding position. Some Norman work; Elizabethan wooden effigy.

61a Sunderland: Holy Trinity. Built in 1719, the church has a pleasant red brick and stone exterior with a good tower. Font has richly ornamented cover.

61a Monkwearmouth: St Peter. Church of Saxon monastery founded in 674 AD by Benedict Biscop. Much altered between 7th and 11th centuries. Contains fine collection of Saxon carved stones.

61e Seaham: St Mary the Virgin. Saxon or early Norman church in gaunt setting near the sea. Roman stones are in the walls; double piscina with curious design; pleasant glass by Kempe.

63d Bewcastle: St Cuthbert. Originally 13th century church with Georgian tower. In the churchyard is one of Britain's finest Anglo-Saxon relics: Bewcastle Cross, a patterned 7th century cross.

63g Lanercost Priory. A tranquil ruin tucked into a secluded corner by the River Irthing. The priory was founded in 1144 by Robert de Vaux for the Augustinian ·canons. The church is exceptionally well preserved, the nave and north aisle being restored in the 19th century and now serving as the parish church. Behind the church are many interesting monuments and tombs. *Daily from 0930 (Sundays from 1400).*

63g Brampton: St Martin. Imaginative church built in the late 19th century by Webb. Woodwork by local craftsmen; glass by William Morris and Edward Burne-Jones.

63h Upper Denton. Small church built by Saxons with stone from Roman wall. Original Roman arch in chancel, one of only two in any English church.

63i Haltwhistle: Church of the Holy Cross. Mainly 13th century church with an interior containing a stepped sedilia and mediaeval monuments, including an effigy of 1389.

64g Haltwhistle. See 63i.

65b Kirkwhelpington: St Bartholomew. Church with good 12th and 13th century work in the tower and porch. Good 18th century chancel with plastered walls and ceiling.

65h Hexham Abbey: Priory Church of St Andrew. Of the first church built in 673, the crypt remains intact. The rest of the church is of the 12th and 13th centuries. The interior has many mediaeval features: Saxon Frith stool, unique monk's night staircase, a 15th century wooden pulpit, some 15th century stalls and misericords, and many effigies.

65h Corbridge: St Andrew. The most important Saxon church in the county. Part of the tower

Durham Cathedral (60i)

dates from 786 AD· or earlier; the Roman arch in the tower is probably from Corstopitum. Good lancet windows.

66b Hartburn: St Andrew. Delightful 13th century church with some later rebuilding. 13th century font and many good 18th century headstones in the churchyard.

66b Bolam: St Andrew. Church with late Saxon tower and mainly Norman interior in parkland setting. Recumbent effigy of a 14th century knight.

66f Ponteland: St Mary the Virgin. Church with 12th century tower and 13th century transept of great character. Beautiful undecorated font of 14th century and some contemporary heraldic glass.

66h Heddon-on-the-Wall: St Andrew. Saxon and Norman church with a 12th century vaulted sanctuary and fine zig-zag chancel arch.

66h Ovingham: St Mary the Virgin. Church with Saxon tower and magnificent 13th century nave, chancel and transepts. Fine heraldic monument in black marble and a memorial to Thomas Bewick.

66i Walbottle - Newburn: St Michael and All Angels. Fine church of rubble stonework, with Norman tower and 13th century aisles.

67e Seaton Delaval: Our Lady. Small Norman church of great beauty set in grounds of Vanbrugh's house. Outstanding mediaeval stone shields and 14th century effigies inside.

67f Tynemouth Priory. Ruined abbey with some fine upstanding remains, dating from the 11th to 13th centuries. *Daily from 0930 (winter Sundays from 1400).* 🏰

67g Newcastle: Cathedral of St Nicholas. Dating mainly from the 14th and 15th centuries, this former parish church achieved cathedral status in 1882. Most notable feature is the 194ft crown spire surmounted by an open lantern on flying buttresses. Inside are a 14th century nave and choir.

St Andrew, Newgate Street. Church with 12th century chancel arch and nave arcading. Also a 15th century unpainted font cover of elaborate design; an early Georgian porch; and Royal Arms of George III.

Blackfriars, between Stowell Street and Low Friar Street. Restored 13th century Dominican priory, one of the most complete in England. After the dissolution of the monasteries, the buildings were used by city's craft guilds; now a tourist and crafts centre. *April to September: Tuesday to Friday and bank holiday Mondays 1000-1800; weekends 1000-1630. October to*

March: Tuesday to Saturday 1000-1300, 1400-1630. 🍵 🖼 🍴 🚻

St John the Baptist, Westgate Road. Mediaeval church with 17th century font cover and an impressive 17th century pulpit.

67h Jarrow: St Paul. Church founded in 681 AD in which the Venerable Bede worshipped, it contains the only Saxon window with Saxon stained glass in the world, plus Bede's chair and late mediaeval choir stalls. Also at this site are the extensive remains of both Saxon and Norman monasteries. At nearby Jarrow Hall is a display of Saxon life. *Tuesdays to Saturdays and bank holiday Mondays 1000-1730, Sundays 1430-1730.* 🍵

71d Elsdon: St Cuthbert. Church built of rubble stonework dating from the 12th and 14th centuries. Fine Renaissance tablet in the nave and good plain glazing.

71f Rothbury: All Saints. Mediaeval church with 13th century transepts and chancel. Fine font with mid-17th century bowl, supported by part of an Anglo Saxon cross shaft.

71f Brinkburn Priory. Augustinian foundation of 1135 in lovely river setting. The church still survives in its entirety, having been restored in 1858. The lancet windows contain fragments of 13th century glass. *Daily from 0930 (winter Sundays from 1400).*

71h Kirkwhelpington. See 65b.

72e Rothbury. See 71f.

72f Brinkburn Priory. See 71f.

72g Kirkwhelpington. See 65b.

72h Hartburn. See 66b.

73b Warkworth: St Lawrence. Church with Norman chancel arch and 12th century vaulted chancel. Also: 15th century porch with room above; fine 17th century wrought-iron rails; some fragments of 15th century glass.

73b Hermitage: Warkworth Hermitage. 14th century hermitage and chapel cut in solid rock. Access by rowing boat from castle. *April to September: daily from 0930 (Sundays from 1400).* 🏰

73h Bothal: St Andrew. 13th and 14th century church in beautiful setting. Contains many fragments of mediaeval glass, 17th century altar rails and a 16th century alabaster table tomb.

75a Kirknewton: St Gregory. Ancient church with unusually low chancel and vaulting. Fine stone carving on chancel arch.

77g Alnwick: St Michael and All Angels. One of the most important 15th century churches in Northumberland. Some fine 14th century effigies and fragments of 15th century glass. Royal Arms of 1st Hanoverian period.

78e Norham: St Cuthbert. Church of reddish stone with Norman chancel and chancel arch, 14th century effigy and Stuart Royal Arms.

79c Farne Island: Inner Farne Chapel. Sole memorial of religious activity on the Farnes is this 14th century chapel. ♣ 🚶

79d Ancroft: St Anne. Norman church raised by Holy Island monks, with 14th century fortified tower built into the west end.

79e Holy Island: St Mary the Virgin. Late 13th century church of Early English style, with long chancel and 18th century bellcote.

Lindisfarne Priory. Ruins of a monastery dating from 1090. It was the centre of Christianity in the north: the first monastery was started by St Aidan in 635 AD. Collection of Anglian and Viking stones and mediaeval pottery. *Daily from 0930 (winter Sundays from 1400).* ❀ 🏰 🏛 🍴 🚻

79i Bamburgh: St Aidan. Church is a mixture of styles from 13th to 15th centuries. Fine 13th century crypt under the chancel. Grace Darling is buried here.

Bird Watching

These pages list the most popular bird watching sites and those of ornithological significance. Birds confined to aviaries or otherwise in captivity are included in the section on Wildlife in Captivity on page 108.

18b Knaresborough Ringing Station. Several thousand interesting birds ringed each year, including a variety of warblers in the autumn.

20b Duddon Sands. An area of inter-tidal sands with numerous waders on passage in the spring. Some wildfowl, mainly pintail and greylag geese. Marks at Green Road, Millom Marsh, Angerton Marsh and Dunnerholme.

20c Duddon Sands. See 20b.

20i Barrow-in-Furness Docks. Excellent place for storm-driven seabirds and duck in hard weather.

20i Rampside Sands. Haunt of waders, grebes, divers and wildfowl.

20i Foulney Island. Nature reserve with breeding grounds for birds like common terns. Waders and wildfowl can also be seen in appreciable numbers on passage. *Access by permit only* from Cumbria Trust for Nature Conservation, tel. Ambleside (096 63) 2476.

20i South End: Walney Island. Tel. Barrow (0229) 41066. Nature reserve with the largest colony in Europe of lesser black backed and herring gulls; the southernmost British breeding station of eider duck. In the south there is one of the largest wader roosts in Lancashire. *Access by permit only* from Cumbria Trust for Nature Conservation, tel. Ambleside (096 63) 2476.

21a Barker Scar: Leven Estuary. Waders are present at all seasons, but are most numerous in autumn.

21c Low Meathop: Meathop Marsh and Estuary. Good for waders including rarities. Black tern are regular in autumn and wildfowl are also numerous.

21c Arnside: The Promenade. Greylag geese can be seen on the estuary in winter as well as many waders throughout spring, autumn and winter.

21c Sandside: The Promenade. Similar bird watching station to Arnside (above); mainly waders.

21d Bardsea: Leven Estuary. Waders are most numerous in autumn as well as wigeon, pintail and other wildfowl in winter.

21d Bardsea Country Park. Includes an area of tidal sands on which can be seen waders and sea duck. ♣ ⅏

21e Grange-over-Sands: Castle Head Field Centre. Tel. (044 84) 4300. Bird watching holidays organised around Morecambe Bay and south Lakeland. Minimum age 5 years. *October to February.*

21f Silverdale Green: Leighton Moss Nature Reserve. Tel. (0524) 701413. Owned by the RSPB, there is a reception centre with displays and 5 bird watching hides. Among the attractions are bittern, reed warbler, and large numbers of wildfowl and waders. *April to September: Wednesdays, Thursdays, weekends and bank holidays 1000-1700. January to March and October to December: weekends and Wednesdays only 1000-dusk.* ♿

21f Keer Channel. An extensive area of saltings, attracting large numbers of shelduck in late summer as well as many waders and wildfowl.

21h Half Moon Bay: Morecambe Bay. A huge area of inter-tidal sand, one of the most

Royal Society for the Protection of Birds

The RSPB is a charity, supported by over 300,000 members, whose objective is the protection and conservation of wild birds and their habitats. One of the main ways in which it achieves this is the aquisition of land for nature reserves. Visitors are welcome at the sites listed in the entries on these pages, but are asked to observe the following rules:

- Members are admitted free to all reserves. Charges to non-members are made on arrival but are refunded to anyone enrolling as a member during the visit.
- Parties of 10 or more people must book in advance - at least one month.
- No dogs are allowed, other than on public footpaths.
- Visitors must keep to the marked paths and trails.
- Photography is only allowed from the paths or hides.

For details of membership apply to the RSPB, The Lodge, Sandy, Beds SG19 2DL, tel. (0767) 80551.

Nature Reserves

Nature reserves, and the nature trails which run through them, exist for several reasons: the area may be of scientific or educational interest; or a particular kind of habitat or species of wildlife needs to be preserved. The reserves are controlled by such organisations as the RSPB, the Nature Conservancy Council or a County Naturalists Trust, but these bodies often do not own the land, so that access is frequently limited. It is, therefore, vital when visiting a nature reserve to keep to the marked path or trail and to observe the Country Code (see page 80). For details of any particular reserve contact the organisation concerned or the nearest ℤ (see page 122).

important wader sites in western Europe. Oystercatcher, knot, bar-tailed godwit, sawbills and sea duck in good numbers in winter.

21i Morecambe: Morecambe Bay. See 21h (above).

21i Hest Bank: Morecambe Bay. See 21h.

22a Arnside. See 21c.

22a Sandside. See 21c.

22d Silverdale Green. See 21f.

22d Keer Channel. See 21f.

22g Hest Bank. See 21h Morecambe Bay.

23b Dentdale: Whernside Cave and Fell Centre. Tel. Dent (085 75) 213. Bird watching courses arranged for junior members of RSPB. Excursions to Leighton Moss and Morecambe Bay. *May to July.* ▲

23e Ingleborough. The open moorland around this summit and Pen-y-ghent (23f) attracts birds like dipper, redshank, golden plover, curlew, wheatear, raven and buzzard; most birds common to moors can also be sighted. ▲

23f Pen-y-ghent. See Ingleborough (23e). ▲

24d Pen-y-ghent. See Ingleborough (23e).

24h Malham Tarn Field Centre. Tel. Airton (072 93) 331. Bird study courses arranged in summer

and autumn. Bird watching is done in the Yorkshire Dales where the common moorland birds, as well as raptors like the merlin and the peregrine, can be seen. ♣

25e Gouthwaite Reservoir. A beautiful setting, good for watching wildfowl in winter, especially whooper swan. Dipper, grey wagtail and Canada goose are present in summer.

27c Helmsley: Freedom of Ryedale Holidays, 23a Market Place. Tel. (0439) 70775. Bird watching holidays arranged. ♣ ☽

28a Helmsley. See 27c.

30c Filey Brigg. Excellent for watching seabirds in autumn, this mile-long reef is also notable (at low tide) for waders. In winter sea duck and grebes can be seen offshore.

31d Bempton Cliffs. Notable as the only mainland breeding site of the gannet in Britain. Also seen in profusion are kittiwakes, guillemot, razorbill, puffin and rock doves.

31e Flamborough Head. Good for large numbers of breeding kittiwake in summer, the Head is also a good vantage point for observing a wide variety of seabirds in spring and autumn.

31g North Sands: Bridlington to Sewerby. Good numbers of waders, especially in Bridlington Bay, including dunlin and sanderling. Little gulls are also noted most winters.

32e Ravenglass: Drigg Dunes Nature Reserve. Best known for the largest British breeding colony of black-headed gulls as well as numerous waders and four species of tern. *Access by permit only,* from Cumberland County Council, The Courts, Carlisle.

35g Killington Reservoir. Holds a small number of wildfowl, some of which breed on the islands. Outstanding flock of goosander. ⚠ 🐟

35i Dentdale. See 23b.

36g Dentdale. See 23b.

41g Helmsley. See 27c.

41i Sutherland Lodge Activity Centre. Tel. Cropton (075 15) 228. Multi-activities include bird watching holidays. ♣ ▲ ☽

42c Whitby: Northern Field and Activity Centre. Larpool Hall. Tel. (0947) 4073. Holiday courses arranged in ornithology. ♣

42g Sutherland Lodge. See 41i.

42h Low Staindale: Staindale Lake. A small conservation lake frequented by waterfowl.

44b Mine: Siddick Pond. Although the pond suffers great disturbance, especially during the breeding season, it still holds a variety of species: duck; waders on passage; sedge warbler and corn bunting in the reedbeds.

44g St Bees Head. The high cliffs are one of England's most notable seabird breeding stations, with guillemot, razorbill, puffin, kittiwake and fulmar.

51b Hurworth Burn Reservoir. Small population of the commoner duck species. Also usually a passage of waders, terns and little gulls in autumn.

51c Middleton Lighthouse. Good for watching seabirds, especially grebes, gulls and auks.

51c Hartlepool Docks. In rough weather seabirds take shelter here. Notable are scoter and a variety of other sea ducks, divers and auks.

51c Seaton Carew. A good spot to watch sea ducks in winter, along with waders, gulls, auks, grebes and divers. In autumn shearwaters and skua pass offshore.

51f Cowpen Marsh. RSPB bird reserve with a particularly rich wetland habitat. Large numbers of waders and duck are seen here in spring and summer. For access contact Mr N. Sills, 315 Wolviston Back Lane, Billingham, Teesside.

51f Seal Sands. Public hide at Long Drag for watching the numerous wildfowl on the sands.

52a Middleton. See 51c.

52a Hartlepool Docks. See 51c.

52a Seaton Carew. See 51c.

52b North Gare Breakwater. Good for watching seabirds, especially in winter and autumn.

52d Seal Sands. See 51f.

52d Cowpen Marsh. See 51f.

52e South Gare Breakwater. Good for watching seabirds offshore, including skua, sea duck, divers and gannets. 🐟

54b Grune Point: Moricambe Bay. An excellent migration centre which gathers numbers of interesting passerines as well as seabirds offshore.

54c Anthorn: Moricambe Bay. Large expanses of salting attract numerous waders in winter and on passage. Wigeon, sea duck and geese are also present in winter.

60c Washington Wildfowl Refuge, Middle Barmston Farm. Tel. (0632) 465454. The attractive landscaped park contains a comprehensive display of wildfowl from every continent. Comfortable hides are situated around the reedbeds and ponds in the park, where many ducks and waders find refuge, particularly in winter and on passage. *Daily 0930-1730 (or dusk if earlier).* 🐷 🏠 🐃

61h Hurworth Burn Reservoir. See 51b.

61i Middleton. See 51c.

62g Rockcliffe Marsh. Large area of salting backed by water meadows on which geese are numerous in winter, particularly pink-footed and barnacle geese. Also numerous duck and waders.

64i Grindon Lough. Upland water which holds whooper swan, goosander and goldeneye in winter, bean goose, duck and curlew in spring and the black-headed gull in summer. *Lough is private: view only from the road.*

65i Welton Hall: Whittle Dene Reservoirs. These series of small lakes are attractive to many species of wildfowl, especially tufted duck, goosander, pochard and smew. 🐟

66g Welton Hall. See 65i.

67d Gosforth Lake. One of the best inland waters for duck in the county; preserved as a sanctuary. *Access by permit only* from the Northumberland and Durham Natural History Society, Hancock Museum, Barras Bridge, Newcastle-upon-Tyne NE2 4PT. Tel. Newcastle (0632) 326386.

67e Holywell Ponds. Haunt of a variety of wildfowl, including many duck and whooper swans. Passage waders are also common. *View from public footpaths.*

67e Seaton Sluice. An area of rocky coastline with extensive dunes attracting large numbers of sea duck and commoner waders in winter.

67e St Mary's Island. Large flocks of waders are present in winter when sea duck, divers and auks are frequently noted. During passage periods, especially autumn, there is excellent sea watching.

67e Rising Sun Farm: Swallow Ponds. Formed by mining subsidence, the ponds attract wild swans in winter and a variety of waders on passage. *Ponds*

Common species in flight

A few of the more frequently seen species are shown below, all drawn to scale. Colour pictures of birds commonly seen on freshwater lakes and along the sea shore can be found in the introductory section of this book, on pages 12 and 13.

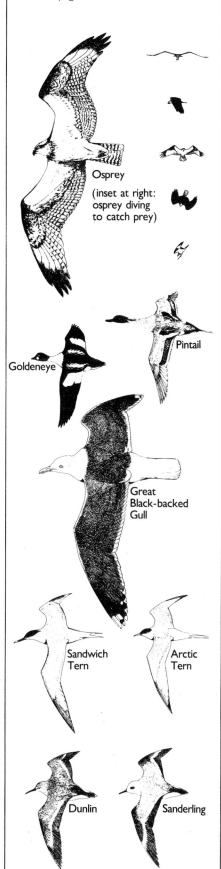

Osprey
(inset at right: osprey diving to catch prey)

Goldeneye

Pintail

Great Black-backed Gull

Sandwich Tern

Arctic Tern

Dunlin

Sanderling

private: view only from footpath.

67i Marsden Rocks. Cliff footpath leads to good sea watching area, especially interesting in winter and autumn. In summer Marsden Rock, a high offshore stack, is a breeding ground for fulmars, cormorants, shags and kittiwakes.

73b Low Hauxley. Numerous waders on passage can be seen on the shore in autumn whilst the area is excellent for sea watching, especially July to October.

73e Blakemoor Farm: Cresswell Ponds. The proximity of the ponds to the sea makes them attractive to a large variety of waders and other migrants. The foreshore is frequented by waders and sea duck whilst the small mixed woodland to the south west is the haunt of the commoner chats, flycatchers and warblers. 🌳

76i Glanton: World Bird Research Station. Tel. Powburn (066 578) 257. Wild bird sanctuary which looks after injured birds of any species except seabirds. Also exhibitions of work and expeditions around the research station. *End May to mid-September, daily 1400-1700.* ❀

77b Seahouses. The sandy foreshore north to Bamburgh (79i) is very good in winter for Slavonian and red-necked grebes, divers and sea duck. In autumn a variety of waders are seen on passage; Arctic and great skuas are common in summer.

77e Low Newton-by-the-Sea: Newton Pool. Haunt of both wildfowl and waders; good numbers of sea duck in winter. *View from footpath on seaward side of pool.*

77f Castle Point. Especially good sea watching in autumn when skuas, terns and gannets are noted. In summer the cliffs are the haunt of breeding seabirds and a colony of cliff-breeding house martins. 🏚

77f Cullernose Point. Cliffs north to Castle Point are good for sea watching. See previous entry.

79a Berwick-upon-Tweed: Tweed Estuary. Good area for watching seabirds in winter. The sandy beach just north of pier is good for waders.

79c Farne Islands. A group of small islands which in summer become the breeding ground for 20 different species of seabird, including puffin, kittiwake, eider duck, guillemot, fulmar and tern. Access to Inner Farne and Staple Island by permit only. All information on tickets and sailings from 🅸 or Seahouses (0665) 720651. *April to end September; restricted access during breeding season from mid-May to mid-July.* 🌳

79e Lindisfarne National Nature Reserve. This magnificent coastal reserve includes Holy Island, and much of the adjacent sands. The whole area is noted for migrants in season, greylag and pink-footed geese, sea duck, grebes and divers. See following entries for best viewpoints.

79e Beal. See Lindisfarne Nature Reserve (79e).

79e Fenham. See Lindisfarne Nature Reserve (79e).

79e The Links. See Lindisfarne Nature Reserve (79e).

79e Lindisfarne. See Lindisfarne Nature Reserve (79e).

79h Elwick. See Lindisfarne Nature Reserve (79e).

79i Ross Links. See Lindisfarne Nature Reserve (79e).

79i Heather Cottages. See Lindisfarne Nature Reserve (79e).

79i Bamburgh. The foreshore south to Seahouses (77b) is good for grebes, divers and sea duck in winter. A variety of waders can be seen in autumn on passage, whilst Arctic and great skuas are a common sight in summer.

Industry Past and Present

From industrial archaeology to the latest nuclear power stations, including open-air museums, craft workshops, modern factories and collieries. Preserved railways offering rides to the public are, however, detailed in the section on Tourist Railways (page 107).

18e Crimple Viaduct. Built in 1847 by the York & Midland Railway Company to carry the Leeds to Thirsk line ½ mile over Crimple Beck.

19f York: National Railway Museum. Leeman Road, tel. (0904) 21261. This magnificent modern museum, only a short walk from the BR mainline station, is the official home of over 50 standard and narrow gauge preserved locomotives, ranging from the replica of Stephenson's *Rocket* built for the Rainhill 150 celebrations in 1980, through the fastest steam loco in the world, the 126 mph *Mallard*, to the gas turbine prototype of the tilting Advanced Passenger Train. There are dozens of steam locomotives, including a fascinating Merchant Navy class 4-6-2 which has been sectioned and - with the help of a podium full of buttons - lights up to show its inner workings; also diesel and electric locos and a huge collection of rolling stock, including many royal coaches. Despite its massive size - over 2 acres - the main museum building can display only a fraction of the available exhibits, and these are therefore changed at frequent intervals. The building is also connected to the British Rail tracks outside and many of the standard gauge steam locos are maintained in working order, being used to haul BR steam specials or loaned to preservation societies. As if all that were not enough, the museum also contains one of the largest collections anywhere of railway equipment and material, plus many working models; film shows, reference library and educational facilities. *Daily 1000-1800 (Sundays from 1430). Free.* 🍽

Derwent Valley Railway. Layerthorpe Station, tel. 58981. Unique standard gauge line which escaped nationalisation in 1948 and has since been operated independently. Although passenger services were run until 1979, the line was finally closed in 1981.

20b Hallthwaites: Country Matters, Old Bull Pen, tel. Millom (0657) 2068. Traditional herbal produce. *Thursday to Tuesday 1030-1900.*

20b Millom Folk Museum, St George's Road, tel. (0657) 2555. Full scale model of an iron ore drift; also replica miner's cottage kitchen, blacksmith's forge and many agricultural relics. *Easter week, then May to mid September: Sunday/Monday 1300-1700, Tuesday to Saturday 1000-1700.*

20b Hodbarrow. Desolate remains of a 19th century iron ore mine which once produced over 340,000 tons per year. Part of the workings have now been modelled in the Millom Folk Museum (see previous entry).

20e Barrow-in-Furness: Docks. Massive yards used by Vickers Limited to build ships, mainly for the Royal Navy and other navies. The Vickers-Armstrong collection of ships' models can be seen in the Furness Museum (see 🖼 for details).

Town Centre Trail, starting from the railway station. Passes many examples of Victorian architecture. Details from 🗎 ; 1¾ miles.

21a Ulverston: Wendy Todd Textiles, Corn Mill Galleries, Old Town Mill, tel. (0229) 54600. Screen printing of clothing and furnishings in what was once a 17th century corn mill; also a small museum. *Tuesday to Saturday 0930-1730.* 🍽

Cumbria Crystal, Lightburn Road, tel. 54400. Glassblowing, cutting and engraving of lead-crystal wineglasses, decanters, etc., mostly to 17th and 18th century designs. *Weekdays 0900-1600; also occasional Saturdays (AM only).* ♿

Studio Galleries, 5 Theatre Street, tel. 56141. Stained and engraved glass. No animals. *Tuesday to Saturday 1000-1630.*

21f Silverdale: Wolf House Gallery, Gibraltar, tel. (0524) 701405. Pottery and woodworking displays; craft gallery. *Summer: Tuesday to Sunday, 1030-1730. Winter: weekends only, 1030-1730.* 🍽

21h Heysham Head: Nuclear Power Station. Tel. (0524) 53131. Twin stations, the first of which has been operational since late 1981. Visits to this station can be arranged for groups; both can be seen from a purpose built observation tower. *Tower open: April to end September, daily 1000-dusk. Free.*

21i Lancaster: Hornsea Pottery, Wyresdale Road, tel. (0524) 68444. Modern factory with high temperature kilns producing ceramic tableware. Factory tours; miniature golf; children's playground. 🍽 ♣ 🚐 🚗

22a Levens Hall Steam Collection. Tel. Sedgwick (0448) 60321. Fine range of working industrial and traction engines; also some steam powered vehicles, models and hot-air engines. *Easter Sunday to end September: Sundays, Tuesdays to Thursdays and bank holiday Mondays 1400-1700 (steam working on Sundays and bank holiday Mondays only).* ☕ ❀ 🏛

22d Silverdale. See 21f.

22d Carnforth: Steamtown Railway Museum, Warton Road, tel. (052 473) 4220 or 2625. Huge ex-British Rail engine shed now housing over 30 standard gauge preserved locomotives from mainline and industrial railways in Britain and Europe, including such famous steam locos as *Flying Scotsman, Sir Nigel Gresley* and the replica *Novelty;* also a wide range of rolling stock, from Pullman saloons and buffet cars to steam cranes and mineral wagons. The 37 acre site also contains all the paraphernalia of steam loco operations and fully equipped engineering workshops. Most locos are in working order and many are used on BR's own steam specials. Souvenir shop, collector's corner and model railway. *Daily 0900-1600 (1700 in summer).* 🍽 🚗 🚐

22g Lancaster. See 21i.

23d Low Bentham: Bentham Pottery, Oysterber Farm, tel. (0468) 61567. *Weekdays 0900-1700.*

24g High Trenhouse, Malham Moor, tel. Airton (072 93) 322. Multi-activity centre includes courses in dairywork, weaving and spinning, carpentry, farming, etc. ▲

25h Pateley Bridge: Nidderdale Museum, Council Offices, tel. Harrogate (0423) 711225. Old Victorian workhouse now displays many thousands of items depicting the history of the area, including farming and crafts. *Easter to Spring Bank Holiday, weekends; then daily until the end of September; then Sundays only until Easter; 1400-1700.* 🖼

26e North Stainley: Lightwater Valley. Tel. Ripon (0765) 85321. Major leisure complex includes a Craft Centre with free demonstrations of pottery, glass blowing and wood carving; also a working pig farm. *April/May weekends and bank holidays 1030-1730; June to end August daily 1030-1900; September weekends 1030-1600.* 🍽 🚐 🚗 ☆

27a Thirsk Station: Treske Ltd Furniture Workshop. Tel. (0845) 22770. Old premises housing modern factory where only Yorkshire ash is used. Both machine and hand work can be seen from specially-built 300 ft viewing gangway. *Daily 0900-1700. Free.*

27b Kilburn: Robert Thompson Craftsmen. Tel. Coxwold (034 76) 218. Wide range of furniture, mostly in oak, with famous mouse trademark, produced in modern workshop. *Weekdays 0800-1200, 1245-1645; Saturdays 1030-1200.*

27d Sessay: Albert Jeffray. Tel. Hutton Sessay (084 53) 323. Church and domestic carvings and furniture, including many small items, mostly made of English Oak. *Weekdays 0900-1700; weekends and bank holidays by appointment.*

29a Pickering: Beck Isle Museum of Rural Life, off Bridge Street, tel. (0751) 73707. Regency house with 17 rooms each devoted to a different aspect of life in the area, including domestic, medical, agricultural and printing items; also a range of village shops and craft workshops. *Easter to mid October: daily 1030-1230, 1400-1730 (later in August).* 🍽 🖼

29a Zoo: Flamingo Land. Tel. Kirby Misperton (065 386) 287. Working farm with milking parlour and chicken hatchery; also pottery workshop. Many other attractions on this 350 acre site (see other sections for details). 🍽 ♿ ❀ 🐘 🦜 🐾 ♫ ☆

32b Calder Hall: Windscale Nuclear Power Station. Tel. Seascale (094 02) 333 ext 220. The world's first commercial nuclear power station, opened in 1956. Now a major experimental site - the large sphere houses an Advanced Gas-Cooled Reactor - it is perhaps best known for its work on reprocessing used nuclear fuels. *By appointment only: weekdays at 1000 and 1330 for 2-hour tours.*

32e Ravenglass: Railway Museum. Tel. (065 77) 226. Models, photographs and other relics, plus two steam locomotives are housed in an old engine shed devoted to the history of 15 inch gauge railways, including the adjacent Ravenglass & Eskdale. Slide shows. *April to end October: daily by request. Other months: by appointment.* 🍽 🚐 🗎

32f Muncaster Castle: Watermill. The mill race carries water ¾ mile from the River Mite to a 13ft overshot wheel, which powers three pairs of millstones, two elevators, flour separators and a hoist. Flour milled here can be bought. Trout farm nearby sells fish. *Easter to end September: Sunday to Friday.* 🍽 ♣ ❀ 🏛 🐾

33c Grasmere: White Bridge Forge. Tel. (096 65) 414. Traditional blacksmith. *Weekdays 0800-1800; Saturdays 0800-1200.*

Chris Reekie & Sons, The Old Coach House, Stock Lane, tel. 221. Weaving. *Monday to Saturday 0900-1800; also summer Sundays from 1000.*

33c Skelwith Bridge: Kirkstone Galleries. Tel. Ambleside (096 63) 3296. Green slate building materials and hand-crafted gifts. *Workshops open weekdays 0800-1700.*

33e Coniston: Gondola. Restored steam yacht providing trips on the lake. (See ⛴ for details).

33f Hawkshead: Old Courthouse, ½ mile north of town centre; tel. Ambleside (096 63) 3003. Objects and photographs depict many aspects of domestic and working life, notably the swillmaking and weaving trades, since mediaeval times. *Easter weekend, then May to October: Tuesday to Sunday and bank holiday Mondays; 1400-1700.* 🏛

33g Hallthwaites. See 20b.

34a Grasmere. See 33c.

34a Skelwith Bridge. See 33c.

34d Hawkshead. See 33f.

34e Bowness-on-Windermere: **The Steamboat Museum**, Rayrigg Road, tel. (096 62) 5565. Unique collection of vessels kept under cover and in working order, including a 1780 sailing boat, steamboats dating from 1850 to 1911, 1922 and 1938 speedboats and an 1898 motor boat. Many other items show the development of navigation on the lake. *Easter to October: Monday to Saturday 1000-1700; Sundays 1400-1700.* 🍵 🏕

    Craftsmen of Cumbria, Falbarrow Road, tel. 2959. Pottery, leatherwork, jewellery and brass-rubbing are among the skills on show. *April to September: Thursday to Sunday (daily June to August) 0930-1730.* ♿

    Stonecraft Design, Longlands, tel. 3600. Stonework by master mason. *April to October: Thursday to Sunday (also daily June to August) 0930-1730.* ♿

34f Staveley: **Peter Hall Woodcraft**, Danes Road, tel. (0539) 821633. Traditional furniture and antique restoration. *Weekdays 0900-1800; Saturdays 0900-1300.* ♿

34i Kendal: **Museum of Lakeland Life and Industry**, Abbot Hall, tel. (0539) 22464. Objects and photographs depict local life and industry, including equipment used by farmers, blacksmiths, wheelwrights, miners, brewers, mechanics and weavers; old children's classroom and much else. *Weekdays 1030-1700; weekends 1400-1700.* 🍵 ♿ 📷 🏛

    Susan Foster, 9 Windermere Road, tel. 26494. Weaving, spinning and dying. *Wednesdays, Fridays and Saturdays (Monday to Saturday in July and August) 1000-1700.*

    Illingworth's Tobaccos, Aynam Mills, tel. 21898. Snuff factory established 1867 and now making 18 varieties of perfumed and medicated snuff. Visitors get a 1 hour tour covering the history of snuff, plus a free sample. *By arrangement only (call 2 weeks in advance). Free.*

34i Levens. See 22a.

34i Levens Hall. See 22a.

35h Sedbergh: **Pennine Tweeds**, Farfield Mill. Tel. (0587) 20558. Weaving factory. *Weekdays 0930-1200, 1330-1700; Saturdays AM.*

36b Winton: **Langrigg Pottery**. Tel. Kirkby Stephen (0930) 71542. *Tuesday to Saturday 0900-1700 (later in summer).*

36b Kirkby Stephen: **Dent Glass**, Crossfield Mill, tel. (0930) 71543. Sandblast engraving of tableware, windows, etc. *Weekdays 0900-1600.*

36i Hawes: **Outhwaite Ropemakers**, Town Foot. Tel. (096 97) 487. Ropes for agriculture, church bells, skipping, sailing, etc., are made by traditional methods, fascinating to watch. Children's playground opposite. *Weekdays 0900-1700; Saturdays 1000-1200. Free.*

37f Reeth: **Swaledale Folk Museum**, Reeth Green, tel. (074 884) 373 *(evenings)*. Illustrates many aspects of local life, including sheep and cattle farming and lead mining. 📷 📖

38c Middleton Tyas: **The Herb Centre**. Tel. Barton (032 577) 686. Fresh and dried herbs, plus products containing herbs. *Easter to end September: Saturday to Thursday 1400-1700.*

38d Reeth. See 37f.

41h Hutton-le-Hole: **Ryedale Folk Museum**. Tel. Lastingham (075 15) 367. Folk park covering 2½ acres, with agricultural and craft tools, unique mediaeval glass kiln, blacksmith's shop and large collection of farm waggons. Also much non-industrial material, including reconstructed buildings, etc. (see 📷 for details). *Easter to end October: daily 1100-1715.*

42b Grosmont Station. Locomotive shed of the North Yorks Moors Railway (see 🚂 for details). Houses the line's two dozen or so locos, most of them steam, plus a very extensive range of historic rolling stock. Inspection gallery for visitors. *Easter to end October: daily.* 🍵

44c Cockermouth: **Balnakeil Forge**, Lamplugh Corner, tel. (0900) 823169. Blacksmith's shop. *Weekdays 0800-1730; Saturdays 0800-1300.*

44e Branthwaite: **Ron Dickens**. Tel. Workington (0900) 3814. Wood carving. *By arrangement.*

44g Whitehaven: **Museum**, Market Place, tel. (0946) 3111 ext 289. Upper gallery includes displays on the town's industrial past, especially shipping and coal mining. *Monday to Saturday 1000-1700. Free.* 📷

    Workshop, 48 Roper Street. Pottery, batik and screen printed fabrics. *Monday to Saturday 1000-1730 (closed Wednesday PM).*

45f Keswick: **Cumberland Pencil Centre**, Southey Works, tel. (0596) 72116. The history of pencil making machines, factory shop and some drawings on display. *May to October: Monday to Saturday 0900-1630.*

    Lakeland Stonecraft, 13 High Hill, tel. 72994. Range of stonework. *Weekdays 0900-1630.*

46c Penrith: **Wetheriggs Country Pottery**, Clifton Dykes, tel. (0768) 62946. Working pottery, weaver and farrier; also a museum of clay processing and pottery making, plus steam powered machinery, children's play area, etc. *Daily 1000-1700.* 🍵 ♿ 🏕

47h Crosby Ravensworth: **Cumbria Stone Quarries**, Silver Street, tel. Ravensworth (093 15) 227. Stonework. *By appointment only.*

48g Winton. See 36b.

48h Dowgill Head: **Ian & Rhona Mathews**. Tel. Brough (093 04) 465. Jewellery, clocks and polished stonework. *Easter to late December: weekdays 1000-1800, but telephone first.*

50e Shildon: **Timothy Hackworth Museum**, Soho Street, tel. Spennymoor (0388) 816166 ext 290. The home of one of the unsung heroes of railway development, engineer to George Stephenson and first manager of the Stockton & Darlington Railway. The 16 rooms are now furnished as they would have been during his lifetime; adjacent engine shed houses full size replica of Hackworth's famous 1829 loco

Sanspareil, plus one of his surviving locos, the 1837 *Braddyll*; Rail Trail (leaflet from museum) takes in much of Shildon's industrial past. *April to end September: Wednesday to Sunday 1000-1800.* 🍵

50i Darlington: **Railway Museum**, North Road. Tel. (0325) 60532. The world's oldest station at which trains still stop, this was the terminus of the Stockton & Darlington Railway, and is now a halt on the Darlington Bank Top to Bishop Auckland line. The 1842 building has been magnificently restored to house seven historic steam locos, notably Stephenson's No 1 *Locomotion* of 1825, plus rolling stock, a large '00' scale model of the S & DR as it was in 1829, documents and other railwayana. *Easter to end September: Monday to Saturday 1000-1700, Sundays 1100-1600. October to Easter: Monday to Saturday 1000-1500.* 🍵

50i Works: **Broken Scar Waterworks**. Steam powered compound rotative beam engine built in 1904; also a 1913 gas engine. *By appointment only; contact the superintendent.*

51c Hartlepool **Maritime Museum**, Northgate, tel. (0429) 72814. Displays cover fishing, shipbuilding, marine engineering, etc.; restored fisherman's cottage, ship's bridge, gas lit lighthouse. *Monday to Saturday 1000-1700. Free.*

51h Preston **Hall Museum**. Tel. Eaglescliffe (0642) 781184. Includes a transport section with old cars, bicycles, commercial vehicles, motor bikes, horse drawn vehicles and an 1870 steam locomotive. *Monday to Saturday 1000-1800; Sundays 1400-1800. Free.* 🍵 📷

51i A174: **Newham Grange Leisure Farm**. Tel. Middlesbrough (0642) 245432. Complete working farm, plus buildings devoted to agricultural history: farmhouse kitchen, 19th century veterinary surgery, merchant's shop, etc. Visitors Centre gives history since 17th century; audio/visual room links farm to regional history. *Easter to end October: daily 0930-1730. November to Easter: Sundays only, 0930-dusk.* 🍵 🏕 🐄

51i Seamer. See 40b.

52a Hartlepool. See 51c.

52d Middlesbrough. See 51f.

52g A174. See 51i.

52g Seamer. See 40b.

55c Linstock: **Carlisle Pottery**. Tel. Carlisle (0228) 26833. *Weekdays 1000-1600.*

55c Carlisle: **Habbick & Campbell**, 2nd Floor, 54 Lowther Street. Jewellery, silversmith and knitwear. *Monday to Saturday 1030-1600.*

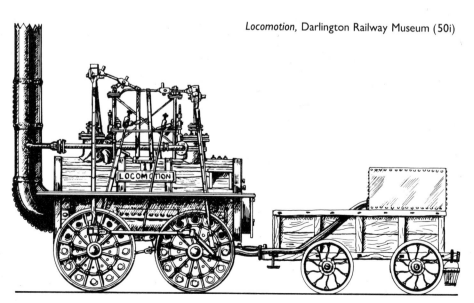

Locomotion, Darlington Railway Museum (50i)

55h Greenhead: **Anne Utting**, Greenrigg Cottage, Caldbeck Common, tel. Caldbeck (069 98) 679. Master weaver. *Daily (closed Friday AM.)*

56a Linstock. See 55c.

56a Carlisle. See 55c.

56b Wetheral Viaduct. One of Britain's first major railway viaducts, built during the 1830's; the 5 arches are almost 100ft high.

56c Hallbankgate: **Frank Mercer**, Eastern Cottage, tel. 309. Weaving. *Any time, but telephone first.*

57c Keenley: **Museum of Printing and Graphic Art.** Tel. Whitfield (049 85) 279. History and development since the 15th century; working antique machinery; demonstrations of all stages of printing. *By appointment only.*

57e Alston: **South Tynedale Railway Preservation Society,** The Railway Station, tel. (049 83) 696. Visitor centre with displays about the now defunct branch line to Haltwhistle (63i). *May to September: daily PM. Free.* 🔲.

Society members are building a 2ft gauge tourist railway along the old trackbed, planning to complete the first 1½ miles in 1982. This will later run to Slaggyford (57b).

58a Keenley. See 57c.

59e Consett: **Hownsgill Railway Viaduct,** south of town. Built of brick and stone in 1858 for the Stanhope & Tyne Railway. Now a public footpath. *Any time. Free.*

60b Tanfield Causey Arch. The world's oldest railway bridge, built in 1725 to carry what was then a horse hauled waggonway. Soon to carry trains again, when the Tanfield Railway is extended (see 🚋 Marley Hill).

60b Beamish: **North of England Open Air Museum.** Tel. Stanley (0207) 31811. Over 200 acres devoted to the social and industrial heritage of Northumbria, concentrating on the late Victorian era. The scale of the place is astonishing, including as it does a reconstructed colliery, with winding gear, fully furnished pit cottages and a processing plant; a complete village market square, with shops and houses from all over the North East rebuilt brick by brick; two railways and an electric tramway (see 🚋 for details); Home Farm with its Durham shorthorn cows and other animals, plus a huge collection of mainly 19th century farm tools and machinery; the re-opened Mahogany Drift mine, where visitors can walk through real coal; and a large transport museum with cars, lorries and many other vehicles. Plenty for all the family to see: allow at least one full day. *April to end September: daily 1000-1700. October to end March: Tuesday to Sunday 1000-1600.* 🍵 🚐 🔲 🚋

60c Springwell: **Bowes Railway Wagon Works.** Tel. Newcastle (0632) 461847. Well equipped engineering workshops whose achievements included the construction of working replica of Stephenson's *Rocket* for the 1980 Rainhill 150 celebrations. Much old rolling stock is also on show. *Most weekends 1045-1630.* 🍵 🚋

60c Washington: **'F' Pit Industrial Museum,** Albany Way, District 2, tel. (0632) 467640. Old colliery engine house with well preserved steam engine (now worked electrically). Short colour film of the pit when working. *Weekdays 1000-1600; weekends 1400-1600.*

60c Washington: **Studio Pottery,** Old Hall Smithy, The Green, District 4. Stone tiles, sculpture, etc. made to mediaeval designs. *Monday to Saturday 0930-1700; Sundays 1300-1730.*

60c Penshaw: **Victoria Railway Viaduct.** One of the first high stone railway viaducts, it was finished in 1838. One of the arches spans 160ft and rises to 128ft, believed to be the largest arch in Europe.

61a Monkwearmouth Station Museum, North Bridge Street, tel. Sunderland (0783) 77075. Imposing 1848 station building restored to Edwardian glory, containing displays showing the history of land transport in the North East. Model trains and trams, Victorian and Edwardian bicycles, rebuilt Atlantean bus cab in which children can 'drive' and - outside - a small collection of standard gauge steam locos and rolling stock. *Monday to Saturday 1000-1800; Sundays 1400-1700. Free.*

61a Sunderland: **Vaux Brewery,** Castle Street, tel. (0783) 76277. All stages of brewing and bottling are shown on guided tour, which includes stables used by the shire horses which still haul local deliveries. *Weekdays, by arrangement only.*

Wearmouth Railway Bridge. Built in 1879, believed to be the largest surviving single span wrought iron hog back girder bridge.

61b Ryhope Engines Museum, Ryhope Pumping Station (opposite General Hospital). Tel. Sunderland (0783) 210235. Two 100hp steam beam engines preserved in full working order; small museum devoted to water supply, including working water wheel and fascinating display of sanitary ware. *Easter to end December: static display every weekend 1400-1700: steam working bank holiday weekends.* 🍵

61e Cold Hesleden: **Dalton Pumping Station.** Tel. Sunderland (0783) 57123. Steam powered Cornish beam engine built in 1879. *By appointment only.*

61i Hartlepool. See 51c.

63h Hallbankgate. See 56c.

65i Newton: **Hunday National Tractor and Farm Museum.** Tel. Stocksfield (066 15) 2553. Converted farm buildings now house a massive and fascinating collection of agricultural implements and machinery, ranging from hand tools to a complete steam thresher and a working water mill (all indoors!); also blacksmith's shop, joiner's, many working models and, of course, the unique collection of over 250 veteran and vintage tractors. Outside are small animal enclosures, 'junk' tractor for kids to play on and some narrow gauge railway stock. *Summer: daily 1000-1800. Winter: reduced hours (telephone first). Working days most bank holidays.* 🍵

66h Wylam Railway Museum, Falcon Centre, tel. (066 14) 2174. Material from the many lines of the Tyne valley, including work by Stephenson, Hackworth and others. *Tuesdays and Thursdays 1400-1730; Saturdays 0900-1200; also June to September Sundays 1430-1630. Also by arrangement: tel. 3520.*

67b Blyth Railway Museum, Princess Louise Middle School, tel. (067 06) 3125. Local exhibits, mainly from the Blyth & Tyne Railway. *Mondays (not bank holidays) 1800-2030.*

67d Killingworth: **Dial Cottage.** Home of George Stephenson from 1805 to 1823; a plaque commemorates his first steam locomotive, *Blucher.*

67g Newcastle upon Tyne: **Museum of Science and Engineering,** Blandford House, West Blandford Street, tel. (0632) 326789. Displays devoted to engineering, shipbuilding, mining and transport, including the colliery locomotive *Billy* and many models. *Daily. Free.*

Museum of the Department of Mining Engineering (Newcastle University), Queen Victoria Road, tel. 328511 ext 3118. Many small items from local pits, notably a large collection of safety lamps; also watercolour paintings of Northumbria colleries in 1830-40. *By appointment only.*

Scottish & Newcastle Brewery, Gallowgate, tel. 325091. Conducted tours show every stage of beer making at the home of the famous Newcastle Brown Ale, with samples to follow. *Weekdays at 1430, but must book in advance.*

High Level Bridge. Fascinating combined bridge carrying A1 road and the main London to Edinburgh railway over the Tyne; it was designed by Robert Stephenson and Thomas Harrison in 1849.

Blackfriars Craftworkers Trust, between Stowell Street and Low Friar Street, tel 328630. Group of local craftsmen whose products include leather, soft toys, jewellery, etc. *Weekdays 1000-1700; Saturdays 0900-1600.* 🍵 🔲 ✝ 🔲

67h Willington Viaduct. Dramatic viaduct built for the Newcastle & North Shields Railway; the present iron structure dates from 1869.

68i Kielder Viaduct. One of the finest stone skew-arch railway bridges in Britain, it was built in 1862 and now stands disused, its piers lapped by the head-waters of the new reservoir.

69g Kielder Water. Major new reservoir covering 2684 acres, making it one of Europe's largest man made lakes, holding over 41 million gallons of water. The dam (mainly earth) and the valve tower behind it are over 170ft high. Water is released into the River North Tyne to flow down to Riding Mill (65i), where it is extracted into a 20 mile underground pipeline with outlets on the River Wear at Frosterley (59g) and the River Tees at Eggleston (49e). The reservoir itself is being extensively developed for leisure use (see other sections for details). 🚐 ⛵ 🎣 🔲

71c Cragside Iron Bridge. Now undergoing restoration, it is thought to have been built in the factory of armaments king Lord Armstrong; he owned the adjacent house (see 🏠), which was the first in the world to be lit by electricity generated by water. *April to end October daily; November to end March weekends; from 1030.* 🌳 🏠 🔲

72b Cragside. See 71c.

77e Dunstan Steads Farm Centre. Tel. Embleton (066 576) 221. Old blacksmith's forge; also an implement shed containing much modern farm machinery (children can sit on a combine harvester), used on modern working farm. *Easter, Whitsun, then mid July to early September: daily. Also weekends in May and June. 1300-1700.* 🍵 🐓

77f Craster: **Robson & Sons Kipper Curers,** Haven Hill. Tel. Embleton (066 576) 223. Complete process of smoking herrings is explained; fish can be bought when available. *June to mid September: weekdays 0930-1200, 1300-1700; Saturdays 0930-1200.*

78i Heatherslaw Mill. Tel. Crookham (089 082) 224. Well restored 19th century water driven corn mill in full working order; also a display of millwright's tools. *April to end October: daily 1100-1800.*

79a Berwick-upon-Tweed: **Royal Border Bridge.** Built by Robert Stephenson in 1850; it carries the main East Coast railway line 720 yds over the Tweed on 28 arches, at a height of 126ft.

79e Holy Island: **Lindisfarne Liquers,** St Aidan's Winery, tel. (0289) 89230. Showroom where famous Lindisfarne Mead can be sampled (by over 18's); also alcoholic jam, marmalade and lemon curd. Customs & Excise forbid visitors to actual winery. *Easter to end September: daily 1000-1700.* 🍵 ❄ 🏰 🏠 ✝ 🔲

Tourist Railways

These are railways on which the public can ride and include both standard and narrow gauge lines, together with some of the most impressive miniature systems. Where trains can only be watched, they are listed under Industry Past and Present (pages 104-106).

21b Lakeside and Haverthwaite Railway. Tel. Newby Bridge (0448) 31594. The whole atmosphere of this standard gauge line is that of a 1950s British Rail branch line, which it once was, having run from Ulverston (21a) until closure in 1965. Enthusiasts rescued the northern 3¼ miles in 1973 and now offer 15 minute rides behind a whole range of steam locomotives, notably a pair of 2-6-4 Fairburn tanks. There are also several interesting diesels, while most of the coaches are ex-BR Mk I stock. Trains connect at Lakeside with Sealink steamers to Windermere and combined tickets are available. *Easter weekend, Sundays only in April, then May to September daily 1100-1700 (steam trains hourly); also October Sundays.*

22d Carnforth: Steamtown Railway Museum. Tel. (052 473) 4220. The largest collection of working steam locos in northern England is housed in this 37 acre motive power depot (see ⌂ for details). Many of the locos are used on British Rail summer steam specials on the Cumbrian Coast Line via Ulverston and Barrow, and rides are also offered along almost one mile of standard gauge track within the museum area; there is also a passenger-carrying 15 inch gauge miniature railway of 1000 yds. *Steam rides: Easter to October Sundays and bank holidays, also daily in July and August; 0900-1700.*

21i West End: Morecambe Pleasure Park Railway, West End Promenade. Single-track 20 inch gauge line covering ⅓ mile, with diesel locos disguised as steam. *Easter to October daily 1000-2200.*

26e North Stainley: Lightwater Valley Railroad. Tel. Ripon (0765) 85321. Just one of the attractions at this leisure complex is a 15 inch gauge miniature line covering over 1 mile, with steam haulage on most trains. *April/May weekends and bank holidays 1030-1600; June to end August daily 1030-1700; September weekends 1030-1600;*

26i Newby Hall Miniature Railway. Tel. Boroughbridge (090 12) 2583. Miniature 10¼ inch gauge line covering ½ mile through attractive grounds beside the River Ure. Locos include steam-powered 4-6-0 Royal Scot. *Easter Saturday to 2nd Sunday in October: Wednesdays, Thursdays, weekends and bank holidays 1400-1830.*

29a Pickering. See 42b.

29a Zoo: Flamingoland Miniature Railway. Tel. Kirby Misperton (065 386) 287. Continuous 10¼ inch gauge loop 350 yds long; haulage by gas powered model of Flying Scotsman. Many other attractions on 350 acre site. *Easter to September daily 1000-1600.*

32e → 33d Ravenglass and Eskdale Railway. Tel. (065 77) 226. Nicknamed Ratty, this is the oldest narrow gauge line in England, having been opened in 1875 to carry iron ore. Abandoned in 1913, it was rebuilt as a 15 inch gauge tourist line in 1915 and operated thus until the late 1950s. Ratty was saved by hefty private donations, re-opened in 1960, and now carries passengers and freight for 7 miles through the beautiful but rugged valley from Ravenglass ( ) via Muncaster ( ) to Dalegarth ( ), taking about 40 minutes each way. Summer tourist trains are steam hauled, locos including 2-8-2 *River*

Mite and 2-6-2 *Northern Rock*; interesting diesel stock includes *Shelagh of Eskdale*, a miniaturised BR design. Coaches for disabled passengers. *March weekends, then April to end October daily 0745-1920; also one diesel train each way on winter weekdays.*

32f Ravenglass and Eskdale Railway. See 32e.

33d Dalegarth Station: Ravenglass and Eskdale Railway. See 32e.

33i Lakeside and Haverthwaite Railway. See 21b.

34g Lakeside and Haverthwaite Railway. See 21b.

42b → 42g North Yorkshire Moors Railway (Moorsrail). Tel. Pickering (0751) 72508. One of the major preserved lines in Britain and certainly the most important in the North Country, the NYMR is a real railway, connecting with British Rail at its northern end and offering a realistic service over the 18 miles from Grosmont ( ) to Pickering ( ). The line is of historical interest, having been built by George Stephenson for horse and rope haulage as long ago as 1836. Steam trains first ran in 1865, after which the line survived until Beeching; the standard gauge tracks were not pulled up, however, and enthusiasts re-opened the line in 1973. Today's journey takes around 1 hour each way, much of it through the 400ft deep Newtondale Gorge, which takes the railway into the heart of the North Yorks Moors National Park. Because of the restrictions imposed by the National Park, only a few through trains are steam-hauled, most being diesel-hauled, but the timetables are very clear about which is which. There are over 20 steam locos, including the Stanier Black Five 4-6-0 George Stephenson and a pair of powerful 0-6-2 tanks which make light work of hauling six coaches over the Ellerbeck summit; visiting engines also work the line quite often. Volunteer helpers are always welcome - tel. Darlington (0325) 63063 between 1900 and 2100 for details. Through tickets to/from Whitby and Middlesbrough are available from British Rail. *Easter to early November: daily 0930-1800 (trains hourly in June, July and August). Talking Timetable: tel. (0751) 73535.*

42c Whitby: Westcliff Miniature Railway, Westcliff Sports Ground. Roughly circular 10¼ inch gauge line covering 300 yds; diesel haulage. *Summer only: daily.*

43h North Bay Railway, Northstead Manor Gardens. Britain's largest council-owned miniature railway, this 20 inch gauge line covers just under 1 mile, with diesel locos disguised as steam. *Easter to early October: daily (trains every 20 mins).*

49i Whorlton: Lido Railway. Tel. (083 37) 397. Miniature 15 inch gauge line through ½ mile of beautiful scenery on the south bank of the River Tees; locos include 4-4-2 steam unit. *Easter to end September: weekends (daily in school holidays).*

60b Beamish: North of England Open Air Museum. Tel. Stanley (0207) 31811. This remarkable 200 acre site contains no less than three rail-borne transport systems: two standard gauge railways plus an electric tramway. The major undertaking is a 1 mile steam railway based on Rowley Station, which was removed from its site in the Consett hills and rebuilt brick by brick in the museum. Several steam locos include a North Eastern Railway 0-6-0, the last survivor of 201 built in the late 18th century. A separate ¼ mile track is used by a full-scale replica of Stephenson's *Locomotion*, behind which visitors can occasionally ride. The tramway offers rides in vintage cars from Gateshead, Sunderland and Sheffield, all in immaculate condition. *April to end September: daily 1000-1700. October to end March: Tuesday to Sunday 1000-1600.*

60b Marley Hill: Tanfield Railway. Tel. Newcastle (0632) 742002. The world's oldest existing railway, this standard gauge line started life as a wooden waggonway in 1725, progressing through horse and rope haulage to steam power by 1881; it finally closed to traffic in 1964. The first section of track was restored to use in 1977, and about 1 mile is currently open, from Sunniside south to the engine shed at Marley Hill. Eventually, the line will run a further two miles to East Tanfield, via the picturesque Causey Dene and the famous Causey Arch (see ⌂). The line retains its industrial character, with a collection of around 20 steam locos all built for colliery or other private railways. Most were also built locally, ranging from the 0-4-0 Black Hawthorn saddle tank *Wellington* (built 1873) to a 53 ton 0-6-0 saddle tank built in Newcastle by Stephenson & Hawthorns in 1957. Most passenger coaches are modern replicas, but there is much historical rolling stock, including a steam crane. *Easter to August: bank holiday Sundays and Mondays; also all Sundays in July and August. Marley Hill shed open for viewing only every Sunday 1000-1700.*

60c Springwell: Bowes Railway. Tel. Newcastle (0632) 461847. The world's only standard gauge rope-hauled railway in preservation, it has actually been designated a Scheduled Ancient Monument. What remains once formed part of the Pontop and Jarrow Railway, which was started by George Stephenson in 1826 and eventually linked 13 local collieries to the main line at Pelaw. The rope hauled sections comprise two inclines: 750 yds at 1 in 15, and 1170 yds at 1 in 70; the rest of the site includes old waggonways, and about 1¼ miles of conventional trackbed on which steam-hauled rides can be had. The line has its own wagon works (see ⌂ for details). Owned by the county council and run as a charity, the railway welcomes volunteer helpers, who should contact the Tyne and Wear Industrial Monuments Trust, tel. (0632) 816144 ext 259. *Operating days: Easter Monday, then first Sunday of each month until October, 1200-1700.*

60c Lambton Park. Railway now closed.

67h The Leam: Bowes Railway. See 60c Springwell.

67i South Shields: Lake Shore Railroad, South Marine Park. Miniature 9½ inch gauge line covering 500 yds around the boating lake. Steam locos, including 4-6-2 *Mountaineer*, are all American types. *Easter to end November.*

Wildlife in Captivity

Including zoos, aviaries, aquaria and outdoor safari parks. Animals in the wild are included in the sections on Countryside (pages 80-83) or Bird Watching (pages 102-103).

18b Conyngham Hall Zoological Gardens. Tel. Harrogate (0423) 862793. Specialises in snakes, including some of the largest in captivity anywhere; also lions, tigers, panthers, pumas, llamas, wallabies and sea lions. *Daily 1000-1600 (later in summer).* 🐘 &

18h Harewood House: Bird Garden. Over 200 species of exotic birds from all over the world, including penguins, emus, macaws and snowy owls. *April to end October: daily from 1000; also limited opening in winter.* 🐘 & ✱ m ⌂ ✕

21a High Hay Bridge: Deer Museum. Tel. Greenodd (022 986) 283 or 412. Wild deer enclosures and displays relating to their upkeep. No dogs. *By appointment only.* ♣ ⌂

21h Heysham Head. See ☆ for details.

21i Morecambe: Marineland, Stone Jetty, Promenade, tel. (0524) 414727. Oceanarium houses turtles, penguins, alligators and mink; also dolphins and sea lions which perform daily shows. Aquarium holds hundreds of freshwater and marine fish species. *Summer: daily 1000-1830.*

21i Lancaster: Rare Breeds Survival Unit, Hornsea Pottery, Wyresdale Road, tel. (0524) 68444. Collection of rare domestic and farm animals, covering 19 acres on a site with many other attractions. Children's playground. *Daily from 1030.* 🐘 & ♣ ⌂ ⌑

22d Leighton Hall. Tel. Carnforth (0524) 734474. Collection of birds of prey, with free flying eagles released daily at 1530 (unless raining). *May to September: Tuesdays, Thursdays and Sundays 1400-1700.* 🐘 ⌂ ✱ ⌂ ☆

22g Lancaster. See 21i.

29a Zoo: Flamingo Land. Tel. Kirby Misperton (065 386) 287. Extensive pleasure park covering over 350 acres, most of which is devoted to wildlife. Over 1000 animals, birds and reptiles represent about 80 species, including elephants, big cats, apes and monkeys, bears, seals and sea lions, crocodiles, and, of course, several types of flamingo (one of which eats dog biscuits!). Also a working farm and pets' corner. *First Sunday in March to end October: daily 1000-1600.* 🐘 & ⌂ ✱ ⌑ ⌂ ♪ ☆

31g Sewerby Hall Zoo. Tel. Bridlington (0262) 73769. Deer and wallabies run free in the park; there is also a miniature zoo and aviary. *Daily 0900-dusk.* 🐘 ✱ ⌑

32f Muncaster Castle. Tel. Ravenglass (065 77) 614. Tropical bird garden, flamingo pool and rare Himalayan bears. *Easter to early October: Saturday to Thursday 1200-1700.* 🐘 & ♣ ✱ ⌂

33i High Hay Bridge. See 21a.

34g High Hay Bridge. See 21a.

43h Scarborough: Zoo. Now closed.

46f Lowther Wildlife Park. Tel. Hackthorpe (093 12) 523. Mixture of rare farm breeds, deer, birds and European wild animals (including polecats, wolves, badgers, boars, etc.) in 230 acres of parkland. Dog kennels. *April to October 1000-1700.* 🐘 & ⌂ m

47f Appleby Castle. Tel. (0930) 51402. Conservation centre for the Rare Breeds Survival Trust, with a collection of unusual farm animals and waterfowl. *Easter weekend, then early May to late September: daily 1030-1700.* ☕ ♣ ⌑

51i A174: Newham Grange Leisure Farm. Tel. Middlesbrough (0642) 245432. Complete range of common farm animals, some of which can be fed by children; also a collection of rarer breeds. *Easter to end October: daily 0930-1730. November to Easter: Sundays only 0930-dusk.* 🐘 ⌂ ⌑

51i Marton: Stewart Park. Tel. Middlesbrough (0642) 311211. Extensive parkland includes an aviary with many species of parakeet; also various animal breeds and birds. *Summer: daily 1000-1800. Winter: daily 0900-1600. Free.* 🐘 & ⌑

52g A174. See 51i.

60a Stanley Zoo. Now Closed.

60b Beamish: Home Farm, part of the North of England Open Air Museum, tel. Stanley (0207) 31811. Restored farm buildings now house many agricultural exhibits (see ⌑ for details), plus a selection of local farm animals, including Durham shorthorn cows. *May to end August daily; rest of year Tuesday to Sunday; 1000-1800.* 🐘 ⌂ ⌑ ⌑ ⌑

60c Washington Wildfowl Refuge, Middle Barmston Farm, tel. (0632) 465454. Wildfowl from every continent, with over 1000 birds, many of them very rare. Visitor Reception building overlooks whole park; children's play area. *Daily 0930-1730 (dusk if earlier).* 🐘 & ⌂ ⌑

60c Lambton Park. Now closed.

76c Chillingham: Wild Cattle, Home Farm, tel. Chatton (066 85) 213. Large park containing the famous herd of white cattle which have been there for 700 years. They are the only animals of their kind which have never been crossed with domestic cattle. Castle not open to public. *April to end October: Mondays and Wednesday to Saturday 1000-1200, 1400-1700; Sundays 1400-1700.*

77e Dunstan Steads Farm Centre. Tel. Embleton (066 576) 221. Working farm with sheep, laying hens, rabbits, pigs, cattle, donkey, goat, etc. Children's play area. Old or waterproof footwear recommended. No dogs near farm. *Easter, Whitsun, then mid July to early September: daily; also weekends in May and June; 1300-1700.* 🐘 ⌑

Cruising by Boat

Includes all kinds of boat trips: sea cruises, ferries, island visits, river and canal boats, on all of which you can relax while someone else does the driving. Self-drive boating is dealt with on pages 109-110.

19c York: Hills Boatyard, Lendal Bridge, tel. (0904) 23752. One hour cruises to the Archbishop of York's Palace and back. *April to September.*

Ouse Cruises, Skeldergate Bridge, tel. 32530. Pleasure cruises on the River Ouse. *April to September.*

21a Ulverston: Nor' West Sailing, tel. Newby Bridge (044 83) 821. Yacht sailing in the North Sea.

30c Filey. Boat trips from the beach. *Summer only.*

31g Bridlington. Cruises around Flamborough Head. *Summer only.*

33e Coniston: *Gondola*. Tel. Ambleside (096 63) 3003. 1859 steam yacht restored by National Trust now plys the lake carrying 86 passengers. Opulent steam-heated Victorian saloon. *Good Friday to end September: Sunday to Friday.* △ ♪

34e Windermere. Four ferries ply the lake, calling at Lakeside (🐘 ⌑), Bowness and Ambleside. Booking from all three piers, or tel. Sealink on Newby Bridge (0448) 31539. *March to early October: every ½ hour Bowness-Ambleside; six/eight daily sailings around lake.*

34e Bowness-on-Windermere: Windermere Lake Holidays Afloat, Shepherds Boatyard, tel. (096 62) 3415. Motor and sailing cruises on the lake in fully equipped boats. *March to November: weekly. Rest of year: 3 days.*

34e Ferry House. Car and passenger ferry across Lake Windermere. *Monday to Saturday 0650-2150; Sundays 0910-2150; every 20 mins.*

42c Whitby. Pleasure cruises leave from the pier. *Summer only.*

43h Scarborough. Speedboat trips and pleasure cruises from the harbour. *Summer only.*

45e Derwent Water. Motor launches cruise the lake and can be boarded at Keswick, Ashness Gate, Lodore, High Brandelhow, Low Brandelhow and Hawse End. For details tel. (0596) 72263. *Easter to October daily: every 30 mins, plus guided evening trip.* 🐘

46e Howtown. See 46f Pooley Bridge.

46f Pooley Bridge: Ullswater Navigation Company, tel. Kendal (0539) 21626. Cruises by motor launch via Howtown (46e) to Glenridding (46g), taking about 1 hour each way. *Easter to October: three trips daily.* 🐘

46g Glenridding. See 46f Pooley Bridge.

60i Durham: Brown's Boat House, Elvet Bridge, tel. (0385) 64292. 40 minute pleasure trips on the River Wear. *Easter to October.* △

67g Newcastle Quayside. River trips on the Tyne are operated by Mid-Tyne Ferries, tel. (0632) 832172, and by Nigel Gray, tel. Hexham (0434) 603755.

77b Seahouses. Cruises to the Farne Islands on the *Glad Tidings*, tel. (0665) 720308, the *St Cuthbert*, tel. 720388, and the *Britannia*, tel. 720317. Round trip takes about 2½ hours.

Sailing and Boating

Sailing clubs and schools where temporary membership and/or other facilities are available to the short term visitor. Also: canoeing, rowing and power boating centres; and places where you can hire - for long or short term -canal boats, yachts, dinghies, and motor boats.

21b Staveley-in-Cartmel: Nor' West Sailing. Tel. Newby Bridge (044 83) 821. Dinghy sailing holidays arranged on Lake Windermere. RYA instruction. *Easter to October.*

21b Fell Foot Country Park. Tel. Newby Bridge (0448) 31273. Canoeing, rowing, club sailing and yachts for hire. Dinghy park. Launch fee. *Daily, subject to weather conditions.* 🚩 ♿ 🏕 ♣

25h Pateley Bridge: North Pennine Outdoor Pursuits. Tel. Harrogate (0423) 711197. Multi-activity courses which include canoeing; minimum age 11 years. *All year.* ▲

31g Bridlington: Royal Yorkshire Yacht Club, Windsor Crescent, tel. (0262) 72041. Temporary membership available. Annual regatta held in August.

33c Grasmere. Tel. (096 65) 409. Canoes and sailing craft; no power boats. Launching fee. *Easter to October.* ⛵

33e Coniston Water. All types of small boats can be used on the lake. Maximum speed of 10 nautical mph for powered craft. For launching see Monk Coniston (33f). ⛵

33f Monk Coniston: Coniston Boating Centre, Lake Road, tel. (096 64) 366. Rowing boats and small craft for hire. Launching facilities. *March to October: daily 0900-1800.*

33f Esthwaite Water. Tel. Hawkshead (096 66) 331. Rowing boats only; permits from Hawkshead Post Office. Boats for hire. ⛵

34c Bowness-on-Windermere: Lake District Outdoor Pursuits Centre, Fallowbarrow Hall, tel. Windermere (096 62) 5454. Holiday Courses provided in canoeing, sailing and raft-building. ▲
Windermere Marina, Nab Wood, tel. 2891. Good facilities for holiday sailors. *Daily.*
Windermere Aquatic, Glebe Road, tel. 2121. Extensive facilities; boats for hire. *Weekdays 0800-1715; weekends 0700-1800.*
Lake Warden's Complex, Ferry Nab Road, tel. 2244. Dinghy park; slipway; visitors berths. *Daily from 0900.*

34d Esthwaite Water. See 33f.

34g Staveley-in-Cartmel. See 21b.

34g Fell Foot. See 21b.

35g Killington Reservoir: Killington Sailing Association. Temporary membership available from The Bursary, Sedburgh School. ⛵⛵

42c Whitby Yacht Club, The Pier. Tel. (0947) 603623. Cruising in coastal waters. Racing season from March to September.

43h Scarborough Yacht Club, Lighthouse Pier, tel. (0723) 73821. Temporary membership available.

45b Bassenthwaite Lake Sailing Club. Tel. (059 681) 341. Many facilities. Only sailing boats allowed on the lake.

45d Crummock Water. Rowing boats for hire. Contact The Scale Hill Hotel, Loweswater, tel. Lorton (090 085) 232.

45e Derwent Water: Derwentwater Boat Club. Tel. Keswick (0596) 72912. Temporary membership available on a daily basis.
Keswick Launch Company. Tel. 72263. Small craft and rowing boats for hire.
Nichol End Marine. Tel. 73013. Motor boats and rowing boats for hire.

45g Buttermere. Sailing boats only allowed on the lake. Permits from the National Trust.

46e Watermillock House: Ullswater Sailing School. Tel. Pooley Bridge (085 36) 438. Boats for hire; RYA sailing tuition.

46g Glenridding: Tindal Ltd. Tel. (085 32) 393. Motor boats for hire.

48f Selset Reservoir: Selset Sailing Club. Sailing and windsurfing are controlled by the club, whose clubhouse is beside the dam. ⛵

49d Grassholme Reservoir. Rowing boats for hire from the warden at the site. ⛵

49d Hury Reservoir. Rowing boats can be hired from the warden at the site. ⛵

51c Hartlepool Yacht Club. Tel. (0429) 74931. Temporary membership available. 🚩 ⛵

51f Middlesbrough: Eccles Marine. Tel. (0642) 211756 or 219965. Small boats and cruising sail boats for hire. ⛵

52a Hartlepool. See 51c.

52d Middlesbrough. See 51f.

56c Talkin Tarn Country Park. Tel. Brampton

Wind Speed

This is normally indicated by a numerical scale of force, known as the Beaufort Scale after Sir Francis Beaufort (1774-1837), the English admiral who invented it.

Beaufort Number	Wind Speed (mph)	Description of conditions on land and sea
0	0-1	**Calm** Smoke rises vertically.
1	1-3	**Light Air** Smoke drifts.
2	4-7	**Light Breeze** Can be felt on the face.
3	8-12	**Gentle Breeze** Moves leaves and small twigs. Small waves
4	13-18	**Moderate Breeze** Raises dust and waste paper; thin branches move. Waves 4-5ft; 'white horses' form.
5	19-24	**Fresh Breeze** Small trees sway. Waves 6-8ft.
6	25-31	**Strong Wind** Large branches move; wind is distinctly audible. Waves up to 12ft; crests foaming.
7	32-38	**High Wind** Large trees move; resistance to walking against the wind. Waves up to 16ft, breaking in gusts.
8	39-46	**Gale** Breaks twigs off trees; difficult to walk against wind. Waves 20-25ft; sea 'boiling' in places.
9	47-54	**Severe Gale** Tears tiles off roofs; picks up relatively large objects. Waves up to 30ft; sea foaming everywhere; poor visibility in spray.
10	55-63	**Storm** Uproots trees; damages buildings. Waves up to 40ft; difficult to see through spray.
11	64-75	**Hurricane**
12	75 plus	**Hurricane**

Slipways

No details of individual slipways are given, but the location of all those with public access is accurately marked. Please note that in some cases permission may be needed and/or a small fee may have to be paid for access; also that launching times may be restricted by the tide. Check locally before using any slipway.

Safety

However experienced you are, the seas in this region can be treacherous and there are a number of safety precautions which must always be taken. Before setting out, always obtain a weather forecast - the local coastguard station is the best source for this; they are marked CG on the maps, or you can obtain the telephone number from the nearest Tourist Information Office (see page 122). Whenever a gale of Force 8 or above is expected within 6 hours, warning flags are hoisted at coastguard stations and at harbours.

Always leave details of your trip with someone, or leave a note on the car windscreen, so that people know when you are missing and can instigate a search. The information needed is: a description of your boat (length, colour, name, type); the number of people on board; a list of any safety equipment carried; when you set sail and when you expect to return.

Carry some extra clothing (especially waterproofs) even in summer, as you could be stranded or becalmed and it can become very cold at sea at any time of year. Always wear an approved design of life jacket.

If you fall overboard, remove your shoes and any heavy clothing immediately, but retain the rest of your garments, as these will help keep you warm. Tread water as slowly as possible to preserve energy, although a proper life jacket will keep you afloat with no effort on your part. Recognised distress signals include: standing up with arms apart, raising and lowering them as if imitating a bird; waving a flag or any item of clothing; flying the Red Ensign (normally flown from the stern) high in the rigging or upside down. If you see any of these, dial 999 and ask for the coastguard.

Although the general rule is that steam gives way to sail, you must bear in mind that modern supertankers and the like simply cannot manoeuvre with any speed at all - it can take them a couple of miles to stop, for example! - and that in narrow or crowded sea lanes large vessels may have no choice but to maintain their course. Standard horn signals are: 1 blast "am turning to starboard", 2 blasts " am turning to port", 3 blasts "am reversing".

(069 77). Boats for hire. Permits issued for sailing, rowing and canoeing. No power boats. ✦

59a **Derwent Reservoir: Sailing Club.** Tel. Blanchland (043 475) 258. Day tickets available to visitors.

59a **Pow Hill Country Park: Sailing Club.** Rowing boats and yachts for hire. For details contact the Sunderland and South Shields Water Company, tel. Sunderland (0783) 210610. ⛵ ♣

60i **Durham: Brown's Boathouse,** Elvet Bridge, tel. (0385) 64292. Rowing boats for hire. *Easter to October: daily 0900-1800.*

61a **Sunderland Yacht Club.** Tel. (0783) 75133. Temporary membership available.

61i **Hartlepool.** See 51c.

63c **Low Cranecleugh: Kielder Water.** See 68i.

64a **Low Cranecleugh: Kielder Water.** See 68i.

66a **Bolam Lake.** Canoeing, dinghy sailing and inflatables. Maximum depth of water: 6ft in winter, less in summer. *Daily. Free.* ⛵ ♣ ✦

67b **Blyth: Royal Northumberland Yacht Club.** Tel. (067 06) 3636. Temporary membership available.

67d **Killingworth Lake.** Tel. North Shields (0632) 575544. Canoeing.

67f **Tynemouth Sailing Club.** Tel. North Shields

(0632) 572617. Temporary membership available. Facilities for berthing visiting yachts.

68i/69g **Kielder Water.** This huge new reservoir is being developed for dinghy and yacht sailing, along with many other water-based leisure activities. At Low Cranecleugh (69g) there are extensive facilities, including moorings for 200 yachts. All activities on the lake are controlled by the Northumbrian Water Authority: tel. Gosforth (0632) 843151. ⛵ ⌁ ✦ ✚

76c **Belford: Windy Gyle Outdoor Centre.** Tel. (066 83) 289. Adventure holidays include canoeing and dinghy sailing; instruction. No experience necessary; minimum age 16. *June to September.* ▲ ∪ ☆

79a **Berwick-upon-Tweed Sailing Club.** (secretary tel. 0289 2181). Temporary membership is available.

Water Sports

Sub-aqua, waterskiing and windsurfing centres; also organisations offering holidays and/or tuition in these and other water sport activities. Sailing and Boating are covered in the previous section.

18d **Harrogate: Sub-aqua Club,** Coppice Pool (secretary tel. 0423 888977). *Thursdays 1945.* ✐

19f **York: Sub-aqua Club,** St Peter's School Swimming Baths (secretary 0904 400495). *Tuesdays 1930-2030.* ✐
   Windsurfing Centre, Moor Lane, Dringhouses, tel. 58063. Tuition and boards for hire.

20e **Barrow-in-Furness: Lakeland Windsurfer School,** St George's Square, tel. (0229) 24740. Windsurfing on Lake Windermere; must be able to swim. *April to October: daily courses.*
   Barrow-Cuda. Sub-aqua Club, Abbey Baths. *Tuesdays 2100-2200* ✐
   Furness Sub-aqua Club, Abbey Baths. *Thursdays from 2000.* ✐

20h **Walney Channel: South Cumbrian Water Ski Club.** Comprehensive waterskiing facilities.

23i **Settle: North Ribblesdale Sub-aqua Club,** Swimming Pool (secretary Earby 028 284 3039). *Mondays 2030-2130.* ✐

26e **Ripon Sub-aqua Club,** Ripon Spa Baths, on B6265 west of town. *Wednesdays 2000-2100.* ✐

31g **Bridlington.** Waterskiing is allowed within designated areas. For details contact the Foreshore Manager (tel. 0262 78255). ✦

32a **Egremont: West Cumbria Sub-aqua Club,** Wyndham Swimming Pool. *Thursdays 2000* ✐

34e **Troutbeck Bridge: Kendal and Lakes Sub-aqua Club,** Troutbeck Pool (secretary tel. Windermere 0524 761662). *Tuesdays 2000.* ✐

42c **Whitby Sub-aqua Club,** 73 Upgang Lane, tel. (0947) 5782.

43h **Scarborough: Water Ski Club,** The Mere. Facilities for visiting waterskiers. *April to October.*
   Sub-aqua Club (secretary tel. 0723 72036). Teachers Training College, Filey Road *(September to May)*; South Bay Open Air Pool, *(May to September: Thursdays from 2000).* ✐

44a **Solway Sub-aqua Club,** Sherbrook Pool. *Sundays 2000-2200.* ✐

44h **Egremont.** See 32a.

46e **Sandwick: Ullswater Ski Club.** Facilities include a jump and a slalom course. *April to October.*

48i **Balderhead Reservoir: Water Ski Club,** club house at north end of the dam (secretary tel. Washington 0632 469097). *Summer only.* ✦

50b **Bishop Auckland: Sub-aqua Club,** Bishop Auckland Baths, Woodhouse Lane, *Mondays 2000-2100.* ✐

50i **Darlington: Sub-aqua Club,** Branksome School Baths. *Thursdays 1900-2100.* ✐

51c **Hartlepool: Yacht Club.** Tel. (0429) 74931. Facilities for visiting waterskiers. ✦ ⚠

51f **Middlesbrough: Sub-aqua Club,** Berwick Hill Baths. *Fridays 2000-2100.* ✐
   Eccles Marine. Tel. (0642) 211756 or 219965. Instruction in sub-aqua diving. ⚠

52a **Hartlepool.** See 51c.

52f **Redcar: Dorman Long Water Ski Club.** Tel. (064 93) 2015. Facilities for visiting waterskiers. *April to October.*

52f **Saltburn-by-the-Sea: Cleveland Divers,** Sub-aqua Club, Saltburn Leisure Centre. *Mondays from 2030.* ✐

52d **Middlesbrough.** See 51f.

60i **Durham Sub-aqua Club,** City Baths. *Sundays from 0930.* ✐

61a **Sunderland Sub-aqua Club,** High Street Baths. *Mondays 1700-1900.* ✐

61i **Hartlepool.** See 51c.

65g **Hexham Sub-aqua Club,** Community Centre and Baths (secretary tel. 0434 604975). *Mondays 2000-2200.* ✐

66c **Morpeth Sub-aqua Club,** Swimming Baths (secretary tel. 0670 55563). *Thursdays 2030* ✐

67b **Blyth Sub-aqua Club,** The Pool. *Wednesdays from 2100.* ✐

67g **Newcastle: Divers Club,** Shipcote Baths. *Fridays from 2000.* ✐
   Trail-a-Boats, 159 Westgate Road, tel. (0632) 615367. Hire of windsurfing equipment and wet-suits. *Mondays, Tuesdays and Thursday to Saturday.*

71e **Fontburn Reservoir: Water Ski Club.** Facilities for visiting waterskiers with their own boats. *Wednesdays and weekends.* ✦

72d **Fontburn Reservoir.** See 71e.

73g **Morpeth.** See 66c.

77e **Newton Windsurfing Centre.** Tel. Embleton (066 576) 666. Tuition; hire of boards and wet-suits.

Swimming Pools

No details of individual pools are given here, but the symbols indicate the existence of all known pools with public access. Indoor and outdoor, heated and non-heated, sea and freshwater swimming pools are included. Opening times and charges can usually be obtained from the nearest Tourist Information Office (see page 122).

Fishing

18b Knaresborough - River Nidd. Right bank for ¾ mile. Coarse. Permits from Smith's TS, High Street, Knaresborough.

18e Thistle Hill - River Nidd. Right bank south to Birkham Woods. Coarse and game. Permits from farmer or TS in Knaresborough.

18f River Wharfe. Either bank for 2 miles upstream. Coarse and game. Permits from TS and George and Dragon, Wetherby.

18f Ox Close House - River Nidd. Right bank for 1 mile downstream. Coarse. Permits from Crown Inn, Kirk Hammerton. *June to February.*

18h Roundhay Park Lakes. Coarse and trout *(late March to February)* in Waterloo Lake; coarse *(June to February)* in the upper lake. Permits from Leeds TS.

18i Boston Spa - River Wharfe. Right bank for ½ mile upstream. Coarse and game. Permits from Spa Baths.

19a Toll - River Ouse. Right bank for 3 miles upstream. Coarse. Permits from Anchor Inn, Dunsforth. *June to February.*

19a Lock - River Ouse. For 1½ miles to Kyle Mouth. Coarse. Permits from Fotherby's Garage, Newton-on-Ouse or York TS. *June to February.*

19a Beningbrough Hall - River Ouse. Left bank downstream to Rawcliffe (19e). Coarse. Permits from York TS. *June to February.*

19b Laund House - River Ouse. Right bank downstream to Nether Poppleton (19e). Coarse. Permits from Post Office, Nether Poppleton. *June to February.*

19c Earswick - River Foss. Section on right bank. Coarse. *Free.*

19d Skip Bridge - River Nidd. Right bank for ¾ mile downstream. Coarse. Permits from Skip Bridge Garage. *June to February.*

19e Nether Poppleton - River Ouse. Right bank for 3 miles downstream. Coarse. Permits from Leeds AA, 75 Stoney Lane, Beckett Street. *June to February.*

19f York - River Ouse. For 1½ miles in city boundary. Coarse. *Free.*

19f Manor - River Ouse. Downstream on left bank to Naburn Sewage Works (19i). Coarse. Permits from Hoe's Bakery, Fulford. *June to February.*

19g Newton Kyme - River Wharfe. Upstream to Boston Spa Gasworks. Coarse and game. Permits from Spa Baths, Boston Spa.

19g Tadcaster - River Wharfe. Either bank for 2 miles centred on the town. Coarse. Permits from Brittania Inn or Webb's TS, Kirkgate, Tadcaster.

19h Ulleskelf - River Wharfe. Right bank for 3 miles upstream. Coarse. Permits from Leeds TS or Ulleskelf Arms. *June to February.*

19h Ryther - River Wharfe. Right bank for 2 miles downstream. Coarse. Permits from Ulleskelf Arms, Ulleskelf. *June to February.*

20a Southfield. Shore. Shallow water fishing for bass from Summer Hill (north) to Haverigg Haws (south).

20c Kirkby-in-Furness - Kirkby Pool (river). Upstream to Reeks Bridge. Coarse, trout and some sea trout. Permits from Furness FA, 22 Derbyshire Road, Barrow-in-Furness.

20e Haverigg Point. Shore. Cod and flatfish from

rocks and beach. Worm bait available locally.

20e Hodbarrow Point. Shore. Rock and beach fishing for cod and flatfish. Worm bait available.

20e Duddon Sands. Offshore. Flatfish, mainly plaice and flounder, from deep water channel between shore and main expanse of sand.

20e Roanhead Ponds. Coarse in 8 ponds; trout in only 1. Permits from kiosk at site (*summer only*) or Furness FA, 22 Derbyshire Road, Barrow-in-Furness NWWA.

20e Ormsgill - Lower Reservoir. Brown and rainbow trout; coarse includes tench and carp. Permits from Tally Ho Pub near reservoir. NWWA.

20f Roanhead Ponds. See 20e.

20f Urswick Tarn. Coarse, including bream. Rowing boat available. Permits from bailiff at site or Derby Arms, Urswick.

20f Gleaston - Gleaston Beck. Downstream to the sea. Permits from Furness FA, 22 Derbyshire Road, Barrow-in-Furness. *Opens 1 April.*

20h Biggar. Shore. Quality bass on west facing beach from *May to September.*

20i Roa Island. Shore. Bass, cod, dab, flounder, plaice, silver eel, tope and whiting from causeway.

20i Foulney Island. Shore. Bass, cod, flatfish, mackerel, silver eel, tope and whiting from the causeway.

20i Piel Island. Offshore. Worthwhile fishing for bass, cod, tope and whiting. Crab bait from Roa Island.

21a Lowick Bridge - River Crake. Right bank. Trout, sea trout and salmon. Permits from Lowick Mill Farm, Lowick Bridge.

21b Newby Bridge - River Leven. Right bank for 300 yards. Trout. Permits from Swan Hotel, Newby Bridge.

21c Halforth - River Kent. For 2 miles upstream. Trout, salmon. Permits from Low Levens Farm, Sampool Lane, Kendal.

21a Ulverston Canal. Left bank of the entire canal. Coarse. Permits from keeper on site or Parker's TS, 23 Market Street, Ulverston.

21i Morecambe. Shore. Bass, conger, dab, flounder, plaice and whiting caught from local beaches, Battery Skeer, Grosvenor and Central Pier.

Offshore. Good numbers of bass, cod, dogfish, mackerel, pouting, ray and whiting in the bay. Worm bait available locally.

22a Halforth. See 21c.

22c Kirkby Lonsdale - River Lune. For 2 miles. Trout, sea trout, salmon. Permits (5-day ticket only) from Kirkby Lonsdale TS. *February to October.*

22f Whittington - River Lune. Right bank for 400 yards. Trout, salmon. Permits from Whittington Farm.

22g Lancaster - River Lune. Sea trout, salmon and coarse (above weir). Permits from Darwen and Gough TS, 6 Moor Lane, Lancaster or Station Hotel, Caton.

22h Halton - River Lune. Coarse (above weir), sea trout and salmon. Permits from Darwen and Gough TS, 6 Moor Lane, Lancaster or Station Hotel, Caton.

22h Halton Park - River Lune. For 5 miles upstream. Trout, salmon and sea trout; in some places fly only. Permits from Darwin and Gough TS, 6 Moor Lane, Lancaster or Station Hotel, Caton.

22i Hornby - River Wenning. From bridge to River Lune. Trout, fly only. Permits from Castle Hotel, Hornby.

23c Green Field Beck - Greenfield Lake. Trout, fly only. Permits from Buck Inn, Buckden (24e). YWA. *April to September.*

23d Ingleton - River Greta. For 4 miles above and below town. Trout, fly only. Permits from Wells TS, Main Street, Ingleton. *Mid-March to September.*

23d Park Foot - River Greta. For 7 miles upstream. Trout, sea trout, salmon; mainly fly. Permits from Well's Newsagent, Ingleton.

23i Settle - River Ribble. For 4½ miles centred

112

on the town. Trout and salmon, fly only. Permits from Royal Oak, Settle. *April to October.*

24a Green Field Beck. See 23c.

24e Buckden - River Wharfe. For 3½ miles above and below town. Coarse and trout (fly only). Boat available. Permits from Buck Inn, Greenfield Garage or Mrs Lambert, the keeper.

24g Settle. See 23i

24h Malham Tarn. Trout, fly only. Boat for hire. Permits from Field Centre. YWA. *May to September.* ♣ ⚓

24i Grassington - River Wharfe. Area of 2½ miles. Coarse (grayling), trout (fly only). Permits from Devonshire Arms or Post Office, Grassington. *Trout April to September; grayling October to February.*

24i River Wharfe. Downstream to Drebley (25g). Coarse (grayling), trout (fly only). Permits from Skipton TS or Red Lion Hotel and Fell Hotel, Burnsall. *Trout June to September; grayling October to February.*

25b River Cover. From River Ure to Hall's Bridge. Trout, fly only. Permits from Coveridge Inn, Middleham or East Witton Estate Office, Leyburn.

25b Leighton Reservoir. Trout. Permits from machine at fishing hut in car park.

25d Scar House Reservoir. Trout. Permits from ticket machine at site.

25g Appletreewick - River Wharfe. Left bank for ½ mile. Coarse and game. Permits from New Inn, Appletreewick.

26c Pickhill - River Swale. For 2 fields at New Leys Farm. Coarse and game. Permits from Thornaby AA, 5 Melsonby Grove, Hartburn, Stockton-on-Tees.

26c River Swale. Left bank for 3 miles upstream. Coarse. Permits from Buck Inn, Maunby. *June to February.*

26c Skipton upon Swale - River Swale. For ½ mile above and below bridge. Coarse and game. Permits from Moss's TS, Thirsk.

26c Catton - River Swale. Right bank downstream for 1 mile. Coarse and game. Permits from Moss's TS, Thirsk.

26e Birkby Nap - River Laver. Downstream to Rustic Bridge, Ripon. Trout, fly only. Permits from Hodgson's TS, Ripon. *April to September.*

26e Ure Bank - River Ure. For 7 miles upstream. Coarse and game. Permits from Brewer's Arms, Ripon.

26e Studley Roger - Rogers Quarry. Coarse. Permits from Brewer's Arms, Ripon. YWA.

26e Ripon - River Ure. Right bank for 1 mile downstream. Coarse and game, fly only. Permits from Hodgson's TS, Ripon. *April to May.*

26f Topcliffe - River Swale. Either bank for 1½ miles centred on the town. Coarse and game. Permits from Black Bull, Topcliffe. *April to February.*

26h Ox Close House - Ripon Canal. Tow path for 1½ miles upstream. Coarse and game. Permits from Brewer's Arms, 2 Bondgate Green, Ripon. YWA.

26i Mulwith - River Ure. Either bank for 1 mile downstream. Coarse. Permits from Newby Hall Estate Office, Skelton-on-Ure.

26i Boroughbridge - River Ure. Right bank to Hall Arm Lane. Coarse. Permits from Post Office.

27d The Grange - Cod Beck. Right bank for 1½ miles. Coarse and game. Permits from Moss's TS, Thirsk.

27g Ellenthorpe Hall - River Ure. Left bank for 1 mile. Coarse. Permits from Ellenthorpe Hall Farm.

27g Toll. See 19a.

27h Lock. See 19a.

28b Riccal House - River Riccal. Right bank on the Nunnington Estate, Coarse and game. Permits from Estate Office, Nunnington Hall, tel. Nunnington (043 95) 202. *April to September.*

28b Nunnington - River Rye. For 1½ miles upstream. Trout, fly only. Permits from keeper, tel. (043 95) 247 or Estate Office, Nunnington Hall, tel (043 95) 202. *April to September.*

28b West Ness - River Rye. For 1 mile upstream. Course and game. Permits from keeper, tel. Nunnington (043 95) 247 or Estate Office, Nunnington Hall, tel (043 95) 202. *April to September.*

28f Great Lake, Castle Howard. Fine coarse fishery with excellent catches of tench, bream, perch, pike and roach. Permits from keeper at site. YWA.

29a Zoo - Costa Beck. For 3 miles downstream from Flamingoland (🛒 ❀ 🍴 ↓T ☆). Coarse and game. Permits from Kirkby Misperton Caravan Site. *April to February.*

29b Foulbridge - River Derwent. Either bank 3 miles downstream. Coarse and game. Permits from Providence Inn, Yedingham. *April to February.*

30a West Ayton - River Derwent. Upstream to Langdale End (42i). Trout, fly only. Permits from Hackness Grange Hotel and Everley Hotel, Hackness. *April to September.*

30b Scarborough Mere (lake). Coarse. Permits from bank. YWA.

30c Filey Brigg. Shore. Rock marks, like Crab Hole, The Spittles, Binks Gulley and Ling Rock, produce good catches of coalfish, cod, dab, mackerel, pollack and wrasse. Plentiful lug locally.

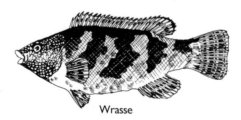

Wrasse

30c Filey. Shore. Good sand fishing for dab and other flatfish in the bay, notably at Coble Landing.
Offshore. Mostly drift fishing over rocky marks by Flamborough Head and Bempton Cliffs for cod, coalfish and haddock.

31g Bridlington. Shore. Beaches and rocky marks within the bay, as well as the North Pier and South Pier, provide good fishing for cod, dab and flounder. ⤬

31h South Landing. Offshore. Excellent fishing in sheltered water for bass, coalfish, dogfish, flatfish, mackerel, pollack and thornback ray.

32a Sellafield - River Ehen. Upstream to Ennerdale Water (44i) through Cleator Moor (44h). Coarse and game. Permits from the Post Office, Cleator Moor. *Late March to October.*

32c Wast Water. Trout (*late March to October*), salmon (*April to October*), sea trout (*May to October*) and char. Permits from Estate Office at Cockermouth Castle.

32e Seascale. Offshore. Good launching for marks giving bass, cod, flatfish, ray, tope and whiting.

32e Barn Scar. Shore. Excellent fishing for bass, cod and flatfish. Worm bait available locally.

32f Muncaster Castle - River Esk. Left bank ½ mile downstream. Trout and salmon. Permits from Pennington Arms, Ravenglass.

33a Burnmoor Tarn. Trout and pike in water owned by the National Trust. *Free.*

33b Cobdale Tarn. Perch and some trout. *Free.*

33c Grasmere. Trout, char and most coarse fish. *Free.* ⛺

33c Rydal Water. Perch, pike and reasonable trout. Permits from TS at Ambleside, Bowness and Windermere.

33c Ambleside - River Rothay. Upstream to Grasmere. Mostly trout with some perch and pike. Permits from TS at Ambleside, Bowness and Windermere.

33c Loughrigg Tarn. Coarse fishing for pike and perch. Permits from Tarn Foot Farm at the southern end of the water.

33c Elter Water. Trout, char and coarse fish. *Free.*

33c Brathay Hall - River Brathay. Right bank for 2 miles upstream. Coarse and game. Permits from TS at Ambleside, Bowness and Windermere.

33d Eel Tarn. Trout fishing. NWWA. *Free.*

33e Seathwaite Tarn. Trout and char. Permits from local TS.

33e Goats Water. Trout and char, mostly small. *Free.*

33e Coniston Water. Trout (NWWA), pike, perch, and char. Rowing boats for hire. *Free.* ⛺

33f Tarn Hows - Yew Tree Tarn. Trout fishery. Permits from Coniston TS.

33f High Arnside Tarn. Brown trout fishery, fly only. Permits from TS at Ambleside, Bowness and Windermere.

33f Esthwaite Water. Trout (*mid-March to end September*) and coarse (*mid-June to mid-March*). Boats for hire. Permits from Hazel Seat Lodge, Graythwaite. ⛺

33f Grizedale Beck. Either bank for 2 miles downstream. Trout. Permits from shop at camp site. *Easter to September.*

33h Lowick Bridge. See 21a.

33i Newby Bridge. See 21b.

34a Grasmere. See 33c.

34a Rydal Water. See 33c.

34a Ambleside. See 33c.

34a Loughrigg Tarn. See 33c.

34a Elter Water. See 33c.

34a Brathay Hall. See 33c.

34b Small Water. Trout. *Free.*

34b Troutbeck - Trout Beck. Left bank for 1 mile. Trout and perch. Permits from local TS.

34d Tarn Hows. See 33f.

34d High Arnside. See 33f.

34d Esthwaite Water. See 33f.

34d Grizedale Beck. See 33f.

34e Bowness-on-Windermere - Windermere. Trout, char, and coarse (pike and perch). Boats for hire. NWWA for trout and char. *Entire lake free.*

34e Hag End - School Knot Tarn. Trout, fly only. Permits from TS at Ambleside, Bowness and Windermere.

34f Staveley - River Kent. Upstream to Kentmere (34c). Boats for hire. Permits from Staveley Newsagents.

34f Burneside - River Kent. Downstream to Sedgwick (34i). Trout and salmon. Permits from Kendal TS. *November to August.*

34f Millcrest - River Sprint. Trout and salmon. Permits from Kendal TS.

34g Newby Bridge. See 21b.

34i Kendal - River Kent. Section known as Kendal Town Water. Trout, sea trout and salmon. *Free.*

34i Sedgwick - River Kent. Upstream to Burneside (34f). Trout and Salmon. Permits from Kendal TS. *November to August.*

34i Halforth. See 21c.

35d Browfoot - Whinfell Tarn. Coarse with rudd, perch and pike the main species. Permits from the farm by the lake.

35d Edgebank - Skelsmergh Tarn. Roach and rudd. *Free.*

35d Skelsmergh Hall - River Mint. Downstream on either bank to River Kent. Trout and salmon. Permits from Kendal TS.

35e Copplethwaite - River Lune. For 3 miles. Trout and salmon. Permits (weekly only) from Sedbergh TS.

35g Killington Reservoir. Trout *(March to September)* and coarse *(June to March)*. Permits from keeper at site or Kendal TS.

35h Sedbergh - Rivers Clough, Dee and Rawthey. Trout and salmon (Rawthey only). Permits from Sedbergh TS.

36b Halfpenny House - River Eden. Trout, fly, only. Permits from Thornaby AA, 5 Melsonby Grove, Hartburn, Stockton-on-Tees.

Brown Trout

36b Lammerside Castle - River Eden. Trout, fly only. Permits from Thornaby AA, 5 Melsonby Grove, Hartburn, Stockton-on-Tees.

36e Outhgill - River Eden. For 1½ miles. Trout, fly only. Permits from Thornaby AA, 5 Melsonby Grove, Hartburn, Stockton-on-Tees.

36h River Ure. Downstream to Cams House (37g). Trout and coarse (grayling). Permits (weekly only) from Hawes AA, 2 Chapel Street, Hawes.

37f Grinton - River Swale. Right bank for 5½ miles upstream. Trout. Permits from Thornaby AA, 5 Melsonby Grove, Hartburn, Stockton-on-Tees.

37g Cams House - River Ure. Upstream to 36h. Trout and coarse (grayling). Permits (weekly only) from Hawes AA, 2 Chapel Street, Hawes.

37g Bainbridge - River Ure. Either bank for 6 miles centred on the town. Trout *(April to September)*, and coarse, including grayling *(June to February)*. Permits from keeper at Semer Water or Rose and Crown, Bainbridge.

37g River Bain. For 1 mile downstream. Trout. Permits from Rose and Crown, Bainbridge.

37g Semer Water. Trout and coarse, including excellent bream. Permits from keeper or Rose and Crown, Bainbridge. YWA.

37h Woodhall - River Ure. Left bank for ½ mile. Trout. Permits from Skipton AA, 18 Beech Hill Road, Carelton, Skipton.

37i Aysgarth Force - River Ure. Coarse and game. Permits from Palmer Flatt Hotel, Aysgarth.

38d Grinton. See 37f.

38e Marske - River Swale. Either bank downstream to Great Langton (39d). Coarse and trout. Permits *(limited in October to February)* from Richmond TS.

38f Catterick Bridge - River Swale. Coarse and game. Permits from Thornaby AA, 5 Melsonby Grove, Hartburn, Stockton-on-Tees.

38h Middleham - River Ure. For 1½ miles upstream to Iron Bridge and 2 miles downstream. Coarse and game. Permits from Old Horn Inn, Spennithorne. *April to February.*

38h Hollins House - River Ure. For 1 mile upstream *(April to end February)* and 1½ miles downstream (fly only) of Ullshaw Bridge. Coarse and game. Permits from Blue Lion Inn, East Witton or Old Horn Inn Spennithorne.

38h River Cover. See 25b.

39a Croft-on-Tees - River Tees. For 5 miles north to Darlington and 5½ miles downstream. Coarse and trout. Permits from Thornaby AA, 5 Melsonby Grove, Hartburn, Stockton-on-Tees.

39b Neasham - River Tees. Left bank opposite village green. Coarse. *Free.*

39d Catterick - River Swale. Right bank for 1 mile. Coarse. Permits from Bridge House Hotel, Catterick.

39d Great Langton - River Swale. Either bank upstream to Marske (38e). Coarse and trout. Permits *(limited in October to February)* from Richmond TS.

39h Morton upon Swale - River Swale. Either bank downstream for 4 miles. Coarse and game. Permits from keeper in Morton. *May to December.*

39h River Swale. See 26c.

39h Pickhill. See 26c.

40e Black Shar - Cod Beck Reservoir. Trout, fly only. Permits from Hambleton District Council, 72 High Street, Northallerton. YWA.

40f Malkin Bower - River Seph. Right bank downstream to Broadway Foot (40i). Trout, fly only. Permits from Hawnby Hotel.

40i New Hall - River Rye. For 4 miles downstream. Trout, fly only. Permits from Hawnby Hotel.

40i Broadway Foot - River Seph. Upstream to Malkin Bower (40f). Trout, fly only. Permits from Hawnby Hotel.

42b Sleights - River Esk. Downstream to pier end in Whitby (42c). Trout, sea trout and salmon. Permits from Whitby TS; Mrs Perry, River Gardens, Sleights or R. Swaby, Millbeck, The Carrs, Ruswarp.

Salmon

42c Whitby. Shore. The East and West Piers fish well for bass, cod, flatfish, mullet and whiting.

Offshore. Boat fishing can add catches of conger, dogfish, haddock, ling, pollack and ray. Lug from east side of harbour at low tide.

42h High Dalby House - Dalby Beck. For 3 miles. Trout. Permits from Chief Forester, Low Dalby.

42i Langdale End - River Derwent. Downstream (south) to West Ayton (30a). Trout, fly only.

Permits from Pritchard's TS, Eastborough or Hackness Grange Hotel and Everley Hotel, Hackness. *April to September.*

43h Scarborough - Shore. Bass, cod, coalfish, dab, flounder, mackerel, plaice and whiting caught from rock marks at The Basin, The Horseshoe and East Pier. Sandy marks at Marina Drive and West Pier are good for flatfish.

Offshore. Marks in South Bay off Marina Drive for flatfish and off Scalby Mills for the above plus conger, dogfish, haddock, ling and pollack.

43h Scarborough Mere. See 30b.

44b Maryport Shore. Prime beach marks along Grasslot and Promenade beaches but all types of shorefishing good. Species caught include bass, cod, dab, flounder, plaice, pollack and whiting.

Offshore. Good catches of ray, tope, dogfish, mackerel and coalfish. Rag from shore at golf course.

44b Seaton. Shore. Good catches of dab, flounder, cod, mackerel, plaice, silver eel and whiting. Lug available locally.

44c Cockermouth - River Cocker. Section known as the Town Water. Trout, sea trout and salmon. Permits from the Town Hall.

River Derwent. Sections known as the Town Water and the Egremont Estate Water. Trout, sea trout and salmon. Permits from Town Hall.

44d Harrington. Shore. Good for catches of cod, dab, flounder, mackerel, plaice, silver eel and whiting.

44d Parton. Shore. Good rock fishing mark from which can be caught cod, mackerel, silver eel and whiting.

44e Workington. Offshore. Very good boat fishing a mile out for cod, dogfish, mackerel, ray, tope and whiting. Worm and lug available locally.

44f Loweswater. Pike, perch and trout. Boats for hire. Permits from Cockermouth TS or Kirkstile Inn, Loweswater.

44f Congra Moss (reservoir). Trout, fly only. Permits from Cockermouth TS. *April to September.*

44g Whitehaven. Shore. Fishing marks at Wellington beach and Whitehaven Pier are good for flatfish, cod, mackerel, silver eel and whiting.

Offshore. As well as the above species catches are made of dogfish, pouting, ray and tope.

44g St Bees Head. Shore. Very similar fishing to Parton (see 44d).

44h Meadley Reservoir. Trout. Permits from Post Office, Cleator Moor or Wath Brow and Ennerdale AA, 11 Crossings Close, Cleator Moor. *Late March to October.*

44i Ennerdale Bridge - River Ehen. Downstream to Sellafield (32a) through Cleator Moor (44h). Coarse and game. Permits from the Post Office. Cleator Moor. *Late March to October.*

44i Ennerdale Water. Trout with the chance of char, salmon and sea trout. Permits from Post Office, Cleator Moor. *Late March to October.*

45b Bassenthwaite Lake. Trout, perch and pike, with the occasional salmon. Boats for hire. Permits from Bassenthwaite Post Office.

45e Portinscale - River Derwent. Either bank for 1½ miles downstream. Trout *(late March to mid-September)* and salmon *(April to September)*. Permits from Temple's TS, Station Street, Keswick.

45e Derwent Water. Coarse and trout. Boats for hire. Permits from Temple's TS, Station Street, Keswick.

45f Keswick - River Greta. Right bank for ½ mile. Trout *(late March to September)* and salmon *(April to October)*. Permits from Temple's TS, Station Street, Keswick.

114

45g Crummock Water. Coarse and game. Boats for hire. Permits from Kirkstile Inn, Loweswater or the Gun Shop, Cockermouth.

45g Buttermere. Trout, char and coarse (pike and perch). Permits from Croft House Farm, Buttermere, Kirkstile Inn, Loweswater or Cockermouth TS.

45i Watendlath Tarn. Trout and pike (large). *Free.*

45i Blea Tarn. Good trout and perch. Permits from Keswick TS.

46e Ullswater. Trout *(late March to mid-September)*, salmon *(mid-January to mid-October)*, sea trout *(May to mid-October)* and coarse fish. *Free* fishing but some access is private.

46e High Force - Aira Beck. National Trust water. Trout. *Free.*

46g Red Tarn. Trout and the chance of gwyniad. *Free.*

46g Grisedale Beck. Entire stream. Trout. *Free.*

46g Deepdale Beck. Trout. *Free.*

46g Grisedale Tarn. Trout. *Free.*

46h Goldrill Beck. Trout. *Free.*

46h Brothers Water. Pike, perch and trout. *Free* but some access is private and permission must be obtained from the owner.

46h Hartsop Beck. Entire stream. Trout. *Free.*

46h Small Water. See 34b.

47e Bank - River Eden. Upstream to Sandford (47i) through Appleby (47f). Coarse. Permits from Appleby TS, Market Place. *October to January.*

Rudd

47i Sandford - River Eden. Downstream to Bank (47e) through Appleby (47f). Coarse. Permits from Appleby TS, Market Place, Appleby *October to January.*

48b Cow Green Reservoir. Trout. Permits from Ticket Office at site. NWA.

48b Caldron Snout - River Tees. Left bank downstream to Newbiggin (48f). Trout, fly only. Permits from Raby Estate Office, Middleton-in-Teesdale. *Late March to September.*

48f Newbiggin - River Tees. Upstream to Caldron Snout (48b). Trout, fly only. Permits from Raby Estate Office, Middleton. *Late March to September.*

48f Selset Reservoir. 625 acres of brown and rainbow trout, fly only. Permits from ticket machine at site. NWA.

48g Sandford. See 47i

48i Balderhead Reservoir. 576 acres of trout. Permits from ticket machine at site. NWA.

49d Middleton-in-Teesdale - River Tees. Right

bank. Trout, fly only. Permits from Cleveland Arms, Middleton or Turnbull Estate Agents, Chester-le-Street. *Late March to September.*

49d Grassholme Reservoir. 250 acres of brown and rainbow trout. Rowing boats for hire. Permits from ticket machine at site. NWA.

49d Hury Reservoir. 204 acres of brown and rainbow trout. Rowing boats for hire. Permits from ticket machine at the site. NWA.

49g Blackton Reservoir. 110 acres of brown trout. Permits from ticket machine at site. NWA.

49h Barnard Castle - River Tees. Between Stone and Thorngate Bridge. Trout. *Free.*

50a Holme House - River Wear. Upstream to A68 Bridge. Trout, sea trout and salmon. Permits from The Cottage, Witton-le-Wear or Estate Office, Lambton Park, Chester-le-Street.

50b Willington - River Wear. For 4 miles above and below the town. Trout and sea trout. Permits from Bond's TS, 80 High Street, Willington.

50i Croft-on-Tees. See 39a.

51c Hartlepool. Shore. Marks at Heugh Breakwater, Lighthouse Corner, Carr House Sands, Staincliff and North Gare for cod, dogfish and haddock.

Offshore. Boats available for hire. Main species caught include cod, coalfish, dab, flounder, plaice, pouting, and whiting.

51h Aislaby - River Tees. Right bank downstream to River Leven. Coarse. Permits from Flynn's TS, 12 Vard Terrace, Stockton-on-Tees.

52a Hartlepool. See 51c.

52e South Gare Breakwater. Shore. Cod, conger, dab, flounder, mackerel, plaice, pollack, sole and whiting. Worm bait available locally.

52e Bran Sands. Shore. The Tees estuary and adjoining coastline fish well for coalfish, cod, dab, flounder, gurnard, mackerel, plaice and sole.

52e Coatham Sands. Shore. The beaches east to Redcar are very productive for the species listed above at Bran Sands.

52f Redcar. Shore. Good marks along the sands and rocks of this area. Species caught include cod, conger, flatfish, mackerel, pollack and whiting.

52f Marske-by-the-Sea. Shore. Good casting beach which gives catches of codling and flatfish.

52f Saltburn Pier. Shore. Fishes well for coalfish, codling, flounder, mackerel and whiting.

52i Lockwood Beck Reservoir. 60 acres of trout, fly only. Rowing boats for hire. Permits from ticket machine at site. NWA. *May to October.*

53d Saltburn-by-the-Sea - Penny Hole. Shore. A popular venue for codling.

53h Scaling Dam Reservoir. 105 acres of brown trout *(April to September)* and rainbow trout *(April to October)*. Permits from ticket machine at site. YWA.

53i Sandsend Ness. Shore. Sand fishing between here and Happy Valley is good for bass, cod, flatfish, mullet, mackerel and whiting.

Sea Bass

54c Whitehill - River Waver. From Solway Firth upstream through 54f and 55d. Trout and sea trout. *Free* but permission for access must be sought from relevant farmers.

54f Abbeytown - Crummock Beck. Upstream from junction with River Waver. Trout. *Free.*

54g Maryport. See 44b.

54h Low Leathes - River Ellen. Upstream to Allhallows (54i). Trout, sea trout and salmon. Permits (weekly only) from The Colour Shop, Aspatria.

54i Brayton Park - Brayton Pond. Coarse. Permits from Keepers' Cottage close to lake. NWWA.

54i Allhallows - River Ellen. Downstream to Low Leathes (54h). Trout, sea trout and salmon. Permits (weekly only) from The Colour Shop, Aspatria.

55a Whitrigg - River Wampool. Most of river upstream to West Curthwaite (55e). Trout and sea trout. *Free.*

55b Thurstonfield Lough. Trout, fly only. Rowing boats for hire. Permits from keeper at site. NWWA.

55c Carlisle - River Eden. For 7 miles centred on the town. Trout and salmon. Permits from Carlisle TS. *Mid-January to mid-October.*

55c Rickerby - River Eden. Downstream to railway bridge west of Carlisle. Coarse. Permits from Taylor's TS, Grove Lane, Carlisle. *October 15 to January 16.*

55e West Curthwaite - River Wampool. Downstream to Whitrigg (55a). Trout and sea trout. *Free.*

56a Carlisle. See 55c.

56a Rickerby. See 55c.

56b Ryeclose - Rivers Irthing and Gelt. Fishing area shown on map with ticket. Coarse and trout. Permits from Sports Shop, Front Street, Brampton.

56b Warwick - River Eden. In grounds of Warwick Hall. Trout and salmon. Rowing boats for hire. Permits from the Hall or Crown Hotel, Wetheral.

56c Talkin Tarn. Coarse including pike, perch and roach. Rowing boats for hire. *Free.*

57e Alston - River South Tyne. For 7 miles in upper reaches as described on ticket. Trout, sea trout and salmon. Permits from Alston TS.

58b Allendale Town - River East Allen. As detailed on maps available with ticket. Trout, fly only. Permits (fortnightly only) from Allendale Post Office.

58f Blanchland - River Derwent. Trout, fly only. Permits from Lord Crewe Arms, Blanchland.

58h Cowshill - River Wear. Downstream to Westgate (58i). Trout. Permits from the pub in St. John's Chapel.

58h Burnhope Reservoir. 408 acres of trout. Permits from Ticket Office at site. NWA.

58i Westgate - River Wear. Upstream to Cowshill (58h). Trout. Permits from the pub in St. John's Chapel.

58i Eastgate - River Wear. Downstream to Stanhope (59g). Trout, sea trout and salmon, fly only. Permits from Phoenix Hotel, Stanhope.

59a Derwent Reservoir. Seven miles of bank fishing. Brown and rainbow trout, fly only. Rowing and motor boats for hire. Permits from the Utilities Building at the site. NWA. *May to mid-October.*

59d Waskerley Reservoir. Trout. Permits from Ticket Office at site. NWA.

59e Smiddy Shaw Reservoir. Trout. Permits from Ticket Office at site. NWA.

59g Stanhope - River Wear. Upstream to Eastgate (58i). Trout, sea trout and salmon, fly only. Permits from Phoenix Hotel, Stanhope.

59h Tunstall Reservoir. 112 acres of fly fishing for rainbow and brown trout. Permits from ticket machine at Fishing Lodge. NWA. *May to October.*

60f Finchale Priory - River Wear. South bank for 2 miles. Trout. Permits from Farmhouse Shop at caravan site, tel. Durham (0385) 66528.

60h Willington. See 50b.

60i Durham - River Wear. Left bank from Milburngate to sewage works and right bank from below ice rink to Kepier Priory Farm. Trout and salmon. *Free.*

61a Sunderland - River Wear estuary. Shore. Cod, coalfish, dab, flounder, haddock, mackerel, plaice, pouting and whiting.

61b Roker. Shore. Marks from pier north to Whitburn Bay yield cod, coalfish, flatfish, haddock, mackerel, pouting and whiting.

61b Ryhope. Shore. The beaches south to Hawthorn Hive (61e) give good catches of cod, dab, flounder, haddock, mackerel, plaice, pollack and ray.

61e Seaham. Shore. One of the few beaches in the area that can be well fished for ray, as well as cod, flatfish, mackerel, pouting and whiting.

Offshore. Large numbers of conger, haddock, ling, dogfish, pollack, ray and whiting can be caught at many marks offshore.

61e Hawthorn Hive. Shore. Beaches north to Ryhope (see 61b.)

61i Hartlepool. See 51c.

62e Oakbank (gravel pit). Coarse. Permits from Border Coarse AC, 9 Bruton Crescent, Carlisle.

62i Ryeclose. See 56b.

63g Brampton - River Irthing. Trout, fly only. Various sites in area. Permits from Brampton TS.

63i Featherstone Castle - River South Tyne. Downstream to Bardon Mill (64h) through Haltwhistle. Trout, sea trout and salmon. Permits from Wallace Arms, Featherstone or TS in area.

64g Featherstone Castle. See 63i.

64h Bardon Mill - River South Tyne. Upstream to Featherstone Castle (63i/64g). Trout, sea trout, salmon. Permits from Wallace Arms, Featherstone or TS in the area.

65b Sweethope Loughs. One lake offers fly fishing for trout and the other coarse fishing. Rowing boats and ghillies for hire on trout lake. Permits from keeper at Lake House, tel. Kirkwhelpington (0803) 4249.

65d Chollerford - River North Tyne. Left bank for 1½ miles. Coarse and game. Permits from the George Hotel, Chollerford.

65h Hexham - River Tyne. Right bank for 1 mile upstream. Trout and salmon, fly only. Permits from Tynedale District Council, Hexham, tel. (0434) 604011.

65i Welton Hall - Whittle Dene Reservoirs. Brown and rainbow trout (fly only) in 7 reservoirs north and south of B6318. Permits from keeper, tel. Wylam (066 14) 3210. 🐦

66a Bolam Lake. Coarse. NWA. *Free.* ♣ 🏕️⛵

66c Stannington Bridge - River Blyth. Downstream to Bedlington (67a). Coarse, especially grayling and roach, and trout. Permits from Bedlington and Blagdon AA, 8 Moorland Drive, Bedlington. NWA.

66g Welton Hall. See 65i.

66i Winlaton Mill - River Derwent. Right bank to Lintz Ford. Trout. Permits from Axwell Park and Derwent Valley AA, 14 Naylor Avenue, Winlaton Mill.

67a Sheepwash - River Wansbeck. For 2½ miles in Wansbeck Park. Trout. Permits from Park warden. ♣ 🏕️

Do you need permission?

The right to fish a river, reservoir or pond is always controlled by its owner. In some cases rivers and the like are available to the angler free, i.e. access is not restricted and permits are not required, and this is denoted in the text by *Free*. And sea fishing from or off our shore is not restricted by permits at all, except on municipal piers, etc. However, on all other inland waters some form of permission is required. This usually means buying a ticket issued daily or weekly. Sources for these permits are indicated in the text by the following abbreviations:

TS - Tackle Shop, usually a sports shop or, in the case of small villages or ports, a newsagent

AA - Angling Association

AC - Angling Club

FA - Fishing Association

In many instances permission is also needed from the local water authority. They issue rod licences, usually one per rod, and these may be needed in addition to any ticket or permit. The following abbreviations indicate that a rod licence is required and the water authority from which they are available:

NWA - Northumbrian Water Authority, Northumbrian House, Regent Centre, Gosforth, Newcastle upon Tyne NE3 3PX. Tel. Gosforth (0632) 843151

NWWA - North West Water Authority, New Town House, Buttermarket Street, Warrington WA1 2QG. Tel. Warrington (0925) 53999

YWA - Yorkshire Water Authority, West Riding House, 67 Albion Street, Leeds LS1 5AA. Tel. Leeds (0532) 448201

However, it is very important that before any angling expedition you telephone or write to the person in control of the water you wish to fish, especially with angling clubs. This will avoid any disappointment if conditions and ownership have changed.

67a Bedlington - River Blyth. Upstream to Stannington Bridge (66c). Coarse and trout. Permits from Bedlington and Blagdon AA, 8 Moorland Drive, Bedlington. NWA.

67b River Blyth estuary. Shore. The staithes upstream beyond the ferry can produce coalfish, codling, eel, dab, flounder and plaice.

67b Blyth Pier. Shore. Fishes well for codling, dab, eel, flounder, gurnard, plaice and whiting.

67b Link House - Blyth Beach. Shore. A popular spot for catches of codling, coalfish and flatfish.

67d Brunswick Village - Big Waters. Coarse on 1 lake and 1 pond. Permits in advance from Big Waters AC, c/o 12 Bellister Grove, Fenham, Newcastle (SAE).

67i Marsden Bay. Shore. Fishing marks extend from Lizard Point to South Shields and yield coalfish, cod, dab, flounder, haddock, mackerel, plaice, pouting and whiting.

67i Roker. See 61b.

68f Kielder Castle - River North Tyne. Brown trout on the river and several burns in the area. Permits from Kielder Castle. 🎣 ♣ 🏕️ ⓩ

68i Kielder Water. Stocking with brown and American brook trout. Permits from ticket machine at the Fishing Lodge. ⚠️

69e Blakehopeburnhaugh - River Rede. Trout fishing on 1 mile. Permits from Kielder Castle. ♣

69g Falstone - River North Tyne. For ¼ mile on either bank. Trout and salmon. Permits from Black Cock Inn, Falstone.

69g Kielder Water. See 68i.

70e Blakehopeburnhaugh. See 69e.

70g Falstone. See 69g.

70i Otterburn - River Rede. For 3½ miles downstream. Coarse and game. Permits from Tower Hotel, Otterburn.

71e Hepple - River Coquet. Either bank downstream to Cragend (71f). Trout and salmon. Permits from Rothbury TS.

71e Fontburn Reservoir. 87 acres of native brown trout. Permits from ticket machine at Fishing Lodge. 🎣

71f Rothbury - River Coquet. Salmon and brown trout. Permits from Rothbury and Thropton AC, 'Sandhaig', Hillside, Rothbury.

71f Cragend - River Coquet. Either bank upstream to Hepple (71e). Trout and salmon. Permits from Rothbury TS.

72d Hepple. See 71e.

72e Rothbury. See 71f.

72e Cragend. See 71f.

72e Fontburn Reservoir. See 71e.

72f Low Headley - River Coquet. Salmon and trout. Permits from Anglers Arms, Weldon Bridge, Morpeth.

73b Alnmouth. Shore. Good and extensive beach fishing for cod, flatfish and mackerel.

Offshore. Good launching for marks in Alnmouth Bay. Lug from the estuary sand.

73b Warkworth Harbour. Shore. Good sport for dab, flounder, mackerel and plaice from the two local piers. *Note* in rough weather the piers are exposed and therefore dangerous.

73b Amble. Shore. Good shallow water fishing from sand strip between the headlands for winter codling.

73b Hauxley Haven - Hauxley Point. Good rock fishing mark for winter codling. 🐦

73h Sheepwash. See 67a.

77b Shoreston Dunes. Shore. Good rock fishing venue known as the Tumblers for coalfish, codling, flatfish, mackerel and whiting.

77b Seahouses. Shore. Good marks at main pier, harbour and Cherwick Sands. Species caught include coalfish, codling, flounder, and plaice.

Offshore. Main launching point for boat fishing around Farne Islands and Longstone (79c). Catches from these marks include cod, dogfish, flatfish, monkfish, haddock, gurnard and ray.

77b Snook Point. Shore. Good rock fishing venue similar to Shoreston Dunes (77b).

77g Alnwick Abbey - River Aln. Downstream to Alnmouth Bridge (B1338) (77h). Trout, fly only. Permits from TS and Midland Bank, Alnwick. NWA. *Late March to September.*

77h B1338 (Alnmouth Bridge) - River Aln. Upstream to Alnwick Abbey (77g). Trout, fly only. Permits from TS and Midland Bank, Alnwick. NWA. *Late March to September.*

77h Alnmouth. See 73b.

78e Norham - River Tweed. For 3 miles above and below the bridge. Coarse and trout. Permits from the Masons Arms, Norham.

78f Horncliffe - River Tweed. Downstream to Berwick-upon-Tweed (79a). Coarse and trout. *Free.*

79a Berwick-upon-Tweed - River Tweed. Upstream to Horncliffe (78f). Coarse and trout.

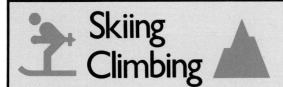

Skiing Climbing

18a Harrogate: Skiing. Harrogate Ski Centre, Hookstone Wood Road, tel. (0423) 55457. 100 metre artificial slope with tow facilities. ☕

21i Lancaster: Skiing. College of Further Education, Morecambe Road, tel. (0524) 66215 ext. 50. One 50 metre artificial slope.

22g Lancaster. See 21i.

23b Dentdale: Whernside Cave and Fell Centre, tel. Dent (058 75) 213. Holiday courses in caving, pot-holing, fell walking and mountaineering. ☕

23b Whernside: Hill Walking. Highest point in North Yorkshire at 737 metres; well marked path to the summit from Bruntscar.

23f Pen-y-Ghent: Hill Walking. Best ascent is via the Pennine Way from the south. This summit, together with Ingleborough (23e) and Whernside (23b), is an objective of the Three Peaks Walk. The Three Peaks of Yorkshire Club is based at Pen-y-Ghent Cafe: to become a member all three peaks must be climbed within 12 hours. ⚑

23e Ingleborough: Hill Walking. Several routes to the summit include a path from Ingleton (23d).

23f Hull Pot and Hunt Pot: Caving. Two of the many suitable caves in the area. Dangerous for beginners; contact Cave Centre, Dentdale (23b).

24d Pen-y-Ghent. See 23f.

24d Hull Pot and Hunt Pot. See 23f.

25h Pateley Bridge: North Pennine Outdoor Pursuits Co Ltd, Kings Court, tel. Harrogate (0423) 711197. Caving, climbing, gorge running and orienteering holidays. ☕ ⚑ ⚠

29b Thornton Dale. See 42h Low Dalby.

32f Eskdale Green: Outward Bound. Tel. (094 03) 281 or London (01) 491 1355. Holiday courses in caving, climbing, hiking, and orienteering

33a Great Gable: Hill Walking. Many routes to the summit: from the top of Honister Pass (45h) via Grey Knotts, Brandreth and Green Gable, probably the easiest and most attractive route; from Seathwaite via Sour Milk Gill and Green Gable; from Seathwaite via Sty Head; from Wasdale via Sty Head; and from Gatesgarth (45h) via Brandreth and Green Gable.
    Rock Climbing. Many testing climbs on the north face. In poor conditions they can become extremely greasy and unsafe.

33a Scafell Pike: Hill Walking. Highest English mountain (977 metres). There are 3 main routes: from Borrowdale (45h) via Sty Head and Great End; from Hardknott Roman Fort (m 33d) up the Esk valley, Cam Spout and Mickledore; and from Wasdale Head via Lingmell Gill.
    Rock Climbing. To the west, across Hollow Stones, Pike's Crag has a large, broken surface providing numerous climbs of a high standard.

33a Sca Fell: Hill Walking. Easiest ascents are from the west: from Wasdale Head via Lingmell Gill and Brown Tongue, the most popular route; and from Eskdale over Slight Side. A more difficult route from the east is from Mickledore via Lord's Rake, but this is only for the experienced and is dangerous in icy conditions.
    Rock Climbing. One of the birthplaces of rock climbing. Many magnificent climbs of up to 400 ft and of every degree of difficulty.

33a Heron Crag: Rock Climbing. Several very severe routes of up to 250ft on a steep outcrop.

33b Pavey Ark: Rock Climbing. Climbs of all standards, up to 300 ft long.

33b Langdale: Rock Climbing. White Ghyll Crag has several routes of up to 250ft for experienced climbers only.

33c Ambleside: Brathay Exploration Group, Old Brathay, tel. (096 63) 3042. Courses in mountain craft for those aged 16 to 22. *March to April and August.*

33d Wallowbarrow Crag: Rock Climbing. Short but testing climbs.

33e Dow Crag: Rock Climbing. Many routes here, up to 400ft long and suitable for all standards. Longest routes at the southern end. One of the birthplaces of rock climbing, it can be very crowded in summer.

33e Old Man of Coniston: Hill Walking. Main routes to the summit (starting east and going clockwise) are: Church Beck and Low Water, the shortest and easiest route; Heathwaite and Goats Water, past the popular climbing area on Dow Crag (see previous entry); Long House east to Brown Pike and then north; Seathwaite Tarn, with routes on both sides of the lake giving access from the north; Wrynose, a tough route from Three Shire stone (m 33b) via the secondary summits of Carrs and Great How; Low Fell (33b) and Holme Fell (33f), both paths converging at the summit of Wetherlam, from which paths lead south to Church Beck or west to Great How to follow previously described routes.

33i Lakeside: YMCA National Centre, tel. Newby Bridge (0448) 31758. Courses in caving, fell walking, orienteering and rock climbing.

34a Ambleside. See 33c.

34b Tongue House: Rock Climbing. Several 100ft climbs up Tongue Scar.

34b Rainsborrow Crag: Rock Climbing. Short climbs on vegetation-covered crag.

34b Troutbeck: Skiing. Limefitt Park Ski Centre tel. Ambleside (096 63) 2300. Facilities for grass-skiing include a lift and hire equipment. *April to September daily.* ☕ ⚲

34c Goat Scar: Rock Climbing. Broken crag with one route to the top.

34e Windermere: Mountain Goat Holidays, Victoria Street, tel. (096 62) 5161. Fell walking in the Lake District; 4 graduated walks end in ascents of Helvellyn (46g) and Scafell Pike (33a). Equipment may be hired. *April to October.*

34g Lakeside. See 33i.

35i Dentdale. See 23b.

36b Birkdale: Hill Walking. High Pike Hill (642 metres high) is most easily reached from B6270 to the north. Path runs along Mallerstang Edge to Black Fell Moss (36e).

36e Wild Boar Fell: Hill Walking. Numerous routes to wide, flat summit. Best access from south; best views to north.

36e Black Fell Moss: Hill Walking. This peak straddles the Cumbria-Yorkshire border. The easiest route to the summit is from the north, via Mallerstang Edge.

36f Great Shunner Fell: Hill Walking. Lies on the Pennine Way (see page 15). Easiest access is from Thwaite (37d).

36f Lovely Seat: Hill Walking. Easiest route is from the road near Butter Tubs.

36g Dentdale. See 23b.

37a Rogan's Seat: Hill Walking. Several routes to

the summit, which is marked by a small cairn.

38f Catterick Camp: Skiing. Catterick Indoor Ski Slope, Loos Road, tel. Richmond (0748) 833788. Two dry ski slopes and tow facilities. *Tuesday to Friday 1930-2200; Sundays 1230-1700; winter Saturdays 1400-1630.*

40c Hasty Bank: Rock Climbing. Many easy and moderate climbs from 25 to 40ft long.

40f Bilsdale East Moor: Rock Climbing. Two routes on the main crag and four more on the offshoot to the south.

41a Easby Moor: Rock Climbing. Several easy, short climbs in Potter's Quarry.

41d Bransdale Moor: Fell Walking. Start of the toughest part of the Lyke Wake Walk, the route of which is marked on the maps. See ♣ 40e (page 81) for details.

41i Sutherland Lodge Activity Centre. Tel. Cropton (075 15) 228. Multi-activity holidays include orienteerings, climbing, etc. ⚑ ⚲

42c Stainsacre Hall, North Yorkshire YO22 4NT. Weekend and weekly courses in mountaineering and fell walking. Adults only. *Open all year.*

42f Ulla Howe: Fell Walking. Eastern edge of the upland section of the Lyke Wake Walk (see 41d).

42g Sutherland Lodge. See 41i.

42h Low Dalby: Orienteering. Wayfaring (orienteering for beginners) course. Maps from Forestry office; access via toll road. ♣ ⛺

44g St Bees Head: Rock Climbing. Very steep cliffs of New Red Sandstone offer climbs of up to 300ft; most routes are between the lighthouse steps and Three Castles buttress. For highly experienced climbers only. ⚑ ⚲

44h Cleator: Skiing. West Cumbria Ski Club, c/o Ehenside School. 25 metre artificial slope. *September to May.*

45a Lambfoot: Higham Hall, tel. Bassenthwaite Lake (059 681) 276. Multi-activity holidays include fell walking, pony trekking and orienteering.

45b Skiddaw: Hill Walking. 3 routes to the summit: from the southeast on Lonscale Fell (45f) a footpath leads directly to the top, first passing Little Man; from the south at Millbeck (45e) via Carl Side; from the northwest by the stream near Barkbeth (45b) via Skiddaw, the longest and most interesting route.

45e Whinlatter Pass: Orienteering. Permanent wayfaring (basic orienteering) course begins from the Visitors' Centre. ♣ ⛺ 🚻

45g Pillar: Hill Walking. 2 routes to the summit: from Buttermere (45g) via Scarth Gap, Black Sail Pass and Looking Stead; and from Gillerthwaite (45g) along the River Liza.
    Rock Climbing. Many magnificent climbs up to 500 ft long and of all standards. Least difficult are to the east; best and longest climbs are on the west and north faces, especially on Pillar Rock, a northern outcrop with a maze of dead ends and vertical gullies. Descents can be hazardous in mist or bad weather; more groups have been forced to bivouac on this crag than on any other in the Lake District.

45h Lodore Cascade: Rock Climbing. Shepherd's Crag buttresses provide numerous climbs ranging from easy to extremely severe.

45h Grange: Rock Climbing. Two crags. Black Crag is split into two buttresses: the right-hand buttress provides wall, groove and slab climbing and has the easier routes; the left-hand buttress is steeper with overhangs, and has several hard climbs. Great End Crag is partially vegetated, but has some severe climbs.

45h Dale Head: Rock Climbing. Buckstone How has many steep climbs of 150 to 300ft. It should be attempted by experienced climbers only.

45h Great Gable. See 33a.

46e Outward Bound Mountain School, tel. Pooley Bridge (085 36) 347 or London (01) 491 1355. Two or three-week courses in mountaineering, hill walking, climbing and mountain rescue.

46g Helvellyn: Hill Walking. Most popular mountain in the Lake District with many routes to the summit. Anti-clockwise from Thirlspot (45i) these are: Thirlspot (King's Head public house) via the path annually waymarked with whitewash; from Wythburn Church (46g) by Whelp Side, the easiest route but takes about 3 hours; via Grisedale Tarn; via Striding Edge, dangerous in icy conditions or high wind and for experienced walkers only; via Swirrel Edge to the north of Red Tarn (🥄), only slightly easier than Striding Edge.

46h High Raise: Hill Walking. Best ascent is from Howtown to the north via Fusedale Beck and High Street Roman Road (m 46f).

47c Cross Fell: Hill Walking. Highest of the Pennines, at 890 metres. Three routes lead to the summit: the shortest and easiest is from Great Dun Fell, crossing the source of the River Tees; from Kirkland (47b) via Kirk Dale and the Pennine Way, the final approach is on the northwest face; and from Fiends Fell (57g), the highest route runs via Knapside Hill and Melmerby Fell.

47f Backstone Edge: Hill Walking. The easiest route to this summit is from Dufton.
Rock Climbing. See 48d.

48a Viewing Hill: Hill Walking. Most easily reached from the track directly west; also accessible from Herdship Fell (48b). The top is flat and boggy, making walking difficult.

48b Ski-tow. Slopes and tow can also be used for grass skiing.

48c Ski-tow. Runs from the upper slopes of Fendrith Hill; used for grass skiing.

48c Newbiggin Common: Hill Walking. Summit, is accessible from the minor road to the west.

48d Backstone Edge: Rock Climbing. Several climbs of up to 50ft on High Cup Nick, a spectacular ravine with a sheer rock face rising vertically for 100ft.
Hill Walking. See 47f.

49c Toll - Hamsterley Forest: Orienteering. Permanent Forestry Commission wayfaring (basic orienteering) course. Maps from the Information Centre or from Hamsterley village post office. ♣

49g Goldsborough Carr: Rock Climbing. Broken gritstone edges give climbs of up to 100ft.

50b Westerton: Rock Climbing. Gritstone quarry with about 30 climbs of up to 30ft.

52h Eston Nab: Rock Climbing. Partially quarried crag has about 40 climbs.

52h Roseberry Topping: Rock Climbing. 'The Matterhorn of Cleveland' has a few climbs on its southeast face; the southwest face is dangerous.

52h Easby Moor. See 41a.

52i Guisborough: Skiing. Ski Club, Hunters Hill, tel. (0287) 35431. Grass ski slope, equipment hire and instruction. *April to September: Sundays 1400-1800.*

52i Guisborough Moor: Rock Climbing. On Highcliffe Nab are steep routes of up to 70ft.

55c Carlisle: Skiing. Carlisle Ski Club (secretary tel. Burgh-by-Sands 022 876 562). Artificial 50 metre ski slope; instruction. *October to March.* ☛

56a Carlisle. See 55c.

57d Black Fell: Hill Walking. See 57e Grey Nag.

57d Hartside Height. See 57e Grey Nag.

57e Grey Nag: Hill Walking. North end of a ridge stretching south to Black Fell (57d) and Hartside Height; all 3 can be reached in a single walk, passing Tom Smith's Stone (631 metres) marking the boundary of Cumbria and Northumbria. Access to southern end from A686; access to northern end from the Pennine Way near Whitley Castle (m 57e).

57g Fiends Fell: Hill Walking. Swiftest ascent from the highest point of A686; also may be reached along the ridge from Cross Fell (57h).

57h Cross Fell: Hill Walking. See 47c.

57i Flinty Fell: Hill Walking. Easy climb from the minor road to the north.

57i Viewing Hill. See 48a.

58d Killhope Moor: Hill Walking. Dominating the moorland, Killhope Law (670 metres) is reached by a path from Allenheads up the northwest face.

58e Allenheads Lodge Outdoor Activities Centre, tel. (043 485) 239. Holidays with snow and grass skiing, rambling, back packing, rock climbing and orienteering. Minimum age 12.

58e Puddingthorn Moor: Hill Walking. Easy ascent from B6295; more interesting route along bridleway from the south near Mount Pleasant.

58e Burtree Fell: Hill Walking. Summit is exactly 2000ft (610 metres). Easily reached from a car park on B6295 near the county boundary.

58g Flinty Fell. See 57i.

58g Viewing Hill. See 48a.

58h Ski-tows. See 48b and 48c.

64e Broomlee Lough: Rock Climbing. Queen's Crag, a quartz outcrop, has some short climbs.

64e Crag Lough: Rock Climbing. Quartz dolerite crag, the finest in the area, with nearly 50 climbs, of all standards and up to 80ft long.

69h Greenhaugh: Family Activity Holidays. Among the pursuits arranged are climbing, fell walking, deer stalking (gun or camera) and orienteering. Tel. R Hodgson (0660) 40245.

70h Greenhaugh. See 69h.

71d Sandy Crags: Rock Climbing. Many climbs of 35ft on fell sandstone.

71e Ravensheugh: Rock Climbing. About 35 climbs of 15 to 40ft.

71e Simonside: Rock Climbing. Fell sandstone outcrop with 40 climbs, most relatively easy.

71e Selby's Cove: Rock Climbing. Compact sandstone crag with several routes.

71g Wishaw Pike: Rock Climbing. Small sandstone crag with a few climbs.

72d Sandy Crags. See 71d.

72e Ravensheugh. See 71e.

72e Simonside. See 71e.

72e Selby's Cove. See 71e.

75c Wooler: Ewart Outdoor Centre. YMCA-run weekly courses in climbing, fell walking, grass skiing and orienteering. Tel. C Jones, Fencehouses (038 579) 2822.

75d Auchope Cairn: Hill Walking. Named after a British general killed in the Boer War, this cairn stands between two unnamed summits (726 and 737 metres high). It can be reached from The Cheviot; via the Pennine Way; or from Cocklawfoot to the west, a duller route.

75d The Cheviot: Hill Walking. The highest mountain in Northumbria (816 metres). It can be reached: from Langleeford (75e) via Harthope Burn and Cairn Hill, the shortest and most beautiful route, via the Pennine Way which crosses it north-south; or from Auchope Cairn.

75e Langlee Crags: Rock Climbing. Some 30-ft routes on good sandstone.

75e Comb Fell: Hill Walking. Best route is from the northeast, from Langleeford.

75g Windy Gyle: Hill Walking. Summit straddles the England-Scotland Border and is marked by a large cairn. There are four routes to the summit: from Bloodybush Edge; from Barrow Lane via Hindside Knowe and The Street footpath to the Pennine Way; via the Pennine Way itself; or from Cocklawfoot in Scotland.

75g Bloodybush Edge: Hill Walking. Two paths lead to this 610 metre summit: from Uswayford to the east, the shorter route (under 1 hour); or from Heigh to the south, via Cushat Law.

75h Cushat Law: Hill Walking. This 616 metre summit can be reached from Heigh to the southwest.

76b Wooler. See 75c.

76c Belford Moor: Rock Climbing. Bowden Doors is an extensive sandstone crag with short climbs of all grades.

76c Belford: Windy Gyle Outdoor Centre, West Street, tel. (066 83) 289. Adventure holidays including rock climbing and fell walking. Minimum age 16. *June to September.* △ ∪ ☆

76d Langlee Crags. See 75e.

76d Comb Fell. See 75e.

76g Cushat Law. See 75h.

77f Cullernose Point: Rock Climbing. Quartz dolerite promontories with numerous vertical faults and chimneys providing several climbs of a very high standard.

79h Belford Moor. See 76c.

79h Belford. See 76c.

Wind Chill

Shows the effect of wind speed (expressed on the Beaufort Scale, details of which can be seen on page 109) on temperature (m degrees Fahrenheit). The temperatures listed on the top row are those which would be shown on a thermometer protected from any wind; those below are the equivalents at the various wind speeds. The area coloured blue represents the danger zone, in which there is risk of exposed flesh suffering frostbite. Remember that freezing point is +32°F.

Wind Force	Temperature +50	+40	+30	+20	+10	0	−10	−20
2	+48	+37	+27	+16	+ 6	− 5	−15	−26
3	+40	+28	+16	+ 4	− 9	−21	−33	−46
4	+36	+22	+ 9	− 5	−18	−36	−45	−58
5	+32	+18	+ 4	−10	−25	−39	−53	−67
6	+29	+15	− 1	−17	−31	−46	−61	−77
7	+27	+11	− 4	−20	−35	−49	−67	−82
8+	+26	+10	− 6	−21	−37	−53	−69	−85

Riding and Pony Trekking

Includes riding schools, pony trekking and hacking centres, and race courses (Flat and National Hunt). Always telephone the school or hire centre in advance for booking information. The figure towards the end of most entries denotes the number of horses or ponies for hire.

18a Markington: Yorkshire Riding Centre. Tel. Bishop Monkton (076 581) 207. Instruction; riding holidays. 45.

18c Minskip: Prospect Stables, Prospect Villa, tel. Boroughbridge (090 12) 2791. Trekking; hacking; children only (ages 3-13). 8.

18d Harrogate: Belmont Riding School, 193 Forest Lane, tel. (0423) 886997. Hacking. 17.

18d Brackenthwaite: Harrogate Equestrian Centre, Brackenthwaite Lane, Burn Bridge, tel. (0423) 871894. Hacking; instruction; riding holidays. 55.

18e Barrowby Riding Centre. Tel. Harewood (0532) 886201. Instruction. 4.

18f Wetherby Racecourse. Tel. (0937) 62035. National Hunt racing. *September to May: meetings every month.*

19c Wiggington: Moor House Riding Centre, Sutton Road, tel. York (0904) 769029. Instruction; riding courses. 15.

19f York Racecourse. Tel. (0904) 22260. International Flat racing, including such famous meetings as the Benson and Hedges Gold Cup, and the historic Ebor, Gimcrack and Great Voltigeur. *May to October: 2- or 3-day meetings every month.*

21b Bigland Hall Riding Centre. Tel. Newby Bridge (0448) 31728. Trekking; hacking; instruction. 15.

21b Cartmel Racecourse. Tel. (044 854) 313. National Hunt racing. *Spring Bank Holiday and late Summer Bank Holiday: Saturday and Monday.*

21e Birkby Hall, Birkby Cottage, tel. (044 854) 319. Instruction.

21e Guides Farm. Tel. Grange (044 84) 2165. Trekking; hacking. 10. *April to September.*

21f Far Arnside: Leisure Riding Centre, Hollins Farm. Tel. Silverdale (0524) 701767. Trekking; hacking. *April to October.*

22b Elmsfield Park Equestrian Centre. Tel. Milnthorpe (044 82) 2891 or 3896. Hacking; instruction. 32.

22d Far Arnside. See 21f.

22h Caton School of Equitation, Quernmore Road. Tel. (0524) 770694. Hacking; instruction. 25. *June to September.*

25c Low Swinton: Swinton Riding and Trekking Centre, Home Farm, tel. Masham (076 582) 636. Trekking; riding holidays. 15.

25h Pateley Bridge. Centre closed.

26a Low Swinton. See 25c.

26e Ripon Racecourse. Tel. (0765) 2156. Flat racing. *April to end August: a total of ten days' racing.*

26h Markington. See 18a.

26i Minskip. See 18c.

27a Thirsk Racecourse. Tel. (0845) 22276. Flat racing, the most famous race being the Thirsk Hunt Cup. *April to September; a total of 10 days racing.*

27c Helmsley: Freedom of Ryedale Holidays, 23a Market Place. Tel. (0439) 70775. Trekking; instruction; riding holidays.

28a Helmsley. See 27c.

29a Pickering: Beck Isle Riding Stables, The Rookers, New Bridge Road, tel. (0751) 72982. Trekking; hacking; riding holidays.

29c Granary Farm: The Heights Pony Trekking Centre. Tel. Scarborough (0723) 85321. Instruction.

29c Snainton Riding Centre. Tel. Scarborough (0723) 85218. Trekking; hacking; instruction; riding holidays. 22.

29e Rillington Manor Riding School. Tel. (094 42) 246. Hacking; instruction. 9.

30f Grindale: The Forge Trekking Centre. Tel. Bridlington (0262) 601543. Trekking, multi activity holidays. *Easter to September.*

32b Fleming Hall Riding School. Tel. Seascale (094 02) 455. Trekking; hacking; instruction. 10.

32i Bootle: Beckside Farm. Tel. (065 78) 736. Trekking; instruction. *April to October.*

33e Bowmanstead: Spoon Hall Pony Trekking. Tel. Coniston (096 64) 391. Trekking. *April to September.*

33f Hawkshead Hill: Tarn Hows Hotel. Tel. (096 66) 330. Trekking. 9. *March to November.*

34b Troutbeck: Limefitt Park. Tel. Ambleside (096 63) 2564. Trekking. 25. *April to October.*

34d Hawkshead Hill. See 33f.

34e Oakland: Wynlass Beck Stables. Tel. (096 62) 3811. Trekking; hacking; instruction; riding holidays. 11.

34e Windermere: Craig Level Riding School. Tel. (096 62) 3572. Trekking; hacking; instruction.

34f Crook: Greenhills Stables. Tel. Staveley (0539) 821327. Hacking; instruction. 6.

34i Larkrigg Stables. Tel. Sedgwick (0448) 60245. Instruction.

35d Meal Bank: Hishow Farm. Now closed.

35g Ellenwray: Holmescales Farm Riding Centre. Tel. Kendal (0539) 22292. Trekking; hacking; instruction. 20.

37g Sedbusk Pony Trekking Centre. Tel. Hawes (096 97) 403. Instruction; riding holidays. 28.

38e Brokes: Brook Farm Equitation Centre. Tel. Richmond (0748) 3937. Instruction. 11.

38f Catterick Racecourse. Tel. Redcar (0642) 484068. International Flat and National Hunt racing. *All year: meetings every month.*

39e Yafforth Lodge Equestrian Centre. Tel. Northallerton (0609) 2679. Hacking; instruction; riding holidays. 14.

40i Broadway Foot: Bilsdale Riding and Trekking Centre, Shaken Bridge Farm. Tel. Bilsdale (043 96) 252 or 225. Trekking; instruction; holidays.

41g Helmsley. See 27c.

41i Sutherland Lodge Activity Centre. Tel. Cropton (075 15) 228. Multi-activity centre includes pony trekking holidays.

42g Sutherland Lodge. See 41i.

42g Pickering. See 29a.

42i Granary Farm. See 29c.

43d Robin Hood's Butts: Browside Pony Trekking Centre, Ladysmith Farm, tel. Whitby (0947) 880295. Trekking; hacking; riding holidays. 20. *Easter to October.*

44b Seaton Riding School, Seaton Road. Tel. Workington (0900) 3027. Trekking; hacking; instruction. 8.

44b Little Clifton: Marron Pony Trekking Centre, Clifton Green Farm, tel. Workington (0900) 61448. Trekking; instruction.

44f Birk Bank: Wood Farm Stables. Tel. Cockermouth (0900) 823403. Trekking; instruction. *April to October.*

44h Meadley Reservoir: Low Cock How, Kinniside. Tel. Lamplugh (094 686) 354. Trekking.

45b Robin Hood Riding Centre. Tel. Bassenthwaite Lake (059 681) 296. Trekking; hacking; instruction. 12.

45b Bassenthwaite: Hill Farm. Tel. (059 681) 498. Trekking. 7.

45e Little Crosthwaite: Old Windebrowe Stables. Tel. Keswick (0596) 72254. Instruction. *March to November.*

46d Lofshaw Hill: Lakeland Trekking, Troutbeck Hotel. Tel. Greystoke (085 33) 243. Trekking. 11. *April to September.*

46d Troutbeck: Rookin House Farm. Tel. Greystoke (085 33) 561. Trekking. 35. *April to mid-September.*

46f Elderbeck: Ellerslea Trekking Centre, Roe Head Lane. Tel. Pooley Bridge (085 36) 405. Trekking. 20. *April to October.*

Roe Head Trekking Centre, Roe Head Farm. Tel. (085 36) 459. Trekking. 25. *April to September.*

46h Patterdale: Side Farm Trekking Centre. Tel. Glenridding (085 32) 337. Trekking. 25. *April to October.*

47d Clifton: White House Stables. Tel. Penrith (0768) 64486. Trekking; hacking; instruction; riding holidays. 8.

47f Murton: Ash Lea. Tel. Appleby (0930) 51259. Trekking; hacking; instruction. 4. *March to October.*

47f Stoneriggs. Tel. Appleby (0930) 51354. Trekking. *Spring Bank Holiday to October.*

48d Murton. See 47f.

48d Stoneriggs. See 47f.

48g Mains House: Grey Horse Riding Stables. Tel. Brough (093 04) 651. Trekking; hacking; instruction 12. Pony and trap for hire.

49c Ravensford: Hamsterley Riding School and Livery Stables. Tel. Witton-le-Wear (038 888) 328. Hacking. 16.

49d Thringarth: West Park. Tel. Middleton-in-Teesdale (083 34) 380. Hacking; instruction. 10. *March to October.*

49d The Cross: Park House Farm Riding Centre. Tel. Teesdale (0833) 50474. Trekking; instruction; riding holidays. *March to December.*

50i Darlington: Newstead Riding Centre, Blackbanks Lane. Tel. (0325) 64592. Instruction. 25.

51a Sands Hall: Sedgefield Racecourse. Tel. Stockton (0642) 557081. National Hunt racing. *September to end May; total of 18 fixtures.*

51f Field House: Greatham Riding Centre. Tel. Hartlepool (0429) 870250. Instruction.

52d Field House. See 51f.

52f Redcar Racecourse. Tel. (0642) 484068. Flat racing. *May to end October: a total of 15 days racing.* 🏇

52h Eston Equitation Centre, Jubilee Road. Tel. Eston Grange (064 95) 452260. Trekking; hacking; instruction. 20. *July to September.*

52i Skelton: Cleveland Riding Centre. Tel. Guisborough (0287) 50303. Hacking; riding holidays. 35.

54b Holiday Camp: Silloth Riding School. Tel. (0965) 31667. Trekking; hacking. 25. *April to September.*

54h Allonby Riding School. Tel. (090 084) 273. Trekking; hacking; instruction. 24.

55b Bow: Stonerigg Riding Centre. Tel. Burgh-by-Sands (022 876) 253. Hacking; instruction. 11.

55c Cargo Riding Centre. Tel. Rockcliffe (022 874) 300. Trekking; hacking; instruction. 10. ♿

55e Carlisle Racecourse. Tel. Hexham (0434) 603320. Flat and National Hunt racing. *Meetings all year, except in March and August.*

56a Carlisle Racecourse. See 55c.

56c Castle Carrock Riding Centre. Now closed.

58b Thornley Gate: Allendale Riding School. Tel. Allendale (043 483) 378. Hacking. 8.

60d Maiden Law: Langley Close Equestrian

Centre. Tel. Lanchester (0207) 520925. Instruction. 12.

62h Blackdyke Farm. Tel. Rockcliffe (022 874) 633. Hacking; instruction. 8.

62h Cargo. See 55c.

63g B6318: Thorney Moor. Tel. Brampton (069 77) 3019. Trekking; hacking; instruction. 10.

64b Tarset Castle: Redmire Riding. Tel. Bellingham (0660) 40263. Trekking; instruction.

65g High Yarridge: Hexham Racecourse. Tel. (0434) 603320. National Hunt racing. *March to May, then September to December; at least one fixture per month.*

65g Plover Hill Riding School and Trekking Centre, Yarridge Road. Tel. Hexham (0434) 602888. Trekking; hacking; instruction. 4.

66c Netherton Park Training School (North of England Equestrian Centre). Tel. Stannington (067 089) 428. Instruction. Telephone first: may be closed.

67d Middle Brunton: Barton Stud Equitation Centre. Tel. Newcastle (0632) 362088. Instruction. 20.

67d Gosforth Park: Newcastle Racecourse. Tel. (0632) 362020. National Hunt racing, top races being the Eider Chase and the Fighting Fifth

Hurdle Race; flat racing, with main races being the Northumberland Plate, Pattern Race and the Seaton Delaval Stakes. *October to August, total of 27 fixtures.* 🏇

67e Murton House Riding School. Tel. North Shields (0632) 571369. Instruction. 13.

68f Ravenshill: Trekking and Trail Riding Centre. Tel. Kielder (0660) 50251. Trekking; trail riding; instruction; riding and hunting holidays. 35.

69h Track: Crag House. Tel. Bellingham (0660) 40259. Instruction. 25. *April to October.*

69h Tarset Castle. See 64b.

70g Track. See 69h.

70h Tarset Castle. See 64b.

71a Harbottle: Kidlandlee Trail Riding. Tel. Rothbury (0669) 50254. Trail Riding. *May to October.*

71f Whitton Farm House Hotel. Tel. Rothbury (0669) 20811. Instruction. 7.

72e Whitton. See 71f.

76c Belford: Windy Gyle Outdoor Centre. Tel. (066 83) 289. Holidays arranged, including riding and instruction. *June to September.* ⚓ ▲ ⛷

77h Alndyke: Windy Edge Stables. Tel. Alnwick (0665) 2284. Hacking; instruction. 12.

79h Belford. See 76c.

Aviation Motor Sport

Aviation entries include flying clubs, aircraft museums, popular gliding and hang gliding venues. Motor sport information includes permanent and temporary race tracks (for cars, karts and bikes); also hill climb and sprint courses.

Rallies. The three main forest areas of the North Country are all used regularly for high-speed special stage events organised at local, national and international level. Major events include the Mintex International *(February)* in the North Yorkshire forests west of Scarborough; the Lakeland Stages *(March)* and the Tour of Cumbria *(September)* in the Lake District forests; the Hadrian *(May)* and the Lindisfarne *(August)* in Kielder Forest, north west of Newcastle. All three forest areas are also used for the World Championship RAC Rally *(November)*. For details of the organising clubs to contact for further information, call the Royal Automobile Club Motor Sport Division on London (01-) 235 8601.

18h Harewood Park: Motor Sport. 1090-yard hill climb used for events organised by the BARC's Yorkshire Centre, tel. M S Wilson on Morley (0532) 533722. *April to October: usually 5 meetings.*

21e Holker Hall: Ballooning and Parachuting. Tel. Flookburgh (044 853) 328. Displays of hot air balloons and parachuting are among many events and activities available here. *Weekends only, weather permitting.* 🏇 ♿ ♣ ❄ 📷 ☆

21h Heysham Head: Kart Racing. Permanent track used for meetings organised by Morecambe & Heysham Kart Club (secretary tel. Lancaster 0524 811294). World Cup held each May. *Frequent weekends.* 🏇 ☆

22c Barbon Manor: Motor Sport. 890-yard hill climb used for meetings organised by Westmorland Motor Club (secretary tel. Kendal 0539 25887). National championship *(May)*.

27b Sutton Bank: Yorkshire Gliding Club. Tel. (0845) 597237. Instruction for individuals and groups; 5-day residential courses; full time instructors; minimum age 18. *April to October.* 🏇

28b Wombleton Aerodrome: Windsports Centre, the Control Tower, tel. (0751) 32356.

One-day and 4-day courses in powered hang gliding.

28f Castle Howard: Motor Sport. 400-yard hill climb used for events organised by Yorkshire Sports Car Club (secretary tel. Bradford 0274 684508). *Two meetings, usually March and October.* 🏇 ❄ 📷 🏕

30b Olivers Mount: Motor Sport. Spectacular permanent race circuit with tight hairpin bends, used for solo motor cycle races and occasionally by rallies. Several bike meetings each year: details from 🛈.

30b Staxton: Northern Hang Gliding Centre. Tel. Sherburn (094 44) 333. Courses lasting 5 days and including instruction towards Pilot I Certificate; all equipment supplied; no experience needed; minimum age 16.

30i Carnaby: Bridlington Aerodrome. Midweek, weekly and fortnightly courses in parachuting; flying tuition; aircraft for hire; accommodation available; minimum age 16; some equipment needed. Contact: British Skysports, tel. (0262) 77367.

Motor Sport. Carnaby Raceway is used for occasional car sprint meetings; also for kart races (national meetings in May, July and September); all organised by Auto 66 Club (secretary tel. Driffield 0377 84727).

39h Leeming: RAF Central Flying School. Tel. Northallerton (0609) 2441. Small collection of historic aircraft, including Spitfire, Javelin, Meteors and Vampires. *By permission only.*

42e High Horcum: Hang Gliding. Venue used by Northern Hang Gliding Centre. See 30b.

44i Rowrah: Kart Racing. Permanent circuit used for meetings organised by Cumbria Kart Racing Club (secretary tel. Penrith 0768 63220). *Frequent weekends.*

59b Currock Hill: Northumbria Gliding Club. Tel. Ebchester (0207) 561286. Five-day courses for individuals and groups; flights up to 30 mins/6000ft; self-catering accommodation; all equipment supplied; no experience necessary; ages 14-65. *May to September.*

61a Sunderland Airport: North East Aircraft Museum. Tel. (0632) 693417. Collection of post Second World War aircraft, including Vampire, Meteor, Hunter, Super Sabre, Gyroglider, Dragonfly and other civil and military machines; also some ancillary equipment. *Sundays PM.*

Parachute Centre, Washington Road. Tel. Durham (0385) 65315. Weekend and weekly courses for individuals or groups; bunkhouse or motel accommodation; all equipment supplied; no experience necessary; minimum age 16.

66d Ouston Moor: Motor Sport. Disused airfield perimeter track at Albermarle Barracks used for sprint races over 1400-yard course; also for occasional rallies. All events organised by Tynemouth & District Motor Club (secretary tel. Whitley Bay 0632 533697).

66f Newcastle Airport (Woolsington): Newcastle upon Tyne Aero Club. Tel. (0632) 861321 or 860966 ext 317. Flying tuition, including courses for private licence, night rating, etc.

66h Currock Hill. See 59b.

73d Bockenfield: Felton Kart Track. Permanent circuit used for meetings organised by Northumbrian Kart Club (secretary tel. Whitley Bay 0632 521579). *Frequent weekends.*

76c Belford: Windy Gyle Parachute Centre, Border Ventures Ltd, West Street, tel. (066 83) 289. Weekend and 7-day courses in sport parachuting; accommodation provided; no experience necessary; minimum age 16. *April to September and most weekends.* ⚓ ▲ ↺

79h Belford. See 76c.

Golf
18 Courses

Only courses where visitors and/or temporary members can play have been included. Each course is marked on the map together with its number of holes (see panel below). Some organisations offering golfing holidays are also listed.

18b Scriven: Manor Vale GC. Tel. Kirkbymoorside (0751) 31525. Moorland; 18 holes; 5600 yds; Par 68. ☕

18d Oakdale GC. Tel. Harrogate (0423) 67162. Parkland; 18 holes; 6291 yds; Par 72. ☕

18g Alwoodley GC. Tel. Leeds (0532) 681680. Heathland; 18 holes; 6755 yds; Par 72. ☕

18h Alwoodley Gates: Moortown GC. Tel. Leeds (0532) 681682. Heathland; 18 holes; 6606 yds; Par 69.

18h Slaid Hill: Moor Allerton GC. Tel. Leeds (0532) 661154. 27 holes; 6953 yds; Par 72. The only British course designed by the American golf architect, Robert Trent Jones. ☕

18h Roundhay GC. Tel. Leeds (0532) 662695. Municipal parkland; 9 holes; 5390 yds; Par 70. ☕ ❄ ♪

19e Askham Bryan: Pike Hills GC. Tel. York (0904) 70656. Parkland; 18 holes; 5960 yds; Par 71. **H** ☕

19f Heworth GC. Tel. York (0904) 24204. Meadowland; 11 holes; 5888 yds; Par 69.

19f Fulford GC. Tel. York (0904) 55212. Parkland; 18 holes; 6779 yds; Par 72. **H** ☕

20h Vickerstown: Furness GC. Tel. Barrow-in-Furness (0229) 41232. Links; 18 holes; 6340 yds; Par 71. ☕

21b Grange Fell GC. Tel. Grange-over-Sands (044 84) 2536. Gentle downland; 9 holes; 5278 yds; Par 70.

21d Ulverston GC. Tel. (0229) 52824. Parkland; 18 holes; 6200 yds; Par 71. **H** ☕

21i Bare: Morecambe GC. Tel. (0524) 412841. Seaside; 18 holes; 5731 yds; Par 67. ☕

22g Bare. See 21i.

22g Lancaster: Lansil GC. Tel. (0524) 65252. Parkland; 9 holes; 5608 yds; Par 70. ☕

23d High Bentham: Bentham GC. Tel. (0468) 61018. Meadowland; 9 holes; 5850 yds; Par 72.

23i High Paley Green: Settle GC. Parkland; 9 holes; 4590 yds; Par 64.

25c Masham GC. Tel. (076 582) 379. Parkland; 9 holes; 4934 yds; Par 64.

26a Masham. See 25c.

26e Ripon City GC. Tel. (0765) 3640. Parkland; 9 holes; 5780 yds; Par 70. ☕

27a North Kilvington: Thirsk & Northallerton GC. Tel. Thirsk (0845) 22170. Meadowland; 9 holes; 6150 yds; Par 65. ☕

29d Malton & Norton GC. Tel. (0653) 2959. Parkland; 18 holes; 6401 yds; Par 72. ☕

29f Ganton GC. Tel. Sherburn (094 44) 329. Outstanding inland links course; 18 holes; 6693 yds; Par 72. Harry Vardon was once the professional here; venue of the 1981 PGA Championship. ☕

30a Ganton. See 29f.

31e Flamborough GC. Tel. Bridlington (0262) 850333 Undulating seaside course; 18 holes; 5404 yds; Par 66. ☕

32e Seascale GC. Tel. (094 02) 202. Links; 18 holes; 6307 yds; Par 71. ☕

34e Windermere GC. Tel. (096 62) 3123. Undulating parkland; 18 holes; 4940 yds; Par 67. ☕

34i Kendal GC. Tel. (0539) 24079. Moorland; 18 holes; 5483 yds; Par 66. ☕

35h Sedbergh GC. Tel. (0587) 20659. Moorland; 9 holes; 2100 yds; Par 64.

38c Richmond GC. Tel. (0748) 2457. Parkland; 18 holes; 5704 yds; Par 71.

39i North Kilvington. See 27a.

40g North Kilvington. See 27a.

41h Kirkbymoorside GC. Tel. (0751) 31525. Moorland; 9 holes; 5435 yds; Par 68. ☕

42c Whitby GC. Tel. (0947) 602768. Seaside; 18 holes; 5980 yds; Par 69. ☕

43h Scarborough: North Cliff GC. Tel. (0723) 60786. Parkland; 18 holes; 6284 yds; Par 70. ☕
St Nicholas Hotel, St Nicholas Cliff, tel. (0723) 64101. Golfing holidays include green fees and champagne! *All year.* ☕

44a Hunday: Workington GC. Tel. (0900) 3460. Hilly meadowland; 18 holes; 6202 yds; Par 71. **H** ☕

45f Keswick GC. Tel. Threlkeld (059 683) 324. Parkland; 9 holes; 2600 yds; Par 67.

46c Penrith GC. Tel. (0768) 62217. Parkland; 18 holes; 6026 yds; Par 69. **H** ☕

46d Keswick. See 45f.

47f Appleby GC. Tel. (0930) 51432. Moorland; 18 holes; 5960 yds; Par 68. ☕

49h Barnard Castle GC. Tel. (083 33) 2237. Moorland; 18 holes; 5838 yds; Par 68. ☕

50b Bishop Auckland GC. Tel. (0388) 2198. Hilly parkland; 18 holes; 6340 yds; Par 72. ☕ ♣ ⌂

50i Darlington GC. Tel. (0325) 63936. Wooded parkland; 18 holes; 6272 yds; Par 71. ☕

51c Hartlepool GC. Tel. (0429) 4398. Seaside; 18 holes; 5484 yds; Par 69. **H** ☕

51c Seaton Carew GC. Tel. Hartlepool (0429) 66249. Championship links; 18 holes; 6613 yds.; Par 72. ☕

52f Saltburn-by-the-Sea GC. Tel. (028 72) 2812. Meadowland; 18 holes; 5803 yds; Par 70. **H** ☕

54b Silloth-on-Solway GC. Tel. (0965) 31179. Links; 18 holes; 6343 yds; Par 72. ☕

54g Maryport GC. Tel. (090 081) 2605. Links; 11 holes; 6270 yds; Par 71. ☕

Notes

🚩9 🚩13 🚩14 🚩18 🚩27

The above symbols are used on the maps to show the actual number of holes available at each course; in keeping with golfing convention, however, all yardage and par figures given in the text apply to a round of 18 holes. Membership qualifications and the dates on which visitors can play vary and you should always check with the club beforehand. **H** indicates that an official handicap or proof of golf club membership is required.

56c Brampton GC. Tel. (069 77) 2255. Heathland; 18 holes; 6258 yds; Par 73. ☕

57e Alston GC. Tel. (049 83) 675. Moorland; 9 holes; 4894 yds; Par 66.

58b Allendale GC. Tel. (043 483) 412. Meadowland; 9 holes; 4408 yds; Par 64.

60d Ousterley: South Moor GC. Tel. Stanley (0207) 32848. Parkland; 18 holes; 6405 yds; Par 71. ☕

60f Chester-le-Street GC. Tel. (0385) 883218. Parkland; 18 holes; 5936 yds; Par 70. ☕

60h Langley Moor: Durham City GC. Tel. Durham (0385) 780069. Parkland; 18 holes; 6100 yds; Par 71. ☕

60h Brancepeth Castle GC. Tel. Meadowfield (0385) 780075. Parkland; 18 holes; 6300 yds; Par 70. ☕

61a Wearside GC. Tel. Hylton (078 324) 2518. Parkland; 18 holes; 6315 yds; Par 71. **H** ☕

61h Castle Eden & Peterlee GC. Tel. (042 981) 220. Parkland; 18 holes; 6339 yds; Par 70. ☕

64c Bellingham GC. Tel. (0660) 20281. Downland; 9 holes; 5220 yds; Par 67.

65g Hexham GC. Tel. (0434) 693072. Parkland; 18 holes; 6228 yds; Par 70. ☕

65g Tyne Green: Tynedale GC. Tel. (0434) 604011. Municipal; 9 holes; 5640 yds; Par 70.

66f Whorlton Grange: Westerhope GC. Tel. Newcastle (0632) 869125. Wooded parkland; 18 holes; 6407 yds; Par 73. ☕

67d Gosforth Park GC. Tel. (0632) 853495. Parkland; 18 holes; 5962 yds; Par 69. ☕ ∪

67d Gosforth: City of Newcastle GC. Tel. (0632) 851775. Meadowland; 18 holes; 6454 yds; Par 72. ☕

67g Newcastle United GC. Tel. (0632) 864693. Moorland; 18 holes; 5853 yds; Par 69.

67g Wallsend GC. Tel. Newcastle (0632) 621973. 18 holes; 6601 yds; Par 72.

67i Whitburn GC. Tel. (0783) 292144. Parkland; 18 holes; 5993 yds; Par 70. ☕

69i Bellingham. See 64c.

70h Bellingham. See 64c.

71e Rothbury GC. Tel. (0669) 20694. Meadowland; 9 holes; 5200 yds; Par 68.

73b Alnmouth Village GC. Tel. (066 573) 370. Seaside; 9 holes; 6100 yds; Par 70. ☕

73b Warkworth GC. Tel. (066 588) 596. Seaside; 9 holes; 5856 yds; Par 70.

73i Newbiggin-by-the-Sea GC. Tel. (0670) 817344. Seaside; 18 holes; 6444 yds; Par 72. ☕

77b Seahouses GC. Tel. (0665) 70794. Seaside; 18 holes; 5370 yds; Par 67.

77i Alnmouth. See 73b.

79a Berwick-upon-Tweed: Magdalene Fields GC. Seaside; 18 holes; 6551 yds; Par 72.

79d Goswick: Berwick-upon-Tweed GC. Tel. Ancroft (0289) 87256. Links; 18 holes; 6437 yds; Par 72. ☕

79i Bamburgh Castle GC. Tel. (066 84) 378. Seaside; 18 holes; 5495 yds; Par 68. ☕

Special Interest

A potpourri of leisure parks, caves, miniature villages, mediaeval banquets and other fascinating activities which simply could not be listed under any other heading.

19f The York Story, The Heritage Centre, Castlegate, tel. (0904) 28632. The finest of its kind in Britain, this combination of films, tapestries, models, craftwork and audio/visual displays exhibits the social and architectural history of York in a converted 15th century church. A guide to the major buildings of the city is available (see ⌖ for many of these). *Daily 1000-1700 (Sundays PM).*

21e Holker Park. Tel. Flookburgh (044 853) 328. Family leisure complex including baby animal farm, children's adventure playground, toy museum, model railway, a collection of curios and much more. *Easter to September daily 1100-1800 (but closed some Saturdays)* ♥ ⚘ ❋ ▣ ⌖ ✩

21h Heysham Head Leisure Park, Barrows Lane, tel. (0524) 52391. Sports complex includes an indoor roller skating rink, trampolines, a skateboard track, crazy golf and a children's playground. *Summer: daily 1000-1800.* ♥ ✈ ⚡

21i Morecambe: Leisure Park and Superdome, Marine Road, tel. (0524) 419419. Family entertainment centre with roller skating rink; evening events (including Miss Great Britain heats every Wednesday); swimming pool has wave machine. *Daily 1000-1700.* ♥ ✈

Pleasure Park, West End, tel. 410024. Lancashire's answer to Disneyland, with over 50 exciting rides, including the Giant Wheel, Skyrider, Wave Swinger, Ghost Train, Scream Machine, etc,; Kiddies Park; Fun City. *Summer: daily from 1100.* ♥

22d Leighton Hall: Antique Dolls House. 12ft by 5ft by 7ft scale models of sumptuous 18 room American home. It took over 18 years to build, and is filled with over 1200 tiny antique fittings, including furniture, glassware, china - even a sewing machine and a chess set. *May to September: Sundays, Tuesday to Thursday and bank holiday Mondays 1400-1630.* ♥ ⛺ ❋ ⌖ 🐘

23d Ingleton: White Scar Caves. Tel. (0468) 41244. Underground waterfalls, stalactites and stalagmites and rock formations, all impressively illuminated in a ½ hour tour. No special clothing needed. *February to November daily 1000-dusk.*

23e Gaping Gill Hole. Britain's deepest pot hole, into which water flows and falls 365ft in a single jet. Noisy and spectacular. Visitors can be winched down *(Spring and August bank holidays only).*

23e Ingleborough Cavern. Tel. Clapham (046 85) 242. Guided tours through illuminated rock formations, stalagmites and stalactites. 1¼ mile nature trail through nearby woods. *March to October daily; rest of year weekends; 1030-1730.*

26e North Stainley: Lightwater Valley. Tel. Ripon (0765) 85321. Family leisure complex, with Fort William, mini-bikes, cyclo-cross track, boating lake and practice/playing facilities for golf, archery, tennis, cricket, football, frisbee, etc. *April/May weekends and bank holidays 1030-1730; June to end August daily 1030-1900; September weekends 1030-1730.* ♥ ⛺ ⚡ ⚡

28b Nunnington Hall: Carlisle Miniature Rooms. Tel. (043 95) 283. Series of model rooms fully furnished in different periods. *April to end October: Tuesday to Thursday, weekends and bank holiday Mondays, 1100-1800.* ♥ ⌖

29a Zoo: Flamingo Land. Tel. Kirby Misperton (065 386) 287. Large pleasure park mainly devoted to animals, but including many children's attractions: Jungle Cruise raft ride through Zulu villages, Gnomeland, adventure playground, funfair, giant Hornby model railway, etc. Accommodation available in holiday village (tel. 300). *First Sunday in March to end October: daily 1000-1600.* ♥ ⛺ ⚡ ❋ ⚡ 🐘 🐄 ✈

33c Ambleside: Dolls House Museum, Fair View Road, tel. (096 63) 2358. Large collection of dolls, plus 12 mainly Victorian dolls houses. *Easter to end October: Wednesday to Friday 1030-1300, 1400-1700.*

34a Ambleside. See 33c.

39f East Harlsey: Yorkshire Horse Drawn Caravans, The Old Post Office, tel. (060 982) 262. Four berth horse drawn caravans for weekly hire (Saturday to Saturday) over established routes in the Cleveland and Hambleton Hills. No unaccompanied children. *April to October.*

40d East Harlsey. See 39f.

43h Scarborough: Mazes. Two privet hedge mazes, in Victoria Park (40yds by 30yds) and on The Esplanade (32yds by 22yds).

50i Darlington Museum: Observation Beehive. Live honey bees in action; also displays of beekeeping equipment. *Weekdays 1000-1800 (Thursdays AM only); Saturdays 1000-1730.*

51c Hartlepool: HMS Warrior, Coal Dock. The world's first ironclad warship, launched in 1860; now Britain's only surviving battleship! She was the most powerful (40 guns), largest (420ft long) and fastest (17½ knots) warship in the world, so formidable that she never had to fire a shot in anger. Despite languishing for 50 years as a dockside pontoon in Wales, the wrought iron hull has survived well and is now undergoing restoration before eventually being moved to Portsmouth to. See 30b.

52a Hartlepool. See 51i.

58h Ireshopeburn: Rancho del Rio. Tel. Wearhead (095 63) 391. Converted schoolhouse offering wild west version of the mediaeval banquet fad, with finger lickin' food, square dancing, cowboy and indian souvenirs, etc. *Daily*

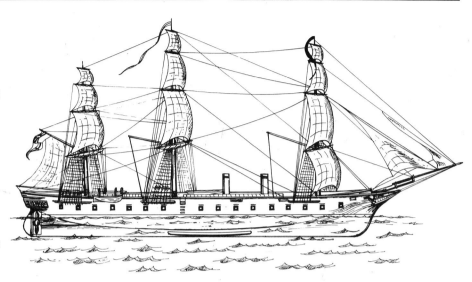

HMS *Warrior* as she looked in 1860. Her remains are now moored at Hartlepool (51c)

from 1930 by arrangement only.

60c Lambton Park. Now closed.

60f Lumley Castle: Elizabethan Banquets. Tel. Durham (0385) 883267. Usual combination of wine, women and song, here set in Elizabethan times. Accommodation available. *Telephone for details.* ⚡

61i Hartlepool. See 51c.

65c Wallington Hall. Tel. Scots Gap (067 074) 283. Stately home with many collections, including about 20 old dolls houses, one of which is a 36 room mansion with electric lighting, running water and over 70 tiny dolls. Also a full size children's room with old toys, games and books and a Noah's Ark. *Mid April to end September: Wednesday to Monday, 1300-1800. Also October Wednesdays and weekends, 1400-1700.* ♥ ⚘ ❋ ⌖ ⓘ

66a Wallington Hall. See 65c.

67e Seaton Delaval Hall: Mediaeval Banquets. Tel. (0632) 481759. Usual combination of mead, maidens and minstrels, this one actually set in mediaeval times. *Telephone for details.* ⌖

67g Newcastle: Bagpipe Museum. The Black Gate, St Nicholas Street, tel. (0632) 327938. Once the gatehouse of New Castle, it now houses over 100 sets of Scottish, Irish, Northumbrian, French, Indian and Egyptian pipes, all arranged chronologically. Also documents, photographs and other bagpipe memorabilia. *Wednesday to Saturday 1200-1600.*

67i South Shields: Tyne Lifeboat. Only the third ever built, it saved 1028 lives between 1833 and 1893 and now stands preserved near the town centre.

71h Wallington Hall. See 65c.

72h Wallington Hall. See 65c.

78i Ford: Lady Waterford Hall. Tel. Crookham (089 082) 224. Old village school with 19th century mural of Old and New Testament Bible scenes, all featuring local children and their parents. *Daily 0930-1830.* ⚘

Tourist Information Offices

Including those run by tourist boards and local authorities; also by such organisations as the National Trust, national parks, etc. Each entry gives the area covered; "beds" means that accommodation enquiries can be handled; *Summer* usually means Easter to September.

18b Knaresborough. Regional, beds: Market Place, tel. (0423) 866886. *Summer only.*

18d Harrogate. National, beds: Royal Baths Assembly Rooms, Crescent Road, tel. (0423) 65912.

18f Wetherby. Local: Council Offices, 24 Westgate, tel. (0937) 62706/9.

19f York. National, beds: De Grey Rooms, Exhibition Square, tel. (0904) 21756/7.
 Yorkshire & Humberside Tourist Board, 312 Tadcaster Road, YO2 2HF, tel. 707961.
 National Trust Yorkshire Regional Office: 32 Goodramgate, YOI 2LG, tel. 29621.

20b Millom. Local: St George's Road, tel. (0657) 2555. *Summer only.*

20e Barrow-in-Furness. Local, beds: Civic Hall, Duke Street, tel. (0229) 25795.

21a Ulverston. Local: The Renaissance Centre, 17 Fountain Street, tel. (0229) 52299.

21e Grange-over-Sands. Local, beds: Council Offices, Main Street, tel. (044 84) 4026. *Summer.*

21i Morecambe. Regional, beds: Marine Road Central, tel. (0524) 414110.

21i Lancaster. National, beds: 7 Dalton Square, tel. (0524) 2878.

22c Kirkby Lonsdale. Local, beds: 18 Main Street, tel. (0468) 71603.

22g Lancaster. See 21i.

23d Ingleton. Regional, beds: Community Centre Car Park, tel. (0468) 41049. *Summer only.*

23d Bentham. Local, beds: Station Road, tel. (0468) 61043. *Summer only.*

23e Clapham. Yorkshire Dales National Park Centre: tel. (046 85) 419. *Summer only.* ♣

23i Settle. Regional, beds: Town Hall, Market Place, tel. (072 92) 3617. *Summer only.*

24g Settle. See 23i.

24h Malham. Yorkshire Dales National Park: The Car Park, tel. Airton (072 93) 363. *Summer.* ♣

24i Grassington. Yorkshire Dales National Park: Colvend', Hebden Road, tel. (0756) 752748.

25h Pateley Bridge. Regional, beds: Southlands Car Park, High Street, tel. (0423) 711147 *Summer only.*

26e Ripon. Regional, beds: Wakemans House, Market Place, tel. (0765) 4625. *Summer only.* ▣

27a Thirsk. Local, beds: 16 Kirkgate, tel. (0845) 22755. *Summer only.*

27b Sutton Bank. Local, North Yorks Moors National Park, beds: tel. (0845) 597426. *Summer only.* ♣ ☆

27c Helmsley. Regional, beds: 23a Market Place, tel. (0439) 70775.

28a Helmsley. See 27c.

29a Pickering. Local, North Yorks Moors National Park, beds: The Station, tel. (0751) 73791. 🛏

30c Filey. Local, beds: John Street, tel. (0723) 512204. *Summer only.*

31g Bridlington. National, beds: Garrison Street, tel. (0262) 73474 or 79626. *Summer only. In winter, tel. 78255.*

32a Egremont. Local, beds: Lowes Court Gallery, Main Street, tel. (0946) 820693. *Summer.*

32e Ravenglass. Regional, beds: Car Park, Ravenglass & Eskdale Railway Station, tel. (065 77) 278. *Summer only.* ☕ 🛏

33c Grasmere. Local, beds: Broadgate Newsagency, tel. (096 65) 245.

33c Ambleside. Regional, Lake District National Park, beds: Old Courthouse, Church Street, tel. (096 63) 2582. *April to October.*
 National Trust North-West Regional Office: Rothay Holme, tel. 3883.

33e Coniston. Local, Lake District National Park, beds: Car Park, tel. (096 64) 533. *Summer only.*

33f Hawkshead. Local, Lake District National Park, beds: next to main car park, tel. (096 66) 525. *April to October.*

33f Waterhead. Lake District National Park: in car park at head of lake. *Summer.* ☕ ♣ ▣

34a Grasmere. See 33c.

34a Ambleside. See 33c.

34d Hawkshead. See 33f.

34e Brockhole. Lake District National park Centre, tel. Windermere (096 62) 2231. *April to November.* ☕ ♣ ⊓ ❋

34e Windermere. Regional, beds: Victoria Street, tel. (096 62) 4561. *Summer only.*
 Cumbria Tourist Board, Ellerthwaite, LA23 2AQ, tel. 4444/7. *Letters or telephone calls only.*
 Camping/Caravanning Advice: Lake District Special Planning Board, tel. 5515 or 5555. *Mid-April to mid-September PM only.*
 Weather Information covering the Lake District National Park: tel. 5151/4. *Summer only.*
 Teletourist: recorded information for visitors. Tel. 6363.

34e Bowness-on-Windermere. Local, Lake District National Park, beds: Bowness Bay, tel. Windermere (096 62) 2895 or 2244 ext 43. *April to December.*

34i Kendal. Regional, beds: Town Hall, tel. (0539) 25758.

35h Sedbergh. Local, beds, Yorkshire Dales National Park: 72 Main Street, tel. (0587) 20125. *Summer only.*

36i Hawes. Yorkshire Dales National Park: Station Yard, tel. (096 97) 450. *Summer.* ▣ ⬇T

37f Reeth. Local: Swaledale Folk Museum, tel. (074 884) 373. *Summer evenings only.* ▣ ⬇T

37h Askrigg. Office now closed.

37h Aysgarth Falls. Yorkshire Dales National Park: Car Park, tel. (093 93) 424. *Summer only.* ♣

38d Reeth. See 37f.

38f Richmond. Regional, beds: Friary Gardens, Queen's Road, tel. (0748) 3525. *Summer only.*

38h Leyburn. Local, beds: Commercial Square, tel. Wensleydale (0969) 23069. *Summer only.*

39g Leeming. Regional, beds: Service Area at junction A1/A684, tel. (0677) 23611 ext 41. *Summer only.*

41b Danby. Local, North Yorks Moors National Park, beds: Danby Lodge, Lodge Lane, tel. Castleton (028 76) 654. *Summer only.* ☕ ♣ ▣

41g Helmsley. See 27c.

41i Pickering. See 29a.

42c Whitby. Regional, beds: New Quay Road, tel. (0947) 602674.

42g Pickering. See 29a.

43h Scarborough. National, beds: St Nicholas Cliff, tel. (0723) 72261 or 73333.

44b Maryport. Local, beds: I Senhouse Street, tel. (090 081) 3738.

44c Cockermouth. Regional, beds: Riverside Car Park, Market Street, tel. (0900) 822634. *Summer only.*

44e Workington. Office now closed.

44g Whitehaven. National, beds: Market Place, tel. (0946) 5678.

44h Egremont. See 32a.

45f Keswick. Regional, beds: Moot Hall, Market Square. *April to December.* In winter tel. (0596) 72645.
 Lake District National Park: same address, tel. 72803. *April to December.*

45h Seatoller. Lake District National Park: next to village car park, tel. Borrowdale (059 684) 294. *April to October.*

46c Penrith. Local, beds: Robinson's School, Middlegate, tel. (0768) 64671 ext 33. *Summer.*

46f Pooley Bridge. Local, Lake District National Park, beds: Caravan, Eusemere Car Park, tel. (085 36) 530. *Summer only.*

46g Glenridding. Local, Lake District National Park, beds: Caravan, Beckside Car Park, tel. (085 32) 414. *Summer only.*

47f Appleby. Regional, beds: The Moot Hall, tel.(0930) 51177. *Summer only.*

48h Brough. Regional, beds: The 'One Stop' Shop, tel. (093 04) 260.

49c Castlewood (Wear Valley). Office now closed. ♣ ⊓

49h Barnard Castle. Regional: 43 Galgate, tel. Teesdale (0833) 38481.

50a Castlewood. See 49c.

50i Darlington. Regional, beds: Branch Library, Crown Street, tel. (0325) 62034 or 69858.

51c Hartlepool. Regional, beds: Victory Square, tel. (0429) 68366.
 Local: Hartlepool Docks, tel. 74922. *Summer.*

51f Middlesbrough. Regional: 125 Albert Road, tel. (0642) 245432 ext 3580, or 245750.

52a Hartlepool. See 51c.

52d Middlesbrough. See 51f.

54b Silloth. Local: The Green, Waver Street, tel. (0965) 31944.

54f Abbey Town. Office now closed.

55c Carlisle. Regional, beds: Old Town Hall, Greenmarket, tel. (0228) 25517 or 25396.

56a Carlisle. See 55c.

56c Brampton. Local: Moot Hall, tel. (069 77) 3433. *Summer only.*

56d Southwaite M6 Service Area. National, beds: tel. (069 93) 445 or 446. ☕

57e Alston. Local, beds: Railway Station, tel. (0498) 81696.

59i Castlewood. See 49c.

60h Peterlee. National, beds: The Upper Chare, tel. (0783) 864450.

60i Durham. National, beds: 13 Claypath, tel. (0385) 43720.

61i **Hartlepool.** See 51c.

62e **Longtown.** Local, beds: 21 Swan Street, tel. Carlisle (0228) 791201.

63g **Brampton.** See 56c.

63i **Haltwhistle.** Local, beds: Tynedale District Council Sub Office, Sycamore Street, tel. (0498) 20351.

64c **Bellingham.** Office now closed.

64g **Haltwhistle.** See 63i.

64h **YH.** Northumberland National Park: Once Brewed, Military Road, tel. Bardon Mill (049 84) 396. *Summer only.*

65c **Wallington Hall.** National Trust Northumbria: tel. Scots Gap (067 074) 234. ☕ ♣ ❀ 🏛 ☆

65h **Hexham.** National, beds: Manor Office, Hallgates, tel. (0434) 605225.
Northumberland National Park: Eastburn, South Park, tel. 605555.

65h **Corbridge.** Regional, beds: Vicar's Pele Tower, Market Place, tel. (043 471) 2815. *Summer only.* ⛏

66a **Wallington Hall.** See 65c.

66h **Prudhoe.** Office now closed.

67e **Whitley Bay.** Regional: The Promenade, tel. (0632) 524494. *Summer only.*

67g **Newcastle upon Tyne.** National, beds: Central Library, Princess Square, tel. (0632) 610691.
Regional: Blackfriars, Friars Street, tel. 615367. ☕ 📺 ⬆
Northumbria Tourist Board, covering Cleveland, Durham, Northumberland and Tyne & Wear: 9 Osborne Terrace, NE2 1NT, tel. (0632) 817744.

67g **Gateshead.** Regional, beds: Central Library, Prince Consort Road, tel. (0632) 773478.

67h **North Shields.** National, beds: Tyne Commission Quay, tel. (0632) 579800. *Summer only.*

67i **South Shields.** Regional, beds: South Foreshore, tel. (0632) 557411. *Summer only.*

67i **Jarrow.** Regional, beds: Jarrow Hall, Church Bank, tel. (0632) 892106.

69b **Byrness.** Northumberland National Park: 9 Otterburn Green, tel. Otterburn (0830) 20622. *Summer only.*

69i **Bellingham.** See 64c.

70a **Byrness.** See 69b.

70h **Bellingham.** See 64c.

71a **Harbottle.** Northumberland National Park: Forestry Commission Car Park. *Summer weekends only.*

71f **Rothbury.** Northumberland National Park: Church House, Church Street, tel. (0669) 20877. *Summer only.*

72e **Rothbury.** See 71f.

72h **Wallington Hall.** See 65c.

75c **Wooler.** Regional, beds: High Street Car Park, tel. (066 82) 602. *Summer only.*

75f **Ingram.** Northumberland National Park: Old School House, tel. Powburn (0665) 78248. *Summer only.*

76b **Wooler.** See 75c.

76e **Ingram.** See 75f.

77b **Seahouses.** Regional, beds: 16 Main Street, tel. (0665) 720424. *Summer only.*

77g **Alnwick.** Regional, beds: The Shambles, tel. (0665) 603120. *Summer only.*

79a **Berwick-upon-Tweed.** National, beds: Castlegate Car Park, tel. (0289) 7187. *Summer only.*

Index

Abbreviations

B.	Bay	Pt.	Point
Hd.	Head	R.	River
I.	Island	Res.	Reservoir
L.	Lake, Loch		
Ls.	Lakes		

Clev.	Cleveland
Dumf./Gal.	Dumfries & Galloway
Cumb.	Cumbria
Humber.	Humberside
Lancs.	Lancashire
N.Yorks	North Yorkshire
N'land	Northumberland
Tyne/Wear	Tyne & Wear
W.Yorks.	West Yorkshire

Abberwick *N'land* 77g
Abbeytown *Cumb.* 54f
Acaster Malbis *N.Yorks.* 19h
Acaster Selby *N.Yorks.* 19h
Acklam *Clev.* 51i
Acklam *N.Yorks.* 29g
Acklington *N'land* 73a
Acomb *N.Yorks.* 19e
Acomb *N'land* 65h
Aglionby *Cumb.* 62a
Aikton *Cumb.* 55a
Ainderby Quernhow
    N.Yorks. 26c
Ainderby Steeple *N.Yorks.* 39h
Ainstable *Cumb.* 56f
Ainthorpe *N.Yorks.* 41b
Aira Force *Cumb.* 46e
Aiskew *N.Yorks.* 39g
Aislaby *N.Yorks.* 41i
Aislaby *N.Yorks.* 42b
Akeld *N'land* 75b
Aldborough *N.Yorks.* 27g
Aldbrough St. John
    N.Yorks. 50h
Aldcliffe *Lancs.* 21i
Aldfield *N.Yorks.* 26d
Aldingham *Cumb.* 21d
Aldro *N.Yorks.* 29g
Aldwark *N.Yorks.* 27g
Allanton *Borders* 78b
Allen, R. *N'land* 64h
Allendale Town *N'land* 58a
Allenheads *N'land* 58e
Allerby *Cumb.* 54h
Allerston *N.Yorks.* 29b
Allerton Mauleverer
    N.Yorks. 18c
Allithwaite *Cumb.* 21e
Allonby *Cumb.* 54g
Aln, R. *N'land* 77h
Alne *N.Yorks.* 27h
Alnham *N'land* 75i
Alnmouth *N'land* 77i
Alnwick *N'land* 77g
Alston *Cumb.* 57e
Alwinton *N'land* 75g
Alwoodley *W.Yorks.* 18g
Amble *N'land* 73b
Ambleside *Cumb.* 34a
Amotherby *N.Yorks.* 28f
Ampleforth *N.Yorks.* 27c
Ancram Res. *N'land* 25d
Ancroft *N'land* 79d
Angram *N.Yorks.* 19h
Annfield Plain *Durham* 60a
Anthorn *Cumb.* 54c
Appersett *N.Yorks.* 36i
Appleby *Cumb.* 47f
Applethwaite *Cumb.* 45e
Appleton-le-Moors
    N.Yorks. 41h
Appleton-le-Street *N.Yorks.* 28f
Appleton Roebuck
    N.Yorks. 19h
Appleton Wiske *N.Yorks.* 39c
Appletreewick *N.Yorks.* 25g
Arkendale *N.Yorks.* 26i
Arkengarth Dale *N.Yorks.* 37b
Arkholme *Lancs.* 22e
Arlecdon *Cumb.* 44h
Armathwaite *Cumb.* 56e
Arncliffe *N.Yorks.* 24e
Arnside *Cumb.* 21c
Arrad Foot *Cumb.* 21a
Arthington *W.Yorks.* 18g
Asenby *N.Yorks.* 26f
Ashington *N'land* 73h
Askam in Furness *Cumb.* 20e
Askham *Cumb.* 46f
Askham Bryan *N.Yorks.* 19e
Askham Richard *N.Yorks.* 19d
Askrigg *N.Yorks.* 37g
Aspatria *Cumb* 54h
Austwick *N.Yorks.* 23e
Aydon *N'land* 65i
Ayle *N'land* 57e
Aynsome *Cumb.* 21b
Aysgarth *N.Yorks.* 37h
Azerley *N.Yorks.* 26d

Backbarrow *Cumb.* 33i
Bagby *N.Yorks.* 27a
Baileyhead *Cumb.* 63a
Bainbridge *N.Yorks.* 37g
Balderhead Res. *Durham* 48i

Baldersby *N.Yorks.* 26c
Baldersby St. James
    N.Yorks. 26f
Baldersdale *Durham* 49g
Baldwinholme *Cumb.* 55e
Balk *N.Yorks.* 27b
Bamburgh *N'land* 79i
Bampton *Cumb.* 46i
Barbon *Cumb.* 22c
Bardon Mill *N'land* 64h
Bardsea *Cumb.* 21d
Bardsey *W.Yorks.* 18h
Barlow *N'land* 66i
Barnard Castle *Durham* 49h
Barningham *Durham* 49i
Barrasford *N'land* 65d
Barrow-in-Furness *Cumb.* 20e
Barton *N.Yorks.* 39a
Barton-le-Street *N.Yorks.* 28f
Barton-le-Willows *N.Yorks.* 28i
Bassenthwaite *Cumb.* 45b
Bassenthwaite L. *Cumb.* 45b
Battersby *N.Yorks.* 41a
Baugh Fell *Cumb.* 36d
Baycliff *Cumb.* 21d
Baysdale *N.Yorks.* 41a
Beadlam *N.Yorks.* 41g
Beadnell *N'land* 77b
Beal *N'land* 79e
Beanley *N'land* 76f
Bearl *N'land* 65i
Bearpark *Durham* 60e
Beauclerc *N'land* 65h
Beaumont *Cumb.* 54i
Beck Hole *N.Yorks.* 42e
Beckermet *Cumb.* 32a
Beckermonds *N.Yorks.* 24a
Beckfoot *Cumb.* 54e
Bedale *N.Yorks.* 39g
Bedlington *N'land* 67a
Beetham *Cumb.* 22a
Belford *N'land* 79h
Belle Isle *Cumb.* 34e
Bellerby *N.Yorks.* 38e
Bellingham *N'land* 64c
Belsay *N'land* 66b
Beltringham *N'land* 64h
Bempton *Humber.* 31d
Beningbrough *N.Yorks.* 19b
Benthall *N'land* 77b
Benwell *Tyne/Wear* 66i
Berwick Hill *N'land* 66f
Berwick-upon-Tweed
    N'land 79a
Bewcastle Fells *Cumb.* 63a
Bewerley *N.Yorks.* 25h
Bewshaugh *N'land* 68i
Bickerton *N.Yorks.* 18f
Biggar *Cumb.* 20h
Bilbrough *N.Yorks.* 19h
Billingham *Clev* 51e
Billy Row *Durham* 60g
Bilsdale *N.Yorks.* 40i
Bilton *N'land* 77h
Bilton *N.Yorks.* 19d
Bilton Banks *N'land* 77h
Bingfield *N'land* 65e
Binsoe *N.Yorks.* 26a
Birdsall *N.Yorks.* 29g
Birdsall Brow *N.Yorks.* 29g
Birk Beck *Cumb.* 35a
Birk Dale *N.Yorks.* 36c
Birkby *Cumb.* 54g
Birkby *N.Yorks.* 39b
Birling *N'land* 77h
Birstwith *N.Yorks.* 26g
Birtley *N'land* 65a
Birtley *Tyne/Wear* 60c
Bishop Auckland *Durham* 50b
Bishop Dale *N.Yorks.* 37h
Bishop Middleham *Durham* 51a
Bishop Monkton *N.Yorks.* 26h
Bishop Thornton *N.Yorks.* 26g
Bishopthorpe *N.Yorks.* 19f
Bishopton *Durham* 51d
Bishopton *N.Yorks.* 26e
Black Hambleton *N.Yorks.* 40e
Black Heddon *N'land* 66d
Blackaburn *N'land* 63i
Blackadder Water *Borders* 78a
Blackburn *Durham* 60e
Blackburn L. *N'land* 71c
Blackford *Cumb.* 62h
Blackhall Colliery *Durham* 61h
Blackton Res. *Durham* 49g
Blakehopeburnhaugh
    N'land 69e

Blakelaw *N'land* 66i
Blanchland *N'land* 58f
Blawith *Cumb.* 33h
Blaydon *Tyne/Wear* 66i
Blencarn *Cumb.* 47b
Blencathra *Cumb.* 45f
Blencogo *Cumb.* 54f
Bleng, R. *Cumb.* 32b
Blennerhasset *Cumb.* 54i
Blindcrake *Cumb.* 54i
Blitterlees *Cumb.* 54b
Bloodybush Edge *N'land* 75g
Blyth *N'land* 67b
Blyth, R. *N'land* 66c
Boggle Hole *N.Yorks.* 43a
Bolam *Durham* 50e
Bolam L. *N'land* 66b
Boldon *Tyne/Wear* 67i
Boldron *Durham* 49h
Boltby *N.Yorks.* 40h
Bolton *Cumb.* 47e
Bolton *N'land* 76i
Bolton Fell *Cumb.* 62f
Bolton-le-Sands *Lancs.* 22g
Bolton Low Houses
    Cumb. 55d
Bolton Percy *N.Yorks.* 19h
Bolton upon Swale
    N.Yorks. 39d
Boltonfellend *Cumb.* 62f
Boltongate *Cumb.* 54i
Bolts Law *N'land* 58b
Bomarsund *N'land* 73h
Bonjedward *Borders* 74d
Boosbeck *Clev* 52i
Boot *Cumb.* 33d
Boothby *Cumb.* 63g
Bootle *Cumb.* 32h
Bootle Fell *Cumb.* 32i
Border Forest Park
    N'land 63/68/69
Boroughbridge *N.Yorks.* 26i
Borrow Beck *Cumb.* 35d
Borrowby *N.Yorks.* 39i
Borrowdale *Cumb.* 45h
Borrowdale Fells *Cumb.* 45h
Borwick *Lancs.* 22e
Bossall *N.Yorks.* 28i
Boston Spa *W.Yorks.* 18i
Bothel *Cumb.* 54i
Boulmer *N'land* 77i
Bournmoor *Durham* 60c
Boustead Hill *Cumb.* 55a
Bouth *Cumb.* 33i
Bouthwaite *N.Yorks.* 25e
Bow Fell *Cumb.* 33b
Bowburn *Durham* 60i
Bowder Stone *Cumb.* 45h
Bowes *Durham* 49g
Bowmanstead *Cumb.* 33e
Bowmont Water *Borders* 74c
Bowness-on-Windermere
    Cumb. 34e
Bowscale Fell *Cumb.* 45c
Bowsden *N'land* 78f
Boynton *Humber.* 30i
Brackenthwaite *Cumb.* 45d
Brafferton *N.Yorks.* 27d
Braithwaite *Cumb.* 45e
Bramham *W.Yorks.* 18i
Bramhope *N.Yorks.* 18g
Brampton *Cumb.* 47f
Brampton *Cumb.* 63g
Brancepeth *Durham* 60h
Brandon *Durham* 60h
Branch End *N'land* 66g
Brandsby *N.Yorks.* 27f
Bransdale *N.Yorks.* 41d
Branthwaite *Cumb.* 44e
Branton Green *N.Yorks.* 27g
Branxton *N'land* 78h
Brathay, R. *Cumb.* 33c
Brawby *N.Yorks.* 28c
Breamish, R. *N'land* 76f
Brearton *N.Yorks.* 26h
Brenkley *Tyne/Wear* 66f
Bridekirk *Cumb.* 44c
Bridge End *Cumb.* 55f
Bridge End *N'land* 63i
Bridge End *N'land* 65h
Bridlington *Humber.* 31g
Briggswath *N.Yorks.* 42b
Brigham *Cumb.* 44c
Brignall *Durham* 49i
Brigsteer *Cumb.* 34i
Broadwath *Cumb.* 56b
Brockie Law *Borders* 68b

Brockwoodlees Dumf./Gal. 62b
Bromfield Cumb. 54f
Brompton N.Yorks. 39f
Brompton N.Yorks. 29c
Brompton on Swale N.Yorks. 38f
Brookhouse Lancs. 22h
Broomhaugh N'land 65i
Broomhill N'land 73e
Broomlee L. N'land 64e
Broomley N'land 65i
Brotherlee Durham 58i
Brothers Water Cumb. 46h
Brotton Clev. 53d
Brough Cumb. 48h
Brough Sowerby Cumb. 48g
Broughton N.Yorks. 28f
Broughton Beck Cumb. 21a
Broughton in Furness Cumb. 33g
Broughton Moor Cumb. 44b
Brown Moor N'land 64f
Brownhart Law Borders 74i
Brownrigg Head N'land 69f
Broxa N.Yorks. 43g
Broxa Forest N.Yorks. 42f
Brunstock Cumb. 62h
Brunswick Village Tyne/Wear 67d
Brunton N'land 77b
Buck Fell N'land 68h
Buckden N.Yorks. 24e
Buckden Pike N.Yorks. 24c
Buckstone Moss Borders 68d
Buckton Humber. 31d
Buckton N'land 79h
Budle N'land 79i
Budle B. N'land 79i
Budle Pt. N'land 79i
Bulbeck Common N'land 58f
Bulmer N.Yorks. 28h
Burdale N.Yorks. 29h
Burgh by Sands Cumb. 55b
Burgh Marsh Cumb. 62g
Burn Hope Durham 58g
Burn Moor Lancs./N.Yorks. 23g
Burneside Cumb. 34f
Burneston N.Yorks. 39g
Burngrange Moor N'land 69d
Burnhope Durham 60d
Burnhope Moor Durham 58g
Burnhope Res. Durham 58h
Burniston N.Yorks. 43g
Burnopfield Durham 60a
Burnsall N.Yorks. 25g
Burnsall and Thorpe Fell N.Yorks. 24i
Burnt Yates N.Yorks. 26g
Burradon N'land 71a
Burradon Tyne/Wear 67d
Burrill N.Yorks. 39g
Burtersett N.Yorks. 37g
Burtholme Cumb. 63g
Burton Agnes Humber. 30i
Burton Fell Cumb. 48d
Burton Fleming Humber. 30e
Burton in Kendal Cumb. 22e
Burton in Lonsdale N.Yorks. 23d
Burton Leonard N.Yorks. 26h
Burtree Fell Durham 58e
Burythorpe N.Yorks. 29g
Butterknowle Durham 49f
Buttermere Cumb. 45g
Buttermere Fell Cumb. 45g
Butterwick N.Yorks. 28f
Butterwick N.Yorks. 30d
Buxley Borders 78a
Byermoor Tyne/Wear 60a
Byers Green Durham 60h
Byland Abbey N.Yorks. 27c
Byrness N'land 69b
Bywell N'land 65i

Caldbeck Cumb. 55h
Caldbeck Fells Cumb. 55h
Caldbergh N.Yorks. 38g
Caldbergh Moor N.Yorks. 25b
Calder, R. Cumb. 32b
Calder Bridge Cumb. 32b
Caldew, R. Cumb. 55f
Caldron Snout Cumb./Durham 48b
Caldwell N.Yorks. 50g
Calf, The Cumb. 35e
Calthwaite Cumb. 56g
Cam Beck N.Yorks. 23c
Cam Fell N.Yorks. 23c
Cambo N'land 71h
Cambois N'land 73i
Camerton Cumb. 44b
Camperdown Tyne/Wear 67d
Camptown Borders 74g
Canonbie Dumf./Gal. 62e
Cantsfield Lancs. 22f
Capelstone Fell N'land 68h
Capheaton N'land 65c
Cargo Cumb. 55c
Cark Cumb. 21e
Carlesmoor N.Yorks. 25f
Carleton Cumb. 47a
Carleton Cumb. 56a
Carlisle Cumb. 55c
Carlton Clev. 51d
Carlton N.Yorks. 37i
Carlton N.Yorks. 41g
Carlton Husthwaite N.Yorks. 27e
Carlton in Cleveland N.Yorks. 40b
Carlton Miniott N.Yorks. 26c
Carlton Moor N.Yorks. 37i
Carnaby Humber. 30i
Carnforth Lancs. 22d
Carperby N.Yorks. 37h
Carr End N'land 77b
Carr Shield N'land 58d
Carrock Fell Cumb. 55h
Carrs, The N.Yorks. 29c
Carrville Durham 60f
Carter Bar Borders 74g
Carter Fell Borders/N'land 69a
Carter Moor N'land 66c
Carthorpe N.Yorks. 26b
Cartmel Cumb. 21b
Cartmel Fell Cumb. 34h
Cartmel Sands Cumb. 21d
Carvoran N'land 63i
Casterton Cumb. 22c
Castle Bolton N.Yorks. 37i
Castle Carrock Cumb. 56b
Castle Eden Durham 61h
Castle Howard N.Yorks. 28f
Castle Pt. N'land 77f
Castleside Durham 59e
Castleton N.Yorks. 41b
Castleton Ridge N.Yorks. 41b
Castletown Tyne/Wear 61a
Castley N.Yorks. 18g
Catcleugh Res. N'land 69a
Cateran Hill N'land 76f
Catlowdy Cumb. 62f
Caton Lancs. 22h
Caton Moor Lancs. 22h
Catrigg Force N.Yorks. 24g
Cattal N.Yorks. 18f
Catterlen Cumb. 46c
Catterick N.Yorks. 39d
Catterick Bridge N.Yorks. 38f
Catterick Camp N.Yorks. 38f
Catterick Moss Durham 59g
Catterton N.Yorks. 19g
Catton N.Yorks. 26c
Catton N'land 58a
Caulside Dumf./Gal. 62b
Causey Hill N'land 65g
Cautley Spout Cumb. 35f
Caw Cumb. 33d
Cawton N.Yorks. 28e
Cayton N.Yorks. 30b
Cayton B. N.Yorks. 30b
Cessford Borders 74e
Chapel Fell Durham 58h
Clapel le Dale N.Yorks. 23e
Chapel Stile Cumb. 33c
Chapelknowe Dumf./Gal. 62d
Charlton N'land 69i
Chatto Craig Borders 74e
Chatton N'land 76c
Chatton Moor N'land 76c
Chester-le-Street Durham 60c
Chesterholm N'land 64h
Chesterhope N'land 70i
Chesterhope Common N'land 70i
Chesterwood N'land 64i
Cheswick N'land 79d
Cheswick Sands N'land 79d
Chesters N'land 68c
Chesters Pike N'land 63i
Chevington Drift N'land 73e
Cheviot, The (Great Cheviot) N'land 75d
Cheviot Hills Borders/N'land 69/70/74/75
Chillingham N'land 76c
Chilton Durham 50c
Chirdon Burn N'land 63c
Chirnside Borders 78b
Chirton Tyne/Wear 67e
Chollerford N'land 65d
Chollerton N'land 65d
Chop Gate N.Yorks. 40f
Choppington N'land 73h
Chopwell Tyne/Wear 59c
Chopwell Wood Tyne/Wear 59c
Christon Bank N'land 77e
Claife Heights Cumb. 33f
Clapham N.Yorks. 23e
Clappersgate Cumb. 33c
Clara Vale N'land 66h
Claughton Lancs. 22h
Clawthorpe Cumb. 22b
Claxton N.Yorks. 28h
Clayton Fell N'land 71i
Cleadon Tyne/Wear 67i
Cleasby N.Yorks. 50h
Cleator Cumb. 44h
Cleator Moor Cumb. 44h
Clennell N'land 75h
Cleveland Hills N.Yorks. 40/41
Cliburn Cumb. 47d
Clifford W.Yorks. 18i
Clifton Cumb. 47d
Clifton N.Yorks. 19e
Clougha Lancs. 22h
Cloughton N.Yorks. 43e
Cloughton Newlands N.Yorks. 43e
Coalcleugh N'land 58d
Coanwood Common N'land 57b
Coastley N'land 65g
Coatham Sands Clev. 52e
Cochrane Pike N'land 75i
Cockayne N.Yorks. 41d
Cocker, R. Cumb. 44c
Cockermouth Cumb. 44c
Cockfield Durham 49f
Cod Beck N.Yorks. 27a
Coe Burn N'land 76i
Colburn N.Yorks. 38f
Colby Cumb. 47e
Cold Fell Cumb. 57a
Cold Hesledon Durham 61e
Cold Kirby N.Yorks. 40i
Cold Law N'land 75e
Coldbeck Cumb. 35c
Coldsmouth Hill Borders/N'land 75a
Coldstream Borders 78g
College Burn N'land 75a
Colliery Row Tyne/Wear 60f
Collin Hags Dumf./Gal. 62a
Collingham W.Yorks. 18i
Collis Ridge N.Yorks. 41g
Colsterdale N.Yorks. 25b
Colsterdale Moor N.Yorks. 25b
Colt Crag Res. N'land 65a
Colthouse Cumb. 33f
Colton Cumb. 33i
Colton N.Yorks. 19h
Colwell N'land 65e
Comb N'land 69e
Comb Fell N'land 75e
Commondale N.Yorks. 52i
Commondale Moor N.Yorks. 52i
Coneysthorpe N.Yorks. 28e
Coniston Cumb. 33e
Coniston Fells Cumb. 33e
Coniston Water Cumb. 33h
Conistone N.Yorks. 24i
Conistone Moor N.Yorks. 24f
Consett Durham 59e
Constable Burton N.Yorks. 38h
Coomb Edge Borders 68e
Copeland Forest Cumb. 32c
Copgrove N.Yorks. 26i
Copley Durham 49f
Copmanthorpe N.Yorks. 19h
Copt Hewick N.Yorks. 26f
Coquet, R. N'land 73a
Coquet I. N'land 73b
Corbridge N'land 65h
Corney Fell Cumb. 32i
Cornforth Durham 60i
Cornhill-on-Tweed N'land 78h
Cornsay Durham 59f
Corsenside Common N'land 70i
Cotehill Cumb. 56e
Cotherstone Durham 49e
Cotherstone Moor Durham 48i
Cottonshope Burn N'land 69b
Coulderton Cumb. 32a
Coulton N.Yorks. 28d
Coundon Durham 50b
Coundon Grange Durham 50b
Countersett N.Yorks. 37g
Coupland N'land 75b
Cover Dale N.Yorks. 25a
Coverham N.Yorks. 38h
Cow Green Res. Cumb./Durham 48b
Cowan Bridge Lancs. 22f
Cowesby N.Yorks. 40h
Cowledge Burn N'land 77g
Cowpen N'land 67b
Cowpen Marsh Clev. 52d
Cowshill Durham 58h
Cowthorpe N.Yorks. 18f
Coxhoe Durham 60i
Coxwold N.Yorks. 27e
Crackenthorpe Cumb. 47e
Crackpot N.Yorks. 37e
Cracoe N.Yorks. 24i
Crag Hill Cumb. 23a
Crag L. N'land 64h
Cragdale Moor N.Yorks. 24b
Craghead Durham 60e
Craik Moor Borders 74f
Crailing Borders 74d
Crake, R. Cumb. 21a
Crambe N.Yorks. 28i
Cramlington N'land 67d
Craster N'land 77f
Crathorne N.Yorks. 39c
Crawcrook Tyne/Wear 66h
Crawley Side Durham 59g
Cray N.Yorks. 24b
Crayke N.Yorks. 27f
Cresswell N'land 73e
Cringle Moor N.Yorks. 40c
Croft-on-Tees Durham 50i
Croglin Cumb. 56f
Croglin Fell Cumb. 57d
Cronkley Fell Durham 48b
Crook Cumb. 34f
Crook Durham 60g
Crookhall Durham 59f
Crookham N'land 78h
Crookham Eastfield N'land 78h
Crooklands Cumb. 22b
Cropton N.Yorks. 41i
Cropton Forest N.Yorks. 41i
Crosby Cumb. 54g
Crosby Garrett Fell Cumb. 35c
Crosby Ravensworth Cumb. 47h
Crosby Ravensworth Fell Cumb. 47h
Cross, The N'land 69g
Cross Fell Cumb. 57h
Crossbow Hill Borders 68d
Crosscanonby Cumb. 54g
Crossgates N.Yorks. 30b
Crossthwaite Common Durham 48f
Crosthwaite Cumb. 34h
Crummock Water Cumb. 45d
Croxdale Durham 60i
Culgaith Cumb. 47b
Cullercoats Tyne/Wear 67f
Cullernose Pt. N'land 77f
Cummersdale Cumb. 55c
Cumrew Cumb. 56f
Cumrew Fell Cumb. 56c
Cumwhinton Cumb. 56a
Cumwhitton Cumb. 56b
Cundall N.Yorks. 27d
Cunning Pt. Cumb. 44d
Curr, The Borders 75d
Currock Hill N'land 66h
Cushat End Borders 74f
Cushat Law N'land 75h

Dacre Cumb. 46e
Dacre N.Yorks. 25i
Daddry Shield Durham 58h
Dalby N.Yorks. 28d
Dalby Forest N.Yorks. 42h
Dale Cumb. 56f
Dale Head Cumb. 45h
Dalehouse N.Yorks. 53h
Dallowgill Moor N.Yorks. 25e
Dalston Cumb. 55f
Dalton N'land 58c
Dalton N'land 66e
Dalton N.Yorks. 27d
Dalton N.Yorks. 38b
Dalton-in-Furness Cumb. 20f
Dalton-le-Dale Durham 61e
Dalton Piercy Clev. 51c
Dalton upon Tees N.Yorks. 39a
Danby N.Yorks. 41b
Danby High Moor N.Yorks. 41b
Danby Low Moor Clev. 53g
Danby Low Moor N.Yorks. 41b
Danby Rigg N.Yorks. 41b
Danby Wiske N.Yorks. 39e
Darden L. N'land 71d
Darley N.Yorks. 25i
Darlington Durham 50i
Darnbrook Fell N.Yorks. 24d
Darques Burn N'land 69f
Darras Hall N'land 66e
Davyshiel Common N'land 70f
Deadwater Moor N'land 68f
Dean Cumb. 44f
Dean Moor Cumb. 44e
Deanscales Cumb. 44f
Dearham Cumb. 54g
Debdon L. N'land 71c
Deep Dale Durham 49g
Deep Dale N.Yorks. 42i
Deepdale Cumb. 35i
Deepdale N.Yorks. 24b
Deepdale Common Cumb. 46g
Deerness, R. Durham 60g
Deighton N.Yorks. 19i
Deighton N.Yorks. 39f
Delves Durham 59f
Dent Cumb. 35i
Dentdale Cumb. 35i
Denwick N'land 77h
Derwent, R. Cumb. 44c
Derwent, R. Durham/Tyne/Wear 59e
Derwent, R. N.Yorks. 28f
Derwent Fells Cumb. 45h
Derwent Res. N'land/Durham 59a
Derwent I. Cumb. 45e
Derwent Water Cumb. 45e
Detchant N'land 79h
Devil's Water N'land 65h
Devoke Water Cumb. 32f
Dilston N'land 65h
Din Fell Borders 68d
Dinlabyre Borders 68h
Dinley Fell Borders 68d
Dinmont Lairs N'land 68i
Dinnington Tyne/Wear 66f
Dipton Durham 59c
Dipton Wood N'land 65h
Dirt Pot N'land 58e
Dishforth N.Yorks. 26f
Distington Cumb. 44e
Dockray Cumb. 46e
Dod Burn Borders 68a
Dod Fell Borders 68e
Dodd, The N'land 69g
Dodd Fell N.Yorks. 36i
Dodd Wood Cumb. 45e
Doddington N'land 79g
Doddington North Moor N'land 78i
Doe, R. N.Yorks. 23e
Dollywaggon Pike Cumb. 46g
Dormanstown Clev. 52e
Dove, R. N.Yorks. 28b
Dovenby Cumb. 44c
Dow Crag Cumb. 33e
Downholme N.Yorks. 38e
Dowston Burn Borders 68e
Doxford N'land 77d
Drigg Cumb. 32e
Drigg Pt. Cumb. 32e
Drumburgh Cumb. 55a
Druridge B. N'land 73e
Dubmill Pt. Cumb. 54d
Dudley Tyne/Wear 67d
Duddo N'land 78f
Duddon, R. Cumb. 33d
Duddon Bridge Cumb. 33g
Duddon Sands Cumb. 20e
Dufton Cumb. 47f
Dufton Fell Cumb. 48a
Duggleby N.Yorks. 29h
Duncombe Park N.Yorks. 28a
Dungeon Ghyll Force Cumb. 33b
Dunmoor Hill N'land 75e
Dunnerdale Fells Cumb. 33g
Dunsley N.Yorks. 53i
Durham Durham 60i

Eaglescliffe Clev. 51h
Eaglesfield Cumb. 44f
Ealinghamrigg Common N'land 64c
Eamont, R. Cumb. 46f
Eamont Bridge Cumb. 46c
Earle N'land 75b
Earsdon N'land 73d
Earsdon Tyne/Wear 67e
Earsdon Hill N'land 73d
Earswick N.Yorks. 19c
Easby N.Yorks. 38f
Easby N.Yorks. 40c
Easedale Cumb. 33c
Easington Clev. 53h
Easington Durham 61e
Easington Beck Clev. 53h
Easington Colliery Durham 61e
Easington Lane Tyne/Wear 61d
Easingwold N.Yorks. 27e
East Allen, R. N'land 58b
East Allen Dale N'land 58b
East Ayton N.Yorks. 43g
East Barnby N.Yorks. 53i
East Baugh Fell Cumb. 36g
East Bolton Moor N.Yorks. 37e
East Cowton N.Yorks. 39b
East Denton Tyne/Wear 66i
East Harlsey N.Yorks. 39f
East Hauxwell N.Yorks. 38f
East Hedleyhope Durham 59i
East Herrington Tyne/Wear 61a
East Heslerton N.Yorks. 29f
East Keswick W.Yorks. 18h
East Kielder Moor N'land 69d
East Layton N.Yorks. 50g
East Lutton N.Yorks. 29f
East Ness N.Yorks. 28b
East Ord N'land 78c
East Rainton Tyne/Wear 61d
East Rigton W.Yorks. 18h
East Rounton N.Yorks. 39c
East Sleekburn N'land 67b
East Thirston N'land 73d
East Witton N.Yorks. 38h
East Woodburn Common N'land 70i
Eastfield N.Yorks. 30b
Eastgate Durham 58i
Easton Cumb. 55a
Ebberston N.Yorks. 29b
Ebchester Durham 59c
Eccup W.Yorks. 18g
Eccup Res. W.Yorks. 18g
Eckford Borders 74d
Eden, R. Cumb. 62g
Edlingham N'land 76i
Edmondbyers Durham 59d
Edmondbyers Common Durham 59d
Edmondsley Durham 60e
Edrom Borders 78a
Eel Crag Cumb. 45d
Egglescliffe Clev. 51h
Eggleston Durham 49e
Eggleston Common Durham 49b
Eglingham N'land 76f
Eglingham Burn N'land 77d
Egremont Cumb. 44h
Egton N.Yorks. 42b
Egton Bridge N.Yorks. 42a
Egton High Moor N.Yorks. 41f
Ehen, R. Cumb. 32a

Elilaw N'land 75h
Elishaw N'land 69f
Ellen, R. Cumb. 54h
Ellerby N.Yorks. 53h
Ellergreen Cumb. 34f
Ellerton N.Yorks. 39d
Ellingham N'land 77a
Ellingstring N.Yorks. 25c
Ellington N'land 73h
Elrington N'land 64i
Elsdon N'land 71d
Elsdon Burn N'land 70i
Elterwater Cumb. 33c
Elton Clev. 51h
Eltringham N'land 66g
Elwick Clev. 51b
Emblehope Moor N'land 69d
Embleton N'land 77e
Embleton B. N'land 77e
Emmethaugh N'land 69g
Ennerdale Bridge Cumb. 44i
Ennerdale Fell Cumb. 44i
Ennerdale Forest Cumb. 45g
Ennerdale Water Cumb. 44i
Eppleby N.Yorks. 50g
Eryholme N.Yorks. 39b
Escomb Durham 50b
Escrick N.Yorks. 19i
Esh Durham 60d
Esh Winning Durham 60g
Eshott N'land 73d
Esk, R. Cumb. 32f
Esk, R. Cumb./Dumf./Gal. 62e
Esk, R. N.Yorks. 41c
Esk Hause Cumb. 33a
Eskdale Cumb. 33d
Eskdale Fell Cumb. 33a
Eskdale Green Cumb. 32f
Esthwaite Water Cumb. 33f
Eston Clev. 52e
Etal N'land 78h
Evenwood Durham 50d
Evertown Dumf./Gal. 62d
Ewe Hill N'land 69d
Ewe Moor N.Yorks. 24g
Exelby N.Yorks. 39g

Faceby N.Yorks. 40b
Fadmoor N.Yorks. 41h
Fairfield Cumb. 46g
Falling Foss N.Yorks. 42c
Fallowfield N'land 65d
Falstone N'land 69g
Fangdale Beck N.Yorks. 40f
Farlam Cumb. 56c
Farleton Cumb. 22b
Farlington N.Yorks. 28g
Farndale N.Yorks. 41d
Farndale Moor N.Yorks. 41d
Farnham N.Yorks. 26i
Fatfield Tyne/Wear 60c
Faugh Cumb. 56b
Fearby N.Yorks. 25c
Featherstone Common N'land 63i
Featherwood N'land 69c
Feetham N.Yorks. 37e
Felixkirk N.Yorks. 40h
Felkington N'land 78f
Fell Head Cumb. 35e
Fellgate Tyne/Wear 67h
Felling Tyne/Wear 67g
Felton N'land 73d
Felton Common N'land 72c
Fenham Flats N'land 79h
Fenton Cumb. 56b
Fenton Town N'land 78i
Fenwick N'land 65f
Ferrensby N.Yorks. 26i
Ferryhill Durham 50c
Ferryhill Station Durham 50c
Field Broughton Cumb. 21b
Filey N.Yorks. 30c
Filey B. N.Yorks. 30c
Filey Brigg N.Yorks. 30c
Fimber Humber. 29h
Finsthwaite Cumb. 33i
Finghall N.Yorks. 38i
Firbank Cumb. 35e
Fishburn Durham 51a
Flamborough Humber. 31e
Flamborough Hd. Humber. 31e
Flawith N.Yorks. 27h
Flaxby N.Yorks. 18c
Flaxton N.Yorks. 28h
Fleetwith Pike Cumb. 45h
Fletchertown Cumb. 54f
Flimby Cumb. 44b
Flixton N.Yorks. 30b
Flixton Wold N.Yorks. 30e
Flodden N'land 78h
Flookburgh Cumb. 21e
Folkton N.Yorks. 30b
Follifoot N.Yorks. 18e
Font, R. N'land 72i
Fontburn Res. N'land 71e
Football Hole N'land 77b
Ford N'land 78i
Fordon Humber. 30e
Forest Hall Tyne/Wear 67d
Forge Valley N.Yorks. 43g
Foss, R. N.Yorks. 27i
Foston N.Yorks. 28h
Foulburn Gair N'land 75d
Foulden Borders 78c
Foulney I. Cumb. 20i
Foulplay Knowe N'land 70f
Fountains Fell N.Yorks. 24d
Fourlawhill Top N'land 65a
Fourstones N'land 65g
Foxholes N.Yorks. 30d
Foxup N.Yorks. 24d
Fozy Moss N'land 64e
Fraisthorpe Humber. 30i
Framwellgate Moor Durham 60e
Fremington Edge N.Yorks. 37f
Frenchman's Bay Tyne/Wear 67i
Frizington Cumb. 44h
Frosterley Durham 59g
Froswick Cumb. 34b
Fulbeck N'land 73g
Fulford N.Yorks. 19f
Fulwell Tyne/Wear 67i
Furness Fells Cumb. 33e
Fylingdales Moor N.Yorks. 42f

Gainford Durham 50g
Gaitsgill Cumb. 55f
Galphay N.Yorks. 26d
Gamblesby Cumb. 57g
Gammersgill N.Yorks. 25a
Ganthorpe N.Yorks. 28e
Ganton N.Yorks. 30d
Ganton Wold N.Yorks. 30d
Garleigh Moor N'land 71f
Garnett Bridge Cumb. 34f
Garrigill Cumb. 57i
Garsdale Cumb. 36g
Garthside Cumb. 63g
Gateshead Tyne/Wear 67g
Gawthrop Cumb. 35i
Gayle N.Yorks. 36i
Gayle Beck N.Yorks. 23b
Gayle Moor Cumb./N.Yorks. 22b
Gayles N.Yorks. 38b
Gayles Moor N.Yorks. 38a
Gelt, R. Cumb. 56b
Geltsdale Middle Cumb. 57a
Giggleswick N.Yorks. 23i
Gilcrux Cumb. 54h
Gilderdale Forest Cumb. 57d
Gilesgate Moor Durham 60f
Gillamoor N.Yorks. 41h
Gilling East N.Yorks. 28d
Gilling West N.Yorks. 38c
Gilsland Cumb. 63h
Girdle Fell N'land 69d
Gisborough Moor Clev. 52i
Glaisdale N.Yorks. 41c
Glaisdale Moor N.Yorks. 41e
Glaisdale Rigg N.Yorks. 41e
Glantlees Hill N'land 72c
Glanton N'land 76i
Glaramara Cumb. 45h
Glasshouses N.Yorks. 25i
Glasson Cumb. 55a
Glassonby Cumb. 56i
Gleaston Cumb. 20f
Glen, R. N'land 75b
Glenderamackin, R. Cumb. 46d
Glendhu Hill N'land 68i
Glendue Fell N'land 57a
Glenridding Cumb. 46g
Glenridding Common Cumb. 46g
Goathland N.Yorks. 42e
Goathland Moor N.Yorks. 42e
Goldsborough N.Yorks. 18c
Goldsborough N.Yorks. 53i
Goodber Common Lancs. 22i
Gordale Scar N.Yorks. 24h
Gormire L. N.Yorks. 27b
Gosforth Tyne/Wear 67d
Gosforth Cumb. 32b
Gosforth L. Tyne/Wear 67d
Gouthwaite Res. N.Yorks. 25e
Grafton N.Yorks. 27g
Grange Cumb. 45h
Grange-over-Sands Cumb. 21e
Grange Villa Durham 60b
Grangetown Clev. 52e
Grantley N.Yorks. 25f
Grasmere Cumb. 33c
Grasmoor Cumb. 45d
Grassholme Res. Durham 49d
Grassington N.Yorks. 24i
Grassington Moor N.Yorks. 25d
Grayrigg Cumb. 35d
Graythorp Clev. 51f
Great Asby Cumb. 47i
Great Ayton N.Yorks. 52h
Great Barugh N.Yorks. 28c
Great Bavington N'land 65b
Great Borne Cumb. 44i
Great Broughton Cumb. 44b
Great Broughton N.Yorks. 40c
Great Busby N.Yorks. 40b
Great Clifton Cumb. 44b
Great Corby Cumb. 56b
Great Crakehall N.Yorks. 39g
Great Crosthwaite Cumb. 45e
Great Dod Cumb. 46d
Great Easby Cumb. 63g
Great Edstone N.Yorks. 28b
Great End Cumb. 33a
Great Fencote N.Yorks. 39d
Great Fryup Beck N.Yorks. 41c
Great Gable Cumb. 45h
Great Habton N.Yorks. 28f
Great Haw N.Yorks. 25a
Great Hetha N'land 75a
Great Langdale Beck Cumb. 33b
Great Langton N.Yorks. 39d
Great Lumley Durham 60f
Great Mell Fell Cumb. 46d
Great Moor N'land 75e
Great Musgrave Cumb. 48g
Great Ormside Cumb. 47i
Great Orton Cumb. 55b
Great Ouseburn N.Yorks. 27g
Great Ryle N'land 75i
Great Salkeld Cumb. 56i
Great Scar N.Yorks. 24g
Great Shunner Fell N.Yorks. 36f
Great Sled Dale N.Yorks. 36f
Great Smeaton N.Yorks. 39b
Great Stainton Durham 51d
Great Strickland Cumb. 47d
Great Swinburne N'land 65d
Great Urswick Cumb. 20f
Great Whernside N.Yorks. 24f
Great Whittington N'land 65e
Greatmoor Hill Borders 68d
Greatham Clev. 51f
Greatrigg Man Cumb. 46g
Green, The Cumb. 33g
Green Fell Cumb. 57h
Green Hammerton N.Yorks. 19a
Green Rigg Cumb. 62c
Green Rigg Cumb. 63e
Greendykes N'land 76c
Greenhaugh N'land 69h
Greenhead N'land 63i
Greenlee L. N'land 64e
Greenodd Cumb. 21a
Greenrow Cumb. 54b
Greenside Tyne/Wear 66h
Gressingham Lancs. 22e
Greta, R. Durham 49h
Greta, R. Lancs./N.Yorks. 22f
Gretna Dumf./Gal. 62g
Gretna Green Dumf./Gal. 62g
Grewelthorpe N.Yorks. 26d
Grey Friar Cumb. 33e
Greygarth N.Yorks. 25f
Greyhound Law N'land 69b
Greysouthen Cumb. 44c
Greystoke Cumb. 46b
Grimwith Res. N.Yorks. 25g
Grindale Humber. 30f
Grindale Field Humber. 30f
Grindon N'land 78e
Grindon L. N'land 64h
Grinton N.Yorks. 37f
Grisedale Cumb. 46g
Grisedale Forest Cumb. 46g
Grisedale Pike Cumb. 45d
Gristhorpe N.Yorks. 30c
Grizebeck Cumb. 33h
Grizedale Cumb. 33f
Grizedale Forest Cumb. 33f
Grosmont N.Yorks. 42b
Grubbit Law Borders 74f
Guide Post N'land 73h
Guisborough Clev. 52h
Gunner Box N'land 71e
Gunnerside N.Yorks. 37e
Gunnerton N'land 65d
Gunson Height Cumb. 20c
Guyzance N'land 73a

Hackforth N.Yorks. 39d
Hackness N.Yorks. 43g
Hackthorpe Cumb. 47d
Haggerston N'land 79d
Haggie Knowe Borders 68f
Haile Cumb. 32b
Haisthorpe Humber. 30i
Hale Cumb. 22a
Half Moon B. Lancs. 21h
Halidon Hill N'land 78c
Hall Dunnerdale Cumb. 33d
Hall Moor N.Yorks. 19b
Hallbankgate Cumb. 63g
Halleypike L. N'land 64f
Hallgarth Durham 60f
Hallin Fell Cumb. 46e
Hallington N'land 65e
Hallington Reservoirs N'land 65e
Halton Lancs. 22g
Halton N'land 65h
Halton Gill N.Yorks. 24d
Haltwhistle N'land 64g
Hambleton Hills N.Yorks. 40h
Hampsthwaite N.Yorks. 18a
Hamsterley Durham 49c
Hamsterley Durham 59c
Hamsterley Common Durham 49b
Hamsterley Forest Durham 49b
Hanlith N.Yorks. 24h
Harbottle N'land 71a
Hard Knott Pass Cumb. 33d
Hardknott Castle Cumb. 33d
Hardraw N.Yorks. 36i
Hare Law N'land 75a
Harehope N'land 76f
Hareshaw Common N'land 69i
Harewood W.Yorks. 18h
Harewood Park W.Yorks. 18h
Harker Cumb. 62h
Harkers Hill Borders 74e
Harkerside Moor N.Yorks. 37e
Harlow Hill N'land 66d
Harmby N.Yorks. 38h
Harome N.Yorks. 28b
Harpham Humber. 30i
Harrogate N.Yorks. 18a
Hart Clev. 61h
Hart Burn N'land 71h
Hart Crag Cumb. 46g
Hartburn N'land 71i
Harter Fell Cumb. 33d
Harter Fell Cumb. 34c
Harthope Burn N'land 75e
Hartlepool Clev. 52a
Hartlepool B. Clev. 52a
Hartley Cumb. 36b
Hartley N'land 67b
Hartleyburn Common N'land 57a
Hartlington N.Yorks. 25g
Harton N.Yorks. 28h
Hartsop Cumb. 46h
Harwood Dale N.Yorks. 43d
Harwood Dale Forest N.Yorks. 43d
Harwood Dale Moor N.Yorks. 43d
Harwood Forest N'land 71d
Haswell Durham 61d
Haswell Plough Durham 61g
Haughton Common N'land 64e
Hauxley N'land 73b
Hauxley Haven N'land 73b
Haverigg Cumb. 20b
Haverigg Pt. Cumb. 20d
Haverthwaite Cumb. 21a
Hawcoat Cumb. 20e
Hawes N.Yorks. 36i
Haweswater Res. Cumb. 46i
Hawkhill N'land 77h
Hawkhope Hill N'land 69g
Hawkshead Cumb. 33f
Hawkshead Hill Cumb. 33f
Hawkshead Moor Cumb. 33f
Hawkswick N.Yorks. 24e
Hawkswick Clowder N.Yorks. 24e
Hawnby N.Yorks. 40i
Hawnby Moor N.Yorks. 40i
Haws Pt. Cumb. 20i
Hawthorn Durham 61e
Haxby N.Yorks. 19c
Haycock Cumb. 45g
Haydon Bridge N'land 64i
Hayton Cumb. 54h
Hayton Cumb. 56b
Hazlerigg Tyne/Wear 67d
Hazon N'land 73a
Headlam Durham 50d
Heads Nook Cumb. 56b
Healaugh N.Yorks. 19d
Healaugh N.Yorks. 37e
Healey N.Yorks. 25c
Heathfield Moor N.Yorks. 25g
Heaton Lancs. 21i
Heaton Tyne/Wear 67g
Hebburn Tyne/Wear 67h
Hebden N.Yorks. 25g
Hebden Moor N.Yorks. 25g
Hebron N'land 73g
Heddon Hill N'land 75f
Heddon-on-the-Wall N'land 66h
Hedley on the Hill N'land 66h
Heighington Durham 50e
Heiton Borders 74b
Helm Crag Cumb. 33c
Helmington Row Durham 60g
Helmsley N.Yorks. 28a
Helperby N.Yorks. 27d
Helperthorpe N.Yorks. 29f
Helton Cumb. 46f
Helvellyn Cumb. 46g
Hendon Tyne/Wear 61b
Henshaw N'land 64h
Henshaw Common N'land 64e
Hepburn Wood N'land 76f
Hepple N'land 71d
Hepscott N'land 73g
Herdship Fell Durham 48b
Hermitage Hill Borders 68d
Hermitage Water Borders 68g
Heron Pike Cumb. 33c
Hertford R N.Yorks. 30b
Hesleden Durham 61h
Heslerton Carrs N.Yorks. 29e
Heslington N.Yorks. 19f
Hessay N.Yorks. 19e
Hest Bank Lancs. 21i
Hethersgill Cumb. 62i
Hethpool N'land 75a
Hett Durham 60i
Hetton Downs Tyne/Wear 61d
Hetton-le-Hole Tyne/Wear 61d
Heugh N'land 66e
Heversham Cumb. 22a
Heworth N.Yorks. 19f
Hexham N'land 65h
Hexhamshire Common N'land 58b
Heysham Lancs. 21h
High Angerton N'land 71i
High Ash Head Moor N.Yorks. 25e
High Bentham N.Yorks. 23d
High Buston N'land 77h
High Callerton N'land 66f
High Capon Edge N'land 64b
High Church N'land 73g
High Conniscliffe Durham 50h
High Countess Crag N'land 69a
High Crag Cumb. 45g
High Crindledike Cumb. 62h
High Cup Gill Cumb. 48d
High Dales N.Yorks. 43g
High Ellington N.Yorks. 25c
High Etherley Durham 50a
High Fells Cumb. 45f
High Force Durham 48c
High Green Cumb. 34b
High Harrogate N.Yorks. 18b
High Haswell Durham 61d
High Hawsker N.Yorks. 42c
High Hesket Cumb. 56e
High Hesleden Durham 61h
High Hutton N.Yorks. 28i
High Lorton Cumb. 45d
High Mark N.Yorks. 24h
High Newton Cumb. 21b
High Newton-by-the-Sea N'land 77b
High Pike Cumb. 55h
High Raise Cumb. 46h
High Rochester N'land 69f
High Seat Cumb./N.Yorks. 36e
High Shilford N'land 65i
High Spen Tyne/Wear 66h
High Stand Plantation Cumb. 56e
High Stile Cumb. 45g
High Street Cumb. 46h
High Warden N'land 65g
High Westwood Durham 59c
High White Stones Cumb. 33b
High Yarridge N'land 65g
Highfield Cumb. 63h
Highfield Tyne/Wear 59c
Hill Head N'land 66i
Hilpsford Pt. Cumb. 20i
Hilton Clev. 51h
Hilton Cumb. 48d
Hilton Durham 50d
Hilton Fell Cumb. 48d
Hincaster Cumb. 34i
Hindburn, R. Lancs. 22i
Hinderwell N.Yorks. 53h
Hindhope Hill Borders 74h
Hindhope Law N'land 69e
Hindley N'land 65i
Hipswell N.Yorks. 38f
Hipswell Moor N.Yorks. 38e
Hirsel L. Borders 78g
Hirst N'land 73h
Hobkirk Borders 68b
Hobson Durham 60a
Hoff Beck Cumb. 47f
Hogdon Law N'land 75h
Hogswood Moor N'land 68f
Holburn N'land 79g
Holgate Moor N.Yorks. 37c
Holker Cumb. 21e
Holling Hill N'land 71f
Holme Cumb. 22b
Holme N.Yorks. 26c
Holmrook Cumb. 32e
Holwick Durham 48f
Holwick Fell Durham 48f
Holy I. N'land 79f
Holy I. Sands N'land 79e
Holystone N'land 71a
Holystone Common N'land 71d
Holywell N'land 67e
Honister Pass Cumb. 45h
Hope Moor Durham 37b
Hophills Nob Borders 74g
Hornby N.Yorks. 39b
Hornby N.Yorks. 38f
Horncliffe N'land 78f
Horndean Borders 78e
Horden Durham 61h
Hornsby Cumb. 56e
Horsehouse N.Yorks. 25a
Horseshoe Hill Durham 59d
Horsforth W.Yorks. 18g
Horsley N'land 66h

Horsley N'land 69f
Horton in Ribblesdale N.Yorks. 23f
Horton Moor N.Yorks. 23f
Horton Moor N'land 79g
Houghton Cumb. 55c
Houghton N'land 66h
Houghton-le-Spring Tyne/Wear 61d
Hovingham N.Yorks. 28e
How Cumb. 56b
Howardian Hills N.Yorks. 28d
Howden Dene N'land 65h
Howden-le-Wear Durham 59i
Howdon Tyne/Wear 67h
Howe Cumb. 34h
Howe N.Yorks. 26c
Howick N'land 77e
Howlsyke N.Yorks. 41c
Hownam Borders 74f
Hownam Law Borders 74f
Howsham N.Yorks. 28i
Huby N.Yorks. 18d
Huby N.Yorks. 27i
Hudswell N.Yorks. 38e
Hulne Park N'land 77g
Humble Hill N'land 63b
Humbleton N'land 75b
Humphrey Hd. Pt. Cumb. 21e
Humshaugh N'land 65d
Hundale Pt. N.Yorks. 43e
Hunderthwaite Durham 49d
Hunderthwaite Moor Durham 48i
Hungry Law Borders 69b
Hunmanby N.Yorks. 30f
Hunsingore N.Yorks. 18f
Hunsonby Cumb. 56i
Hunstanworth Durham 58f
Huntington N.Yorks. 19f
Hunton N.Yorks. 38i
Hunwick Durham 50b
Hurst Moor N.Yorks. 37c
Hurworth-on-Tees Durham 50i
Hury Res. Durham 49d
Husthwaite N.Yorks. 27e
Hutton Borders 78b
Hutton Buscel N.Yorks. 29c
Hutton Conyers N.Yorks. 26e
Hutton Henry Durham 61h
Hutton in the Forest Cumb. 56h
Hutton-le-Hole N.Yorks. 41h
Hutton Lowcross Woods Clev. 52h
Hutton Magna Durham 49i
Hutton Mulgrave Wood N.Yorks. 42b
Hutton Ridge N.Yorks. 41e
Hutton Roof Cumb. 22b
Hutton Rudby N.Yorks. 40b
Hutton Sessay N.Yorks. 27e
Hutton Wandesley N.Yorks. 19d
Hycemoor Cumb. 32h

Ilderton N'land 75f
Ill Bell Cumb. 34b
Ill Crag Cumb. 33a
Illgill Head Cumb. 32c
Ilton N.Yorks. 25c
Ingleborough N.Yorks. 23e
Ingleby Arncliffe N.Yorks. 40d
Ingleby Cross N.Yorks. 40e
Ingleby Greenhow N.Yorks. 40c
Ingleton Durham 50d
Ingleton N.Yorks. 23d
Inglewood Forest Cumb. 56g
Ingoe N'land 65f
Ingoe Moor N'land 65f
Ingram N'land 75f
Ireby Cumb. 55g
Ireby Lancs. 23d
Ireleth Cumb. 20f
Ireshope Moor Durham 58h
Ireshopeburn Durham 58h
Iron Crag Cumb. 44i
Irt, R. Cumb. 32f
Irthing, R. Cumb./N'land 63e
Irthington Cumb. 62i
Irton N.Yorks. 30a
Irton Moor N.Yorks. 43g
Ivegill Cumb. 56d
Iveston Durham 59f

Jarrow Tyne/Wear 67h
Jed Water Borders 74d
Jedburgh Borders 74d
Jesmond Tyne/Wear 67g

Kaber Cumb. 48h
Kaber Fell Cumb. 36c
Kale Water Borders 74b
Kearstwick Cumb. 22c
Keasden N.Yorks. 23h
Keer, R. Lancs. 22e
Keld N.Yorks. 37d
Keldholme N.Yorks. 41h
Kelfield N.Yorks. 19i
Kelleth Cumb. 35b
Kelloe Durham 61g
Kelso Borders 74b
Kendal Cumb. 34i
Kent, R. Cumb. 34i
Kentmere Cumb. 34c
Kentmere Res. Cumb. 34b
Kenton Tyne/Wear 67g
Kenton Bank Foot N'land 66f
Kepwick N.Yorks. 40h
Kershope Burn Borders/Cumb. 62c
Kershope Forest Cumb. 62c
Keswick Cumb. 45f
Kettle Ness N.Yorks. 53i
Kettleness N.Yorks. 53i
Kettlewell N.Yorks. 24f
Kexwith Moor N.Yorks. 37c
Kibblesworth Tyne/Wear 60b
Kidlandlee N'land 75g
Kidsty Pike Cumb. 46h
Kielder N'land 68f
Kielder Burn N'land 68f
Kielder Forest N'land 68/69
Kielder Res. N'land 69g
Kielderhead Moor N'land 69d
Kilburn N.Yorks. 27b
Kildale N.Yorks. 41a
Kildale Moor N.Yorks. 41a
Kilham Humber. 30h
Kilham N'land 78h
Killinghall N.Yorks. 18a
Killington Cumb. 35h
Killington Res. Cumb. 35h
Killingworth Tyne/Wear 67d
Kilnsey N.Yorks. 24i
Kilnsey Crag N.Yorks. 24i
Kilton Beck Clev. 53g
Kimblesworth Durham 60e
Kimmerston N'land 78i
King's Meaburn Cumb. 47e
Kingsdale Beck N.Yorks. 23d
Kingstown Cumb. 55c
Kirby N.Yorks. 40c
Kirby Grindalythe N.Yorks. 29h
Kirby Hill N.Yorks. 26i
Kirby Hill N.Yorks. 38b
Kirby Knowle N.Yorks. 40h
Kirby Wiske N.Yorks. 39h
Kirk Deighton N.Yorks. 18f
Kirk Fell Cumb. 45g
Kirk Gill N.Yorks. 24b
Kirk Gill Moor N.Yorks. 24e
Kirk Hammerton N.Yorks. 19d
Kirk Merrington Durham 50c
Kirk Yetholm Borders 74c
Kirkandrews-on-Eden Cumb. 55b
Kirkbampton Cumb. 55b
Kirkbride Cumb. 55a
Kirkby Fleetham N.Yorks. 39d
Kirkby Lonsdale Cumb. 22c
Kirkby Malham N.Yorks. 24h
Kirkby Malzeard N.Yorks. 26d
Kirkby Malzeard Moor N.Yorks. 25e
Kirkby Overblow N.Yorks. 18e
Kirkby Stephen Cumb. 36b
Kirkby Stephen Common Cumb. 36b
Kirkby Thore Cumb. 47e
Kirkby Wharfe N.Yorks. 19g
Kirkbymoorside N.Yorks. 41h
Kirkcambeck Cumb. 63d
Kirkdale N.Yorks. 41h
Kirkham N.Yorks. 28i
Kirkheaton N'land 65f
Kirkhouse Cumb. 63g
Kirklevington Clev. 51h
Kirklington N.Yorks. 26b
Kirklinton Cumb. 62i
Kirknewton N'land 75b
Kirkoswald Cumb. 56i
Kirksanton Cumb. 20a
Kirkstone Pass Cumb. 34b
Kirkwhelpington N'land 71h
Knapton N.Yorks. 19e
Knares, The N'land 63b
Knaresborough N.Yorks. 18b
Knarsdale N'land 57b
Knayton N.Yorks. 39i
Knock Cumb. 47f
Knock Fell Cumb. 47c
Knott Cumb. 45c
Knowe, The Cumb. 34b
Knox Knowe Borders 68c
Kyle, R. N.Yorks. 27h
Kyloe Hills N'land 79g

Ladykirk Borders 78e
Ladyside Pike Cumb. 45d
Lake District National Park Cumb. 32/33/34/44/45/46
Lamb Hill Borders 74i
Lamberton Beach N'land 78c
Lamblair Hill Borders 68e
Lamesley Tyne/Wear 60b
Lancaster Lancs. 22g
Lanchester Durham 60d
Lane End Cumb. 32h
Langcliffe N.Yorks. 23i
Langdale Fell Cumb. 33b
Langdale Fell Cumb. 35e
Langdale Forest N.Yorks. 42f
Langdale Pikes Cumb. 33b
Langdon Common Durham 48c
Langdon Fell Durham 58h
Langholm Dumf./Gal. 62b
Langlee Crags N'land 75e
Langley N'land 64i
Langley Park Durham 60e
Langleydale Common Durham 49e
Langrigg Cumb. 54f
Langstrath Beck Cumb. 45h
Langstrothdale Chase N.Yorks. 24a
Langthorne N.Yorks. 39g
Langthorpe N.Yorks. 26i
Langthwaite N.Yorks. 37b
Langtoft Humber. 30g
Langton N.Yorks. 29g
Langton Burn Borders 78a
Langton Wold N.Yorks. 29g
Langwathby Cumb. 56i
Lank Rigg Cumb. 44i
Larriston Borders 68e
Larriston Fells Borders 68h
Lartington Durham 49h
Lastingham N.Yorks. 41i
Latchly Hill Borders 74f
Laver, R. N.Yorks. 26d
Laversdale Cumb. 62i
Laverton N.Yorks. 26d
Lawkland N.Yorks. 23h
Lazenby Clev. 52e
Lazonby Cumb. 56i
Lazonby Fell Cumb. 56h
Leadgate Cumb. 57e
Leadgate Durham 59c
Lealholm N.Yorks. 41c
Lealholm Moor N.Yorks. 41c
Leap Hill N'land 74h
Leasgill Cumb. 22a
Leavening N.Yorks. 29g
Lebberston N.Yorks. 30b
Leck Lancs. 22f
Leck Fell Lancs. 23a
Leece Cumb. 20f
Leeming N.Yorks. 39g
Leeming Bar N.Yorks. 39g
Lees Hill Cumb. 63g
Leighton N.Yorks. 25b
Leighton Res. N.Yorks. 25b
Leith, R. Cumb. 47d
Leitholm Borders 78d
Lemington Tyne/Wear 66i
Lennel Borders 78g
Leppington N.Yorks. 28i
Lesbury N'land 77h
Levens Cumb. 34i
Levisham N.Yorks. 42h
Levisham Moor N.Yorks. 42h
Lewisburn N'land 68i
Leyburn N.Yorks. 38h
Liddel Water Dumf./Gal./Cumb. 62e
Liddesdale Borders 68g
Lilswood Moor N'land 58b
Lily Mere Cumb. 35h
Lindal in Furness Cumb. 20f
Lindale Cumb. 21c
Lingdale Clev. 52i
Linhope Burn N'land 75e
Linshiels N'land 70c
Linshiels L. N'land 70c
Linstock Cumb. 56a
Linton N.Yorks. 24i
Linton W.Yorks. 18f
Linton-on-Ouse N.Yorks. 27h
Lintzgarth Common Durham 58i
Little Bampton Cumb. 55a
Little Barugh N.Yorks. 28c
Little Benton Tyne/Wear 67g
Little Broughton Cumb. 44c
Little Clifton Cumb. 44b
Little Man Cumb. 45e
Little Ouseburn N.Yorks. 27g
Little Ribston N.Yorks. 18f
Little Salkeld Cumb. 56i
Little Strickland Cumb. 47d
Little Swinburne N'land 65b
Little Thirkleby N.Yorks. 27b
Little Urswick Cumb. 20f
Little Whernside N.Yorks. 25d
Little Whittington N'land 65e
Littlebeck N.Yorks. 42c
Littledale Lancs. 22h
Littlehoughton N'land 77e
Littlemill N'land 77e
Littlethorpe N.Yorks. 26e
Littletown Durham 61d
Litton N.Yorks. 24e
Littondale N.Yorks. 24e
Liverton Clev. 53g
Liza, R. Cumb. 45g
Lockton N.Yorks. 42h
Lockton High Moor N.Yorks. 42e
Lockton Low Moor N.Yorks. 42h
Loft Hill N'land 75a
Lofthouse N.Yorks. 25e
Loftus Clev. 53g
Logan Water Dumf./Gal. 62a
Long Edge N'land 64e
Long Man Hill Cumb. 57h
Long Marston N.Yorks. 19d
Long Marton Cumb. 47e
Long Newton Clev. 51g
Long Sleddale Cumb. 34c
Longbenton Tyne/Wear 67d
Longframlington N'land 72f
Longframlington Common N'land 71c
Longhirst N'land 73g
Longhorsley N'land 72f
Longhorsley Moor N'land 72i
Longhoughton N'land 77h
Longhoughton Steel N'land 77i
Longknowe Hill N'land 75a
Longside Burn Borders 68a
Longtown Cumb. 62e
Lonscale Fell Cumb. 45f
Lorbottle N'land 75i
Lord's I. Cumb. 45e
Lord's Land Cumb. 35i
Lorton Fells Cumb. 45d
Lorton Vale Cumb. 45d
Lough Hill N'land 71e
Lovely Seat N.Yorks. 36f
Low Baring N.Yorks. 41e
Low Dales N.Yorks. 43g
Low Etherley Durham 50a
Low Harker Cumb. 62h
Low Hesket Cumb. 56e
Low Hutton N.Yorks. 28i
Low Mill N.Yorks. 41e
Low Moorsley Tyne/Wear 61d
Low Newton-by-the-Sea N'land 77e
Low Park Cumb. 63d
Low Row N.Yorks. 37e
Low Swinton N.Yorks. 25c
Low Wood Cumb. 21b
Low Worsall N.Yorks. 51g
Lowca Cumb. 44d
Lower Bentham N.Yorks. 23d
Lower Dunsforth N.Yorks. 27g
Loweswater Cumb. 45d
Loweswater Cumb. 44f
Loweswater Fell Cumb.44f
Lowick N'land 79g
Lowick Bridge Cumb. 33h
Lowick Green Cumb. 33h
Lowther, R. Cumb. 46f
Lucker N'land 77a
Ludworth Durham 61g
Lumsden Law N'land 69a
Lund Ridge N.Yorks. 41g
Lune Forest Durham 48e
Lune Moor Durham 48f
Lune, R. Durham 48f
Lune, R. Lancs./Cumb. 22f
Lunedale Durham 49d
Lupton Cumb. 22b
Lyne, R. Cumb. 62h
Lyne, R. N'land 73h
Lyneholme Cumb. 63d
Lynemouth N'land 73h
Lythe N.Yorks. 53i
Lyvennet, R. Cumb. 47e

Madam Law N'land 75a
Malham N.Yorks. 24h
Malham Cove N.Yorks. 24h
Malham Lings N.Yorks. 24h
Malham Moor N.Yorks. 24h
Malham Tarn N.Yorks. 24h
Mallerstang Common Cumb. 36e
Mallyan Spout N.Yorks. 42e
Maltby Clev. 51i
Malton N.Yorks. 28f
Manfield N.Yorks. 50h
Mansergh Cumb. 22c
Mardale Common Cumb. 46i
Marden Tyne/Wear 67e
Marden Rocks N'land 77i
Markington N.Yorks. 26h
Marley Hill Tyne/Wear 60b
Marrick N.Yorks. 37f
Marrick Moor N.Yorks. 37f
Marron, R. Cumb. 44e
Marsden B. Tyne/Wear 67i
Marsett N.Yorks. 37g
Marshall Meadows B. N'land 78c
Marske N.Yorks. 38e
Marske-by-the-Sea Clev. 52f
Marston Moor N.Yorks. 19d
Martindale Common Cumb. 46h
Marton Cumb. 20f
Marton N.Yorks. 27g
Marton N.Yorks. 28c
Marton-le-Moor N.Yorks. 26f
Maryport Cumb. 54g
Masham N.Yorks. 25c
Masham Moor N.Yorks. 25a
Masongill N.Yorks. 23d
Matfen N'land 65f
Matterdale Common Cumb. 46d
Maulds Meaburn Cumb. 47h
Maunby N.Yorks. 39h
Mawbray Cumb. 54e
Maxwellheugh Borders 74b
Meal Bank Cumb. 35d
Mealsgate Cumb. 54i
Meathop Cumb. 21c
Medburn N'land 66e
Medomsley Durham 59c
Melbecks Moor N.Yorks. 37d
Meldon N'land 71i
Meldon Park N'land 71i
Melkridge N'land 64h
Melkridge Common N'land 64h
Melling Lancs 22f
Melmerby Cumb. 57g
Melmerby N.Yorks. 26f
Melmerby N.Yorks. 37i
Melmerby Fell Cumb. 57g
Melmerby Moor N.Yorks. 37i
Melsonby N.Yorks. 38c
Meugher N.Yorks. 25d
Mickle Fell Durham 48e
Mickleby N.Yorks. 53h
Mickleden Cumb. 33b
Mickleton Durham 49d
Mickleton Moor Durham 48f
Mickley N.Yorks. 26d
Mid Fell N'land 68f
Middle Fell Cumb. 32c
Middle Herrington Tyne/Wear 61a
Middleham N.Yorks. 38h
Middlehope Moor Durham 58h
Middles, The Durham 60b
Middlesbrough Clev. 52d
Middlesmoor N.Yorks. 25d
Middlethorpe N.Yorks. 19f
Middleton Cumb. 35h
Middleton N'land 71h
Middleton N'land 79h
Middleton N.Yorks. 41i
Middleton Common Durham 49a
Middleton Fell Cumb. 35h
Middleton in Teesdale Durham 49d
Middleton One Row Durham 51g
Middleton Quernhow N.Yorks. 26c
Middleton St. George Durham 51g
Middleton Tyas N.Yorks. 38c
Middletown Cumb. 32a
Milbourne N'land 66e
Milburn Cumb. 47b
Milburn Forest Cumb. 47c
Milfield N'land 78i
Millbeck Cumb. 45e
Millhead Lancs 22d
Millom Cumb. 20b
Millthrop Cumb. 35h
Milltown Dumf./Gal. 62d
Milnthorpe Cumb. 22a
Milton Cumb. 22b
Milton Cumb. 63g
Mint, R. Cumb. 35d
Mitford N'land 73g
Moat Cumb. 62e
Mockerkin Cumb. 44f
Monk Coniston Moor Cumb. 33f
Monk Hesleden Durham 61h
Monkseaton Tyne/Wear 67e
Monkton Tyne/Wear 67h
Monkwearmouth Tyne/Wear 61a
Moor, The N.Yorks. 29d
Moor Monkton N.Yorks. 19a
Moorhouse Cumb. 55b
Moorsholm Clev. 53g
Moorsholm Moor Clev. 53g
Mordon Durham 51d
Morebattle Borders 74e
Morebattle Hill Borders 74e
Morecambe Lancs. 21i
Morecambe B. Cumb./Lancs. 21d
Moricambe Cumb. 54c
Morland Cumb. 47e
Morpeth N'land 73g
Morton upon Swale N.Yorks. 39h
Mosedale Cumb. 46a
Mossdale Moor N.Yorks. 36h
Moughton Fell N.Yorks. 23e
Moulton N.Yorks. 38c
Mozie Law Borders/N'land 74i
Muggleswick Durham 59d
Muggleswick Common Durham 59d
Muker N.Yorks. 37d
Muker Common N.Yorks. 37d
Mulgrave Wood N.Yorks. 53i
Muncaster Castle Cumb. 32e
Mungrisdale Cumb. 46a
Mungrisdale Common Cumb. 45c
Murk Esk N.Yorks. 42b
Murton Cumb. 47f
Murton Durham 61d
Murton Fell Cumb. 48d
Muston N.Yorks. 30c
Myton on Swale N.Yorks. 27g

Naburn *N.Yorks.* 19i
Nateby *Cumb.* 36b
Natland *Cumb.* 34i
Nawton *N.Yorks.* 41g
Neasham *Durham* 51g
Nedderton *N'land* 67a
Nelly's Moss Ls. *N'land* 71c
Nenthall *Cumb.* 57f
Nenthead *Cumb.* 57f
Ness Point or North Cheek *N.Yorks.* 43a
Nether Kellet *Lancs.* 22g
Nether Poppleton *N.Yorks.* 19e
Nether Silton *N.Yorks.* 40h
Netherton *N'land* 75h
Netherton Colliery *N'land* 67a
Nethertown *Cumb.* 32a
Netherwitton *N'land* 71i
Nettlesworth *Durham* 60e
New Bewick *N'land* 76f
New Brancepeth *Durham* 60h
New Earswick *N.Yorks.* 19f
New Herrington *Tyne/Wear* 61a
New Hutton *Cumb.* 35g
New Marske *Clev.* 52f
New Ridley *N'land* 65i
New Silksworth *Tyne/Wear* 61a
New York *Tyne/Wear* 67e
Newbiggin *Cumb.* 46b
Newbiggin *Cumb.* 47b
Newbiggin *Cumb.*56f
Newbiggin *Durham* 48f
Newbiggin *N'land* 65h
Newbiggin *N.Yorks.* 37h
Newbiggin-by-the-Sea *N'land* 73i
Newbiggin-on-Lune *Cumb.* 35c
Newbottle *Tyne/Wear* 61d
Newbrough *N'land* 65g
Newburn *Tyne/Wear* 66i
Newby *Cumb.* 47d
Newby *N.Yorks.* 23e
Newby Bridge *Cumb.* 33i
Newby East *Cumb.* 56b
Newcastle upon Tyne *Tyne/Wear* 66i
Newcastleton *Borders* 68g
Newcastleton Forest *Borders* 68g
Newfield *Durham* 60h
Newholm *N.Yorks.* 53i
Newpark Wood *N'land* 71i
Newsham *N.Yorks.* 49i
Newsham *N'land* 67b
Newton *Lancs.* 22f
Newton Arlosh *Cumb.* 54c
Newton Aycliffe *Durham* 50f
Newton Dale *N.Yorks.* 42h
Newton Kyme *N.Yorks.* 19g
Newton-le-Willows *N.Yorks.* 38i
Newton-on-Ouse *N.Yorks.* 27h
Newton-on-the-Moor *N'land* 73a
Newton Pt. *N'land* 77b
Newton Reigny *Cumb.* 46c
Newton Tors *N'land* 75a
Newton under Roseberry *Clev.* 52h
Newton Underwood *N'land* 72i
Newtown *Cumb.* 62i
Newtown *N'land* 75c
Nidd *N.Yorks.* 26h
Nidd, R. *N.Yorks.* 25i
Nidderdale *N.Yorks.* 25d
Nilston Rigg *N'land* 64i
Nine Standards Rigg *Cumb.* 36c
Ninebanks *N'land* 57c
Nisbet *Borders* 74a
Norber *N.Yorks.* 23e
Norham *N'land* 78e
Normanby *N.Yorks.* 28c
North Acomb *N'land* 65i
North B. *N.Yorks.* 43h
North Charlton *N'land* 77d
North Choppington *N'land* 73h
North Cowton *N.Yorks.* 39a
North End *N'land* 72c
North Hd. *Cumb.* 44g
North Middleton *N'land* 75f
North Moor *N.Yorks.* 25a
North Rigton *N.Yorks.* 18d
North Sands *Clev.* 52a
North Scale *Cumb.* 20e
North Seaton *N'land* 73h
North Seaton Colliery *N'land* 73h
North Shields *Tyne/Wear* 67h
North Stainley *N.Yorks.* 26e
North Sunderland *N'land* 77b
North Togston *N'land* 73b
North Tyne, R. *N'land* 65d
North Walbottle *Tyne/Wear* 66i
North York Moors National Park *N.Yorks.* 40/41/42
North Yorkshire Moors Railway *N.Yorks.* 42h
Northallerton *N.Yorks.* 39e
Northdale Rigg *N.Yorks.* 41f
Northumberland National Park *N'land* 63/64

Norton *N.Yorks.* 29d
Norton-le-Clay *N.Yorks.* 27d
Nosterfield *N.Yorks.* 26b
Nun Monkton *N.Yorks.* 19a
Nunnington *N.Yorks.* 28b
Nunnykirk *N'land* 71f
Nuns Moor *Tyne/Wear* 67g

Oakenshaw *Durham* 60g
Oakshaw Ford *Cumb.* 63d
Oakwood *N'land* 65h
Ogle *N'land* 66b
Old Bewick *N'land* 76f
Old Byland *N.Yorks.* 40i
Old Cassop *Durham* 60i
Old Hutton *Cumb.* 35g
Old Malton Moor *N.Yorks.* 29d
Old Man of Coniston, The *Cumb.* 33e
Old Park *Durham* 58i
Old Peak or South Cheek *N.Yorks.* 43d
Old Quarrington *Durham* 60i
Old Town *N'land* 70i
Old Town *Cumb.* 22c
Old Wingate *Durham* 61g
Oldstead *N.Yorks.* 27b
Ormesby *Clev.* 52h
Orton *Cumb.* 35b
Osbaldwick *N.Yorks.* 19f
Osgodby *N.Yorks.* 30b
Osmotherley *N.Yorks.* 40d
Osmotherley Moor *N.Yorks.* 40e
Oswaldkirk *N.Yorks.* 28a
Otterburn *N'land* 70f
Otterburn Camp *N'land* 70f
Ottercops Moss *N'land* 71g
Oughterby *Cumb.* 55b
Oughtershaw *N.Yorks.* 24a
Oughtershaw Moss *N.Yorks.* 23c
Oughtershaw Side *N.Yorks.* 24a
Oughterside *Cumb.* 54h
Oulston *N.Yorks.* 27f
Oulton *Cumb.* 55d
Ousby Fell *Cumb.* 57h
Ouse, R. *N.Yorks.* 27h
Ouston *Durham* 60b
Ouston Moor *N'land* 66d
Outhgill *Cumb.* 36e
Over Kellet *Lancs.* 22e
Over Silton *N.Yorks.* 40e
Over Water *Cumb.* 55g
Ovingham *N'land* 66g
Ovington *Durham* 50g
Ovington *N'land* 65i
Oxen Park *Cumb.* 33i
Oxendale *Cumb.* 33b
Oxnam *Borders* 74d
Oxnam Water *Borders* 74d
Oxton *N.Yorks.* 19g

Paddaburn Moor *N'land* 63b
Painshawfield *N'land* 65i
Palmersville *Tyne/Wear* 67d
Pannal *N.Yorks.* 18d
Papcastle *Cumb.* 44c
Pardshaw *Cumb.* 44f
Park *N'land* 63i
Parkbroom *Cumb.* 56a
Parton *Cumb.* 44d
Pateley Bridge *N.Yorks.* 25h
Pateley Moor *N.Yorks.* 25i
Patrick Brompton *N.Yorks.* 38i
Patterdale *Cumb.* 46g
Pawston L. *N'land* 75a
Paxton *Borders* 78c
Peel Fell *Borders/N'land* 68f
Peelwell *N'land* 64i
Pegswood *N'land* 73g
Pelton *Durham* 60b
Pen-y-ghent *N.Yorks.* 23f
Peniel Haugh *Borders* 74a
Pennington *Cumb.* 20f
Penny Bridge *Cumb.* 21a
Penrith *Cumb.* 46c
Penruddock *Cumb.* 46e
Penshaw *Tyne/Wear* 60c
Perkinsville *Durham* 60b
Peterlee *Durham* 61h
Petteril, R. *Cumb.* 56e
Philip Law *Borders* 74h
Pickering *N.Yorks.* 29a
Pickering Beck *N.Yorks.* 42h
Pickhill *N.Yorks.* 26c
Picton *N.Yorks.* 39c
Piel I. *Cumb.* 20i
Piercebridge *Durham* 50h
Pigdon *N'land* 72i
Pike of Blisco *Cumb.* 33b
Pike Fell *Borders* 68b
Pike Rigg *N'land* 57c
Pikeston Fell *Durham* 49b
Pillar *Cumb.* 45g
Pittington *Durham* 60f
Plashetts *N'land* 69g
Plawsworth *Durham* 60e
Plenmeller *N'land* 64g
Plenmeller Common *N'land* 64g

Plumbland *Cumb.* 54i
Plumpton *Cumb.* 56h
Pock Stones Moor *N.Yorks.* 25g
Pockley *N.Yorks.* 41g
Ponsonby *Cumb.* 32b
Pont, R. *N'land* 66e
Ponteland *N'land* 66f
Pool *W.Yorks.* 18g
Pooley Bridge *Cumb.* 46f
Port Clarence *Clev.* 51f
Port Mulgrave *N.Yorks.* 53h
Portinscale *Cumb.* 45e
Pott Moor *N.Yorks.* 25e
Potter Brompton *N.Yorks.* 29f
Potto *N.Yorks.* 40b
Powburn *N'land* 76f
Prendwick *N'land* 75i
Preston *Borders* 78a
Preston *N'land* 77a
Preston *Tyne/Wear* 67e
Preston Hill *N'land* 75d
Preston under Scar *N.Yorks.* 37i
Priest Hutton *Lancs.* 22e
Prior Moor *N.Yorks.* 30e
Prudhoe *N'land* 66h

Quaking Houses *Durham* 60d
Quarrington Hill *Durham* 61g
Quebec *Durham* 60d

Radcliffe *N'land* 73b
Raeburnfoot *Dumf./Gal.* 62d
Rainton *N.Yorks.* 26f
Raisbeck *Cumb.* 35b
Rampside *Cumb.* 20i
Rampside Sands *Cumb.* 20i
Ramsgill *N.Yorks.* 25e
Raskelf *N.Yorks.* 27e
Rathmell *N.Yorks.* 23i
Raven Beck *Cumb.* 56i
Raven Crag *Cumb.* 34a
Ravenglass *Cumb.* 32e
Ravenglass & Eskdale Railway *Cumb.* 32f
Ravenscar *N.Yorks.* 43d
Ravenshill Moor *N'land* 68f
Ravenstonedale *Cumb.* 35c
Ravenstonedale Common *Cumb.* 35c
Ravensworth *N.Yorks.* 38b
Rawthey, R. *Cumb.* 35i
Ray Fell *N'land* 71g
Rayburn L. *N'land* 71f
Raygill House Moor *N.Yorks.* 25d
Raylees Common *N'land* 70i
Reagill *Cumb.* 47h
Red Pike *Cumb.* 45g
Redburn *N'land* 64h
Redburn Common *Durham* 58f
Redcar *Clev.* 52f
Rede, R. *N'land* 70i
Redesdale Camp *N'land* 69f
Redesdale Forest *N'land* 69e
Redesmouth *N'land* 65a
Redheugh *N'land* 69h
Redkirk Pt. *Dumf./Gal.* 62g
Redmarshall *Clev.*51d
Redmire *N.Yorks.* 37i
Redmire Moor *N.Yorks.* 37f
Redpeth *N'land* 63i
Reeth *N.Yorks.* 37f
Reeth Low Moor *N.Yorks.* 37e
Reighton *N.Yorks.* 30f
Rennington *N'land* 77e
Renwick *Cumb.* 56f
Renwick Fell *Cumb.* 57d
Ribble Head *N.Yorks.* 23b
Ribble, R. *N.Yorks.* 23f
Riccall *N.Yorks.* 19i
Riccal Dale *N.Yorks.* 41g
Richmond *N.Yorks.* 38e
Rickerby *Cumb.* 56a
Riding Mill *N'land* 65i
Ridley *N'land* 64h
Ridsdale *N'land* 70i
Rievaulx *N.Yorks.* 40i
Rievaulx Moor *N.Yorks.* 40i
Riggs Moor *N.Yorks.* 25d
Rillington *N.Yorks.* 29e
Rillington Low Moor *N.Yorks.* 29d
Ripley *N.Yorks.* 26h
Ripon *N.Yorks.* 26e
Rise Hill *Cumb.* 36g
Roa I. *Cumb.* 20i
Roadhead *Cumb.* 63d
Robin Hood's Bay *N.Yorks.* 43a
Rochester *N'land* 69f
Rock *N'land* 77e
Rockcliffe *Cumb.* 62g
Rockcliffe Marsh *Cumb.* 62g
Roddam Burn *N'land* 75f
Roe Beck *Cumb.* 55f
Roeburn, R. *Lancs.* 22i
Roecliffe *N.Yorks.* 26i
Rogan's Seat *N.Yorks.* 37a
Roker *Tyne/Wear* 67i
Romaldkirk *Durham* 49d

Rook Hope *Durham* 58f
Rookhope *Durham* 58f
Roseberry Topping *Clev./N.Yorks.* 52h
Rosedale *N.Yorks.* 41e
Rosedale Abbey *N.Yorks.* 41e
Rosedale Moor *N.Yorks.* 41e
Roseden *N'land* 75f
Rosthwaite *Cumb.* 45h
Rothbury *N'land* 71c
Rothbury Forest *N'land* 71e
Rotherhope Fell *Cumb.* 57h
Rothley *N'land* 71h
Rothley Cross Roads *N'land* 71h
Rothley Ls. *N'land* 71h
Roughside Moor *N'land* 64a
Round Top *N'land* 64d
Roundhill Res. *N.Yorks.* 25e
Roundthwaite Common *Cumb.* 35a
Row *Cumb.* 34h
Rowanburn *Dumf./Gal.* 62e
Rowfoot *N'land* 63i
Rowland's Gill *Tyne/Wear* 59c
Roxburgh *Borders* 74a
Roxby *N.Yorks.* 26c
Roxby High Moor *N.Yorks.* 53h
Ruckcroft *Cumb.* 56e
Rudby *N.Yorks.* 40b
Rudland Rigg *N.Yorks.* 41d
Rudston *Humber.* 30i
Rufforth *N.Yorks.* 19e
Ruffside Moor *Durham* 59d
Runswick *N.Yorks.* 53h
Runswick B. *N.Yorks.* 53i
Rushy Knowe *Borders* 68f
Rusland Pool *Cumb.* 33i
Ruston *N.Yorks.* 29c
Ruston Parva *Humber.* 30h
Ruswarp *N.Yorks.* 42c
Ryal *N'land* 65f
Rydal *Cumb.* 33c
Rydal Fell *Cumb.* 33c
Rydal Water *Cumb.* 33c
Rye Dale *N.Yorks.* 27c
Rye, R. *N.Yorks.* 27c
Ryhope *Tyne/Wear* 61b
Ryhope Colliery *Tyne/Wear* 61a
Ryther *N.Yorks.* 19h
Ryton *Tyne/Wear* 66h

Sacriston *Durham* 60e
Sadberge *Durham* 51g
Saddleback *Cumb.* 45f
St. Bees *Cumb.* 44g
St. Bees Hd. *Cumb.* 44g
St. Helen Auckland *Durham* 50d
St. Herbert's I. *Cumb.* 45e
St. John's Beck *Cumb.* 45f
St. John's Chapel *Durham* 58h
St. Marys or Newton Haven *N'land* 77b
St. Sunday Crag *Cumb.* 46g
Saltburn-by-the-Sea *Clev.* 52f
Saltom B. *Cumb.* 44g
Salton *N.Yorks.* 28c
Sand Side *Cumb.* 20c
Sandford *Cumb.* 47i
Sandhutton *N.Yorks.* 26c
Sandsend *N.Yorks.* 53i
Sandsend Wyke *N.Yorks.* 53i
Sandside *Cumb.* 21c
Sandstell Pt. *N'land* 79a
Santon Bridge *Cumb.* 32f
Sark, R. *Cumb./Dumf./Gal.* 62d
Satley *Durham* 59f
Satron *N.Yorks.* 37d
Satterthwaite *Cumb.* 33i
Saughieside Hill *N'land* 75d
Saughtree Fell *Borders* 68e
Sawdon *N.Yorks.* 42i
Sawley *N.Yorks.* 26g
Sca Fell *Cumb.* 33a
Scackleton *N.Yorks.* 28e
Scafell Pikes *Cumb.* 33a
Scagglethorpe *N.Yorks.* 29d
Scalby *N.Yorks.* 43g
Scalby Ness Rocks *N.Yorks.* 43h
Scald Hill *N'land* 75e
Scale Force *Cumb.* 45g
Scalebar Force *N.Yorks.* 24g
Scaleby *Cumb.* 62i
Scales *Cumb.* 20f
Scampston *N.Yorks.* 29e
Scar House Res. *N.Yorks.* 25d
Scarborough *N.Yorks.* 43h
Scarcroft *W.Yorks.* 18h
Scargill *Durham* 49h
Scargill High Moor *Durham* 49g
Scars, The *N'land* 73e
Scawton *N.Yorks.* 27c
Scawton Moor *N.Yorks.* 27c
Scorton *N.Yorks.* 39d
Scotby *Cumb.* 56a
Scotch Corner *N.Yorks.* 38c
Scotland Gate *N'land* 73h
Scotswood *Tyne/Wear* 66i
Scotton *N.Yorks.* 38f
Scrayingham *N.Yorks.* 28i
Scriven *N.Yorks.* 18b
Scruton *N.Yorks.* 39g
Scugdale Beck *N.Yorks.* 40e
Seaham *Durham* 61e

Seahouses *N'land* 77b
Seal Sands *Clev.* 52d
Seamer *N.Yorks.* 51i
Seamer *N.Yorks.* 30b
Seascale *Cumb.* 32d
Seatallan *Cumb.* 32c
Seathwaite Fells *Cumb.* 33e
Seathwaite Tarn *Cumb.* 33e
Seaton *Durham* 61d
Seaton *Cumb.* 44b
Seaton Burn *N'land* 67e
Seaton Carew *Clev.* 52a
Seaton Delaval *N'land* 67e
Seaton Pt. *N'land* 77i
Seaton Sluice *N'land* 67e
Seave Green *N.Yorks.* 40f
Seaville *Cumb.* 54c
Sebergham *Cumb.* 55i
Sedbergh *Cumb.* 35h
Sedbusk *N.Yorks.* 37g
Sedgefield *Durham* 51a
Sedgwick *Cumb.* 34i
Seghill *Tyne/Wear* 67d
Selset Res. *Durham* 48f
Semer Water *N.Yorks.* 37g
Sessay *N.Yorks.* 27d
Settle *N.Yorks.* 23i
Settrington *N.Yorks.* 29d
Seven, R. *N.Yorks.* 28c
Shadforth *Durham* 61g
Shadwell *W.Yorks.* 18h
Shap *Cumb.* 47g
Shap Fells *Cumb.* 34c
Sharper's Hd. *N'land* 79a
Sharperton *N'land* 71a
Sharpness Pt. *Tyne/Wear* 67f
Sheepwash *N'land* 73h
Shepherdshield *N'land* 64e
Shepherdskirk Hill *N'land* 79g
Sheraton *Durham* 61h
Sherburn *Durham* 60f
Sherburn *N.Yorks.* 29f
Sherburn Hill *Durham* 61g
Sherburn Wold *N.Yorks.* 29f
Sheriff Hutton *N.Yorks.* 28h
Shibden Hill *Borders* 74e
Shielcleugh Edge *N'land* 75f
Shilbottle *N'land* 77h
Shildon *Durham* 50e
Shill Moor *N'land* 75h
Shillhope Law *N'land* 75g
Shincliffe *Durham* 60i
Shiney Row *Tyne/Wear* 60c
Shipton *N.Yorks.* 19b
Shiremoor *Tyne/Wear* 67e
Shirlaw Pike *N'land* 71c
Shitlington Common *N'land* 64b
Shopford *Cumb.* 63d
Shoresdean *N'land* 78f
Shotley Bridge *N'land* 59b
Shotleyfield *N'land* 59b
Shotton Colliery *Durham* 61g
Sicklinghall *N.Yorks.* 18e
Sidwood *N'land* 69h
Sighty Crag *Cumb.* 63b
Silecroft *Cumb.* 20a
Silloth *Cumb.* 54b
Silpho *N.Yorks.* 43g
Silver Howe *Cumb.* 33c
Silverdale *Lancs.* 21f
Simonburn *N'land* 65d
Simonside Hills *N'land* 71e
Sinderby *N.Yorks.* 26c
Sinnington *N.Yorks.* 41i
Sir Edward's L. *N'land* 65c
Skeeby *N.Yorks.* 38c
Skell, R. *N.Yorks.* 26e
Skelton *Clev.* 52i
Skelton *Cumb.* 56g
Skelton *N.Yorks.* 19b
Skelton *N.Yorks.* 26i
Skelton Beck *Clev.* 52f
Skelton Pike *Cumb.* 63a
Skelwith Bridge *Cumb.* 33c
Skelwith Force *Cumb.* 33c
Skerne, R. *Durham* 50f
Skewsby *N.Yorks.* 28d
Skiddaw *Cumb.* 45b
Skiddaw Forest *Cumb.* 45b
Skinburness *Cumb.* 54b
Skinningrove *Clev.* 53d
Skipton upon Swale *N.Yorks.*26c
Skirfare, R. *N.Yorks.* 24e
Skirwith *Cumb.* 47b
Skirwith Fell *Cumb.* 57h
Slaggyford *N'land* 57b
Slaley *N'land* 59a
Slaley Forest *N'land* 58c
Sleagill *Cumb.* 47d
Sledmere *Humber.* 29i
Sleights *N.Yorks.* 42b
Slingsby *N.Yorks.* 28e
Slyne *Lancs.* 21i
Smiddy Shaw Res. *Durham* 59e
Smithfield *Cumb.* 62i
Snab Pt. *N'land* 73i
Snab Sands *Cumb.* 20h
Snabdaugh *N'land* 69h
Snainton *N.Yorks.* 29b
Snape *N.Yorks.* 39g
Sneaton *N.Yorks.* 42c
Sneaton High Moor *N.Yorks.* 42f
Snilesworth Moor *N.Yorks.* 40e
Snipe Pt. *N'land* 79e

Snitter N'land 71b
Snook Pt. N'land 77b
Snope Common N'land 57b
Snowhope Moor Durham 58i
Soulby Cumb. 48g
Sourmire Moor N.Yorks. 25b
Soutergate Cumb. 20c
South Bank Clev. 52e
South B. N.Yorks. 43h
South Broomhill N'land 73e
South Charlton N'land 77d
South Hd. Cumb. 44g
South Hetton Durham 61d
South Hylton Tyne/Wear 61a
South Kilvington N.Yorks. 27a
South Middleton N'land 75f
South Otterington N.Yorks. 39i
South Shields Tyne/Wear 67i
South Stainley N.Yorks. 26h
South Tyne, R. N'land/ Cumb. 64h
South Wingate Durham 61h
Southwick Tyne/Wear 61a
Sowerby N.Yorks. 27a
Spadeadam Forest Cumb. 63e
Spark Bridge Cumb. 33h
Spaunton N.Yorks. 41h
Spaunton Moor N.Yorks. 41e
Speeton N.Yorks. 30f
Speeton Field N.Yorks/ Humber. 30f
Spennithorne N. Yorks. 38h
Spennymoor Durham 50b
Spittal N'land 79a
Spofforth N.Yorks. 18e
Springfield Dumf./Gal. 62g
Springwell Tyne/Wear 60c
Sprint, R. Cumb. 34c
Sproxton N.Yorks. 28a
Spy Rigg N'land 63f
Stackhouse N.Yorks. 23i
Staffield Cumb. 56f
Stainburn N.Yorks. 18d
Stainburn Moor N.Yorks. 18d
Staindrop Durham 50d
Stainforth N.Yorks. 23i
Stainmore Common Cumb./ Durham 48i
Stainmore Forest Durham 48i
Stainsacre N.Yorks. 42c
Stainton Clev. 51i
Stainton Cumb. 20f
Stainton Cumb. 35g
Stainton Cumb. 46f
Stainton Durham 49f
Stainton N.Yorks. 38d
Stainton Moor N.Yorks. 38d
Staintondale N.Yorks. 43d
Staithes N.Yorks. 53h
Stakeford N'land 73h
Stamfordham N'land 66d
Stanah Cumb. 45f
Stang Forest, The Durham 37c
Stanhope Durham 59g
Stanhope Common Durham 59d
Stanley Durham 60b
Stanley Burn N'land/Tyne/ Wear 66h
Stannington N'land 66c
Stanton N'land 72i
Stapleton N.Yorks. 50i
Starbotton N.Yorks. 24e
Stargate N'land 66i
Starling Dodd Cumb. 45g
Startforth Durham 49h
Station Town Durham 61h
Staveley Cumb. 34f
Staveley N.Yorks. 26i
Staveley-in-Cartmel Cumb. 34g
Staxton N.Yorks. 30b
Staxton Wold N.Yorks. 30e
Stean N.Yorks. 25d
Stean Moor N.Yorks. 25d
Stearsby N.Yorks. 28d
Steel N'land 58c
Steeple Cumb. 45g
Stewartshiels Burn N'land 70f
Stillingfleet N.Yorks. 19i
Stillington Durham/Clev. 51d
Stillington N.Yorks. 27i
Stobhill N'land 73g
Stockghyll Force Cumb. 34a
Stocksfield N'land 65i
Stockton on Tees Clev. 51e
Stokesley N.Yorks. 40b
Stonegrave N.Yorks. 28b
Stonehaugh N'land 64e
Stonesdale Moor N.Yorks. 36c
Stonethwaite Cumb. 45h
Stony Cove Cumb. 46h
Strensall N.Yorks. 28g
Struther Bog N'land 69f
Studley Royal N.Yorks. 26e
Stutton N.Yorks. 19g
Suffield N.Yorks. 43g
Summer Bridge N.Yorks. 25i
Summer Lodge Moor N.Yorks. 37e
Sunderland Tyne/Wear 61b
Sunderland Bridge Durham 60i
Sunniside Durham 59i
Sunniside Tyne/Wear 60b
Sunnyside N'land 65h
Sunnyside Hill Borders 74c
Sutton Grange N.Yorks. 26e
Sutton Howgrave N.Yorks. 26b
Sutton-on-the-Forest N.Yorks. 27i
Sutton-under-Whitestonecliffe N.Yorks. 27b
Swainby N.Yorks. 40e
Swale Dale N.Yorks. 37e
Swale, R. N.Yorks. 38d
Swale, R. N.Yorks. 27g
Swallow Knowe N'land 71c
Swalwel N'land 66i
Swarland N'land 73a
Swarland Estate N'land 73a
Swarth Fell Cumb 36e
Swaythorpe Humber 30h
Sweethope Loughs N'land 65b
Swinhoe N'land 77b
Swinithwaite N.Yorks. 37i
Swinton Borders 78d
Swinton N.Yorks. 28f

Tadcaster N.Yorks. 19g
Talkin Cumb 56c
Talkin Tarn Cumb 56c
Tallentire Cumb 54h
Tanfield Durham 60a
Tanfield Lea Durham 60a
Tansy Hill Dumf./Gal. 62a
Tantobie Durham 60a
Tarn Crag Cumb 34c
Tarnhouse Rigg Cumb 63h
Tarras Water Dumf./Gal. 62b
Tatham Fells Lancs. 23g
Tebay Cumb 35b
Tebay Fell Cumb 35b
Tees, R. Durham/N.Yorks./ Clev. 49i
Tees B. Clev. 52b
Tees Head Cumb 57h
Tees Mouth Clev. 52e
Teesdale Durham 48f
Teesport Clev. 52e
Temple Sowerby Cumb 47e
Terrington N.Yorks. 28e
Teviot, R. Borders 74a
Thimbleby N.Yorks. 40e
Thirkleby N.Yorks. 27b
Thirl Moor N'land 74i
Thirlby N.Yorks. 40h
Thirlmere Cumb 45i
Thirlwall Common N'land 63f
Thirn N.Yorks. 38i
Thirsk N.Yorks. 27a
Thixendale N.Yorks. 29g
Tholthorpe N.Yorks. 27h
Thoralby N.Yorks. 37h
Thormanby N.Yorks. 27e
Thornaby-on-Tees Clev. 51h
Thornbrough N.Yorks. 26b
Thorner W.Yorks. 18i
Thorngrafton N'land 64h
Thornhill Cumb 32a
Thornholme Humber 30i
Thornington N'land 78h
Thornley Durham 59i
Thornley Durham 61g
Thornthwaite Cumb 45e
Thornthwaite Forest Cumb 45d
Thornton Dale N.Yorks. 29a
Thornton Dale N.Yorks. 42h
Thornton-le-Beans N.Yorks. 39i
Thornton-le-Clay N.Yorks. 28h
Thornton-le-Moor N.Yorks. 39i
Thornton Rust N.Yorks. 37h
Thornton Steward N.Yorks. 38i
Thornton Watlass N.Yorks. 39g
Thorp Arch W.Yorks. 18i
Thorpe N.Yorks. 24i
Thorpe Basset Wold N.Yorks. 29e
Thorpe Thewles Clev. 51d
Thouliestane Hill Borders 74e
Threapland N.Yorks. 24i
Three Pikes Cumb/N'land 57d
Threepwood N'land 64i
Threlkeld Cumb 45f
Threlkeld Common Cumb 46d
Threshfield N.Yorks. 24i
Thrintoft N.Yorks. 39e
Throckington N'land 65b
Throckley Tyne/Wear 66i
Thropton N'land 71b
Thrunton N'land 76i
Thrunton Wood N'land 76i
Thursby Cumb 55e
Thurstonfield Cumb 55b
Thwaite N.Yorks. 37d
Thwaites Fell Cumb 32i
Thwing Humber 30e
Tilberthwaite Fells Cumb 33e
Till, R. N'land 78e
Tindale Crescent Durham 50d
Tindale Fells Cumb 57a
Tinnis Hill Borders 62b
Tinnisburn Forest Dumf./ Gal. 62b
Tirril Cumb. 46f
Titlington N'land 76i
Tockwith N.Yorks. 19d
Todd Hill N'land 72i
Todhills Cumb. 62h
Togston N'land 73e
Tollerton N.Yorks. 27h
Topcliffe N.Yorks. 26f
Torpenhow Cumb. 54i
Torrisholme Lancs. 21i
Torver Cumb. 33e
Tosson N'land 71e
Tosson Hill N'land 71e
Tow Law Durham 59i
Town End Cumb. 21c
Town End Cumb. 34e
Town Moor Tyne/Wear 67g
Town Yetholm Borders 74c
Towthorpe Humber. 29h
Towton N.Yorks. 19g
Trimdon Durham 61g
Trimdon Colliery Durham 61g
Trimdon Grange Durham 61g
Tritlington N'land 73g
Tronshaw Hill Borders 74e
Troughend Common N'land 69i
Trout Beck Cumb. 34b
Troutbeck Cumb. 34b
Troutbeck Bridge Cumb. 34e
Trouts Dale N.Yorks. 42i
Tudhoe Durham 60h
Tunstall Lancs. 22f
Tunstall N.Yorks. 38f
Tunstall Res. Durham 59h
Tweed, R. Borders/N'land 78c
Tweedmouth N'land 78c
Tyne, R. Tyne/Wear 67h
Tyne Green N'land 65g
Tyne Head Cumb. 57i
Tynemouth Tyne/Wear 67f

Ugglebarnby N.Yorks. 42c
Ugthorpe N.Yorks. 53h
Ulcat Row Cumb. 46e
Uldale Cumb. 55g
Uldale Fells Cumb. 55g
Ulgham N'land 73h
Ulleskelf N.Yorks. 19h
Ullock Cumb. 44f
Ullswater Cumb. 46e
Ulpha Cumb. 33g
Ulpha Fell Cumb. 33d
Ulverston Cumb. 21a
Ulverston Sands Cumb. 21d
Underbarrow Cumb. 34i
Unthank Cumb. 57g
Upleatham Clev. 52f
Upper Denton Cumb. 63h
Upper Dunsforth N.Yorks. 27g
Upper Poppleton N.Yorks. 19e
Upsall N.Yorks. 40g
Upsettlington Borders 79e
Ure, R. N.Yorks. 26e
Urra N.Yorks. 40f
Urra Moor N.Yorks. 40f
Ushaw Moor Durham 60e
Usway Burn N'land 75g

Vale of Pickering N.Yorks. 28h
Vickerstown Cumb. 20h

Waberthwaite Cumb. 32f
Wadholme Flow Cumb. 54c
Waitby Cumb. 36b
Walbottle Tyne/Wear 66i
Walden Beck N.Yorks. 24c
Waldridge Durham 60e
Wall N'land 65d
Wall Nook Durham 60e
Wallsend Tyne/Wear 67g
Walltown N'land 63i
Walney I. Cumb. 20h
Walshford N.Yorks. 18f
Walton Cumb. 63g
Walton W.Yorks. 18f
Walwick N'land 65d
Wandylaw N'land 77a
Wansbeck, R. N'land 73g
Warcop Cumb. 48g
Warcop Fell Cumb. 48d
Warden N'land 65g
Wardley Tyne/Wear 67h
Warenford N'land 77a
Wark N'land 64f
Wark N'land 78g
Wark Common N'land 64c
Wark Forest N'land 64a
Warks Burn N'land 64c
Warkworth N'land 73b
Warkworth Harbour N'land 73b
Warton Lancs 22d
Warton Sands Lancs 21f
Warwick Cumb. 56a
Warwick Bridge Cumb. 56b
Wasdale Head Cumb. 33a
Washfold N.Yorks. 37c
Washington Tyne/Wear 60c
Waskerley Durham 59e
Waskerley Park Durham 59d
Waskerley Res. Durham 59d
Wass N.Yorks. 27c
Wast Water Cumb. 32c
Watendlath Cumb. 45i
Watergate Moor N'land 64c
Waterhead Common Cumb.62e
Waterhouses Durham 60g
Wath N.Yorks. 26e
Wauchope Burn Borders 68b
Wauchope Forest Borders 68c
Wauchope Water Dumf./ Gal. 62a
Waver, R. Cumb. 54c
Waverton Cumb. 54f
Wear, R. Durham/Tyne/ Wear 50a
Wear Dale Durham 58i
Weardley W.Yorks. 18g
Wearhead Durham 58h
Weaverthorpe N.Yorks. 29f
Wedder Hill N'land 74i
Weeton N.Yorks. 18d
Welburn N.Yorks. 28i
Welbury N.Yorks. 39f
Well N.Yorks. 26b
Wellhope Knowe N'land 71c
Wellington Cumb. 32b
Welton Cumb. 55e
Wenning, R. Lancs./N.Yorks. 22f
Wennington Lancs. 22f
Wensley N.Yorks. 38g
Wensley Dale N.Yorks. 37h
West Allen, R. N'land 57f
West Allen Dale N'land 57c
West Auckland Durham 50d
West Ayton N.Yorks. 29c
West Barnby N.Yorks. 53i
West Baugh Fell Cumb. 36d
West Burton N.Yorks. 37i
West Chevington N'land 73e
West Common Durham 48b
West Cornforth Durham 60i
West Dipton Burn N'land 65g
West Edmondsley Durham 60e
West Fleetham N'land 77b
West Heslerton N.Yorks. 29e
West Hill N'land 75d
West Kielder Moor N'land 68f
West Lilling N.Yorks. 28h
West Lutton N.Yorks. 29i
West Moor N.Yorks. 24e
West Moor N.Yorks. 37a
West Ness N.Yorks. 28b
West Pelton Durham 60b
West Rainton Durham 60f
West Rounton N.Yorks. 39c
West Scrafton N.Yorks. 25a
West Sleekburn N'land 73h
West Stones Dale N.Yorks. 37a
West Stonesdale N.Yorks. 37a
West Tanfield N.Yorks. 26b
West Thirston N'land 73d
West Witton N.Yorks. 37i
West Woodburn N'land 70i
West Wylam N'land 66h
Westend Town N'land 64h
Westerdale N.Yorks. 41b
Westerdale Moor N.Yorks. 41d
Westerhope Tyne/Wear 66i
Westernhope Moor Durham 58i
Westgate Durham 58i
Westlinton Cumb. 62h
Westnewton Cumb. 54e
Westnewton N'land 75a
Westow N.Yorks. 28i
West Sleddale Res. Cumb. 47g
Wether Hill N'land 70i
Wether Hill N'land 75g
Wether Law N'land 69d
Wetheral Cumb. 56b
Wetherby W.Yorks. 18f
Wetherlam Cumb. 33e
Whalton N'land 66b
Wharfe N.Yorks. 23e
Wharfe, R. N.Yorks./ W.Yorks. 18h
Wharfedale N.Yorks.24b
Wharmley N'land 65g
Whashton N.Yorks. 38b
Whaw N.Yorks. 37b
Wheatley Hill Durham 61g
Wheeldale Moor N.Yorks. 41f
Whenby N.Yorks. 28d
Whernside Cumb./N.Yorks. 23b
Whicham Cumb. 20a
Whickham Tyne/Wear 66i
Whin Rigg Cumb. 32c
Whinfell Common Cumb. 35d
Whinfell Forest Cumb. 47d
Whinlatter Pass Cumb. 45d
Whisperdales N.Yorks. 43g
Whita Hill Dumf./Gal. 62b
Whitaside Moor N.Yorks. 37e
Whitbarrow Cumb. 34h
Whitbarrow Scar Cumb. 34h
Whitbeck Cumb. 20a
Whitburn Tyne/Wear 67i
Whitburn B. Tyne/Wear 67i
Whitby N.Yorks. 42c
White Edge Durham 58e
White Fell Cumb. 35e
White Horse N.Yorks. 27b
White-le-Head Durham 60a
Whiteadder Water Borders/ N'land 78b
Whitehaven Cumb. 44g
Whitehill Moor N'land 63c
Whitestone Hill N'land 74i
Whitfell Cumb. 32i
Whitfield N'land 57c
Whitefield Hill N'land 71e
Whitfield Moor N'land 57c
Whithaugh Borders 68g
Whitley Bay Tyne/Wear 67f
Whitley Chapel N'land 58c
Whitsome Borders 78a
Whitsun Dale N.Yorks. 36c
Whitterhope Edge Borders 68d
Whitterhope Foot Borders 68d
Whittingham N'land 76i
Whittington Lancs. 22f
Whitton Borders 74e
Whitton Clev. 51d
Whitton N'land 71f
Whitton L. Borders 74e
Whittonstall N'land 59b
Whitwell-on-the-Hill N.Yorks. 28i
Whixley N.Yorks. 19a
Whorlton Durham 49i
Whorlton N.Yorks. 40e
Whorlton Moor N.Yorks. 40e
Widdale Beck N.Yorks. 36i
Widdale Fell N.Yorks. 36h
Widdrington N'land 73e
Widdrington Station N'land 73e
Widdybank Fell Durham 48b
Wide Open Tyne/Wear 67d
Wigginton N.Yorks. 19c
Wiggonby Cumb. 55b
Wighill N.Yorks. 19d
Wigton Cumb. 55d
Wike W.Yorks. 18h
Wild Boar Fell Cumb. 36e
Willerby N.Yorks. 30a
Williamston Common N'land 57b
Willington Durham 60g
Wilsill N.Yorks. 25i
Wilsons's Pike Borders 68h
Wilton N.Yorks. 29b
Wilton Carr N.Yorks. 29b
Windermere Cumb. 34e
Windy Gyle Borders 75g
Windy Knowe Borders 68e
Wingate Durham 61g
Wingates N'land 71f
Winksley N.Yorks. 26d
Winlaton Tyne/Wear 66i
Winlaton Mill Tyne/Wear 66i
Winskill Cumb. 56i
Winster Cumb. 34e
Winston Durham 50g
Winterburn Res. N.Yorks. 24h
Winton Cumb. 48g
Winton Fell Cumb. 36c
Wintringham N.Yorks. 29e
Wiske, R. N.Yorks. 39e
Witherslack Cumb. 34h
Witton Gilbert Durham 60e
Witton Moor N.Yorks. 25b
Witton Park Durham 50a
Woden Law Borders 74h
Wold Newton Humber. 30e
Wolds, The Humber. 29i
Wolfcleugh Common Durham 58e
Wolfelee Hill Borders 68b
Wolsingham Durham 59h
Wolsingham North Moor Durham 59h
Wolsingham Park Moor Durham 59g
Wolviston Clev. 51e
Wombleton N.Yorks. 28b
Woodale N.Yorks. 24c
Woodhorn N'land 73h
Woodland Durham 49e
Woodland Fell Cumb. 33h
Woodland Fell Durham 49e
Wooler N'land 75c
Woolsington Tyne/Wear 66f
Wooperton N'land 75f
Workington Cumb. 44a
Worton N.Yorks. 37h
Wray Lancs. 22i
Wrayton Lancs. 22f
Wreay Cumb. 56d
Wreigh Burn N'land 71b
Wrelton N.Yorks. 41i
Wykeham N.Yorks. 29c
Wykeham Forest N.Yorks. 42i
Wylam N'land 66h
Wyndburgh Hill Borders 68b
Wythburn Fells Cumb. 45i

Yafforth N.Yorks. 39e
Yarm Clev. 51h
Yarrow N'land 69g
Yealand Conyers Lancs. 22d
Yealand Redmayne Lancs. 22d
Yearning Law N'land 74i
Yearsley N.Yorks. 27f
Yearsley Moor N.Yorks. 27f
Yeavering N'land 75b
Yeavering Bell N'land 75b
Yedingham N.Yorks. 29b
Yellow Fawns Cumb. 63e
Yetholm L. Borders 74c
Yetlington N'land 75i
Yewbarrow Cumb. 32c
Yockenthwaite N.Yorks. 24b
York N.Yorks. 19e
Yorkshire Dales National Park N.Yorks. 23/24/36/37

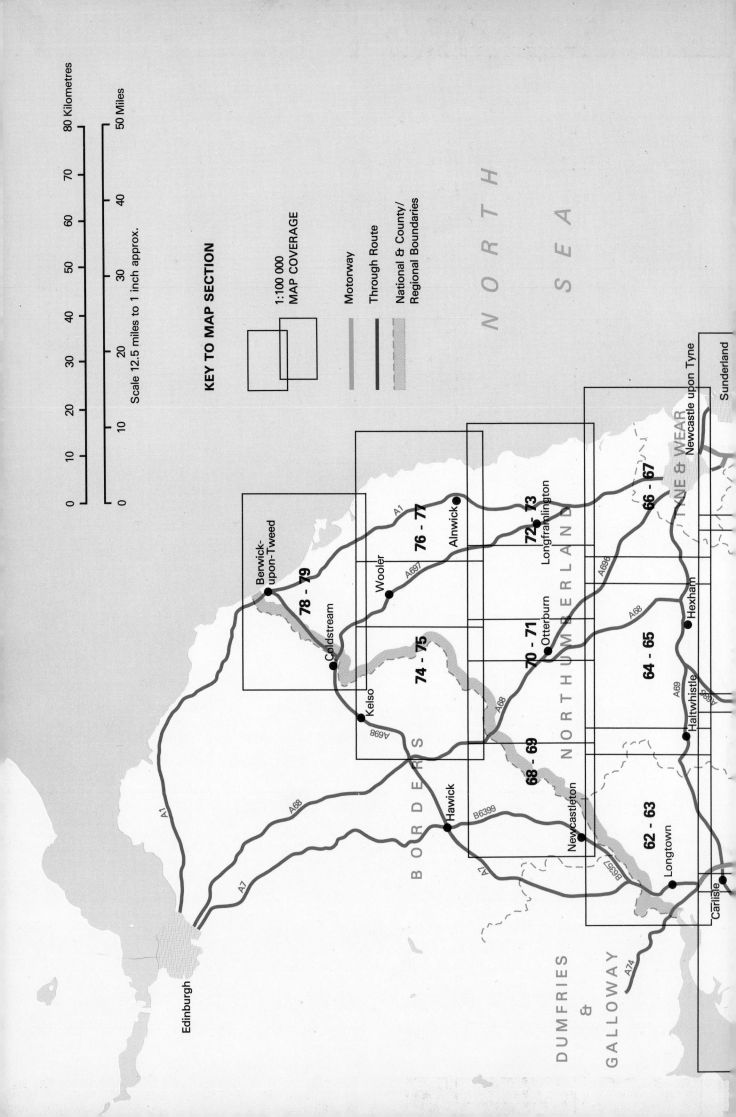

KEY TO MAP SECTION

1:100 000
MAP COVERAGE

Motorway

Through Route

National & County/
Regional Boundaries

80 Kilometres

50 Miles

Scale 12.5 miles to 1 inch approx.

0   10   20   30   40   50   60   70

0   10   20   30   40   50

Edinburgh

A1

A7

A68

A7

BORDERS

Hawick

B6399

A7

A68

A698

Kelso

Coldstream

Berwick-
upon-Tweed

78 - 79

74 - 75

76 - 77

Wooler

A697

A1

Alnwick

68 - 69

Newcastleton

B6357

70 - 71

Otterburn

A68

72 - 73

Longframlington

NORTHUMBERLAND

66 - 67

A696

Newcastle upon Tyne

Sunderland

TYNE & WEAR

62 - 63

Longtown

64 - 65

Hexham

A68

A69

Haltwhistle

A69

Carlisle

DUMFRIES
&
GALLOWAY

A74

NORTH   SEA